Towards Authentic Cornish

Towards Authentic Cornish

A critique of
Kernewek Kemmyn: Cornish for the Twenty-First Century
of Paul Dunbar and Ken George,
Gerlyver Kernewek Kemmyn
by Ken George, and
A Grammar of Modern Cornish
by Wella Brown

by

Nicholas Williams

MA PhD DipCeltStud FLS ITIA
Bard of the Gorsedd of Cornwall
Associate Professor in Celtic Languages
University College, Dublin

evertype
2006

Published by / *Dyllys gans* Evertype, Cnoc Sceichín, Leac an Anfa, Cathair na Mart, Co. Mhaigh Eo, Éire / *Wordhen*. www.evertype.com.

First edition 2006. Reprinted with corrections January 2011.
Kensa dyllans 2006. Daspryntys gans ewnansow Genver 2011.

© 2006 Nicholas Williams.

Editor / *Penscrefer*: Michael Everson.

All rights reserved. No part of this publication may be reproduced, stored in a retrieval system or transmitted, in any form or by any means, electronic, mechanical, photocopying, recording or otherwise, without prior permission of the publishers.
Pub gwyr gwethys. Ny yll ran vyth a'n publysyans ma naneyl bos copyes, sensys aberth yn system daskefyans na truescorrys yn furf vyth oll na dre vayn vyth oll, poken electronek, mechanyk, dre fotocopyans, dre recordyth bo fordh vyth aral, heb cafus cumyas dherag dorn dheworth an dyller.

Y kefyr covath rolyans rag an lyver-ma dhyworth an Lyverva Vretennek.
A catalogue record for this book is available from dhe British Library.

ISBN-10 1-904808-09-3
ISBN-13 978-1-904808-09-1

Typeset in Palatino by Michael Everson.
Olsettys yn Palatino gans Michael Everson.

Cover / *Cudhlen*: Michael Everson

Printed by / *Pryntys gans* LightningSource.

CONTENTS

	Introduction	vii
	Abbreviations and references	xiii
1	My criticisms of Kernowek Kemyn	1
2	General: Ideology	6
3	The Cornish scribal tradition	15
4	A phonemic orthography	24
5	The Prosodic Shift	27
6	The gemination of consonants	42
7	George's two long *o* vowels	51
8	Long *a* in Middle Cornish *tas* 'father'	82
9	Final long *i*; *te/ty* 'thou', *me/my* 'I'	85
10	Vocalic alternation: *y* in monosyllables ~ *e* in disyllables	95
11	The variation *gweth* ~ *gwyth*, *beth* ~ *byth*, *pref* ~ *pryf*	110
12	*Bewnans* 'life' and *clewes* 'to hear'	121
13	*Du* 'black' and *Dew/Du* 'God'	139
14	Pre-occlusion	151
15	*Pesy* 'to pray' and *bohosek* 'poor'	163
16	Unstressed syllables	171
17	Concluding remarks on *KKC21*	184
18	Problems with George's *Gerlyver Kernewek Kemmyn*	188
19	Problems with Brown's *Grammar of Modern Cornish*	235
20	Final observations	282
	Index	285

Instead, we found that the Language Board, which as followers of Morton Nance we had founded to continue his work for Cornish, based on his Unified system, had fallen into the hands of his detractors and Unified's opponents. The work of sixty years of revival, led by a scholar and prophet of true learning and vision, and then continued by the Language Board, had been cast aside and replaced by the theories of a false prophet.

P. A. S. Pool, *The Second Death of Cornish* 7

INTRODUCTION
Background-Foreword (KKC21: 6-7)

0.00 Preliminary Remarks

The present work is in the first place a critique of *Kernewek Kemmyn: Cornish for the Twenty-First Century* (Cornish Language Board 1997) by Paul Dunbar (P.D.) and Ken George (K.G.), a work provoked by my severe criticisms of Kernowek Kemyn in *Cornish Today* (CT; Kernewek dre Lyther 1995). *Kernewek Kemmyn: Cornish for the Twenty-First Century* [KKC21] is in the form of a dialogue between Ken George, referred to throughout as K.G., and Paul Dunbar, whose contributions are preceded by P.D. Ken George is the inventor of Kernowek Kemyn, a synthetic and in my view very mistaken form of revived Cornish. The two authors of KKC21 are described at the beginning of the book as follows:

> Paul Dunbar is a member of the Cornish Language Board and a Bard of the Cornish Gorsedd. He is interested in pedagogic techniques for the teaching of Cornish, and tries out his ideas on a class of learners in Looe.
>
> He is skilled in boat-building and is at present owner of a vineyard near Liskeard. He is the editor of a political magazine named *Kernow*. It is remarkable that he has been able to find time to work on this book, since he is Mebyon Kernow's Parliamentary Prospective Candidate for S.E. Cornwall.
>
> Ken George is a member of the Cornish Language Board and a Bard of the Cornish Gorsedd. He has carried out extensive research on various aspects of Cornish and presented the results at eight international Celtic conferences. He has published over fifty items on Celtic linguistics, including two books and some literary works.
>
> Dr George is Principal Lecturer in Ocean Science at the Institute of Marine Studies, University of Plymouth (KKC21: 3).

0.01 KKC21 as "Catechism"

Although I had always intended to review this work in detail showing why it was so egregiously mistaken, I did not write my critique when the book was first published. This was for two reasons.

A) The format of the whole was not a feature that lent the work any credibility. It is in the form of a dialogue between the omniscient teacher and the eager pupil seeking after truth. As such it has more in common with the polemic catechisms of the Counter-Reformation than with a serious work of scholarship. Moreover I was reluctant to read the work more than once

TOWARDS AUTHENTIC CORNISH

because George and Dunbar descend on occasion to rather childish insults. Here are some examples:

K.G. Leave aside for a moment my opinion that he [i.e. Williams] has made a hash of much of it… (KKC21: 13)

K.G. He's [i.e. Williams] quite wrong but we'll have to show that he is (KKC21: 21)

K.G. It does not matter to Dr Williams, for he is clever enough to be able to transform a language written in such an orthography into its spoken form. Most learners are not that skilled (KKC21: 24)

K.G. Speaking as a beginner in Irish, I would have thought that Dr Williams as a teacher of Irish, would have realized that (KKC21: 23)

K.G. If Dr Williams can't get this one right, then we can have little confidence in the rest of his writings (KKC21: 27)

P.D. Surely Dr Williams can't be so naive as to believe that because they were spelled the same, they were pronounced the same? K.G. I hope not (KKC21: 31)

K.G. His [Williams'] analogy with *dhymmo* therefore falls flat. P.D. And another criticism bites the dust! (KKC21: 43)

P.D. It looks like Dr Williams is wrong yet again (KKC21: 65)

P.D. A cursory look doesn't sound like the meticulous methodology one might expect of a professional Celticist (KKC21: 84)

K.G. Eulogy to *Cornish Today*: What a volume! What a brain!/ Dr Williams writes again/ master of the Celtic pen/ Dr Williams writes again (KKC21: 100)

P.D. So Dr Williams is wrong again. K.G. It would appear so (KKC21: 106)

P.D. Is this one [Williams' criticism 6] rubbish? K.G. Dr Williams must be scraping the barrel (KKC21: 126)

P.D. I find it astonishing that a University lecturer in a department of Celtic studies should make such errors, and worse, propagate them (KKC21: 135)

K.G. Philip Payton notes that "*Cornish Studies* is a fully refereed series", but the referees of Dr Williams' paper failed to realize that most of his ideas on Cornish phonology are dubious if not just plain wrong (KKC21: 160)

P.D. His [Williams'] orthography is lamentable, an absolute non-starter in comparison with *Kernewek Kemmyn* (KKC21: 170)

P.D. What about Dr Williams' reputation as a lecturer in Celtic studies? K.G. It would be improper for us to speculate on that. I will say that, so far as his hypotheses about Cornish are concerned, his credibility is tending to zero (KKC21: 174).

Note, however, that George is curiously inconsistent. Although he says that my "credibility is tending to zero" he also acknowledges his debt to me as a Celtic scholar:

I acknowledge the work done by a long line of Celtic scholars from Edward Lhuyd through Jenner, Nance and Smith to Nicholas Williams (KKC21: 11).

B) I was very unhappy with Kernowek Kemyn. I knew from my extensive reading of the whole of Cornish literature, that Kernowek Kemyn was

INTRODUCTION

mistaken in phonology and inauthentic in spelling. Kernowek Kemyn to me, as to many others, is not Cornish in any real sense. The mere fact that an attempt was being made in KKC21 to vindicate Kernowek Kemyn, which I dislike so very much, was enough to make me put the book aside and to leave the task of dismissing it to others. This they certainly have done. Mills, for example, says of KKC21: "To demonstrate individually that each of George's analyses is wrong would take a very long time, simply because there are a lot of analyses and there is very little that could be said to be right about any ot them" (*Cornish Studies: Seven*: 201). Other academics and commentators who have written against Kernowek Kemyn include Charles Penglase, Michael Everson, Mícheál Ó Searcóid, and Neil Kennedy.

0.02 George's "orthographic profiles"

The first thing one notices about KKC21 is that George throughout uses what he calls "orthographic profiles" as evidence for his views. These are boxes in which the occurrences of different spellings are attested in the various Cornish texts from the *Charter Fragment* to the *Creation of the World*. In these profiles George gives the number of attestations, but never actually quotes any recorded forms. This is a pity. Mills has pointed out that George's data here are often mistaken. He says, for example, of George's "orthographic profile" of the diphthong *ei* that it omits some attestations on the one hand and misrepresents others on the other. Mills adds, "Such omissions and inaccuracies are typical and not the exception in George's analyses. Consequently, one can have little confidence in George's conclusions" *Cornish Studies: Seven*: 202. Mills goes on to show that what George says about the attestations of the diphthong *iw*, the graph *dh* and the spelling of *ty* 'thou' and *why* 'you' are inaccurate. Mills later in his article says, "Furthermore, when one compares the data reported by George with the primary sources, they do not match. His results and conclusions are therefore spurious." *ibid*: 214. My own research confirms Mills's observations.

Even if every instance cited by George everywhere in his work on Cornish were correct and true to the texts, this would not in itself justify his conclusions. George is, I believe, mistaken when he denies that Middle Cornish had a strong scribal tradition. It will, I hope, become apparent to my readers that there was a standard Middle Cornish orthography until the suppression of Glasney in the sixteenth century. As a result of this tradition the way the scribes wrote often hid rather than exhibited their speech patterns. The mere citation of forms without understanding their implications is not enough. This is true for all George's work on Cornish and it is particularly true for KKC21—even were his data correct, which frequently they are not. His discussion of long *o* is an excellent example of the way in which George, I believe, draws the wrong conclusions from his evidence.

If George's data were all accurate and even if George's conclusions were all correct, this would not vindicate Kernowek Kemyn. Kernowek Kemyn is an

TOWARDS AUTHENTIC CORNISH

arbitrary construct that bears no resemblance to Cornish as it was written by Cornishmen at any time in its history. As Pool so aptly puts it:

> Kemyn is something quite different, an entirely artificial creation which does not resemble Cornish as used by Cornish people at any time in history. To those accustomed to Unified, as indeed to those who prefer Kernuak, Kemyn has an alien and somewhat sinister appearance, as if the language had somehow been taken over by robots and reduced to the status of a code (Pool 1995: 6).

0.03 The lack of authenticity in George's spelling

The truth of Pool's observation can readily be seen by comparing the orthography of a selection of words from the Cornish texts with the spellings used in Kernowek Kemyn. For sake of comparison I include the recommended spellings of the same items in my own preferred spelling (Unified Cornish Revised):

KK	spelling in the texts	UCR
arloedh 'lord'	*arluth* PA 4d, OM 336, PC 104, RD 19, etc.	*arluth*
bywnans 'life'	*beunans* OM 682; *bewnans* PA 73b	*bewnans*
bythkweyth 'ever'	*bythqueth* PA 49c, OM 1731, PC 384, etc.	*bythqueth*
diwleuv 'two hands'	*dewle*, PA 131a, OM 2362; *dewla* TH 52	*dewla*
godrevedh 'third day hence'	*gudreva* Lhuyd	*godreva*
goes 'blood'	*goys* BM passim; *gos* OM 812, PC 824, RD 63	*gos*
hwilas 'to seek'	*whelas* PA 257b, OM 1139; *whylas* TH 5a	*whelas*
hwithra 'to examine'	*whythre* OM 1414	*whythra*
imaj 'image'	*ymach* BM 1805	*ymach*
karadow 'beloved'	*caradow* PA 45d, OM 679, PC 73, etc.	*caradow*
kargharow 'shackles'	*carharou* BM 3686	*carharow*
kavoes 'to get'	*cafos* PA 38b; *cafus* OM 647, PC 588, RD 183, etc.	*cafus*
klav 'sick, leprous'	*claff* PA 25b; *claf* OM 1337, PC 1027, RD 724	*claf*
klywes 'to hear'	*clewas* PA 79b, OM 1436; *clowes* BM 3709	*clowes*
koen 'dinner'	*con* BM 1020	*con*
koes 'wood'	*cos* OM 364; *coys* OM 2589	*cos*
kreashyon 'creation'	*creacon* CW 2535; *creacion* TH 14; *creasion* TH 30a	*creacyon*
Krist 'Christ'	*Cryst* PA 59b, 60a	*Cryst*
Kristyon 'Christian'	*crystyen* BM 1327	*Crystyon*
kryghylli 'to shake'	*crehellys* (ppt.) PA 184d	*crehylly*
kwit 'quite'	*quyt* PC 1123, RD 130	*quyt*
okkashyon 'occasion'	*occacion* TH 15a; *occasion* CW 2334	*occasyon*
sita 'city'	*cyte* PA 28d, PC 578, BM 2514; *cyta* TH 31a	*cyta*
skrifa 'to write'	*scryfys* (ppt.) PA 17a; *screfa* TH 48	*screfa*
skwier 'squire'	*squyer* OM 2004, BM 57	*squyer*
toemmder 'heat'	*tomder* PA 58c	*tomder*
ynys 'island'	*enys* OM 2592	*enys*.

INTRODUCTION

0.04 George's approach to the Cornish scribal tradition
George says of me:

> So long as he is hide-bound by a perceived, but quite unnecessary, need to stick as closely as possible to the spellings of the texts, his orthography will remain inferior to that of *Kernewek Kemmyn*. He is fighting with one hand tied behind his back (KKC21: 170).

I am perplexed by this observation. The Cornish revival is attempting to revive an extinct language. It is difficult to ascertain the sound system of Cornish, and there is much disagreement on this score. But we at least have the texts, written by Cornish speakers who knew the language far better than we. It seems to me, that the least we can do, is to attempt as far as possible to write as they did, while trying also to get as close as we can to their pronunciation. Kernowek Kemyn does not do this. First it proposes a phonology which is open to question, and then superimposes upon it a modern, artificial and constructed orthography. George asserts that my orthography will remain inferior to that of Kernowek Kemyn. I hope, whatever imperfections there are in UCR, that nobody will say of it, as I and others say of Kernowek Kemyn, that it is simply not Cornish. Charles Penglase, for example, writes about George's work PSRC:

> There is, therefore, no discussion of the central issue of trying to remain true to traditional Cornish. And yet the underlying assumption involved in a revival movement is the need to restore a traditional language which once existed, and it is this which gives a revival movement its cultural and historical validity. This was overlooked with the invention of a new twentieth-century system in which, as the guiding principles reveal, the real concern was language planning rather than language revival. It is not surprising that the decision by the Cornish Language Board in 1987 to accept George's system should have led to a series of objections, expressed in the words of one leading Cornish scholar who warned that "the Language Board has taken an unjustifiably wrong turn" (*Cornish Studies: Two*: 101).

Mills goes even farther and says: "In fact some people might go as far as to argue that Kernewek Kemmyn has more in common with fictional artificial languages like Quenya and Britheinig than with traditional Cornish" *Cornish Studies: Seven*: 215. That is certainly my view, and I hope to show why in the pages which follow.

0.05 A turning point in the Cornish revival
We are at the moment (2005), however, at a turning-point. The Government has agreed to provide modest funding for the Cornish language It is abundantly clear from the public meetings that the Cornish public want the language movement to agree on a single orthography. Given that the spelling of Kernowek Kemyn is based on the one hand upon a whole series of

misunderstandings and misconceptions and is on the other largely invention, it is imperative that Kernowek Kemyn does not become the system of choice. If, as seems likely, the matter is put in the hands of an independent panel of experts from outside Cornwall, there is little chance that Kernowek Kemyn will be recommended as the Cornish orthography of the future. This book is intended to assist the debate and thus to lessen the use of this unsatisfactory form of Cornish.

ABBREVIATIONS AND REFERENCES

AB = Edward Lhuyd, *Archæologia Britannica* (London 1707 [reprinted Shannon 1971])
ACB = William Pryce, *Archæologia Cornu-Britannica* (Sherborne 1790)
AD = Avoidance of Discussion
B = Breton
BF = O. J. Padel, *The Cornish Writings of the Boson Family* (Redruth 1975)
BK = *Bewnans Ke* [text from the edition of G. Thomas and N. Williams, in press]
BM = Whitley Stokes (ed.), *Beunans Meriasek: the life of St Meriasek, Bishop and confessor, a Cornish drama* (London: Trübner and Co. 1872)
Borlase = William Borlase, *Antiquities of the County of Cornwall* (London 1754)
Breton Grammar = Roparz Hemon, *Breton Grammar* (Tenth Edition), Translated, adapted, and revised by Michael Everson (Dublin 1995)
Campanile = E. Campanile, *Profilo etimologico del cornico antico* (Pisa, 1974)
Carn = *Carn: A link between the Celtic Nations* (Journal of the Celtic League)
CF = *The Charter Fragment*, text from E. Campanile, "Un frammento scenico mediocornico", *Studi e saggi linguistici* 60-80, supplement to *L'Italia Dialettale* 26
CH = Roparz Hemon (ed.), *Christmas Hymns in the Vannes dialect of Breton* (Dublin 1956)
CPNE = O. J. Padel, *Cornish Place-name Elements* (Nottingham 1985)
Cornish-English Dictionary = R. Morton Nance, *Cornish-English Dictionary* (1938) [reprinted Redruth 1990]
CS = Caradar [A.S.D. Smith], *Cornish Simplified* (1955) [reprinted Camborne 1972]
CS2 = Caradar [A.S.D. Smith], *Cornish Simplified: Part Two*, edited by E.G.R. Hooper [Talek], (Redruth 1984)
Cornish Studies = *Cornish Studies: Second Series*, edited by Philip Payton (University of Exeter Press 1993-)
CT = Nicholas Williams, *Cornish Today: an examination of the revived language*, first and second editions (Sutton Coldfield: Kernewek dre Lyther 1995)
CT3 = Nicholas Williams, *Cornish Today: an examination of the revived language*, third edition (Westport: Evertype 2006, ISBN 978-1-904808-07-7)
CTO = Completely Traditional Orthography (see Williams 1997, Appendix E)
CW = Whitley Stokes (ed.), *Gwreans an Bys: the Creation of the World*, (London: Williams & Norgate 1864 [reprinted Kessinger Publishing 1987, ISBN 0-7661-8009-3])
DG = Davies Gilbert, *The Creation of the World with Noah's Flood* (London 1827)
EGC = Stephen J. Williams, *Elfennau Gramadeg Cymraeg* (Cardiff 1960)
ÉC = *Études Celtiques*
George 1992 = Ken George, "An delinyans pellder-termyn toul rag studhya an yeth kernewek" in G. Le Menn and J.-Y. Le Moing, *Bretagne et Pays Celtiques: Mélanges offerts à la mémoire de Léon Fleuriot* (Rennes & St Brieuc 1992)
Gerlyver Kres = Ken George, *The New Standard Cornish Dictionary: An Gerlyver Kres* ([s.l.], Kesva an Taves Kernewek 1998)
GKK = Ken George, *Gerlyver Kernewek Kemmyn* ([s.l.], Cornish Language Board 1993)
GMC1 = Wella Brown, *A Grammar of Modern Cornish* (Saltash: Cornish Language Board 1984) [Unified Cornish]
GMC2 = Wella Brown, *A Grammar of Modern Cornish*, second edition ([s.l.]: Cornish Language Board 1993)

xiii

TOWARDS AUTHENTIC CORNISH

GMW = D. Simon Evans, *A Grammar of Middle Welsh* (Dublin 1964)
HCL = Henry Jenner, *A Handbook of the Cornish Language chiefly in its latest stages with some account of its history and literature* (London 1904)
HMB = D. W. F. Hardie, *A Handbook of Modern Breton (Armorican)* (Cardiff 1948)
HTLO = Hypothesis of the Two Long *o*'s
ID = Incorrect Data
JCH = "Jowan Chy an Horth: John of Chyanhor" [text from AB: 251-53 and BF: 14-19]
Kemysk Kernewek, edited by E. G. R. Hooper (Camborne, An Lef Kernewek 1964)
Kerew = biblical translations by Wella Kerew, edited by J. Loth, *Revue Celtique* 23: 173-200
Kernow
KK = Kernowek Kemyn
KKC21 = *Kernewek Kemmyn: Cornish for the Twenty-First Century*, Paul Dunbar and Ken George ([s.l.], Cornish Language Board 1997)
LAM = Alan M. Kent and Tim Saunders (editors), *Looking at the Mermaid: a reader in Cornish literature 900-1900* (London 2000)
LCB = Robert Williams, *Lexicon Cornu-Britannicum* (Llandovery 1865)
Loth 1900 = J. Loth, "Cornique moderne", in *Archiv für Celtische Lexicographie* (Halle): 224-29
Nance 1952 = R. Morton Nance, *An English-Cornish Dictionary* (Marazion 1952) [reprinted 1978]
Nebbaz Gerriau = Nicholas Boson, *Nebbaz Gerriau dro tho Carnoack* "A few words about Cornish" [text from BF: 24-37]
Norris 1859 = Edwin Norris, *The Ancient Cornish Drama* i-ii (London [reprinted New York/London, Benjamin Blom 1968])
OCV = "Old Cornish Vocabulary" [quoted from Norris 1859 ii: 311-435 and Campanile 1974]
OM = "Origo Mundi" in Norris (1859) i: 1-219
Ordinalia = The three *Ordinalia*, OM, PC and RD from Norris i-ii (1859)
Ó Searcóid (1997) = Mícheál Ó Searcóid. 1997. "A mathematician's view of the use of mathematics in George's 'Long *o*-type vowels in Cornish'". www.evertype.com/gram/searcoid-cornish-maths.pdf
PA = *Pascon agan Arluth* "The Passion of our Lord", text from Harry Woodhouse, *The Cornish Passion Poem in facsimile* (Penryn 2002)
PC = "Passio Domini Nostri Jhesu Christi" in Norris 1859 i 221-479
PNWP = P. A. S. Pool, *The Place-names of West Penwith*, second edition (Penzance 1985)
Pryce *see* ACB
PSRC = Ken George, *The Pronunciation and Spelling of Revived Cornish* ([s.l.]: Cornish Language Board 1986)
RC = *Revue Celtique*
RD = "Resurrexio Domini Nostri Jhesu Christi" in Norris 1859 ii 1-199
SA = *Sacrament an Alter* "Sacrament of the Altar" text quoted from an unpublished edition by D.H. Frost, *Sacrament an Alter: Part II* (St David's College 2003)
Saunders 1990 = Tim Saunders, *Geriadur Arnevez kernauek-brezhonek*, ([s.l.], Imbourc'h 1990)
Pool 1995 = P. A. S. Pool, *The second death of Cornish* (Redruth 1995)
SP = Special Pleading
SWF = Single Written Form (of revived Cornish)

ABBREVIATIONS AND REFERENCES

TH = John Tregear, *Homelyes xiii in Cornysche* (British Library Additional MS 46, 397) [text from a cyclostyled text published by Christopher Bice ([s.l.] 1969)]

UC = Unified Cornish

UCR = Unified Cornish Revised

W = Welsh

Wakelin 1975 = Martyn F. Wakelin, *Language and history in Cornwall* (Leicester: Leicester University Press 1975)

Weatherhill 2005 = Craig Weatherhill, *Place Names in Cornwall and Scilly: A Westcountry Guide* (Launceston 2005)

Williams 1954 = Gwyn Williams, *An Introduction to Welsh Poetry* (London 1954)

Williams 1997 = Nicholas Williams, *Clappya Kernowek: an introduction to Unified Cornish Revised* (Agan Tavas, Portreath 1997, ISBN 1-901409-01-5)

Williams 2006a = "A problem in Cornish phonology" in Nicholas Williams, *Writings on Revived Cornish* (Westport: Evertype 2006, ISBN 978-1-904808-08-4), 1–25

Williams 2006d = "Pre-occlusion in Cornish" in Nicholas Williams, *Writings on Revived Cornish* (Westport: Evertype 2006, ISBN 978-1-904808-08-4) 65–92

Williams 2006f = "Indirect statement in Cornish and Breton" in Nicholas Williams, *Writings on Revived Cornish* (Westport: Evertype 2006, ISBN 978-1-904808-08-4) 111–119

WORC = Nicholas Williams, *Writings on Revived Cornish* (Westport: Evertype 2006, ISBN 978-1-904808-08-4)

YBB = F. Kervella, *Yezhadur bras ar brezhoneg* (La Baule 1947).

Towards Authentic Cornish

CHAPTER 1
My criticisms of Kernowek Kemyn (KKC21: 9-12)

1.00 My criticisms listed
Dunbar and George (KKC21: 10, Fig. 1.1) list my 26 criticisms of Kernowek Kemyn from *Cornish Today* (CT). My criticisms as listed by Dunbar and George read as follows:

C1) Kernowek Kemyn insists of three vocalic lengths: long, half-long and short but Middle Cornish had only long and short.
C2) Kernowek Kemyn distinguishes /ɪː/ and /eː/ although the two had fallen together as /eː/ in Middle Cornish.
C3) Kernowek Kemyn distinguishes /ɔː/ and /oː/ although in standard Middle Cornish the two had fallen together.
C4) Kernowek Kemyn is unaware that /iː/ had become /ej/ in final position in Middle Cornish.
C5) Kernowek Kemyn is unaware that original /ej/ and /aj/ had fallen together as /aj/ in Middle Cornish.
C6) Kernowek Kemyn is unaware that /ow/ and /aw/ were falling together as /aw/ in Middle Cornish.
C7) Kernowek Kemyn is unaware that final /yː/ had become /ɪw/ in Middle Cornish and that final /uː/ had become /ew/.
C8) Kernowek Kemyn distinguishes /i/ and /ɪ/, though the two had fallen together as /ɪ/ in Middle Cornish and /ɪ/ alternated with /e/. Kernowek Kemyn therefore spells 'look', for example, as <mires> with /i/ although it is most frequently spelled *meras* in the texts.
C9) Kernowek Kemyn incorrectly pronounces long /aː/ as [aː] and not [æː].
C10) Kernowek Kemyn is ignorant of the vocalic alternation *y* ~ *e* and as a result posits such non-existent forms as *gwydhenn* 'tree', *hwytha* 'to blow', *ynys* 'island'.
C11) Kernowek Kemyn posits three diphthongs /iw/, /ɪw/ and /ew/ when Middle Cornish had 2 only (or in some cases only 1).
C12) Kernowek Kemyn has *klyw, klywes* and *byw, bywnans* when Middle Cornish had *clew, clewes/clowes* and *byw/bew, bewnans/bownans*.
C13) Kernowek Kemyn attempts to distinguish quality in unstressed vowels even though all unstressed vowels are schwa from the Middle Cornish period onwards.
C14) Kernowek Kemyn posits the impossible /mɪː/ and /tɪː/ for 'I' and 'thou' respectively.
C15) Kernowek Kemyn is unaware that 'to thee' was both /ðɪz/ and /ðiːz/ in Middle Cornish.

1

C16) Kernowek Kemyn spells and pronounces *deghow* 'right' with an unhistorical /e/.
C17) Kernowek Kemyn posits a whole series of geminate consonants in Cornish: /pp/, /tt/, /xx/, etc. none of which existed in the Middle Cornish period.
C18) Kernowek Kemyn has no voiceless sonants /rh/, /lh/, /nh/, even though such items were a feature of Middle Cornish.
C19) Kernowek Kemyn is unaware of the rule that *deg* 'ten', *gwreg* 'wife' always have final /g/ but *medhek* 'doctor' and *gowek* 'mendacious' always have /k/ and the same voice/voicelessness operates with *b*/*p*.
C20) Kernowek Kemyn uses graphs that are at variance with mediaeval and modern practice, e.g. <k> before back vowels as in <Kammbronn>; <kw> for <qu> and <hw> for <wh>.
C21) Because Kernowek Kemyn has half-length, which was absent from Middle Cornish, the system is compelled to geminate letters unhistorically in *mamm* 'mother', *gwann* 'weak', for example.
C22) Kernowek Kemyn is inconsistent with respect to the gemination of consonants: *Kalann* 'Calends', but *lovan* 'rope', [*blydhen* 'year'], but *kribenn* 'comb'.
C23) Kernowek Kemyn is inconsistent in using <oe> for /o:/ in *moes* 'table', for example, but /o-e/ in *aloes* 'aloes'.
C24) Kernowek Kemyn inconsistently uses <sh> to mean [ʃ] in *shap* 'shape' but /sh/ in *leshanow*.
C25) The etymologies underlying Kernowek Kemyn are often wrong and the orthography is inconsistent as well as being mistaken.
C26) The database on which Kernowek Kemyn was constructed is defective; as a result GLKK is replete with omissions and misinformation.

1.01 Note on the word "graph"

Notice incidentally at C20) above, and indeed elsewhere, that George queries my use of the term "graph" rather than "grapheme". I do so deliberately. "Grapheme" means to me a letter or combination of letters used to denote a phoneme. I use the word "graph" in a generic way to mean a letter or combination of letters without specifying its precise function in the phonology of the language in question. Compare the definition in the *Concise Oxford Dictionary* (1995) s.v.:

> **graph**[2] *Linguistics* a visual symbol, esp. a letter or letters, representing a unit of sound or other feature of speech.

1.02 My criticisms: corrections and additions

I should now like to make two alterations to my criticisms of Kernowek Kemyn in the above list. I should now substitute for C3) the following:

MY CRITICISMS OF KERNOWEK KEMYN

C3) Kernowek Kemyn mistakenly believes that Middle Cornish had two long vowels /ɔː/ and /oː/. Middle Cornish originally had /oː/ and /oˑɪ/ but during the Middle Cornish period these two fell together as /oː/ except in final position where /oˑɪ/ remained a diphthong, simplifying to /oj/, e.g. *moy* 'more'.

In C7) I would now omit "and that final /uː/ had become /ew/". This remark was my attempt to explain *plew* 'parish', which I now believe can be better elucidated as an example of metathesis (see **13.06** below).

In addition to the 26 criticisms listed above I should also like to add the following:

C27) Although it ignores the Prosodic Shift, Kernowek Kemyn allows pre-occlusion in pronunciation which is itself a direct consequence of the shift.

C28) The allophone [mː] of /m/ was entirely determined by position. Spellings like <kemmer> and <kemmyn> in Kernowek Kemyn are therefore unnecessary. Kernowek Kemyn, however, believes that /m/ and [mː] were phonemically distinct in Middle Cornish. In which case to spell them identically e.g. in <kemmeres> and <kemmer>, is a repudiation of the phonemic principle, which Kernowek Kemyn claims to espouse.

C29) The proponents of Kernowek Kemyn because they are unaware that the Prosodic Shift is early, misunderstand the function of <nn> in words like *crenna* 'to tremble', *pre(n)na* 'to buy', and *ale(n)na* 'hence'. In consequence discussion of these items in the handbooks of Kernowek Kemyn is mistaken and misleading.

C30) Even if the phonology underlying Kernowek Kemyn could be shown to be correct, the spelling system of Kernowek Kemyn is artificial, arbitrary and quite out of keeping with the orthography of the traditional language. Cornish people are attempting to revive their ancestral language because they value their traditions. In which case using such an unhistorical orthography is illegitimate.

C31) George has now admitted that the database on which he based his *Gerlyver Kernewek Kemmyn* was faulty. Perhaps George could be asked to correct his database and then rewrite Kernowek Kemyn accordingly.

1.03 Inconsistencies in George's Dictionary of Kernowek Kemyn

Gerlyver Kernewek Kemmyn [GKK] contains many notes indicating that George was perplexed by the phonology of Middle Cornish, largely because it does not conform to his own expectations. We shall refer to several of these notes of his below. A detailed analysis of GKK, that I undertook after CT was written, has made me realize that Kernowek Kemyn spellings are even more inconsistent than I previously feared (see C25). Here is a list of some

TOWARDS AUTHENTIC CORNISH

inconsistencies from GKK (based, with additions, on the list I published in *Cornish Studies: Nine*: 248-49):

kavoes 'to get' (< Old Cornish *-uit*) but *eglos* 'church' (Old Cornish < *-uis*)
prena 'to buy' (Welsh *prynu*), *krena* 'to tremble' (Welsh *crynu*) but *warlyna* 'last year' (Welsh *y llynedd*)
bywek 'lively' (Welsh *bywiog*) but *Kernewek* 'Cornish' (Welsh *Cernyweg*)
naw 'nine' and *nawves* 'ninth' but *nownsek* 'nineteen' and *nownsegves* 'nineteenth'
Dewnens 'Devonshire' (Welsh *Dyfnaint*) but *bywnans* (cf. Welsh *bywyd*)
defendya 'to defend' but *difformya* 'to deform'
diskarga 'to discharge' (Breton *diskargañ*) but *dyskybel* 'disciple' (Breton *diskibl*)
politek 'politic' (< Greek *politikos*) but *krytyk* 'critic' (< Greek *kritikos*)
epystyl 'epistle' (Welsh *epistol*) but *pistyll* 'spout' (Welsh *pistyll*)
kyst 'box' (Welsh *cist*) but *trist* 'sad' (Welsh *trist*)
arsmetryk 'arithmetic' but *eretik* 'heretic'
gwerthys 'shuttle' (Breton *gwerzhid*) but *gonis* 'work' (Breton *gounid*)
chalys 'chalice' but *servis* 'service'
palys 'palace' (Welsh *palas*) but *solas* 'solace' (Welsh *solas*)
jentyl 'well-born' (< Old French *gentil*) but *sivil* 'civil' (< Old French *civil*)
kardinal 'cardinal' (< Latin *cardinalis*) but *ordenal* 'ordinal' (< Latin *ordinale*)
pynakyl 'pinnacle', *bytakyl* 'binnacle' but *tabernakel* 'tabernacle'
kopel 'couple' but *kropyl* 'cripple'
favour 'favour' but *sokor* 'succour'
edifia 'to edify', *sertifia* 'to certify' but *justifya* 'to justify'
frya 'to free' but *fria* 'to fry', *fia* 'to flee'
annia 'to vex' but *agrya* 'to agree'
gokki 'foolish', *gokkineth* 'folly' but *gokkyes* 'fools'
trynyta 'trinity', *cheryta* 'charity', *dynyta* 'dignity' but *antikwita* 'antiquity', *kontroversita* 'controversy'
konviktya 'to convict' but *vyktori* 'victory'
vikar 'vicar' (< Old French *vicaire*) but *vytel* 'victuals' (< Old French *vitaille*)
kemmyska 'to mix' (< *ken* + *mysky*; cf. Welsh *cymysgu*) but *kemusur* 'symmetry' (< *ken* + *musur*; cf. Welsh *cymesur*)
demondya 'to demand' (< Old French *demander*) but *kommondya* 'to command' (< Old French *comander*)
gwannder 'weakness' (Breton *gwander*) but *glander* 'cleanness' (Breton *glander*)
klyket 'clicket' but *boekket* 'bucket'
basya 'abate', *klasya* 'to class, to classify' but *passya* 'to pass'
fashyon 'fashion' but *passhyon* 'passion'
dessayt 'deceit' (< Middle English *deceite*) but *resayt* 'recipe' (< Middle English *receite*)
nesa 'to approach' (Welsh *nesu, nesau*) but *nessa* 'next' (Welsh *nesaf*)
klokk 'clock' but *luk* 'luck'
charet 'chariot' but *gargett* 'garter'
fyttya 'to fit' but *akwitya* 'to acquit' (*aquyttya* in the texts)
plattya 'to crouch' but *skwatya* 'to squash'
hwypp 'whip' but *skryp* 'scrip'

MY CRITICISMS OF KERNOWEK KEMYN

hwyppya 'to whip' but *strypya* 'to strip'
brotell 'brittle' but *sotel* 'subtle'
botell 'bottle' but *titel* 'title'
fisek 'physic' but *kymyk* 'chemistry'
referya 'to refer', *preferya* 'to prefer' but *konkerrya* 'to conquer' and *gwerrya* 'to make war'
sertan 'certain' but *bargen* 'bargain'
fesont 'pheasant', *plesont* 'pleasant' but *remenant* 'remnant' and *semlant* (< Middle English *semlant*) 'appearance'
pemont 'payment' (< Middle English *paiement*) but *fisment* 'face' (< Middle English *visement*)
jolyf 'lively' (*iolyf* RD 2013) but *oliv* 'olive' (*olyf* PC 244).
tulyfant 'tulip' but *olifans* 'elephant'
cavach 'cabbage', *trumach* 'sea journey' (pl. *trumajys*) but *imaj* 'image', *vyaj* 'journey', *bysaj* 'face', *damaj* 'damage'.

Notice further **polat** 'fellow' (GKK: 257) but **drogpollat** 'rascal' (GKK: 84). Perhaps the most remarkable inconsistency in GKK involves the form of the word *kyst* 'box'. Under the word *strolgist* 'litter-bin' we are told that the word is a compound of *strol* 'mess, litter' and 2*kist*, that is to say the second of two items spelt *kist*, which each have a separate entry. Oddly enough there is no second *kist*, nor is there a first *kist* either. The word in question is cited only under *kyst* 'box, chest' (see the list above) and this spelling with <y> is also seen in the entry *atalgyst* 'dustbin' < *atal* + *kyst* (GKK: 39). I say in C26 above that George's *Gerlyver Kernewek Kemmyn* is "replete with omissions and misinformation." This George describes as "a calumny" (KKC21: 12). I understand 'calumny' to mean a slander or defamation of a person, and of course I have defamed nobody. I believe now, if anything, I was too kind to *Gerlyver Kernewek Kemmyn* (GKK). When I wrote *Cornish Today* I did not fully realize just how unsatisfactory the dictionary was.

CHAPTER 2
General: Ideology (KKC21: 13-16)

2.00 Absence of theoretical approach in George's work on Cornish.
Penglase has cogently written of George's approach to Cornish phonology in PSRC:

> The use of appropriate research methodology is essential in academic work. There is a number of unusual methodological features in George's dissertation, but there is no point in listing them all. However one crucial omission which deserves mention is the lack of a critical investigation of the validity of Middle Cornish phonology; this is assumed. Whether one thinks a feature is valid or not, it has to be critically examined and supported by firm evidence. In fact, the absence of these requirements makes the application of this phonological system to Cornish an arbitrary imposition on the language (Charles Penglase, *Cornish Studies: Two*: 100).

In fact the deficiencies of George's approach to Cornish phonology and spelling are deeper and more serious still. George lacks any theoretical approach at all. Neither in PSRC nor in his answer to my criticisms does he adopt any unifying theme or idea. Both where he posits in PSRC and where he attempts to refute in KKC21 his assumptions are unexpressed. My critique of Kernowek Kemyn, on the other hand, is based on two premises which I have stated again and again *ad nauseam*: A) that the Prosodic Shift occurred before our earliest Middle Cornish texts and B) that it is illegitimate to clothe a resuscitated language in an arbitrary and newly-constructed orthography, even if our understanding of the phonology is perfect. Given that, in my view, George failed to understand Cornish phonology, Kernowek Kemyn orthography is not an acceptable medium for the revival and ought to be abandoned.

If in KKC21 as a refutation of my criticisms George adduced a whole series of arguments to show that the Prosodic Shift occurred *c*. 1625, as he now believes, his book might carry some weight. This, however, he does not do. He claims, very limply in my view, that the Prosodic Shift of *c*. 1625 lengthened some vowels rather than shortening them. His *[iˑ] in *gwetha* 'keep', *meras* 'look', *syra* 'father', etc. was lengthened, he says, by the shift, and this is the reason for such Late Cornish spellings as *gweetha*, *meero* and *seera*. This is his only attempt at a structural attack on my criticisms. Elsewhere he is content to answer my systematic criticisms *seriatim*, attempting to show case by case that I am mistaken. As evidence for my error he uses "orthographic profiles", in which he does not actually cite any attested forms. It is an easy matter to show that his profiles are inaccurate, as both I and Mills have done. His profiles,

GENERAL: IDEOLOGY

moreover, take no notice of scribal tradition—because George believes that Middle Cornish had none.

Here George's argument is, in my view, completely unconvincing. George believes that Middle Cornish and Late Cornish are very different forms of the language, largely because they are spelt differently. He believes, moreover, that Middle Cornish spelling is based on English. He also believes that Late Cornish spelling is based on English. George does not attempt anywhere to explain, however, how it is that the two orthographies are so different from each other, if they are both have the same basis, i.e. English spelling.

The academic world has been dismissive, quite rightly in my view, of KKC21, George's latest offering in the field of Cornish phonology. Mills has dismissed it out of hand in the most emphatic language: "there are a lot of analyses [in KKC21] and there is very little that could be said to be right about any of them" (*Cornish Studies: Seven*: 201). I do not know of any professional Celticist who has read KKC21 and is convinced by it. In the pages that follow I will have no difficulty in refuting any point that George makes in the work. My advice to George and his supporters is therefore as follows: if you wish to vindicate Kernowek Kemyn, produce arguments based on relevant quotations from the texts to show conclusively that Middle Cornish had a three-fold division of length: long, half-long and short. Quote extensively from the texts to show that the phonology of Kernowek Kemyn is correct. "Orthographic profiles" are insufficient. If you cannot adduce evidence from the texts to prove your phonology, perhaps you should consider rejecting Kernowek Kemyn.

2.01 Traditional Cornish Orthography

George begins his defence of Kernowek Kemyn with a general discussion of his attitude to the spelling of the Middle Cornish texts. Note that I say George, rather than Dunbar and George, because in the dialogue format of this book it is George that makes all the running. We read the following:

> K.G. The following sentence from C[ornish] T[oday] §17.4 is very telling:
> "The lack of method for indicating length [i.e. length of vowels] is perhaps a weakness in Unified Orthography, but it cannot be remedied without doing violence to the spelling of the texts."
> P.D. "violence"!?
> K.G. That's what Dr Williams writes: he appears to hold the orthography of the mediaeval texts as sacrosanct.
> P.D. And you do not?
> K.G. No, I do not.
> P.D. That's an unequivocal admission to make, and one which is bound to cause comment. You'd better explain it.
> K.G. I do not consider that there is any particular intrinsic merit in the orthography of Middle Cornish; it is only one of four different orthographic styles used to write down traditional Cornish, and in the final analysis it is based on contemporary English orthography (KKC21: 15).

In the next chapter I will show how consistent is Middle Cornish orthography from the *Charter Fragment* (?fourteenth century) to the *Creation of the World* (1611). I shall also demonstrate quite clearly that it is not based on contemporary English orthography but is a system unique to Cornish and derives from a number of sources. For the time being, let us just look at the implications of what George says above. George claims to be reviving an extinct medieval language, for which the Middle Cornish texts are by far our most extensive and most complete evidence. George, however, has no particular respect for the medieval scribes who wrote Cornish and indeed who knew Cornish far better than anybody alive today. George believes his orthography, based on his understanding of Cornish phonology, is superior to that of the Middle Cornish writers themselves.

Unlike the traditional spelling of Middle Cornish, George clearly believes that Kernowek Kemyn spells Cornish in such a way as to make the pronunciation immediately apparent. George is mistaken on this point. If the pronunciation of each word in Kernowek Kemyn is obvious, why does George add the pronunciation in phonetic script after so many entries in his *Gerlyver Kernewek Kemmyn*?

But that is not the main argument for opposing Kernowek Kemyn orthography. There are two much more cogent reasons.

2.02 Two theoretical arguments against Kernowek Kemyn

Just suppose for the sake of argument that the phonology on which Kernowek Kemyn is based, turns out to have been mistaken. Then the orthography will have to be reformed. Let us take an obvious example. Assume that the deviser of Kernowek Kemyn mistakenly believed that the variation *s*/*g* (*j*) in words like *kerensa*/*kerenge* 'love' or *pesy*/*pegy* 'pray' indicated two separate palatalized consonants. Assume further that he decided (quite contrary to medieval practice) to spell these consonants <tj> and <dj>. If it could be shown that such items had never existed in the tradtional language, the offending items would have to be removed and replaced by something more traditional, and indeed less bizarre.

Many of my readers will, of course, know that this did indeed happen. Kernowek Kemyn did in its earliest form contain the remarkable graphs <tj> and <dj> . They may also be aware that it was I who first pointed out (Williams 2006a), that these items were unjustified and should be removed. They were indeed excised from Kernowek Kemyn and replaced by <s> and <j> as in Unified Cornish. The Middle Cornish texts on occasion spell *g* in such items with <j>; Unified Cornish's spellings are therefore in agreement with the spelling of the texts. There is an important point of principle here. If we spell as the scribes did, we cannot go wrong. This is what Unified Cornish and my own revision Unified Cornish Revised seek to do. Kernowek Kemyn works differently. It arbitrarily decides how Middle Cornish was pronounced and then imposes upon that doubtful phonology its own artificial spelling. If the phonology can be shown to be mistaken, the spelling will also need to be revised.

The users of Kernowek Kemyn are attempting to revive an extinct medieval language but are using a modern and artificial spelling system. It follows that they are not reviving Cornish at all. George says that by insisting on spelling in traditional orthography I am being "over-sensitive" (KKC21: 14). On the contrary, I am merely making a minimal demand: that Cornish speakers use real Cornish spelling rather than some recently invented system, that may or may not be correct. Kernowek Kemyn orthography is certainly not an accurate reflection of Middle Cornish orthography, but even it it were, it would still be illegitimate. We may only revive the language as it was, not as we should like it to be. Anything else is inauthentic.

2.03 Modern spelling reforms and Cornish

George makes much of the spelling reforms of Irish, Breton and Norwegian and suggests that English could well do with spelling reform—although such is not likely to occur. Irish, Breton, Norwegian and English are completely different from Cornish. *They are all living languages.* In each case we know exactly how they are pronounced, the quality of the consonants, the length of the vowels, the intonation, etc. If we reform the spelling of Norwegian, for example, all we are doing is requiring speakers to spell differently (and more logically) than previously. If we change the orthography of Middle Cornish, we are not merely repudiating those who used the language, we are also making assumptions about a language of which we unfortunately know far too little; and the danger exists that our assumptions may be mistaken.

Because Irish, Breton and Norwegian are still spoken languages, none of them is an adequate parallel for us. The closest parallel is Manx. Native Manx became extinct in 1973. Contemporary revivalists used the traditional orthography, even though it is notoriously difficult for learners; it also has the demerit that it separates Manx from its sister languages, Irish and Scottish Gaelic. In fact of course, Manx though extinct is not exactly parallel with Cornish, because the last native speakers of Manx were recorded and their speech noted in phonetic script. We know much more about the phonology of Manx than we do of Cornish, but nobody has seriously suggested that Manx orthography should be replaced by something more logical or closer to the other Gaelic languages. We spell Manx in the traditional spelling, however awkward and inconvenient that may be, simply because to spell differently would be inauthentic, and thus not Manx in any real sense. Kernowek Kemyn respells Cornish according to George's understanding of Cornish phonology, rather than as the medieval scribes spelt. It is for this reason that I believe Kernowek Kemyn is not Cornish.

2.04 George's database

George admits that the database on which Kernowek Kemyn is based contains "slight defects" (KKC21: 11). In 2001 I drew attention to the inconsistent nature of Kernowek Kemyn's "phonemic spelling" and also to the countless inaccuracies in George's database (*Cornish Studies: Nine*: 247-311). In fact I listed approximately 370 instances in the *Gerlyver Kernewek Kemmyn* where George's "authentication codes" were quite simply incorrect. There are doubtless many more errors in his database, but for reasons of space I confined myself to some of those entries that occurred on average fewer than ten times in the text. George acquired an early draft of my notes from a third party and sent me a postcard explaining why so many occurred in his database. He wrote:

> My a vynn grassa dhis rag an rol a "fowtow" dannvenys dhymm gans [name]. Rann vrassa anedha yw sevys drefenn (a) nag esa genev dasskrif kowal a Pryce; (b) ow thowlenn dhe hwilas henwyn-verb hepken; (c) na wrug vri orth ragskrif Lhuyd in A[rchæologia] B[ritannica] awos y vos "idiosyncratic and highly Cymricised."
>
> [I wish to thank you for the list of "errors" sent me by [name]. The majority of them have arisen because: (a) I did not have a complete copy of Pryce; (b) my computer program searched only for verbal nouns only; (c) I ignored Lhuyd's preface in AB because it was "idiosyncratic and highly cymricized" {a quotation from my article in *Studia Celtica* 32 (1998): 129-54 on pre-occlusion in which I criticize George's phonology}.]*

I leave it to the reader to consult my article in *Cornish Studies: Nine* to see what reply I made to such special pleading. That someone working so intensively upon Cornish should not have had all the necessary texts at his elbow and should moreover have used such an imperfect computer program is itself astonishing. One should note, however, that on his postcard George does indeed admit that his database was faulty, whereas in KKC21 (which was written before my article) he implies that the errors in his database are insignificant.

I should like to make three further points here. In the first place it is ironic that George excuses his having omitted much from Lhuyd's preface on the grounds that Lhuyd's Cornish was to a great extent based on Welsh. In fact George omits much from everywhere in *Archæologia Britannica*, not just from Lhuyd's preface. Yet George asserts in that Lhuyd's orthography of Cornish is the "most scientific and logical of the four [i.e. orthographies]" (KKC21: 14). Moreover George spells 'south' in Cornish <deghow> rather than the attested <dyhow>, <dyghow> "since Breton *dehou* and Welsh *de* both have *e*" (KKC21: 9). Clearly being Cymricized is, in George's view, not always a bad thing.

---

* Now reprinted in WORC, pp. 65–92.

GENERAL: IDEOLOGY

Shortly after Kernowek Kemyn was adopted I wrote to George objecting inter alia to his spelling *Bewnans Meryasek* as **Bywnans Meryadjek*. I probably did not make myself completely clear, because George apparently understood my problem here to be with both *byw* and **bywnans,* rather than with the spelling of **bywnans* only. At all events in his reply to me (26 September 1987) he wrote:

> Ny welav travith kamm gans *byw*; yndelma yth yw skrifys yn Kembrek. An *i* y'n [*recte* yn] hanow *Meriasek* o /j/; trisyllabek o an ger; ytho y skrifav *Bywnans Meryadjek*. Nyndj eus ges omma
>
> [I can see nothing wrong with *byw*; it is so written in Welsh. The *i* in the name *Meriasek* was /j/; the word was trisyllabic; therefore I write *Bywnans Meryadjek*. There is no joke here.]

George at this date (1987) wrote that the spelling **bywnans* was all right, because 'live' was *byw* in Welsh. Yet later he wrote to say that he had avoided Lhuyd when writing his *Gerlyver Kernewek Kemmyn* (1993) because Lhuyd's Cornish was so Cymricized!

2.05 Statistics from the texts

As we shall see in greater detail below, much of what George says about the Cornish texts is inaccurate. This is not necessarily of great importance. It is a truism of historical linguistics that one must always take account of scribal tradition. Very rarely do scribes write as they speak. They write rather as they have learnt to write—and only rarely give themselves away by back-spellings and misspellings. When an English speaker writes *formally* for *formerly*, *principle* for *principal* or *their* for *there*, we know that we are dealing with homophones in his dialect. There is, however, no way of telling from correctly spelt English that the pairs *know* and *no*, *sight* and *cite*, *scene* and *seen* are pronounced identically. Even though the spelling conventions in Cornish were much less rigid, the same kind of thing operated in Cornish as well, as we shall see. It is for this reason that much of George's statistical analysis of Cornish, as well as being inaccurate, is also irrelevant.

2.06 My attitude to the orthography of Revived Cornish

It seems to me that if we are resuscitating an extinct language, we must be as faithful as we can to the literary remains of the language. Cornish was a literary language and the language of most of the people of Cornwall until the Reformation. Thereafter it went into a rapid decline. Its literary tradition and thus its orthographical conventions disappeared. Its speakers dwindled and by the end of the eighteenth century it was dead. It seems to me unwise to base our revived speech on the language of the seventeenth and eighteenth centuries (as Gendall initially sought to do). Rather we seek to revive the latest possible stage of the language before its final decline. It was for this reason that I adopted *Beunans Meriasek*, John Tregear and the *Creation of the World* as my foundation texts for all aspects of Unified Cornish Revised. Fortunately, we now have *Bewnans Ke*, a newly discovered play, whose manuscript was written in the second half of the sixteenth century. The play was originally composed a century or so earlier, probably in the reign of Henry VI (1422-61).

Although I base Unified Cornish Revised on these three (and now four) texts, I deviate from their orthography in two important ways. I use <j> in *crejy* 'believe', *ujy* 'is' and *chanjya* 'to change', for example, though the Middle Cornish texts for the most part use <g> in such cases. I do so because Nance and Jenner both did, and the convention is well established in the revived language. Similarly I use <dh> for the voiced dental continuant rather than <th> (or yogh <ȝ>) used in the texts. Again I do so because Nance and Jenner did, and because the convention in now firmly established in the revived language. I must say, however, that I am not completely convinced that either <j> in *crejy*, *ujy*, etc. or <dh> are entirely defensible. Indeed it appears that Caradar himself thought <th> should be used for both <th> and <dh> in Unified Cornish (see CS2: 38-9). Because of my misgivings about <j> and <dh> in Revived Cornish, I added to Williams 1997, Appendix E in which I spell "Jowan Chy an Horth" (JCH) in a completely traditional spelling, i.e. without <dh> or medial/final <j>.

2.07 George's approach to the orthography of Revived Cornish

It is difficult to know exactly what is George's real approach to Cornish orthography, because he seems to have changed his mind from time to time. In PSRC he wrote:

(a) Because most people learn Cornish from books, the orthography must be as phonemic as possible. (This requirement was not necessary for the MidC in the mystery plays, since all the players, one supposes, knew how to pronounce Cornish, and the writing was merely a "visual adjunct to aural memory"...)

(b) It must not, however, be so phonetic [sic] as to mask the etymology of words, and thereby their relations with Breton and Welsh cognates; i.e. it must not fall into the same trap as Manx vis-à-vis Irish and Scots Gaelic.

(c) Although representing a phonological base dated c. 1500, it should reconcile, as far as possible, the desires of different groups to pronounce Cornish in approximately MidC and LateC fashions.

(d) It should not appear so different from the Unified system as to be rejected by the users of Cornish (PSRC: 93).

It would seem, then, in 1986 George believed an ideal spelling for Revived Cornish should be largely phonemic but should nonetheless recognize the etymologies of words and should also be acceptable to speakers of both Late Cornish and Unified Cornish. There is no mention in any of the above of the authenticity of the proposed spelling. At the time George believed that his phonology of Kernowek Kemyn was very close to the traditional language. He says with remarkable assurance:

> I can therefore state with confidence that Revived Cornish, as exemplified by the phonological base described in the chapter, is closer to the Cornish of 1500 than were either OldC or LateC. What is more, it is closer to the Cornish of 1500 than is, say, the "Geordie" dialect to standard English. I therefore suggest that, were a Cornish speaker from Tudor times suddenly to materialize, present-day speakers would, after some initial adjustments and probably a few laughs, be chatting together without difficulty by the end of the day (PSRC: 91).

George's confidence in Kernowek Kemyn is, I regret, misplaced. The phonology underlying it is, in my view, very unlike Tudor Cornish indeed, and in consequence Kernowek Kemyn is inauthentic.

Having read my criticisms of Kernowek Kemyn in *Cornish Today*, George changed his view of Kernowek Kemyn slightly, or at least lost a little of his belief in the excellence of his system. In a "Provisional Response" to *Cornish Today* published in *Kernow* 34: 8-10 George wrote:

> The orthography of Kernowek Kemyn has got its priorities right: it balances the need for historical authenticity with the need for a phonemic system, giving priority to the latter.

George's assurance is considerably less here than it was in PSRC. Indeed he also says in his "Provisional Response":

> There is a measure of uncertainty ("experimental error") associated with the reconstruction of Cornish. Some is due to the variation within the traditional language. Some is due to the differing interpretations of the data. Dr Williams' description of Kernowek Kemyn as inauthentic means rather that it is at variance with his interpretation of the data. Once a reconstruction approaches traditional Cornish so closely as to be within the zone of uncertainty, then it is as authentic as it can be. It is possible for two reconstructions to be within the zone of uncertainty and yet to differ. Under these circumstances other criteria have to be taken into account.

I disagree with George completely here. There is no "experimental error" and there is no "zone of uncertainty" either. We are talking about historical phonology, not natural science. In historical linguistics we do not run experiments. We read carefully and draw conclusions. If George's use of the terms "experimental error" and "zone of uncertainty" are attempts to excuse his own fundamental errors in devising Kernowek Kemyn, they are ineffective. Kernowek Kemyn is mistaken because George made false assumptions about Cornish and built his entire edifice on untested foundations. The orthography of Kernowek Kemyn depends on its underlying sound-system and is for that reason alone erroneous. It is misconceived anyway, because it is artificial and invented and does not attempt to follow the conventions of the Middle Cornish texts. In fact, however, speakers of Kernowek Kemyn still pronounce their Cornish more or less like Unified. The new orthography is a written system only rather than a spoken one. Since the speakers of Kemyn are still using Unified pronunciation, the shift to Kernowek Kemyn was unnecessary, or as Mills says calls it "an expensive waste of time and energy".

But to return to George's approach to Cornish orthography. In KKC21 his old self-confidence seems to have returned. He says of Kernowek Kemyn:

> There are slight defects in it. The magnitude of the enterprise is such that a small amount of error is unavoidable. The defects do not invalidate the basic structure of *Kernewek Kemmyn*. Remember that the data-base was intially constructed using Unified Cornish.... The important thing is that the phonological structure is correct. Dr Williams is opposed to *Kernewek Kemmyn* because he believes that "the phonological base is erroneous." I am grateful to you [i.e. Paul Dunbar] for this opportunity to show that he is wrong (KKC21: 11).

Actually I am opposed to Kernowek Kemyn not merely because it is based on mistaken phonology but also, as I have said before, because it is an unhistorical and inauthentic orthography, containing Old Cornish, Middle Cornish, Breton and Welsh elements, with some aspects being of George's own invention. In a word I am opposed to Kernowek Kemyn because it is not Cornish.

CHAPTER 3
The Cornish scribal tradition (not in KKC21)

3.00 Is Middle Cornish spelling based on contemporary English?
George says of Middle Cornish orthography: "in the last analysis it is based on contemporary English" (KKC21: 14). When George says that Middle Cornish orthography is based on contemporary English spelling and thus lacks its own scribal tradition he is, I believe, mistaken. Middle Cornish has an autonomous spelling system with a long history, related to, but independent of English.

BM was written by Radulphus (or Richardus) Ton in 1504. If one compares the spelling of BM for example English spelling of the same period, that is to say of Early New English, one finds that the two systems overlap somewhat. This is because both to some degree derive from the spelling conventions brought to Britain by the Normans. Both systems, for example, use the combination <gh> and indeed both use <th> for the dental continuants. Generally speaking, however, Early New English, which is very similar to the spelling of Modern English, and the Cornish of BM are distinct. Early New English uses final mute *-e* everywhere, in such words as *hayle* 'hail!', *devyse* 'advice', *case* 'case', etc. BM does not use the mute *e* in such contexts but writes *heyl, aveys / avys* and *cas*. The mute *-e* is frequently in Early New English a sign of a long vowel in the preceding syllable, e.g. *rose, face* whereas BM spells such long vowels without *-e*, *ros* 'gave' BM 2252, *fas* BM 1361. Forms like *wose* BM 999, *vose* BM 2919, *glowe* BM 1030, *gase* BM 1026, *spede* BM 1090; *lawe* BM 1313; *gothe* BM 1765; *meve* BM 2921 are disyllabic and as such are unlike comparable spellings in Early New English.

Very frequently BM spells long vowels with an unetymological *y* to indicate length: *cays* 'case' BM 1442, 1780; *fays* 'face' BM 1205; *gays* 'lets' BM 1113; *glays* 'blue' BM 1445; *grays* 'grace' BM 992; *tays* 'father' BM 862; *tayl* 'pay' BM 1595; *aleys* 'wide open' BM 1256; *geyl* 'conceals' BM 1438; *weyl* 'sees' BM 1437; *leys* 'advantage' BM 3387; *weyst* 'west' BM 748; *boys* 'to be' BM 1133; *cloys* 'closed' 1728; *doys* 'to come' BM 1397; *moys* 'to go' BM 1398; *noys* 'night' BM 1726; *doyr* 'ground' BM 1278; *foyl* 'mad' BM 920; *moyr* 'sea' BM 2538. Interestingly the scribe of BM spells the English expression *by my troth* as <by my troyth> at BM 1485, which is not an English spelling at all, though the words are English. Cf. *forsoyth* in BK cited below. The use of an unetymological *y* to indicate length is well attested elsewhere in Middle Cornish also. Here are some examples:

A
Long *a*
tays 'father' PA 1a; *ny dayl* 'ought not' PA 85a; *grayth* 'grace' PA 222d; *hays* 'seed' CW 914.

B
Long *e*
seygh 'dry' PA 170d; *heys* 'length' PA 178a, OM 392, RD 2538; *aheys* 'at length' PA 233d; *cleyth* 'left' PA 191a; *steyr* 'stars' PA 211a; *cleyr* 'clear' PA 244c; *gveyth* 'trees' OM 37, 51; *geyth* 'day(time)' OM 39, 385, 458; *wheyl* 'work' OM 1226; *a weyl* 'in sight of' PC 1558; *weyl* 'sees' PC 2304; *seyf* 'stands' RD 2612; *beyth* 'tomb' RD 2083.

C
Long *o*
boys 'to be' PA 49b, 110b, 122a; *goyff* 'smith PA 155a; *ternoys* 'next day' PA 238a; *coyth* 'old' OM 855, BK 755, TH 38a; *forsoyth* 'forsooth' BK 359, 1905, 1994, 2050, 2265; *ow toys* 'coming' TH 9.

In TH *i* often replaces *y* in such spellings, e.g. *bois* 'to be' TH 3, 15a, 17a, 26a, 28; *coith* 'old' TH 27, 28a, 52a; *nois* 'night' TH 52.

This unetymological *y*/*i* is very much a Cornish scribal device but is not used in Early New English. In Middle English a long vowel is shown by doubling, e.g. Chaucer's *estaat* 'estate', *been* 'been', *preest* 'priest', *mooder* 'mother', *stoon* 'stone'. Doubled vowels also indicate length in Early New English, but the Great Vowel Shift has altered the pronunciation of both <ee> and <oo> (see below). In Cornish the unetymological *y* as a mark of length is most frequently used in in the combination <oy>, and I believe the combination <oy> was in fact the origin of the practice of writing *y* after a vowel to denote length. In early Middle Cornish *boys* 'food' had a diphthong and *bos* 'to be' a simple long vowel. By the fifteenth century, if not before, the two had fallen together as [oː]. In consequence the convention of writing <oy> for [oː] was extended to words with [oː] that had never had a diphthong. Then the unetymological <y> was witten as a sign of vocalic length after *a* and *e* as well. Clearly this is a development unique to Cornish, that has no parallel in English spelling.

In Early New English spelling a long vowel followed by [v] is usually written vowel + *ve*, e.g. <prove>, <move>, <save>. In BM on the other hand a long vowel + a final *v* is written vowel + <ff>, e.g. <neff>, <eff>, <doff>. <ff> is also used in <neffra> 'always', an English borrowing, which in the contemporary English spelling is <never>. Similarly a long vowel + *g* is written vowel + *gue* in Early New English, e.g. <league>, <ague>, but appears as vowel + <k> in BM, e.g. <tek>, <whek>. In Early New English [k] after a short vowel is most usually <ck>, e.g. <lack>, <physick>. In BM however [k] in such positions is <k>, e.g. <knak>, <carrek>, <Meriasek>.

In Early New English <gh> is written both at the end of words, e.g. <high>, <plough>, <through> and between syllables in such words as <higher>, <highest>. In BM on the other hand etymological <gh> is confined to final position, e.g. <mogh>, <bogh>, whereas between syllables <h> is used, e.g. <bohes>, <luehes>.

THE CORNISH SCRIBAL TRADITION

BM commonly ends plural imperatives in <ugh>, where the <gh> is almost certainly silent and the whole sequence to judge by later texts means [ow]. An equivalent combination in Early New English from the phonetic point of view is <ow>, e.g. in <window>, <fellow>. Interestingly unstressed [ow] in the plural of nouns is not infrequently represented in BM by <ov> rather than <ow> as in some other Middle Cornish texts. It is noteworthy, therefore that BM renders unstressed [ow] in two different ways according to etymology, a sure sign that we are dealing with well-established scribal practice, rather than with an *ad hoc* spelling based for the nonce on English.

3.01 The combinations <oo>, <oa>, <ee> and <ea> in Early New English spelling

I have already alluded to the doubling of the vowels *e* and *o* in Middle English to indicate length, e.g. in *flee* and *stoon*. Such spellings survive into Early New English but with altered values, i.e. [iː] and [uː] respectively. In Early New English the combinations <ea> and <oa> are used to render [eː] and [oː]. We thus in Early New English find the following: *oo* [uː], e.g. in *food*, *oa* [oː], e.g. in *road*, *ee* [iː], e.g. in *queen*, *see* and *ea* [eː], e.g. in *tea*, *sea*. Doubled vowels are very uncommon in Middle Cornish. In BM, for example, there are a few examples of <ee>, e.g. *lee* 'less' BM 481; *lees* 'advantage' BM 663; *kee* 'hedge' BM 1253; *feer* 'fair' BM 2071; *pee* 'pay' BM 3337 and *cheer* 'chair' BM 3002. In these cases the <ee> is a way of representing [eː] rather than [iː] as would have been the case in English spelling contemporary with BM.

After the dissolution of the monasteries and the suppression of Glasney priory in 1545, the long scribal tradition of Cornish began to be lost. It did not happen immediately, for there were still many men in Cornwall who had learnt to write Cornish in Glasney. By the beginning of the seventeenth century, however, the old spelling was disappearing. This is clear from the *Creation of the World* (1611), in which the old spellings are yielding to new spellings based on English. By the later seventeenth century, the old system has gone and Cornish is being spelt entirely according to the rules of English orthography. It is for this reason that in Late Cornish we find <oo>, <oa> and <ee>, <ea> in common use. Here are some examples:

<oo>
skoothez N. Boson (LAM: 218); *looz* N. Boson (LAM: 220); *cooze* N. Boson (LAM: 220); *booz* J. Jenkins (LAM: 230); *pooz* J. Boson (LAM: 236); *rooz* J. Boson (LAM: 236).

<oa>
moaz Chirgwin (LAM: 228); *moar* J. Jenkins (LAM: 230); *boaz* J. Jenkins (LAM: 230); *moase* O. Pender (LAM: 238); *broaz* J. Boson (LAM: 236).

<ee>
teez N. Boson (LAM: 218); *skreef* N. Boson (LAM: 218); *seer* J. Tonkin (LAM: 226); *teen* J. Boson (LAM: 236); *gweel* J.Tonkin (LAM 226, 228).

<ea>
stean J. Tonkin (LAM: 226), *mean* J. Tonkin (LAM: 226); *pea* J. Tonkin (LAM: 226); *teag* E. Chirgwin (LAM: 230); *greage* J. Jenkins (LAM: 230); *treath* J. Jenkins (LAM: 230).

These four combinations of letters are hardly attested in Middle Cornish, but are common in Late Cornish. The four combinations are based on English, but since they are absent from Middle Cornish orthography, it would seem that the Middle Cornish spelling of vowels was different from the English system. In Late Cornish this was no longer true; the combinations are all frequent in occurrence and have the same values as in the English of the period. I think we can legimately conclude A) that Middle Cornish had its own spelling conventions and that these were independent of English; B) that Late Cornish orthography was very much an English-based system.

3.02 Middle Cornish *gul, gull*; English *gull*
In BM <u> is used, as in Early New English, to represent a short *u*, e.g. *busch* 'flock' BM 3232. Unlike in English <u> is also used to represent a mid-high fronted vowel [œ], for example, in *y fus* 'thou wast' BM 337, *nyns us* 'is' BM 965 and the diphthong elsewhere spelt <yu> or <eu>, e.g. *marrek du* 'a knight of God' BM 352, *du a vercy* 'God of mercy' BM 745, *du a rays* 'God of grace' BM 751. <u> is also used to represent a high fronted vowel [y] in *sur* 'sure' BM 337 and *tus* 'people' BM 335, 805, 806. Note that by the period of BM the word *sure* in English contained a long high back vowel and thus the vowels of Middle Cornish *sur* [sy:r] and English *sure* [ʃu:r] were different.

The various uses of <u> in Middle Cornish are in ways quite unlike those of Early New English and are thus further evidence for the independence of the two spelling systems. This can further be seen in the spelling of the Middle Cornish word for 'to do'. In BM this is *gul*, e.g. BM 377, 652. The same spelling is found elsewhere in the Middle Cornish texts, e.g. OM 487, 519; PC 12, 546, etc. In some Middle Cornish texts, however, the word is spelt *gull*, e.g. PA 3d, 10b; TH 1 x2, 1a, etc. In Early New English <gull> is the name of the sea bird (and also a word for a fool) and has a short high back vowel [ʌ]. In Middle Cornish the word *gul, gull* 'to do' has a long high rounded front vowel [y:]. The word was pronounced [gy:l] but was becoming [gwi:l], this latter being the pronunciation in Late Cornish; e.g. *gweel* N. Boson (LAM: 218), *tho weel* N. Boson (*ibid.*), *gweel* N. Boson (LAM: 220 x 3), *gweel* J. Tonkin (LAM: 228), *gweel* J. Jenkins (LAM: 230). The English word <gull> and the Cornish word <gull> are written identically but pronounced very differently. By the Late Cornish period, however, when the Cornish scribal tradition has been lost, the Middle

THE CORNISH SCRIBAL TRADITION

Cornish word <gul>, <gull> 'to do' is spelt according to English orthographic practice and its actual pronunciation becomes apparent [gwi:l] written <gweel>. It seems to me that the Middle Cornish and Late Cornish spellings of this item are sufficient to show the strength of the Middle Cornish tradition, and to indicate that Middle Cornish was not spelt according to the rules of English orthography.

3.03 The persistence of Middle Cornish spelling

George says "In spite of what Dr Williams says, Cornish has never had its own orthographical tradition" (KKC21: 40). This observation of George's is, I believe, very mistaken indeed. The strength of the Cornish scribal tradition and its persistence throughout the Middle Cornish period can be seen by comparing A) the Middle Cornish spellings of a selection of etyma with B) the spellings of the same items in Late Cornish. In the list below for my Middle Cornish sources I use *Pascon agan Arluth* (PA), the *Ordinalia* (OM, PC, RD), *Beunans Meriasek* (BM), Tregear (TH) and the recently discovered Middle Cornish text *Bewnans Ke* (BK). I do not use the *Creation of the World*, because it contains so many examples of later features, even though its spelling is largely Middle Cornish.

leverel 'to say'
A *leuerell* PA 27c, 59c, 90c, 91a; *leuerel* PA 228a, OM 595, 702, 740, PC 356, 381, RD 570, 585, 589, 961; *leverall* TH 1 x2, 1a x 2, BK 2130; *leverell* TH 1a; *leferel* BM 464, 1383.
B *leverol* N. Boson; *lavarel* N. Boson; *lavaral* Kerew; *laule* Kerew; *laull* Kerew; *laale* Kerew; *lal* J. Tonkins.

lowen 'joyful'
A *lowen* PA 71d, OM 719, PC 2621, RD 2444, BM 747, BK 2631.
B *looan* N. Boson, T. Boson; *loan* Kerew.

kerensa 'love'
A *kerense* PA 223c, OM 2106, PC 549, BM 403, 500, 699; *kerensa* PA 167d, BM 122, 2611, TH 1, 2a, 36a, 48, BK 788, 2970.
B *crengah* Kerew; *crenga* N. Boson; *grensa* T. Boson.

gothfos 'to know'
A *gothfos* OM 822, RD 1750, 2299, 2608; *gothvos* OM 2098, BM 28; *gothuos* PC 1672; *gothvas* BM 104, TH 35a, BK 320; *gothfas* TH 33, 42, 55a; *gothfes* BM 828, 1613.
B *gothaz* Kerew; *guthaz* N. Boson.

drehevel 'to raise, to build'
A *drehevel* OM 1710, PC 896, 2452; **drehevel* BM 2103; *drehevell* TH 22; *drehevall* TH 16, 41.
B *derevoll* N. Boson; *drevel* ACB; *direvall* Borlase.

bohosek 'poor'
A *bohosek* BM 438, 450, 736, 877, 2183; *bohosak* BK 773; *behosek* TH 60; *bohosogyan* PA 37c; *bohosogyon* (pl.) BM 2641; *bohosugyon* (pl.) PC 543; *vohosogyan* (pl.) BM 472; *vohosogyon* (pl.) PA 36c.
B *boadjack* W. Bodinar; *bohodzhak* J. Boson.

pesy, pysy 'to pray'
A *pesy* PA 53c, 54d, 62a, BM 404, 520, 537, TH 9a, 35; *pysy* OM 1607, 2140, 2197, PC 37; *pygy* PC 1162, 2090, RD 1337, 1576; *pegy* BK 133. 2335.
B *pidzha* J. Boson; *pidgee* J. Boson; *peige* T. Boson.

usy, ugy 'which is'
A *usy* BM 1018, 1403, 1214, TH 19a x 2; *ugy* PA 53d, 102a, OM 1398, PC 962, 1044, 3042, RD 782, 2160, TH 20 x 2.
B *ydzhi* Lhuyd; *igge* N. Boson; *igga* N. Boson.

It seems to me quite clear from the above examples that Middle Cornish had a vigorous scribal tradition. Middle Cornish scribes from the period of PA to TH wrote according to a set of conventions which they had learnt when they began to write. Moroever, they tended not to deviate from those conventions. By the period of Late Cornish, however, the scribal tradition was forgotten and those who attempted to write Cornish did so according to English spelling rules.

3.04 Further evidence for the Middle Cornish scribal tradition

In Middle Cornish for 'is' and the word for 'God' have the same vowel in Middle Cornish: /ɪw/ and /dɪw/ (see **13.05** below). Yet Tregear invariably and without any exception that I have noted spells 'is' as <ew> and 'God' he almost always spells as <du> or, with lenited initial, <thu>. The only exception I have noted is *han gweras a thew* 'and the help of God' at TH 10a. Both words are very frequent indeed in TH. George denies that there was a Middle Cornish scribal tradition; if he were correct in this view one might expect to find 'God' written *<dew> in, say 50% of instances. <dew> is, after all, a common spelling elsewhere in Middle Cornish, e.g OM 502, 505, 509, PC 49, BK 188, 566, 2308. TH does not ever write 'God' as <dew> because he had learnt to write this common item as <du>, <thu> and the force of his learnt convention was very strong.

3.05 Spelling of pre-occlusion in CW

Although there are three instances of pre-occlusion in the portion of *Beunans Meriasek* written by the *secunda manus*, it is not until the *Creation of the World* that one finds pre-occlusion frequently marked in spelling: *radn* CW 2356; *gwadn* CW 1275, 1679, 2479; *todn* 1361; *badna* CW 1364; *hedna* 'that' CW 2337, 2491, 2509; *pedn* CW 182, 916, 1019, 1597; *war y bydn* CW 440. There are, however, many places in CW where pre-occlusion is not marked when it might have been, e.g. *henna* CW 17, 96, 122, 127, 136, 148, 153, 171, 206, 245, 259, 380, 501, 503, 557; *hena* CW 448; *splan* CW 28, 97; *splanna* CW 126, 131, 169, 224; *vyn* CW 31, 33, 154, 538; *warbyn* CW 156, 164, 434; *in ban* CW 351; *honna* CW 387; *mynna* (< *myn ef*) CW 470; *banna* CW 506. In fact the occurrences of pre-occlusion are much fewer than those places where pre-occlusion is not indicated. We can, I think, be fairly certain that pre-occlusion was a feature of the dialect of the scribe of CW, William Jordan. Why he writes pre-occlusion so infrequently is to be explained in one of two ways: either A) he was copying from a manuscript which did not show pre-occlusion or showed it only infrequently; or B) Jordan himself learnt to write without pre-occlusion and although it was a normal feature of his dialect the scribal conventions he had learnt did not include it. Given that CW contains an admixture of Middle Cornish spelling and of later English-based orthography, I think the second explanation is probably the more likely. The references to Limbo in CW suggest Jordan's exemplar may have predated the Reformation. If so, the original manuscript was first written before Glasney and its scriptorium were suppressed. In which case the manuscript from which Jordan was copying was almost certainly written in a traditional Middle Cornish orthography, like BM and TH, and the modernizing features of CW are Jordan's own. Given that pre-occlusion occurs so rarely in CW, we can assume that scribal convention was the real reason for Jordan's tendency to let pre-occlusion go unmarked.

3.06 Scribal tradition as part of literary tradition
We cannot separate scribal from literary tradition. If a culture has a strong literary tradition, it is safe to assume that it has strong spelling conventions as well, since both are part of the same continuum: the cultivation of native writing and learning. Now it is undeniable that Middle Cornish had a very vigorous literature, that was quite independent of English. The medieval plays were based on Breton models rather than English ones. Moreover as is clear from the references to places in Cornwall mentioned in them, they are completely nativized. The well-developed metrics of PA and the Middle Cornish plays also indicate a vibrant tradition of writing. There is no imitation of English in the prosody of Middle Cornish. Indeed the predominant seven-syllable line has more in common with the prosody of Wales than with the metres of Brittany. All this suggests to me that medieval Cornwall had its own thriving literary tradition. In which case it is inevitable that it had a vigorous scribal tradition as well.

3.07 George's respelling of Middle Cornish
George denies that there was a Middle Cornish scribal tradition. This has serious implications in two respects. In the first place he does not seem to understand that the strength of the tradition frequently hides changes in speech that the scribes exhibit only on occasion. We have seen above how William Jordan marks pre-occlusion infrequently, even though pre-occlusion

was almost certainly a normal feature of his speech. There are further features of spoken Middle Cornish which are only imperfectly exhibited in the orthography. It seems quite likely, for example, that final long [iː] in words like *dry* 'to carry', *chy* 'house', *ky* 'dog' and *ty* 'to swear' had already diphthongized to [əi] by the Middle Cornish period, but we know that only by the way in which such words rhyme. The actual orthography gives no hint of the sound change.

George takes no account of the fundamental difference between citing spoken forms and citing written ones. Assume that modern linguist in the field noticed the following: that elderly speakers never used a certain phonetic variant Y but always used X, that middle-aged speakers used both X and Y, and that younger speakers used Y only. In such a case the linguist would be justified in assuming that the shift from X > Y was a phonetic change in the process of occurring in the language in question.

A linguist investigating the past history of a language, however, would not be able to draw comparable conclusions about chronology. All he would have in front of him would be texts written hundreds of years before his own time. He would not know the age of any scribe of any text nor probably would he know the precise date of any of the manuscripts on which he was relying. If the language of his texts had been written continuously for many years, his deductions about chronology would of necessity be even less precise. The scribes who wrote the relevant texts would have learnt to read and write from an earlier generation of speakers, who themselves learnt from their predecessors. Scribes would tend therefore to write as they had learnt to write. They would conform to the scribal tradition in which they had been schooled. This would be especially true when they were copying texts rather than composing new ones. If the scribe's dialect was different in small and subtle ways from that of his exemplar, or from that of the person from whom he learnt to write, he might show his dialect on occasion only. Only when he forgot his training and wrote as he spoke, would his own dialect features become apparent. This is exactly the position in Middle Cornish. George's apparent reluctance to allow for a scribal tradition in Middle Cornish and indeed his unwillingness to admit the nature of scribal tradition in general mean that his "orthographical profiles" are not as compelling as he would have us believe. Given that his "orthographical profiles" are frequently less than completely accurate, without precise corroborative evidence they cannot be taken as decisive.

3.08 The transition from Middle to Late Cornish orthography

It is also true that a change in orthography does not in itself imply a change in phonology. As Mills says,

> [I]t does not follow logically that because the orthography changed, this was necessarily accompanied by a simultaneous change in pronunciation. The

THE CORNISH SCRIBAL TRADITION

evidence only shows a change in orthographic practice and there is no associated evidence regarding pronunciation of Cornish (*Cornish Studies: Seven*: 199).

As we have seen the Middle Cornish scribal tradition lasted for a generation or so after the dissolution of Glasney Priory in 1545. This means that by *c.* 1600 the conventional orthography (with all its tolerated variations) was no longer known by writers of Cornish. William Jordan writing CW in 1611 made a fair hand at writing Middle Cornish in much of his play. All native writers after Jordan, however, wrote more or less in an *ad hoc* orthography based on English. Although there is much less Late Cornish than Middle Cornish, the spelling of the later language is much more erratic than that of Middle Cornish. It must be admitted that Late Cornish looks very different from Middle Cornish, and this difference in appearance has led commentators astray. Gendall mistakenly believes that Late Cornish is a simplified and streamlined form of the language, quite different from Middle Cornish. George also believes that Late Cornish is very different from Middle Cornish. And he suggests that the Prosodic Shift, which he dates to *c.* 1600 (or *c.* 1625), is a defining feature of Late Cornish. Both Gendall and George are, I believe, mistaken here. The late Middle Cornish of Tregear and BK is the same language as that of Jordan, Kerew and Nicholas Boson. The only real difference is that of spelling. This is a point to which I will return in my discussion of the Prosodic Shift.

3.09 George's approach to his sources

Because George is unconcerned about the Middle Cornish scribal tradition—indeed he denies it ever existed—he correspondingly has a low opinion of the orthography of the Middle Cornish texts. He tells us that he does "not consider that there is any particular intrinsic merit in the orthography of Middle Cornish". In consequence he is content to respell the language as he sees fit, whether or not his analysis is correct. His analysis I believe to be fundamentally mistaken and I therefore disagree completely with his orthography. On page 123 of KKC21, for example, he lists all the expected forms from PA, OM, PC, RD, BM, TH, SA and CW of the Cornish words for A) 'hear!, hears' and B) 'to hear'. The possible shapes for these two items are A) **clyv/*clyw, clev, clew, clov, clow* and B) **clywes, cleues/cleves, clewes, cloves,* and *clowes*. The only two forms not attested anywhere in any of the texts are **clyv/clyw* and **clywes*. Oddly, these two unattested forms are the basis of Kernowek Kemyn **klyw* 'hear!, hears' and **klywes* 'to hear'. Is it any wonder that I and other commentators are so anxious to discourage the use of Kernowek Kemyn?

CHAPTER 4
A phonemic orthography (KKC21: 17-19)

4.00 Kernowek Kemyn: a phonemic orthography?
The original purpose of Kernowek Kemyn was to produce an orthography for revived Cornish that was as phonemic as possible, although initially George believed that such an orthography should not be so "phonetic" [*sic*] as to obscure the relation of words with Breton and Welsh cognates, and it should be sufficiently close to Unified Cornish as not to be rejected by them (PSRC: 93-4).

George believes that Kernowek Kemyn is, if not wholly phonemic, at least as "phonemic as possible". A phoneme is the smallest segment of significant sound and a phonemic orthography is one in which any phoneme is represented always by the same letter or combination of letters, and only by that letter or combination. By this criterion Spanish, Welsh, Hungarian, and Finnish are pretty well phonemic; English, French, Irish, and Manx are not. Neither is Kernowek Kemyn.

4.01 Inconsistencies in Kernowek Kemyn: <n> and <nn>
It is quite apparent from the list printed at **1.03** above that there are many inconsistencies in Kernowek Kemyn. That is to say that there are many pairs of words in which the same sound is represented by different letters or combinations of letters and in the list cited these inconsistencies may be errors. There are inconsistencies in Kernowek Kemyn, however, that are intentional. In GKK George writes:

> **n** /n/ As *n* in English *nut, tenor, seen*; i.e. [n]
> **nn** /nn/ When stressed, [nn]; [dn] is also acceptable. When unstressed, the length is reduced to [n] (GKK 22).

George is saying here that <nn> is pronounced long [n:] after a stressed vowel, but as short [n] after an unstressed one. This means that <nn> actually represents two phonemes /n:/ and /n/. But /n/ is also written <n>. The system is clearly unphonemic. Were Kernowek Kemyn really been phonemic, it would always write /n/ after unstressed vowels as <n>. As it is Kernowek Kemyn sometimes writes <n> and sometimes <nn>. Kernowek Kemyn writes *blydhen* 'year', *fenten* 'source', *godhen* 'sole of foot', *moren* 'girl', for example, but *benewenn* 'wench', *borlewenn* 'morning star', *dagrenn* 'tear' and *flourenn* 'flower'. This is a deliberate rejection of the phonemic principle by the deviser of Kernowek Kemyn. The words in <nn> are so spelt to assist learners in remembering that the plurals are formed simply by adding *-ow*, whereas the

A PHONEMIC ORTHOGRAPHY

<n> words maintain the single consonant in their plural, e.g. *benewennow*, etc. In fact *borlewenn* has no plural and in traditional Cornish 'tears' are *dagrow* and 'flowers' *flourys*, but there are many other words spelt with <nn> in Kernowek Kemyn which do indeed have -*ennow* in the plural.

But some of George's words in <n> also have <nn> in the plural. One example, is Lhuyd's *bledhynno* 'years' with <nn>. Moreover the commoner plural of *blydhen* in CW exhibits pre-occlusion *vlethydnyow* CW 1862, 2404; *vlethydnyowe* CW 1915. Kernowek Kemyn allows pre-occlusion before *nn* (GKK: 22); it says nothing about *ny*. Tregear, whose dialect does not exhibit pre-occlusion, writes *vlethynnyow* at TH 15 *blethynnyow* at TH 36a, 46a and 51 all with <nny>; yet this is precisely the spelling which "phonemic" Kernowek Kemyn avoids! The spelling *blydhynyow* does not inform learners that pre-occlusion is acceptable in the word. The same is true for *fentynyow*. Welsh, which is almost entirely phonemic, writes *blwyddyn* 'year' and *ffynnon* 'source' with a single final <n> and the plurals *blynyddoedd* and *fynhonnau* have to be learnt individually. Breton writes *bleunienn* 'flower', but the plural *bleunioù* has to be learnt separately. A phonemic spelling would write final <en> rather than <enn> and the inflectional forms would go separately into the lexicon.

The same problem with <nn> for /n/ occurs after /y/; e.g. *asyn* 'donkey', *benyn* 'woman', *bibyn-bubyn* 'shrimp' as against *dervynn* 'demand', *ferdhynn* 'farthing', *telynn* 'harp'. And examples can also be cited for <an> ~ <ann> and <on> ~ <onn>.

4.02 Inconstistencies in Kernowek Kemyn: <i> and <y>

Kernowek Kemyn contains even more remarkable deviations from the phonemic principle. George tells us that /i/ when unstressed is pronounced [ɪ]. This means that it is not /i/ anymore but /ɪ/. But /ɪ/ in Kernowek Kemyn is always written <y>. If the system were truly phonemic <i> would not be written in unstressed syllables at all. Yet we find *bewin* 'beef', *bryntin* 'noble', *elin* 'elbow', *ewin* 'fingernail', *eyrin* 'sloes', *eythin* 'gorse', *gelvin* 'beak', *jardin* 'garden', *jelatin* 'gelatin', *konin* 'rabbit', *kribin* 'wool-card', etc. Presumably the reason for writing the phoneme /ɪ/ as <i> here is to assist the learner with any inflected form in which the i is stressed and therefore *[iˑ]. Yet some of these items in GKK, *bewin, bryntin, jardin, jelatin* and *kribin* for example, are without any inflected form and thus the *i* is always unstressed and therefore [ɪ] in Kernowek Kemyn.

Incidentally the stressed *e* of *bewin* is not entirely happy, given that the expression *bowyn dufunys* 'minced beef' occurs at BM 3224, where the stressed vowel is apparently *o*. Remarkable also is the distinction made in GKK between *Jentil* 'Gentile' and *jentyl* 'gentle.' Tregear writes *Jentyll* 'Gentile' 7a; *Jentyls* 'Gentiles' 14a; *gentyls* 'Gentiles' 45a and *Jentyll* 'gentle' 21a, 38. Moreover Kerew writes *Allale an Gentelles* 'Galilee of the Gentiles' (RC 23: 190). It would seem to me that the Cornish word for 'Gentile' and for 'gentle' are one and the same and neither has a long second syllable. Kernowek Kemyn's distinction appears particularly unjustified.

The same deviation from the phonemic principle occurs in Kernowek Kemyn with what is written in the texts as final <y>, e.g. in *kelly* 'to lose', *predery* 'to consider', *pesy* 'to pray', *cresy* 'to believe', *askelly* 'wings', *lestry* 'vessels', *truesy* 'doleful'. I assume that Kernowek Kemyn spells all these with final <i> because some words of this shape may be used as nouns and thus have a plural, e.g. Kernowek Kemyn *gwariow* 'plays'. What is perplexing, however, is that Kernowek Kemyn also respells English borrowings with a final *y*: *bodi* 'body', *bysi* 'busy', *chevalri* 'chivalry', *drylsi* [dialect] 'drilsy', *falsuri* 'falsehood', *fantasi* 'fantasy', *Kalvari* 'Calvary', *parti* 'party', *remedi* 'remedy'. Few of these have any inflected forms. *Parti* 'party', however, has the English plural—which in Kernowek Kemyn is spelt <partys> rather than *<partis>. It is difficult to see why exactly the singular is spelt <parti> rather than <party>.

The above deviations from the phonetic principle in Kernowek Kemyn occur in the context of the perceived phonemic differences in Cornish between /nː/ and /n/ and between /i/ and /ɪ/. Well before 1500 CE the difference between /nː/ and /n/ had either been lost or had been transformed into the distinction between /ᵈn/ and /n/. By that same token the phonetic distinction between the close /i/ and the open /ɪ/ was entirely one of length: /iː/ ~ /ɪ/. The attempts by Kernowek Kemyn to keep these pairs of phonemes apart are not only unsystematic, they are unnecessary. Kernowek Kemyn is based on mistaken phonology.

CHAPTER 5
The Prosodic Shift (KKC21: 21-7)

5.00 General observations
I have now come to the main part of my task, which is to refute George's defence of Kernowek Kemyn as outlined in KKC21. I believe, as did Jenner, Nance and Caradar, that Middle Cornish had long and short vowels only and that there was no half length. The Prosodic Shift occurred before our earliest Middle Cornish texts were written and indeed was what brought about the change from Old to Middle Cornish. The shift meant that half-long vowels became short, and long vowels increased in intensity but reduced in length to become half-long—which was now the new long. This system is fundamental to Middle Cornish.

5.01 George's methods
The phonology underlying Kernowek Kemyn is, I believe, very mistaken, largely because it dates the Prosodic Shift to the seventeenth century. My 26 criticisms of Kernowek Kemyn, together with the corrections and additions outlined above, I still believe, are valid. In which case, neither George nor anyone else can satisfactorily disprove them. But George has made the attempt and in doing so has used three separate devices.

1. **Inaccurate Data**
   I am not suggesting of course that George has falsified the evidence. It is true, however, that his database of Cornish is very inaccurate, as he himself now admits. Mills has already drawn attention to the way in which the data and George's reporting them do not agree. I also shall be obliged below to point out inaccuracies in George's data. When doing so I shall give any example of misleading or incorrect data the initials [ID].
2. **Avoidance of Discussion**
   When George is confronted with evidence that runs counter to his argument he not infrequently passes over it in silence. He may mention it *en passant* but does not trouble to refute or even discuss it in detail. I will give any example of George's evasions of this kind the initials [AD].
3. **Special Pleading**
   Often when he meets evidence that would undermine his view that the Prosodic Shift is late, George attempts to explain the evidence away by using an *ad hoc* argument. This is perhaps George's

commonest method for dealing with data he does not like. Any examples of such *ad hoc* reasoning I will mark with the initials [SP].

5.02 The date of the Prosodic Shift

George himself is apparently uncertain when exactly the shift occurred. At first he dated it to *c.* 1600 (PSRC: 68). He now seems to believe that it occurred slightly later and he writes "...only after the Prosodic Shift *c.* 1625 did it [the *e* in *alenna*] become short" (KKC21: 153) and "Before our eyes we can see the stable state of Cornish up to and (and) including CW. in 1611, followed by the dramatic increase in the percentage of spellings indicating a shortened vowel" (KKC21: 25). I will assume that George now believes the later date (*c.* 1625) as period at which the Prosodic Shift occurred.

The Prosodic Shift was a major change in Cornish that affected not only vowel length but had repercussions throughout the system. Languages do not undergo such changes overnight. The older generation continue to speak as they always have done; it is the younger speakers who introduce the change. George says that after *c.* 1625 there is a dramatic increase in the percentage of shortened vowels in our surviving texts. This I take to mean that, according to George, the shift began in the first quarter of the seventeenth century. Let us assume then that our younger scribes and writers, say those of about 20 years of age, began *c.* 1625 to write "shifted" Cornish, and this is the cause of the marked increase in shifted spellings. Those between say 25 and 70 years of age would continue to speak unshifted Cornish as they always had and to write it, if they could write. It would then have taken another twenty-five years or so, say *c.* 1645, for our 20-year-olds to become the dominant group, now being 45 years old, while the "unshifted" 25-year-olds of 1625 were now 50 years old and the 70-year olds-are now dead. The shift would not have been complete until the 45-year-olds of 1645 were either dead or no longer writing, i.e. say 70 years of age, and the 20-year-olds of 1625 were now the oldest age-group. This would bring us to after *c.* 1670. We can assume therefore that by George's reckoning the shift was not complete until after *c.* 1670.

Unfortunately George's hypothesis cannot possibly be correct. Nicholas Boson was probably one of our young speakers in 1625. Writing perhaps about 1660-70 in *Nebbaz Gerriau dro tho Carnoack* he tells us that Cornish is so weakened that it is confined to a two separate areas, one from Land's End to the Mount and towards St Ives and Redruth and the other from the Lizard to Helston and towards Falmouth. Moreover the young people are speaking it less and less and the good older speakers are dying out. It is highly doubtful that a major and significant change could have taken place in a language that was fast disappearing and could hardly be described as the language of a community any more.

Major shifts occur in languages that are flourishing and vigorous, and the changes are often the result of important changes in the social life of the speakers. The only significant change in Cornish at the period when George

THE PROSODIC SHIFT

posits the Prosodic Shift was that the language was hastening to its demise. The shift could not have begun *c.* 1625. If it had really been completed in the seventeenth century, i.e. *c.* 1625, it must have started *c.* 1560. In which case TH, SA, BK and CW would all show signs of the shift. George does not believe that the shift is apparent in any of those texts.

I on the other hand believe the Prosodic Shift occurred in the twelfth century. It was triggered by the Norman invasion, the influx of Bretons into Cornwall, the replacement of Anglo-Saxon by Norman French as the administrative language and the renewed contact with Brittany. Anglicized Cornishmen and Cornishwomen began relearning the Celtic language of Cornwall, but brought over into their Cornish an Anglo-Saxon "accent". The lightly stressed and sonorous nature of Old Cornish with its threefold lengths became more vigorous and more heavily stressed. To date the Prosodic Shift as late as *c.* 1625 on theoretical grounds alone is not credible.

5.03 Original half-long vowels in disyllables

As a result of the Prosodic Shift the half-long vowel in words like *scryfa* 'to write', *myres* 'to look' and *gwytha* 'to keep' became short. Because they were shorter than they had been, they were also were more lax, that is to say, the mouths of speakers when pronouncing them were less tense than they had been previously. This meant that original half-long <y> [short i] after the Prosodic Shift had a tendency to be pronounced as a slacker vowel than before and was often (though not always) written as <e>. This is why we sometimes finds *screfa* 'to write', *gwetha* 'to keep' and *meras* 'to look' in the Middle Cornish texts.

George believes that the Prosodic Shift did not occur until the seventeenth century. It was at this point, he says, that half-long became short. George therefore believes that disyllabic words with a "half-long" [i·] e.g. *scryfa*, *gwytha*, *myres*, etc., contained a half-long vowel to the end of the Middle Cornish period. Although he considers that the Prosodic Shift shortened vowels for the most part, at KKC21: 26 George cites evidence evidence purporting to show that in certain words the Prosodic Shift lengthened "half-long" vowels to long. He says "There is clear evidence, especially in the case of the more close vowels /i, ɪ, o/, that the vowels sometimes became long". The Prosodic Shift according to George, then, is the change by which half-long was reduced to short, except in some cases, when it became long! This view that the Prosodic Shift lengthened some "half-long" vowels while shortening others is an excellent example of George's special pleading [SP], and it is entirely without foundation. This is an important point, because this is George's fundamental answer to my criticisms of Kernowek Kemyn. George says that the Prosodic Shift, which he dates unconvincingly to *c.* 1625, shortened half-long to short—except in certain cases, where it lengthened half-long to long. This is not credible. It is unlikely that the Prosodic Shift operated in two diametrically opposite directions at the same time. Either the shift shortened or it lengthened. It is disengenuous of George to suggest that it did both. If the Prosodic Shift did not lengthen, George's defence of Kernowek Kemyn fails. Let us look in detail at George's evidence.

Notice that George in KKC21 cites no example of /o/ lengthening to /oː/. Since [ɪ] was at this period an allophone of /i/. I shall ignore it as a separate entity. George cites evidence for the increase in length at the time of the Prosodic Shift for "half-long" */iˑ/ only. These are the etyma in which his alleged lengthening took place:

A) **Nouns**
pibell 'pipe' in the toponym *Praze-an-Beeble* (Crowan)
skiber 'barn' in *Park an Skeeber* (1649 Constantine), *Gweale Skeeber* (1665 Crowan)
deeber 'saddle' Symonds
peeber 'piper' Anon
seera, zeerah 'father' N. Boson, J. Boson, Kerew, Chirgwin, J.Jenkins, etc.

B) **Verbs**
gweetha 'to keep' Rowe, Tonkin
teera 'to land' N. Boson
wheelas, wheelaz 'to seek' N. Boson, T. Tonkin
meero 'look!' (plural) J. Boson
skreefa 'to write' N. Boson
treegaz 'to dwell' T. Boson.

5.04 George's hypothetical Late Cornish lengthening in nouns

The nouns whose vowels according to George are lengthened in Late Cornish are 1) *pibell* 'pipe', 2) *skiber* 'barn', 3) *deeber* 'saddle', 4) *peeber* 'piper' and 5) *seera* 'father'. The first two are also attested with a short vowel, frequently lowered to [e]:

1) *Parc-an-**bibble**, Wheale **Bebell*** (CPNE: 184).
2) *Gweal **Skeber**, **Skeburia**, **Skebervannel**, Park **Skipper**, **Skibber** Whidden* (CPNE: 206). ***skeber*** Thomas Tonkin (Gendall); ***skebber*** [traditional]

The long vowels in George's list are unrelated to the Prosodic Shift. The lenited form **bybell* occurs in the toponym *Praze-an-Beeble*; similarly the two forms in *Skeeber* are attested from toponyms. Although these are Cornish in origin, they are all attested from English. There is a tendency in English when anglicizing Celtic place-names of this kind, i.e. with a first element with secondary stress and a second element with primary stress, to lengthen [ɪ] > [iː] in the syllable with primary stress, even when it is etymologically short. Thus the Irish toponym *Móinín na gCiseach* (with stressed short *i*), just east of Galway City, is anglicized *Moneen-na-Geeshagh* and the Dublin place-name *Gleann na Mine* (with stressed short *i*) appears as in English as *Glenomena* with a long penultimate [iː]. Something similar appears to have happened in the toponyms

THE PROSODIC SHIFT

Praze-an-Beeble, Park-an-Skeeber and *Gweale Skeeber*. In spoken Middle Cornish the stressed vowel of **pybell* and *skyber* were short and this is reflected in the forms *Parc-an-bibble* and *Wheale Bebell*.

Deeber cited by Symonds, was I suspect taken from a place-name; cf. *Carrack an deeber* (CPNE: 84) and should be explained in the same way as **peeble* in *Praze-an-Beeble* and *skeeber* in *Park-an-Skeeber*, i.e. as an English form. Three forms with a short vowel, however, are cited by Lhuyd:

1) 'C[ornish] **Dibre** [*a saddle*]' s.v. *Dorsuale* 'pack-saddle' AB: 55c
2) 'C[ornish] **Diber**... *sella equina*.' (N.B. *sella equina* = 'horse saddle') AB: 148a
3) '*Galerus*... [C]ornish Hat. **Debre** dour [i.e. sella pluvialis] which some use, seems a late invented word' AB: 62b.

Lhuyd says of the form *debre dour* 'water saddle' (a metaphor for "hat") is used by some. This implies that he heard it in speech rather than read it anywhere. Not only is the stressed vowel short, it has been lowered to [e] as well. We can be quite sure therefore that in Late Cornish the word *diber* 'saddle' was pronounced ['debər] not *['di:bər].

The Late Cornish form *peeber* 'piper' is interesting in the light of the form *peba* 'to pipe' at CW 2546, where the vowel is clearly short and has, in consequence, been lowered. *Peeber* on the other hand has a long vowel by analogy with the simplex **pȳb*, **peeb* 'pipe', which contains long vowel.

5.06 Late Cornish *seera*, Middle Cornish *syre* 'father'

George includes Late Cornish *seera, zeerah* among those words which undergo his putative shift *[i·] > [i:] in Late Cornish. This could not be correct, since *syra* had a long vowel in Middle Cornish. The word *syra* was borrowed either from Old French or Middle English *sire* [si:rə]. It could hardly have been borrowed into Cornish before the Norman Conquest. In Cornish it eventually replaced *tas* 'father', in the same way that *dama* replaced *mam* 'mother'. I assume that *syre* was not borrowed into Middle Cornish until after the operation of the Prosodic Shift, when it came into the language with its long vowel intact. The shift had already shortened half-long to short, but with *syre* the shift was too late. Far from being evidence that the Prosodic Shift was late and lengthened some vowels, as George apparently believes, Late Cornish *seera, zeerah* corroborates my view that the shift was early. Words borrowed after it were not affected by it. This means that *syre* in *syre da* 'father-in-law' at PC 570 has a long stressed vowel.

Although the vowel remained long in *syre, seera*, there was a tendency in Middle Cornish sporadically to shorten long vowels where they occurred in disyllables. This would explain *Me a vyn mose thom* **sera** 'I will go to my father' at CW 1184, where the vowel of *syra* has been shortened and lowered to [e] by analogy with native disyllables.

TOWARDS AUTHENTIC CORNISH
5.07 My "orthographic profile" of some relevant verbs
Before discussing George's views, I should like to look in turn at all the examples of the the disyllabic forms of the verbs *scryfa/screfa* 'to write', *myras/meras* 'to look', *gwytha/gwetha* 'to keep', *whylas/whelas* 'to seek', *tryga/trega* 'to dwell' as attested in the Middle Cornish texts. George believes that all these etyma contained stressed /iˑ/, which Kernowek Kemyn spells <i>. I believe that the Prosodic Shift occurred before the beginning of the Middle Cornish period. In these verbs the original /iˑ/ was shortened. Because it was now short, it untensed and became [ɪ] or [e], which in stressed open syllables were allophones of /ɪ/. Here are the forms in the texts:

1A *scryfa*, etc.
scrife PA 33d; *scriffa* TH 18a, 19, 32 x 2, 33a, 36, 36a, TH 48; *scriffes* TH 2, 3, 44, 45, 51a, 52a; *scriffis* TH 13, 17, 19, 29a, 36; *scriffys* TH 6a, 17a, 29, 43a, 44a x 2, 45; *scryfa* SA 66; *scryfas* PA 33c; *scryffa* TH 19, 38, 45a; *scryfys* PA 17a, PC 78, 95, 101, 138, 435, 748, RD 65, TH 46a, SA 66a; *scryfis* PA 209a; *scryffes* CW 2171; *scryffys* OM 2646, TH 37a, 44a, 46a; *skryffes* TH 6, CW 2178; *skryves* CW 2196.

1B *screfa*, etc.
screfa TH 48; *screfas* TH 48a, 52a x 2; *screfis* BM 394; *screffa* TH 19, 27a, 33, 49; *screffes* TH 43a; *screfys* PA 188d x 2, BM 2766.

2A *myres*, etc.
miras SA 65a; *myras* RD 1179; *myres* OM 774, 1412, 2476, PC 2093, 3178, RD 1536; *myreugh* PC 2404; *myrough* PA 141d, PC 1144, RD 1911; *myrugh* PA 203c; *vyras* BM 196.

2B *meras*, etc.
meras PA 215d, TH 50a, CW 1053; *meres* BM 2690; *merogh* TH 36a; *merough* PA 125c, BK 2808, 3256; *merovgh* BM 95; *merow* TH 28a; *merowgh* TH 49a, CW 736 x 2; *merugh* BM 2086; *veras* OM 2325, BM 4074, TH 2, 3a, 7, 9, 15a; *verays* BM 733; *vereys* BM 1981; *verhan* CW 1626.

3A *gwytha*, etc.
guythe PC 10, 2297, 2445, RD 368, 603, BM 1014, 3857; *guytheugh* RD 366; *guythens* RD 417; *guythes* RD 1537; *guytho* RD 2642, BK 2891; *guythys* PC 41, RD 353, BM 4172; *gvythes* BM 455; *guythys* BM 2640, 3792; *gwythe* PC 111; *gwythys* TH 15; *wythe* OM 422, 488, RD 336, 341, 352, 419, 2107, BM 1077; *omguytha* BM 1339; *omguythe* BM 533, 1346, 1989.

3B *gwetha*, etc.
gwetha TH 14, 19, 23a x 2, 30a, 37, 45a, 49 x 3, SA 59, CW 314; *gweʒe* PA 27d, 127b; *gwethis* TH 33a, 34, 48; *gwethogh* TH 23a; *gwethys* TH 37a; *wetha* TH 21a, 25a, 26, 27, 27a x 3, 29, 37, 45, CW 90, 683, 686; *wethas* TH 47; *wethe* OM 574; *wethen* BM 3933; *omgwetha* CW 1519; *omgwethen* CW 858; *omwetha* TH 3a, 4, CW 1047; *ymwethe* RD 1170.

4A *whylas*, etc.
whyla PC 2262, 3100, RD 222, 1956; *whylas* RD 551, 560, 857, 1646, 2068, 2261, TH 5a, CW 1525, 1742; *whyle* RD 372, 1355; *whyles* RD 1780; *whyleth* RD 853;

THE PROSODIC SHIFT

whyleugh PC 1109, 1116, RD 1288, 1773, 1972, 2213; *whylewhe* RD 537; *whylyes* RD 1680; *whylyth* RD 1640, 1653; *whylsyn* RD 1282; *wyla* BM 918, 2362, 2744; *wyle* BM 860, 3506.

4B ***whelas***, etc.

welas BM 1038; *wele* BM 2964, 3294; *weles* BM 666, 1075, 3106; *whela* PA 21c, 199d, CW 483, 1277, 1734; *whelaf* CW 1695; *whelaff* TH 22a; *whelas* PA 90a, 146d, 156b, 219d, 257b, 257d, OM 1139, BK 3231, TH 3a, 8a, 18a, 22a, 30a, 36a, SA 64a, CW 427, 454, 1691, 1787; *wheleugh* PA 68b, 168d, RD 781; *whelyn* PA 247a; *wheles* TH 27a; *whelys* TH 45.

5A ***tryga***, etc.

drygas TH 15 x 2; *triges* TH 36a; *tryga* OM 1599, 1604, TH 23a; *trygaf* PC 2598; *tryge* OM 317, 350, 1578, PC 542, 808, 2258, RD 2407; *trygens* RD 159; *trygis* BM 39; *trygys* OM 1435, 1483, 1552, 1626, PC 39, 858, 3233, RD 1111.

5B ***trega***, etc.

drega BM 3183, TH 36a, CW 334; *trega* OM 2190, 2665, BK 155, 269, BM 4348, TH 2, 30, 39a, SA 61, 66, CW 981, 1722, 2017; *tregans* CW 296, 933, 1700, 2066; *trege* PA 37b, 214c, OM 566, 1711, BM 947, BM 1344, 2948; *treges* BM 4338; *tregis* PA 46c, 84a, 85d, 89d, 93c, 255d; *tregough* OM 1893; *tregowhe* CW 176; *tregugh* BM 4566; *tregys* PA 7b, BK 45, 1292, BM 687, 816, 1963, 2209, 2284, TH 11a, 36a, 47a, CW 246.

George believes that all these verbs had a half-long high front [iˑ] until the early seventeenth century, when as a result of the Prosodic Shift the vowel was lengthened to [iː]. I say "all these verbs", but this is not strictly true. In GKK published in 1993 he gives 'to dwell' the spelling <tryga> in Kernowek Kemyn and s.v. *tryg* 'position' he adds a note "One would expect /trig/, but the word and its compounds behaved as if they contained /ɪ/ instead of /i/". In *An Gerlyver Kres* (published 1998) he gives *trig* 'position' and *triga* 'to dwell'. Kernowek Kemyn originally claimed to have been scientifically based upon a computer database. In which case it is remarkable that the phonology and orthography of this word in Kernowek Kemyn should appear so hit-and-miss. For my own part I must admit that I certainly would never have expected *tryga* to be *triga with /i/, because I believe the Prosodic Shift was much earlier than c. 1625 and I assume the vowel in *tryga/trega* to be [ɪ] or [e], exactly as the spellings in the texts suggest.

The variation in the stressed vowels of the five verbs gathered above from all the texts seem to suggest that the stressed vowel in them all was in the Middle Cornish period short and lower than /i/. Spellings with <e> occur frequently in all texts and indeed *e*-variants are often the more numerous. To suggest, as George does, that the vowel in all these verbs is [iˑ] throughout seems to me to fly in the face of the evidence. I assume that the stressed vowel had been [i] in all cases, but as a result of the Prosodic Shift, shortened, untensed and was lowered to [ɪ] or [e]. This, of course, means accepting that the Prosodic Shift had occurred before our earliest Middle Cornish texts, which George is unwilling to concede—since that would be to admit that Kernowek

TOWARDS AUTHENTIC CORNISH

Kemyn was based on a fundamental error. Allowing that the Prosodic Shift has occurred before the beginning of the Middle Cornish period is also more logical than George's hypothesis. Such a view assumes that the Prosodic Shift shortened long and half-long vowels, whereas George asserts that the Prosodic Shift ("*c*. 1625") shortened some vowels and lengthened others—hardly a credible hypothesis.

5.08 "Orthographic profile" of *pysy* 'to pray' and *cresy* 'to believe'

Let us look at comparable variation in the disyllabic forms of the following verbs: *pysy/pesy* 'to beg, to pray' and *crysy/cresy* 'to believe'. The attested forms from all the Middle Cornish texts are as follows:

6A ***pysy***, etc.
pygy PC 1013, 1044, 1162, 2090, RD 285, 444, 448, 1337, 1576, 1649, 1932; *pygyn* RD 2394; *pygys* OM 739, PC 2195; *pygyth* RD 852; *pysaf* OM 1390, 1566, PC 3019, RD 148, 902, RD 1157; *pyseygh* PC 2; *pysyn* OM 235; *pysse* OM 2996, RD 873, 2378; *pysso* PC 1890; *pysy* OM 1607, 2140, 2197; *pysys* OM 860.

6B ***pesy***, etc.
pegy BK 133, 2335; *pegyn* BK 2777; *pegys* BK 2423; *pesa* BM 2619, 2778; *pesaf* OM 2255, PC 1166, RD 837, 1356; *pese* BM 4309; *pesef* BM 46, 211; *peseff* BM 323, 1007, 1470, 1835, 2885, 3138, 4286; *pesough* PA 52c, 57b, PC 1076, TH 22; *pesse* BM 193, 3111; *pesugh* BM 2160; *pesy* PA 25c, 53c, 54d, 62a, 65a, 72d, BM 404, 520, 537, 707, 2138, 2141, 2339, 2420, 2506, 2998, 3359, 3475, 3638, 3800, 3845, 4128, 4276, 4288, 4425, 4461, 4554, 4561, TH 35; *pesyn* OM 1973, 2368; *pesys* PA 9a, 10b, 57c, 185b, BM 3615, TH 23.

7A ***crysy***, etc.
crissa TH 19a; *crygy* RD 8, 284, 482, 990, 1016, 1057, 1068, 1078, 1088, 1106, 1114, 1126, 1275, 1345, 1423, 1456, 1462, 1468, 1507, 1514, 1529, 1566, 1709, 2469; *crygyth* RD 1087; *cryses* TH 20; *cryssa* BK 143; *crysy* OM 1435, 1508, PC 2883, TH 38, 54a; *grygy* RD 1046, 1219, 2381; *grysaf* RD 1056; *grysso* RD 1707, 2467; *grysy* RD 1130, 2461; *thyscryssough* 1657; *thyscrysy* OM 1825; *thyscryssys* RD 1040.

7B ***cresy***, etc.
cregy SA 59, 65a; *creseugh* RD 1141, CW 2166; *cresons* OM 1440; *cresough* RD 1300, BK 958; *cresowgh* CW 1434; *cresowh* CW 116; *cresowhe* CW 225; *cresse* BM 1213; *cressef* BM 4415; *cresso* RD 1348, 1555; *cresugh* BM 2681, 3153, 3170; *cresy* OM 233, 241, 1759, 1761, 1784, 2018, BM 834, 971, 4117, 4125, TH 1a, 9a, 19a, 20 x 2, 21, 34, 37a, 50, 53, 53a, 54a, 55, 57, 58 x 2; *cresyae* BM 1865; *cresyn* PA 258d; *cresys* OM 287, TH 34a, 54; *gregy* BK 130; *gresa* PC 216; *gresaf* OM 492, 2752, RD 904, CW 2379; *grese* BM 1530, 1800, 4077, 4372, 4465; *gresough* RD 640; *gresough* OM 1857, PC 2688; *gressa* BK 1194; *gressaf* 1353; *greseff* 4412; *gresso* RD 2478; *gresyn* RD 1549; *gresyth* OM 174.

It will, I think, be admitted that the verbs *pesy* and *cresy* are very similar in the distribution of their stressed vowels to those of *screfa*, *meras*, *gwetha*, *whelas* and *trega* listed above. One should remember also that the monosyllabic forms, for

THE PROSODIC SHIFT

example, of *meras* and *trega* invariably have the vowel <y>, i.e. *myr* and *tryg*, exactly as the monosyllabic forms of *pesy* and *cres* are *pys* and *crys* respectively. Kernowek Kemyn, however, spells the first series of verbs *skrifa*, *mires*, *gwitha*, *hwilas* and *triga* and the latter pair *pysi* and *krysi*. The only reason for this difference in spelling is that the Welsh and Breton cognates of *scryfa*, *myres*, *gwytha*, *whylas* and *tryga* exhibit /i/, whereas the Welsh and Breton cognates of *crysy*/*cresy* and *pysy*/*pesy* are Welsh *credu* and Breton *krediñ* and *pediñ* respectively. In which case one might ask why Kernowek Kemyn does not write **kresi* and **pesi*. At all events the similarities in vocalic variation between the two sets of verbs would suggest that in Middle Cornish they all had similar stressed vowels—and that in none of the verbs was the vowel the close *[i·] <i> of Kernowek Kemyn.

The important point is this: the Welsh and Breton cognates of the seven verbs we have been discussing are of interest in themselves—but they are of little importance when it comes to spelling Cornish. Cornish is not Welsh, neither is it Breton. Cornish has its unique history, because Cornwall's history is particular to Cornwall. Cornwall, unlike Wales, was part of the West Saxon kingdom and was heavily penetrated by English speakers. Breton is unlike Cornish inasmuch as it is a Brythonic language exported to Continental Europe and spoken by people whose original language was Gaulish. Cornish is unique, and the only way in which we can understand Cornish phonology and thus arrive at a satisfactory orthography for the revived language is by studying the Cornish texts. In this matter Welsh and Breton are irrelevant.

Since the stressed vowels of *screfa*, *gwetha*, *meras*, etc., in the texts are spelt similarly to those of *pesy* and *cresy*, it seems the two sets of verbs had similar vowels in speech. In which case *skrifa*, *mires*, *gwitha*, *hwilas* and *triga* of Kernowek Kemyn are without foundation. They ought to be spelt **skryfa*, **myres*, **gwytha*, **hwyles* and *tryga*—and indeed at one time George did indeed spell *triga* as *tryga*, though he was perplexed by the form of the word. At all events, to write *skryfa*, *myres*, *gwytha* and *hwylas* now would mean admitting that the stressed vowel was short. And that would be the same as saying that the Prosodic Shift had occurred in Middle Cornish, an admission that would be fatal for Kernowek Kemyn.

5.09 George's hypothetical Late Cornish lengthening in verbs

One thing is certain: neither *screfa*, *meras*, *gwetha*, *whelas* nor *trega* had a vowel /i·/ in Middle Cornish. As a result George's alleged lengthening of the "half-long" vowel to long [iː] in the seventeenth century is fictitious. And this is so, not only because the vowels were short, but also because the Prosodic Shift shortened vowels. It did not lengthen them.

The verbs affected by George's alleged Late Cornish lengthening (see above) are 1) *gweetha*, 2) *wheelas*, 3) *meero*, 4) *skreefa*, 5) *treegaz* and 6) *teera*. These variants in the case of 1-4 are marginal in Late Cornish; the commoner forms of 1-5 in Late Cornish are identical with the Middle Cornish forms. The verb

35

TOWARDS AUTHENTIC CORNISH

tyra is a special case. There is good evidence (not mentioned by George) to suggest that far from having /iː/ the verbs 1-5 all had a short vowel in Late Cornish, usually spelt <e>. I have collected the following examples from Late Cornish sources:

1)
*travith gwrez tho **gwetha** Curnooack* BF: 25
*rag tho **gwetha** ge Tavaz* BF: 31
*buz gen **guetha** ny deurt droge* BF: 41
*ha **guetha** o Lavarro* BF: 41
*Perh co tra te **guetha** a Suile begenas* BF: 41
*ha bos **gwethys** ena bys vican* Keigwin.

2)
*gworeuh **whellaz** seere rag an flo younk* RC 23: 196
*rag Herod vedn **whelaz** an flo yonk rag e latha* RC 23: 198
*rag ma Herod maraw eva **whellaz** bownaz an flo you[n]k* RC 23: 200
*mee a ved'n moze Da **whelaz** weale da weele* BF: 15
*ha reeg **whelaz** ena weale da weele* BF: 15
***Whelas** tees tha trehe kesow* ACB F f 2
***Whelas** poble tha threhe ithen* ACB F f 2
***Whelas** megouzion tha medge an isse* ACB F f 2
***Whelas** colmurian tha kelme an isse* ACB F f 2
*ez boaze **whelees** car thurt an Tir* LAM: 226.

3)
***meroyow**: an dean yw devethez pocara ha onen anye* RC 23: 185
*ha, **mero**: elez neve theth ha droze thotha* RC 23: 189
***mero**, elez neeve a desquethaz tha Joseph* RC 23: 198
*Ha Deu lavaras, **Mero**, ma res gennam do vy kanifer lushan gen haz* BF: 53
*ha **mero**, tho vo perth da* BF: 53
*dha **meraz** rag an peth es moaz* BF: 58.

4)
*eth yw **screffez** n'ara dean bewah dreath bara e honnen* RC 23: 186
*rag eth ew **screffez*** RC 23: 187
*eth ew **screffez** arta* RC 23: 187
*ryth ew **screffez**: che ra gorthi that arleth Deew* RC 23: 188
*rag andellma thewah **screffez** gen an prophet* RC 23: 195
*Ma goz **screfa** compaz* BF: 46
*Na Re'au gouas koler, rag **screfa** vaze* BF: 46
*Scribo... To write... C[ornish] Dho **skrepha*** AB: 146c
*Scriptus... Written... C[ornish] **Skrephys*** AB: 146c
*veva **skrefyz** arag* AB: 222
*dho **screfa** ketella* AB: 222
*dho **skrefa** neb 'ramatek* AB: 222
*Kernuak ha Godhalek **skrefyz** arag* AB: 222
*a ryganz **skrefa** ragov* AB: 222

THE PROSODIC SHIFT

na ryg me na **skrepha** *bepprez* AB: 223
skrephyz *muy po le* AB: 223
nag ero huei a **skrefa** *an gerrio-ma* AB: 223
tha **screfa** *do why* LAM: 238
buz nagerra termen dem de **screffa** *du straft arta* LAM: 238
ha mouns **screffa** *inna warbedden ni* LAM: 238
Rag na algia ea clappia na **screffa** *Curnoack precarra why* LAM: 238
screfys *gans oleow horen* Keigwin
henwez Mean **scriffez** BF: 27
Scriffas, *Gomar mab Japhet vo en Beas* BF: 48.

5)
ha garah Nazareth e theath ha **tregaz** *en Capernahum* RC 23: 189
Habito... To dwell, to inhabit, to live in; to lodge Dho **trega** AB: 64c
na huath **tregyez** *en an Ulaz-na mui vel padzhar miz* AB: 222.

I find it difficult to believe that George was unaware of these instances. Could it be that he has deliberately suppressed the evidence [AD]?

I have no Late Cornish example of *tyra* 'to land' with a short vowel but the following Middle Cornish examples of disyllables based on the word *tyr* 'land': *tereth* 'land' BM 632, *terathe* 'land' CW 2452, *tereath* 'land' BF: 42; *teryov* 'lands' BM 385, 2594 suggest that such disyllabic forms had a short stressed vowel.

The various verbs cited by George (apart from *whelas*) all have a monosyllabic simplex in the third singular present-future and the second singular imperative, i.e. Middle Cornish *gwyth, myr, scryf* and *tryg*. This monosyllabic simplex represents the root of the verb; it is quite clear that at some period after the operation of the Prosodic Shift, in some dialects of Cornish, the short vowel of *gwytha/gwetha, myres/meras, scryfa/screfa* and *tryga/trega* was analogically replaced by the long vowel of the monosyllabic form. This is exactly comparable with the way Middle Cornish *sevys* 'rose' > *savaz* and *leverys* 'said' > *lavaraz* on the basis of the second singular imperative, *saf* and *lavar* respectively. The Late Cornish *teera* 'to land' is clearly related to the word *tyr* 'land' with a long vowel and it is likely that the noun itself has influenced the verb. *Wheelas* is curious, given that the verb has no monosyllabic simplex. It would seem, however, that it has been drawn into the ambit of the other analogical verbal forms that we have been discussing. At all events *wheelas* is less common in Late Cornish than the expected *whellas*—indeed *wheelas* hardly occurs at all.

Lhuyd is the only scientific observer of Late Cornish. In his vocabulary in AB he cites *Do guitha* 'to keep' (AB: 149c), *Dho huillaz* 'to seek' (AB: 133c) and *Miraz, Do viroz* 'to look' (AB: 173c) all with short vowels. Moreover he gives *Dho skrepha* 'I write' (AB: 146c) and *Dho trega* 'I dwell' (AB: 64a) not only with a short vowel, but a lowered one as well. For Lhuyd these words in Late

Cornish clearly had a short vowel. Where then is the lengthening of *[i·] in them to [iː] posited by George?

Nicholas Boson writes *wheelaz* (LAM: 220) and *skreefez* (LAM: 220) with <ee>, which seems to suggest [iː]. But he also writes *keen point* 'different point' (BF: 15), *geer* 'word' (LAM: 218), *wheeath* 'six' (LAM: 220), *crees* 'peace' (BF: 8) with <ee>, where the vowel can hardly be anything but [eː]. Similarly Kerew writes *geeth* (< *rej eth*) (RC 23: 178. 108), *geer* 'word' (RC 23: 186), *wreeg, wreege* 'wife' (RC 23: 178, 181, 183), *neeve* 'heaven' (RC 23: 184), *steere* 'star' RC 23: 196 and *teege* 'beautiful' RC 23: 187, where the vowel is clearly [eː]. It is not certain therefore that all the forms in <ee> cited by George were actually pronounced with [iː]. It may be that <ee> is merely graphemic for [e].

If forms with [iː] did occur in Late Cornish, they did so alongside the more frequent forms in with a short (lowered) vowel. Late Cornish *gwetha, whellas, mero, skrepha* and *trega* in the examples above are continuations of Middle Cornish *gwetha, whelas, mereugh, screfa* and *trega*; and these forms with their short and lowered vowel are evidence in themselves that the Prosodic Shift has already occurred in Middle Cornish.

5.10 *thyso* and *thys* 'to thee'

In CT §§ 13.7, 18.8 I suggested that the Middle Cornish had two forms of the word written <thys> i.e. [ðiːz] and [ðɪs]. Furthermore I surmised that the short form was by analogy with *thyso* [ðɪso], where the vowel was short. George, because he mistakenly believes Middle Cornish to have had half-length, asserts that the stressed vowel in *thyso* was [i·] and could not therefore have given rise to an analogical form with a short stressed vowel. He says:

> His [Williams'] argument is dependent upon the hypothesis that the stressed vowel in *thyso* was short. We have already seen that the quantity rules were still in operation in Middle Cornish, and the vowel in *thyso* was therefore still half-long. His analogy with *dhymmo* [i.e. > *dhym*] therefore falls flat (KKC21: 43).

George's "proof" that the quantity rules still operated (i.e. that there was half-length in Middle Cornish) depends upon the long vowel [iː] in *gwetha* 'to keep', *whelas* 'to seek', etc., in Late Cornish. We have seen that such forms, if they occur, are marginal and analogical. Late Cornish almost invariably has <e> in such verbs. Moreover, if George allows that *thyso* had a short vowel, he will have to admit that the underlying phonology of Kernowek Kemyn is mistaken. He must therefore continue to insist that the vowel in *thyso* was half-long. It is clear nonetheless that in Middle Cornish the vowel in *thyso* was indeed short. If the vowel had been half-long, the word would always have appeared as <thyso> or similar. As it is, the variant <theso> with lowered vowel is frequently attested. I have collected the following instances:

THE PROSODIC SHIFT

rys yw ʒeso y ʒamnye PA 98d
nyn drossen ny bys deso PA 99d
Ha ʒeso y tanvonas PA 116a
deso benyn yn meʒa PA 198c
Rag trystya theso BK 532
ha ry theso me a ra BK 627
ow ro theso a vyth clere BK 640
Gramersy theso, dremas BK 823
ma na relhans theso bern BK 859
theso bys may tewhellyf BK 1042
Syr Teuthar, mer gras theso BK 1081
Sau ol theso me a'n gaf BK 1097
Desympys rys ew theso BK 1112
theso war ver lavarow BK 1579
theso drys an re erall BK 1989
Me a wor theso mer gras BK 3073
neffra theso ny falla' BK 3213
ha theso ge arluth gwryoneth TH 10
theso ge yma ow pertaynya gwryoneth TH 10
Rag ny ruge kyge na goose desquethes henna theso ge TH 44
ha me a lever theso ge TH 44
me a vyn ry theso ge TH 44
theso ge me a vyn ry TH 44
ʒeso gy par del gotha CW 50
eve a drayle theʒo tha leas CW 739
ow molath these pub preys CW 1267
ow molath theso pub preys CW 1279
theso ny vannaf gava CW 1697
gans an tas theso heb gowe CW 2073
han pythe a long theʒo gye CW 2253
da ew theso ge boes fure CW 2364
my ny gresaf theʒo whathe CW 2379.

For some reason George does not mention the form *theso* in his discussion (KKC21: 43). This is a good example of George's omitting facts that he cannot explain [AD]. But since we have listed them, we can assert that there are two possibilities. A) If in the face of all these examples one can believe that the word *thyso* in Middle Cornish invariably had a half-long [i·], then one can also believe that the phonological basis of Kernowek Kemyn is sound. B) If on the other hand one believes that the spellings with <e> listed above indicate a short and thus lowered vowel, one must also believe that the Prosodic Shift was a *fait accompli* by the Middle Cornish period; which means that the phonological assumptions of Kernowek Kemyn are mistaken. I must admit I espouse the second of those two opinions.

George also says that there are no examples of *thys* 'to thee' with <e> in Middlle Cornish before CW. In this I believe he is mistaken [ID]:

*rag nefre kyn rollen **des*** 'though I give it thee for ever' BM 2593.

This I take to be the same form as is seen in:

*pub ower **thes** rag ʒe weras* 'always for thee to help thee' CW 391
*me a levar **ʒes** fatla* 'I will tell thee how' CW 495
*bethez enna terebah ve dry **thez** geere* 'let him be there until I bring thee word' RC 23: 198
*whetha deth te ra guile whele, ha guile mens es **des** do wele* 'six days thou shalt do work and do as much as there is to thee to do' BF: 41
*En tereath neb a reague de Arlith due ry **dez*** 'The land which thy Lord God gave thee' BF: 42
*Gwra kelmy ow colon **dez*** 'Bind my heart to thee' LAM: 246.

Notice also that *des* 'to thee' is given by Pryce as a headword in his vocabulary. Lhuyd normally marks his long vowels with a circumflex. It would seem, therefore, that the following examples of his have a short vowel:

Dhyz, *dheyz, dhethi and orthyz, Unto thee* AB: 244
*Ema **dhyz**…Thou hast* AB: 247
*Reiz ô **dhyz** Thou wert oblig'd* AB: 247
*me vedn laveral **dhiz*** 'I will tell thee' AB: 253.

Bewnans Ke usually spells 'to thee' as <thys>, but there are seven examples spelt <this>: BK 1874, 1972, 1996, 2364, 2919, 3207, 3215. There is much English in the text of BK, and I suspect that the scribe wrote <this> because he pronounced the word similarly to the English word *this*, i.e. as [ðɪs]. The short form [ðɪs] is derived from *thyso* by analogy: *thymmo* : *thym* / *them* > *thyso* / *theso* : *thes*. This is surely further evidence, that *thyso* in Middle Cornish had a short vowel. I should also point out that Jenner cites the second person singular of the common prepositional pronouns as *genes, dhortas, orthes, ragos, **dhes**, warnas* (HCL: 107), i.e. *dhes* is his only form, and he does not cite *dhys* at all.

Now the question arises, if George is right and *thys* 'to thee' in Middle Cornish always had a long high front vowel [ðiːs], what is the origin of the forms *des, dez, dhiz, dhes*? I believe that *des* and *thes* in Middle Cornish are merely variants of *thys*/*dys* with a short vowel. George on the other hand with his preferred */ðiˑso/* cannot explain them and indeed does not attempt to. This is another example of George's tendency to be silent about what he is unable to explain [AD].

5.11 The Prosodic Shift and George's special pleading
Alleged lengthening in Late Cornish of /iˑ/ in the verbs and nouns posited by George is fantasy. First, because the vowel in all the etyma quoted was already short and already lowered to [ɪ] or [e]. Secondly in many cases the <e> forms

THE PROSODIC SHIFT

are the commoner ones in Late Cornish, evidence which George has failed to note [AD]. Thirdlly the Prosodic Shift was a general process of shortening. To suggest that when the stressed vowel was /i/, it was lengthened by the shift, rather than shortened, is special pleading of the most unconvincing kind [SP]. The Prosodic Shift could certainly not have occurred in the seventeenth century when the language was moribund. The Prosodic Shift involved the shortening of all long and half-long vowels. It did not lengthen any and it occurred before the Middle Cornish period. Kernowek Kemyn is based on mistaken phonology.

CHAPTER 6
The gemination of consonants (KKC21: 23-5)

6.00 George's criticism
George quite fairly criticizes my treatment in *Cornish Today* of this question. I suggested in CT § 2.5, that on occasion etymologically short consonants were written double to indicate that the preceding vowel was short, but I included only a few rather random examples. Since, unlike George, I believe that Middle Cornish had a strong scribal tradition, the relative paucity of unetymological gemination did not bother me. I assumed that scribes wrote single, because that was the convention, even though the preceding vowel was short. I could see that the gemination of historically single consonants was sporadic only in the Middle Cornish texts and my treatment of it was correspondingly cursory in CT. Such occasional gemination was an incidental part of my argument rather than a central one. In view of George's criticisms I will now discuss the question more fully. I should point out before I begin that I disagree strongly with George's views on this matter.

6.01 The Prosodic Shift and long consonants
The Prosodic Shift shortened all half-long vowels to short (that is from two morae to one mora) and all long vowels to half-long (that is from three morae to two morae) which from now on were the new long. As part of the same process all long (or geminate) consonants were reduced to short (or single). This meant that after the shift all disyllabic words contained a short vowel and a single consonant or consonant cluster. Before the shift *kelyn* 'holly' would have had a half-long vowel and a single consonant: /ke·lın/, whereas *kellyn* 'we lose' would have had a short vowel and a geminate consonant: /kel:ın/. As a result of the shift both became /kelın/ and were thus identical in pronunciation. The only part of the system where there could be a distinction in length was in monosyllables, where *tas* 'father' had a long vowel, but *mam* 'mother' a short one. Frequently the Middle Cornish scribes did not trouble to show a long vowel in a monosyllable. If they did wish to show length, they sometimes doubled the vowel, e.g. *haal* 'moor' OM 2708, or they inserted an unetymological <y>, *ny dayl* 'it not fitting' PA 85a. In later texts the mute <e> of English was used: *nyn dale* 'is not fitting' CW 2443.

6.02 Etymologically geminate consonants written single
Because as a result of the Prosodic Shift the difference both between long and short consonants was lost, the Middle Cornish scribes frequently wrote historically geminate consonants as single. Here are some examples of etymologically geminate consonants after stressed vowels written as single

THE GEMINATION OF CONSONANTS

consonants. My examples are from 1) *Beunans Meriasek*, 2) Tregear's *Homilies*, 3) *Bewnans Ke* and the 4) *Creation of the World*; they are not exhaustive.

1 BM

beneth 'blessing' 31; *lemen* 'now' 277, 553, 559, 571, 598, 720, 1084, 1089, 1321, 1336, 1456, 1558, 1638, 1689, 1752, 1819, 1834, 1860, 1967, 2126, 2185, 2209, 2248, 2354, 2386, 2561, 2595, 2703, 2835, 2997, 3016, 3040, 3177, 3203, 3277, 3320, 3398, 3419, 3426, 3522, 3627, 3645, 3681, 3692, 3808, 3923, 4017, 4076, 4155, 4238, 4242, 4273, 4504, 4510, 4525, 4531; *lemyn* 'now' 3214, 3962; *leman* 'now' 4119, 4143; *letris* 'lettered' 2626; *letrys* 'lettered' 290, 752; *melya* 'meddle' 375; *mynen* 'we wish' 414; *ny venen* 'we will not' 3267; *manaff* 'I will' 1860; *a vyna* 'whether she will' 3782; *na thefo* 'so it come not' 415; *a tefes* 'were thou to come' 3827; *gorys* 'put' 437, 3643; *gora* 'to put' 1861; *gore* 'to put' 2331; *wora* 'to put, bury' 4530; *wore* 'to put, bury' 4371, 4378; *oma* 'here' 478, 526, 561, 583, 596, 604, 608, 626, 636, 676. 892, 938, 1233, 1370, 1387, 1401, 1449, 1529, 1592, 1612, 1644, 1702, 1708, 1780, 1919, 1946, 2009, 2097, 2158, 2372, 2969, 2978, 3002, 3321, 3505, 3532, 3538, 3577, 3638, 3644, 3660, 3763, 3792, 3819, 3849, 3884, 3906, 3910, 3925, 3956, 3977, 4056, 4178, 4217, 4279, 4333; *ome* 'here' 3335, 3678; *atoma* 'here is' 1332, 1569, 2806, 3546, 3722; *kemer* 'take, takes' 304, 1899, 2633, 2879, 3395, 3797, 4365; *gemer* 'takes' 1914; *kymer* 4057; *gymer* 'take' 3397, 3674; *omgemer* 'undertakes' 1882; *alema* 'hence' 659, 943, 978, 1027, 1389, 1697, 1742, 2007, 3219, 3434, 3943, 4015, 4506, 4544; *aleme* 'hence' 2689; *lema* 'hence' 2779, 3489; *dymo* 'to me' 734, 1792, 2089, 2543, 3121, 3320, 4090, 4522; *dymovy* 'to me' 1769; *thymo* 'to me' 736, 845, 936, 1410, 1553, 1727, 1780, 1939, 2153, 2424, 2783, 3085, 3124, 3200, 3306, 3373, 3678, 3698, 3765, 3767, 3778, 3787, 3813, 4017, 4056, 4109, 4332; *thymo vy* 'to me' 3594, 3618; *ren tala* 'may he pay it' 755, 3082, 4248; *flatra* 'to beguile' 860; *napya* 'to nap' 958; *hena* 'that' 1031; *gemen* 'bequeathes' 1263, *res pela* 'may he plunder them' 1268; *colonov* 'hearts' 1570, 1582; *ynocens* 'innocents' 1708; *kemys* 'as many' 1782; *teka* 'fairer' 1855, 3146; *weka* 'sweeter' 1856; *terlemel* 'gambol' 2100; *comond* 'commands' 2518, 4030; *rum gueresa* 'may he help me' 2539, 4037; *regen gueresa* 'may he help us' 1221; *regen guerese* 'may he help us' 1758; *letyogh* 'delay!' 2678, 2963; *letya* 'delay' 2731; *comen* 'common' 2710; *meten* 'morning' 2738; *kumyas* 'leave' 2778; *cumyys* 'leave' 2969; *pendreny* (< *pendra ren ny*) 'what shall we do?' 2853; *a reny* (< *a ren ny*) 'we will do' 4950; *mara tuny* (< *mara tun ny*) 'if we come' 3907; *ompenyon* 'brains' 2996; *ompynyon* 'brains' 3038; *setya* 'would attack' 3212; *kemyn* 'common' 3215; *onen* 'ash tree' 3289; *lemyk* 'sup' 3313; *plemyk* 'plummet' 3314; *worhemyn* 'commands' 4141; *othomek* 'needy' 4207; *y tendelas* 'he deserved' 4507.

2 TH

colonow 'hearts' 1, 9, 10a, 18, 19, 23, 26, 28a, 38, 45, 51a, 54a, 55, 57a; *collonow* 'heart' 52; *gora* 'to put' 46a; *woras* 'put, set' 2, 26a, 46a; *ow gora* 'putting' 44; *gorys* 'put' 53; *veny* (< *ven ny*) we were 3a; *ony* (< *on ny*) 'we are' 7a, 9a, 10, 12a; *mar teny* (*mar ten ny*) 'if we happen' 15a; *govenek* 'hope' 9; *lymyn* 'now' 16a, 27a; *comyn* 'common' 21; *anya* 'to vex' 25a; *taclenow* 'things' 27a, 50; *kemer* 31a; *mar menow* 'if you will' 38; *ny vynys* 'thou wilt not' 48a; *galus* 'power' 56.

3 BK
gemer 'take' 142; *ow cokya* 'being foolish' 306; *woky* 'foolish' 577; *goky* 'foolish' 611; *atoma ve* 'here I am' 562; *hedre veny* (< *ven ny*) 'while we be' 622; *re'th gweresa* 'may help thee' 793; *re'th weresa* 'may help thee' 803; *prety* 'pretty' 960; *sopos* 'supposes' 1219; *govenak* 'hope' 1395; *conquerya* 'to conquer' 1484; *ny'th wortesa* 'would not wait for thee' 1963, 1971; *katap onan* 'every one' 2018; *katap huny* 'everybody' 2572; *katap myl* 'every thousand' 2833; *worhemyn* 'command' 2035; *theny* (< *then ny*) 'to us' 2201; *ny venyn* 'we will not' 2739; *in ketela* 'thus' 3016.

4 CW
kymar 'take!' 356, 833, 850, 1165; *gymar* 'take!' 560, 1785; *lemyn* 'now' 32, 115, 217, 337, 359, 367, 423, 558, 810, 874, 1012, 1054, 1083, 1173, 1211, 1388, 1563, 1576, 1647, 1712, 1882, 2201, 2245, 2419, 2422, 2451; *thema* 'to me' 801, 802; *thyma* 'to me' 286, 748, 877, 1144, 1290, 1478, 1638, 1805, 1963, 2166, 2236, 2497, 2505; *thymo* 'to me' 287, 425, 844, 943, 1035, 1090, 1306, 1342, 1367, 1395, 1676, 1692, 1694, 1731, 2435; *theny* 'to us' 2347, 2528; *manaf* 'I will' 313, 471, 503; *ny vanaf* 'I will not' 649, 1524; *ny venyn* 'we will not' 2361; *tenaf* 'I take' 385; *na thefa* 'that he come not' 469; *attoma* 'here is' 977, 1923; *worhemyn* 'command' 1078; *molath* 'curse' 1163, 1164, 1202, 1203, 1268, 1279, 1280, 1341, 1600, 1686; *molathe* 'curse' 1505; *volath* 'curse' 1511, 1631; *gonycke* 'cunning' 1406; *pan defa* 'when might come' 1893; *chala* 'jaw' 1117 x 2.

Note that *govenek* 'hope' BM 2900, *govenak* BK 1395 and *govenek* TH 9, 49 has etymological /n:/ but is always spelt <n>.

6.03 Single consonants written as geminates
Note only do the Middle Cornish scribes on occasion write a single consonant where the consonant is etymologically double, they also not infrequently write consonants double when such consonants are historically single. Here are some examples—the list is not exhaustive:

1 BM
grammer 'grammar' 20, 36; *chappell* 'chapel' 130; *ʒadder* 'goodness' 189, 228; *dadder* 'goodness' 299, 2229, 3173, 4463, 4515; *thadder* 'goodness' 328, 2241, 4271, 4290, 4294; *Connan* PN 423; *nammur* 'not much' 590; *prenna* 'to redeem' BM 868, 2746; *prennas* 'redeemed' 2521; *prennys* (ppt) 'redeemed' 885; *sollebreys* 'already' 1845; *nattur* 'nature' 1973; *ny ammont* 'is of no avail' 2055, 3352, 3624; *anneys* 'unease' 2904; *solladeth* 'already' 2940; *dynnyte* 'dignity' 3025, 3094; *ingynnys* 'engines' 3367; *hellov* 'marshes' 3411; *marrov* 'dead' 3524; *matter* 'matter' 4045.

2 TH
kyffes 'got' 1; *keffys* 'got' 10a; *kyffys* 'got' 11; *skriffes* 'written' 2; *wellas* 'saw' 3; *gwellas* 'to see' 6, 8a, 32a; *wyllyn* 'we see' 50; *asswon* 'to recognise' 6; *daddar* 'goodness' 10, 11a, 12, 26a; *dadder* 'goodness' 11, 25, 26, 30a, 51; *thadder* 'goodness' 30a; *thaddar* 'goodness' 5, 14, 15a; *essa* 'was' 12a, 13; *yth essa* 'was'

THE GEMINATION OF CONSONANTS

56a; *assow* 'ribs' 15a; *vattar* 'matter' 22; *shackys* 'shaken' 31; *shackya* 'to shake' 42; *prophettys* 'prophets' 33 x 2, 42; *esylly* 'members' 35a; *referrya* 'to refer' 23, 36a; *prontyrryan* 'priests' 34; *desyrrya* 'to desire' 38; *braggyas* 'threatened' TH 40; *kentravoggyan* 'neighbours' 40a; *egglossyow* 'churches' 40a; *eddryggys* 'repentant' 40a; *marthussyan* 'marvels' 39, 49a; *reiossya* 'to rejoice' 50a; *blethynnyow* 'years' 36a, 51; *vyllyow* 'thousands' 51; *leuerris* 'said' 52; *dyfferrens* 'difference, different' 53; *vattar* 'matter' 22; *matter* 'matter' 53a; *cristonnyan* 'Christians' 34a, 39a x 2, 54, 54a.

2 BK

prennas 'redeemed' 21, 2030, 2553; *gwyrryon* 'right' 266; *e honnyn* 'himself' 312; *levyrrya* 'to journey' 344; *lavurrya* 'to journey' 1047; *laverrya* 'to journey' 1351, 2366; *lavyrrya* 'to journey' 1369; *carynnyas* 'carcasses' 423; *mettys* 'met' 462; *mettya* 'to meet' 1393; *mettya'* 'I meet' 1443, 1519, 2281; *mettyaf* 'I meet' 1446; *vettya* 'to meet' 2393, 2740; *pytta* 'pity' 616; *myllwyth* 'a thousand times' 922; *cusullya* 'to advise' 988; *gusullyow* 'counsels' 992; *gyrryow* 'words' 1023, 1885, 2148, 2172, 2298; *dyswyllyans* 'atonement' 1090; *vynnys* 'little' 1129; *alenha* (< *alenna*) 'thence' 1309; *Bryttyn* 'Britain' 1645; *negyssas* 'to negotiate' 1902; *negyssyas* 'to negotiate' 1910; *Christonnyon* 'Christians' 1990; *eglynnyon* 'stanzas' 2059; *cannow* 'songs' 2062; *soccor* 'ally' 2498; *socckors* 'supporters' 2069; *soccker* 'ally' 2573; *socckers* 'allies' 2733; *soccors* 'supporters' 2352, 2529; *socker* 'support' 2633; *sockor* 'support' 2812; *matters* 'matters' 2083, 2294; *skettyaf* 'I crush' 2159; *ny dallans* 'they are not worth' 2172; *dufollas* (ppt) 'affronted' 2203; *aquyttya* 'to pay' 2273; *fystynnyn* 'let us hasten' 2735.

4 CW

gollan 'heart' 284; *hollan* 'heart' 734; *gollowe* 'light' 304; *ny wellaf* 'I see not' 1167; *wellas* 'to see' 446, 542, 553, 741, 762, 1246, 1662; *ow gwellas* 'seeing me' 561; *wellas* 'saw' 1916, 2533, 2536; *gwellaf* 'I see' 825; *gwellys* 'seen' 969; *ny wellyn* 'I was not seeing' 1653; *suttall* 'subtle' 455; *sottall* 'subtle' 501, 534, 615; *thewollow* 'devils' 481, 2021; *wylly* 'wily' 512, 816, 1029; *pur verry* 'very merry' 693; *the ballas* 'to dig' 975, 982; *gwicker* 'trader' 1143; *gellas* 'hide' 1245; *cossowe* 'woods' 1520; *assow* 'ribs' 1572; *vyllan* 'scoundrel' 1578; *wollas* 'bottom' 1723, 2033; *allow* 'tracks' 1748; *deffan* 'prohibition' 2130; *planattis* 'planets' 2156; *callys* 'hard' 2191; *kevellyn* 'cubit' 2260; *kevellen* 2262; *gorrow* 'male' 2271; *gorrawe* 'male' 2414.

6.04 Variant spellings in *Beunans Meriasek*

Because the scribes sometimes write historical geminates as single consonants and historically single consonants as geminates, we not infrequently find variant spellings of the same etymon within the same text. For example:

BM

alemma 'hence' 23, 34, 70, 578
aquyttya 'to recompense' 2558
benneth 'blessing' 53, 54, 62, 202
dadder 'goodness' 4463; *ȝadder* 189; thadder 4271

alema 943, 1027, 1389
aquytya 1227
beneth 32
dader 12, 33, 49, 206

45

dymmo 'to me' 521, 669, 719
dynnyte 'dignity' 3094
gymmer 'take(s)' 1112, 1452
gorrys (ppt) 'put' 26
grammer 'grammar' 20, 36
henna 'that' 17, 100, 117
kemmer 'takes' 3079
kemmys 'as many' 4308
lemmen 'now' 57, 703, 941
mannaf, manna 'I will' 2863, 3106, 3854
y fannavy 'I will' 2123
mynnyth 'thou wilt' 919
matter 'matter' 4045
mellya 'interfere' 1128
*metten 'morning' 4420
molleth 'curse' 1049, 3721
nammur 'not much' 590
omma 'here' 29, 222, 658, 664
ompynnen 'brains' 1274
thymmo 'to me' 666, 776
worhemmyn 'commands' 1109

dymo 647, 734
dynyte 1627, 2813, 2856
gemer 1914
gore 'to put' 2331
gramer 76
hena 4109
kemer 1899, 2879
kemys 1782
lemen 346, 571, 599
manaf 1860
y fanaff 2127
mynen 'we will' 414, *menyn* 2334
mater 2694
melya 375
meten 2738
moleth 1022
namur 1414
oma 478, 583, 626, 636, 658, 676
ompenyon 2996; *ompynyon* 3038
thymo 736, 936, 965
worhemyn 1126.

One also finds *onen* 'one' BM 3545, 3801, 3935 and *onen* 'ash tree' BM 3289; *oma* 'here' BM 478, 526, 561, 583, 596, 604, 608, etc., and *oma* 'I am' BM 1359, 1943, 2522, 4120, 4181, 4501. I think we can assume quite reasonably that for the scribe of BM *onen* 'one' and *onen* 'ash' were pronounced the same, as were *oma* 'here' and *oma* 'I am'. That means historically half long vowels for the scribe were short. It seems likely that George would agree. He believes the scribe of BM was more interested in vowel length than in vowel quality. George says:

> Now it was evidently more important to Radulphus Ton, the author of *Beunans Meriasek*, to indicate that certain vowels were long, than to spell them differently because of their quality was different (KKC21: 31).

In which case, according to George, he would not have written *onen* 'one' and *onnen* 'ash tree' as <onen> and *omma* 'here' and *oma* 'I am' as <oma>, had they not had the same length of stressed vowel. If what George is saying about Radulphus Ton is correct, there was no half length in either *onen/onnen* or *oma/omma* in BM. Which is the same as saying that the Prosodic Shift has already occurred.

6.05 Variant spellings in TH, BK and CW

1 TH
commyn 'common' 5, 57a x 2
cristonnyan 'Christians' 26a, 27, 27a
dadder 'goodness' 2, 11, 16a

comyn 21
cristonyan 28, 28a, 29, 56
dader 26a, 30a

THE GEMINATION OF CONSONANTS

dyfferens 'difference, different' 52
egglossyow 'churches' 40a
esylly 'members' 25a, 35a
gallus 'power' 3a, 21, 21a
the gella, y gilla 'one another' 22, 29a
grickys 'Greeks' 56
gwellas 'to see' 6, 32a
keffys 'got' 10a; *kyffes* 1; *kyffys* 11
kemmar 'take(s)' 14a; **kymmer* 1, **kymmar* 34
leuerris 'said' 52
lymmyn 'now' 16, 16a, 18, 19a
nenna 'then' 16a
prontyrryan 'priests' 33a
profettys 'prophets' 42, *prophettys* 42
tacklennow, taclennow 'things' 14, 16 x 2
*trellyas 'turned' 46a
ynnans, innans 'in them' 6a, 38a

defferans 27
egglosyow 36a, 47a
esyly 31a, 58; *esely* 35
galus 56
thy gela, y gyla, y gela 22a, 29a, 32
grekys 26a
gwelas 28a, 29a, 31
kefys 6, 48; *kyfys* 37
kemer 31a
leverys 52; *leueris* 52 x 3
lymyn 16a, 27a
nena 9a, 17a, 18, 19
prontirion 38a, **prontyryan* 39
prophetes 15, 43a
taclenow 27a, 50a
*trelya 'to turn' 50a, 51a
ynans 14.

2 BK

Bryttyn 'Britain' 1645
fystynnyn 'let us hasten' 2755
gallant 'brave' 1741
honnyn 'self' 312
kethtella 'thus' 201, 287
kevennough 'remember!' 1598
mollath 'curse' 740, 2303, 3155, 3156
myllwyth 'thousand times' 922
socckers, sockors 'supports' 2733, 2818
thymmo 'to me' 50, 162, 300
wellys 'I saw' 383
weresso 'may help' 807
worhemmyn 'commands' 1277, 1831

Bretyn 1423
fistenyn 1353
galaunt 2005
honen 466, *honyn* 1436, 2750
ketela 3015
kevenough 1359
molath 740
mylwyth 330, 1548, 1623
sokers, sokors 1732, 1548
thymo 2720
welys 798, 1205
weresa 803
worhemyn 2035.

3 CW

alemma 'hence' 1333, 1709, 1732
*collan 'heart' 284, 734
drog pullat 'evil fellow' 927;
gollowe 'light' 304
gorrawe 'male' 2414
gorrowgh 'put!' 2193
gwellas 'to see' 382, 561; *wellas* 446, 553
gwellys 'seen' 78, 825
hemma 'this' 1786
henna 'that' 439, 445, 501
honna 'that one' (fem.) 20, 394
*kellas 'to hide' 1245
kymmar 'take!' 1448, 688
mannaf 'I will' 314; *vannaf* 507, 648
ny wellaf 'I see not' 1167

alema 1150, 1218, 1287
*colan 306, 1689, 1964, 1998,
drog polat 1441; *droke polat* 769
golowe 45
gorawe 2416
gorowgh 1072
gwelas 132, 1592, 1701
gwelys 475, 2400
hema 1579, 1676 h
hena 418, 625, 814
hona 878
kelas 'to hide' 1807
kymar 356, 833, 1115
manaf 313, 471, 503; *vanaf* 649, 1524
welaf 1461

47

palas 'to dig' 1033	**pallas* 'to dig' 975, 982
tenna 'to draw, shoot' 1554	*tenaf* 'I draw' 385
thymma 'to me' 590	*thyma* 748, 777, 877
thymmo 'to me' 371, 727;	*thymo* 331, 844.

The asterisk indicates that the etymon occurs with mutated in initial at the place indicated. Notice also **dewollow* 'devils' CW 2021, 481 but *dewolow*, *dewolov* BM 145; and *robbys* 'robbed' TH 40a but *robijs* BM 2064.

I assume that the scribes wrote either geminate or single indiscriminately, because the difference was not important. This means that geminate and single consonants were identical in quality and the vowels that preceded them were correspondingly of the same length—and that can mean only one thing: that the vowels were short.

6.06 *Dader* 'goodness' ~ *dadder*

George believes that before a single consonant a stressed vowel in disyllables is half-long in Middle Cornish. He is therefore anxious to explain away the instances of *dadder* with <dd>. In consequence George suggests that *dader/dadder* "appears as a special case". His reason for thinking so is that the <d> is doubled in *dadder* but never in *lader* 'robber', *broder* 'brother', *falladow* 'fail', *caradow* 'beloved', *casadow* 'hateful', *preder* 'thought or *Peder* 'Peter'. Here are all the examples from the texts of both *dader* and *dadder*:

A **dader**
  dadar TH 10, CW 1162; *dader* PC 1296, 3096, BM 13, 33, 49, 61, 206, 210, 261, 4260, TH 26a, 30a; *thader* BM 380.

B **dadder**
  daddar 11a, 12, 26a; *dadder* BM 485, 499, 2229, 3173, 4263, 4514, TH 2, 11, 16a, 25a x 2, 26, 30a, 51; *ʒadder* PA 3b, 189, 228; *thaddar* TH 5, 14, 15a; *thadder* OM 973, PC 3097, RD 1224, BM 528, 2240, 2774, 4271, 4490, 4494, TH 30a.

In KKC21: 23 (fig 4.3) George says there are two forms with /-d-/ in Tregear. I have found three [ID]. George says:

> Thus if *dadder* really contained a short vowel, then it does not necessarily follow that all the other polysyllables containing etymological /-d-/ contained one (KKC21: 23).

This is another example of George's special pleading [SP]. Even if *dadder* had a short vowel, he says, it is not certain that *lader* and *Peder* had a short vowel as well. But this avoids the simple question why *dadder* had a short vowel at all. If the vowel was indeed short, then shortening has occurred in *dadder* at least. In which case the Prosodic Shift had begun by the time of PA. If *dadder* is not

THE GEMINATION OF CONSONANTS

the result of the Prosodic Shift, what caused it to shorten? George does not say [AD].

We have seen from the lists given above that a short vowel was not necessarily indicated. *Omma* 'here' certainly had a short vowel but in BM it is very often written <oma> and is thus identical with <oma> 'I am'. Although it is never written with a geminate <dd>, *lader* almost certainly had a short stressed vowel, as is apparent from the plural *laddron* at PA 90d, 186d, 193d, 229a, PC 336, 2255, RD 125, 1426, etc. Nicholas Boson in the Late Cornish period spells the word *lader* with a single <d>: *Harry an lader* 'Harry the thief' BF: 12. And the plural has a geminate consonant: *leddarn* 'robbers' BF: 17. George would surely concede that both *lader* and *leddarn* had short stressed vowels in Late Cornish, yet only the plural has a geminate—exactly as in Middle Cornish.

If *dadder* is written with a geminate <dd> from the period of PA onwards, we can be certain that it contained a short vowel. George and his supporters have actually suggested that the geminate <dd> in *dadder* may be a reflex of a historical consonant group i.e. *[ɣ+d] or [ɣ+t]. This is not compelling. *Da* 'good' is from **dago*- (cf. Old Irish *dag* 'good'). An early abstract noun **dagotero-*, if the lenited -*g*- survived at all, would have given **daɣter* > **dayder*. If for some reason the loss of internal syllables predated lenition—which is not likely— one would have got **dayter* > **daghter* > *dater* (cf. *myghtern, mytern*). The <dd> in *dadder* in Middle Cornish can, I think, mean only one thing: that the stressed vowel was short.

George asserts that *dadder* is "a special case", though he is prevented by his mistaken belief in half-length in native words in Middle Cornish from seeing why. The two lexemes *da* 'good' and *dader* 'goodness' are without parallel anywhere in Cornish. They A) are transparently related to each other and B) they have differing vocalic lengths in the vowel common to them i.e. *a*. *Da* 'good' < **dago*- has a long vowel, whereas *dader, dadder* by the Prosodic Shift has a short one. There exists in Cornish no other pair of related lexemes which share these two features. Since *da* 'good' is long, someone reading the word *dader* 'goodness' might wish to pronounce it *[da:der] with a long stressed vowel. In order to avoid that possibility the scribes preferred to write <dadder>. There are many pairs of words in Middle Cornish, one a monosyllable and the other a disyllable, in which the vowel length differs. In most cases, however, the difference in vowel length can be shown by vocalic quality: *trega* 'to dwell' ~ *tryg* 'will dwell', *bethaf* 'I will be' ~ *byth* 'be!' This device does not apply in the case of *da ~ dadder*; the only way that the scribes can show the difference in vocalic length is to write *dadder* with a geminate <dd>. The alternation *da ~ dadder* is thus one of the most convincing pieces of evidence we have that the half-long vowels were already short by the Middle Cornish period.

6.07 Conclusions

We can be completely sure that the Prosodic Shift had already occurred in all these texts. The attempt made by Kernowek Kemyn to maintain half-long vowels in words like *dader* 'goodness', *gweles* 'to see', *colon* 'heart', *Breten* 'Britain', etc. is mistaken. Equally mistaken is the attempt to distinguish geminate consonants from their single counterparts. I think we can be fairly certain that in the language of BM, TH, BK and CW the distinction between long and short consonants had been lost. There was no difference for Radulphus Ton, Tregear the scribe of BK or William Jordan between <ll> and <l>, <mm> and <m>, <nn> and <n>, <rr> and <r>, <ss> and <s> or between any other pair of double versus single consonants. In the matter of consonantal length, we have to acknowledge, I think, that Kernowek Kemyn is based on mistaken phonology.

CHAPTER 7
George's two long *o* vowels exemplified in Kernowek Kemyn by <troes> 'foot' and <tros> 'noise' (KKC21: 28-35)

7.00 The question of long *o* in Middle Cornish

Middle Cornish contains many monosyllabic words with long *o*, for example *bōs* 'to be', *bōs* 'food', *mōs* 'to go', *mōs* 'table', *rōs* 'gave', *rōs* 'net', *cōth* 'old', *cōth* 'falls'. The long *o* in some of these etyma is the reflex of earlier short *o* lengthened as a result of the Brythonic new quantity system. In such cases Cornish long *o* corresponds exactly with Welsh and Breton long *o*: *bōs* 'to be' = Welsh *bōd* 'to be' and Cornish *cōth* 'old' = Breton *kōzh* 'old'. In other cases, however, Cornish long *o* is the development of earlier *ui* or *oi* and corresponds to Welsh *wy* and *oe* and to Breton *oa*: Cornish *cōs* 'wood' = Welsh *coed* 'wood', Breton *koat*; Cornish *rōs* 'net' = Welsh *rhwyd* 'net'; Cornish *nōth* 'naked' = Welsh *noeth* 'naked'. Therefore, in Middle Cornish, *ō* (written <o> and <oy> in the texts) corresponds to Welsh *o* in some cases and to Welsh *oe* and *wy* in others.

In Late Cornish the vowel of words that have *wy* and *oe* in Welsh and *oa* in Breton, frequently appears as *ū*: *kûz* 'wood', *bûz* 'food', *rûz* 'net', *lûz* 'grey', etc. whereas the reflex of Middle Cornish *ō* < *o* by lengthening remains *ō* in the later language.

7.01 George's Solution (HTLO)

George's explanation of these phenomena is as follows: he believes that Middle Cornish had two separate and distinct long *o*-vowels. The first was a long open *o* /ɔ:/ and this was the vowel of *bōs* 'to be', *mōs* 'to go' and all the other words that have long *ō* by lengthening of *o*. The second phoneme was /o:/, long closed *o*, which is the reflex of earlier *oi* or *ui* and corresponds to Welsh *oe* or *wy* and Breton *oa*. This long closed *o* George believes was raised to *ū* c. 1625 (PSRC: 129) and thus appears in Late Cornish as /u:/. This hypothesis of George's I will refer to from now on as "the Hypothesis of the Two Long *o*'s" or HTLO. In Kernowek Kemyn George spells his two phonemes differently: /ɔ:/ is written <o>, e.g *mos* 'to go', *bos* 'to be', whereas /o:/ appears as <oe>, e.g. *moes* 'table', *boes* 'food'.

First it should be noted that until very recently no Celtic scholar who has concerned himself with the question has ever suggested such an explanation for the question of Middle Cornish *ō*, Late Cornish *ū*. Neither Pedersen, Lewis, nor Jackson has any hint of such a hypothesis. Similarly none of the great scholars of the revival, Jenner, Nance, or Caradar ever considered that HTLO was necessary. Nance was aware of the problem, but he believed (rightly, in my view) that Late Cornish *ū* in such words as *kûz*, *lûz* was confined to monosyllables ending in *s* < *d*. He appears to have thought (again, rightly, in my view) that the solution to the problem was in this precise phonetic environment. In the introduction to his *Cornish-English Dictionary* of 1938 he says: "In Late Cornish *ō* sometimes becomes *ū*, especially in monosyllables ending in an *s* that represents an older *d* or *t*; e.g. *bōs* (food), *cōs*, *trōs*, *lōs* become *būz, cūz, trūz, lūz*."

HTLO does not, however, appear to be George's own hypothesis. The idea that Middle Cornish had two long-*o* phonemes was first apparently suggested by Tim Saunders in his "New Unified Cornish" of 1975 (Saunders 1990: vi). Moreover Saunders spells /ɔ:/ as <o> and /o:/ as <oe>, exactly as is the case in Kernowek Kemyn. Saunders system of Neo-Cornish is highly schematized and has never gained acceptance among revivalists.

7.02 The spelling <oe>

Kernowek Kemyn uses <oe> for /o:/. This, in my view, is unnecessary anyway, since Middle Cornish never had two separate long *o* phonemes. What is particularly perplexing is why <oe> was chosen for /o:/. <oe> does it is true, occur occasionally in earlier forms of toponyms, e.g. *Cargoes, Bossywoelou, Moelvre, Nancecoethan*, etc.; but <oe> is very uncommon indeed in the texts before the seventeenth century. When <oe> is used in the literature it is seldom used as a reflex of Old Cornish *ui*. I have collected the following examples.

oe
1 disyllabic:
goef 'woe to him' PA 259d, OM 754, 1016, 1889, 2093, PC 750, 871, 2457, RD 176, 615, 757, 1349, 2313, 2350, 2419, BK 415, 1656, 2701; *loer* 'enough' (< *lower*) OM 90; *aloes* 'aloes' PC 3198; *Boecy* 'Boetia' BK 2674.

2 [œ]
oes 'is' BK 904.

3 diphthong [oi]
noe 'Noah' OM 931, 933, 941, 973, 1096, 1157, 1207; *oel* 'oil' OM 327, 841; *noe* 'nephew' BK 2746, 3133, 3196a & b.

4 long /ɔ:/ <o> in Kernowek Kemyn
coeth 'old' BM 1979; *scoen* 'soon' BM 4066; *boes* 'to be' CW 1401; *boese* 'to be' SA 59a x 2; *goer* 'puts' CW 1847, 1857; *doer, thoer* 'earth' CW 294, 353, 924, 952, 1851, 2455; *moer* 'sea' BK 92, CW 355; *cloer* 'mild' CW 351.

5 long */o:/ <oe> in Kernowek Kemyn
noeth 'naked' OM 259, 262, BK 417, 3156; *ov toen* 'carrying' PC 3077; *doen* 'carry' CW 94, 2427; *woer* 'knows' CW 2403.

Notice further that neither *noeth* 'naked', *doen* 'carry' nor *woer* 'knows' exhibits long [u:] in Late Cornish If one really needs to distinguish those words that have Late Cornish *ō* from those that have Late Cornish *ū*, <oe> would seems a rather unsuitable and indeed untraditional spelling. We must remember, however, that Kernowek Kemyn is an arbitrary orthography that bears only a tangential relationship to the texts upon which it claims to have been based.

7.03 George's <oe> type spellings

George refers to "<oe>-type spellings" (KKC21: 29, fig. 5.1) when referring to those spellings of words containing his */o/ but in which the vowel in the texts is written other than <o>. To call them <oe>-type spellings is disingenuous, because the overwhelming majority of them in fact contain <oy> or <oi>. George knows that this, but uses the title "<oe>-type spellings" as a way of suppressing the evidence. This looks like an example of George's misrepresenting the data [ID]. George also omits to mention that <oy>, <oi> has other functions in the texts, being frequently used to represent the diphthong [oi] both in native words and in borrowed ones. Here are some examples from PA and OM:

1 [oi] in native words
moy 'more' PA 21d, 35d, 51d, 72d, 104d, 116d, 128c, 132d, 145c, 180b, 198d, 200d, 209a, 227b, 237b, OM 108, 134, 170, 219, 391, 399, 591, 829, 946, 1092, 1614, 2476, 2793; *the voy* 'the more' OM 2016; *moygha* 'most' PA 112d, 196c; *roy* 'give' OM 444, 680.

2 [oi] in borrowed words
ioy 'joy' PA 21d, 30a, 226a, 251b, 258c, OM 154, 306, 359, 517, 558, 1374, 2476; *poynt* 'point' PA 83d; *coyntis* 'cleverness' PA 109c, 125a; *oynment* 'ointment' PA 235b, 252c; *voys* 'voice' OM 477, 1436, 1487; *oyl* 'oil' OM 694, 703, 741, 815; *noy* 'Noah' OM 1017, 1231; *moyses* 'Moses' OM 1402 x 2, 1433, 1443, 1551, 1572, 1583, 1585, 1627, 1643, 1682, 1702, 1715, 1767, 1777, 1799, 1841, 1863, 1931, 1946, 2644; *oyeth* 'oyez!' 2297, 2419 x 2.

<oy> is also used on occasion in the texts to represent [o:] in borrowed words, e.g. *forsoyth* 'forsooth' BK 359, 1905, 1994, 2050 and 2265. And we shall see below that <oy> and also <oi> are not infrequently used in Middle Cornish to represent what in Kernowek Kemyn is spelt <o>—this latter is a most important consideration.

We must remember, therefore, in all his discussion of what he spells <oe> in Kernowek Kemyn, George is actually talking about <oy> and that this same graph is used to represent a diphthong. This is of crucial significance, since what in Kernowek Kemyn is represented by <oe>, was historically a diphthong, a fact reflected in the traditional spelling.

7.04 The theoretical basis of HTLO

Although HTLO appears at first glance to explain the alternation between Middle Cornish ō and Late Cornish ū coherently and elegantly, the more one examines it, the less tenable it becomes. Let us look at some theoretical objections first.

Welsh has only one /o/, though the long vowel is less open than its short equivalent. Breton has both /oː/ and /ɔː/, though the opposition is quite unlike that proposed for Kernowek Kemyn, since the Breton equivalent of /oː/ <oe> in Kernowek Kemyn is usually *oa*, e.g Kernowek Kemyn *koes* 'wood', Breton *koad*; Kernowek Kemyn *hwoer* 'sister', Breton *c'hwoar*, etc. In Breton some etyma with /ɔː/ in Kernowek Kemyn have /ɔː/, e.g. *to* 'roof', *ro* 'gift', *roz* 'rose', whereas others with /ɔː/ in Kernowek Kemyn have /oː/ in Breton, e.g. Breton *kozh* 'old', Kernowek Kemyn *koth*; Breton *skol* 'school', Kernowek Kemyn *skol*; Breton *mor* 'sea', Kernowek Kemyn *mor*.

The original research that lies behind Kernowek Kemyn was done in Brittany under Breton supervision. The Bretons since Loth have tended to believe that Cornish was little more than a dialect of Breton. This was in some sense true at the very earliest period. By the Middle Cornish period, however, it was certainly not true at all. Cornish was a separate language with a distinctive phonology, morphology and syntax. Given that Modern Breton has an opposition between /oː/ and /ɔː/, it is not astonishing that George should assume the same for Cornish. Many of the errors in George's phonology and therefore in Kernowek Kemyn can be attributed to his underlying view that Middle Cornish and Modern Breton are very similar. Because George believes Breton and Middle Cornish are very close, in my view, he pays insufficient attention to the Middle Cornish texts themselves.

It is apparent incidentally that the schematic orthography of Kernowek Kemyn is also based on Breton. Compare Kernowek Kemyn *hwoer* 'sister' with Breton *c'hoar*, Kernowek Kemyn *terri* with Breton *terriñ* or Kernowek Kemyn *skrifa* with Breton *skrivañ*.

Before we leave the question of the origins of HTLO a further point should be made. In standard Breton the opposition /oː/ ~ /ɔː/ survives until the present day. In Cornish on the other hand HTLO requires that the more closed of these two phonemes became [uː] *c.* 1625. One might ask what other phenomena were occurring *c.* 1625 to induce the raising to [uː]. In English [oː] became [uː] in the fifteenth century, but this was part of a general reshaping of the English vowel system known as the Great Vowel Shift. George believes that [iː] in Cornish became [ei] as a consequence of the English Shift, i.e. starting in the fifteenth century. The change [oː] > [uː] in George's view is presumably part of the (Cornish) Prosodic Shift (see Chapter 5). As we have already seen, George believes that the Prosodic Shift shortened vowels except "half-long" *i* and *o* which it lengthened. Presumably the shift of [oː] > [uː] is part of the same phenomenon. Of course we know on theoretical grounds alone that *c.* 1625 is far too late in the history of Cornish for any major change. George's alleged shift of [oː] > [uː], e.g. *[koːz] 'wood' > [kuːz] is not credible.

GEORGE'S TWO LONG O VOWELS

7.05 *[ɔː] in Middle Cornish

Middle Cornish did have a vowel very close indeed to [ɔː] but it was an allophone of /aː/. Middle Cornish had only one long vowel in the low central area /aː/ which, because it had so much room, appears to have had at least two separate allophones. One was [æː] which on occasion fell together with [eː]. The other was [ɑː] which appears to have occurred after [b] and before [l]. If Middle Cornish really had had /ɔː/ distinct from /oː/, it would have been close to [ɑː]. When /ɔː/ was shortened it would have been correspondingly less tense and would have been very close to indeed to [ɑ]. One ought here mention that Breton short /ɔ/ has a very open allophone (*Breton Grammar*: 87). Irish may also provide a parallel. Ulster Irish has both /oː/ (e.g. *leabhar* /Lʲoːr/ 'book') and /ɔː/ (e.g. *leor* /Lʲɔːr/ 'enough'). When in Ulster and Oriel /ɔː/ shortens in the English version of place-names, it not infrequently gives [a], for example *Tandragee* < *Tóin re Gaoth* in Co. Armagh and *Yellowbatter* < *Bóthar Buí* in Co. Louth.

George believes that the word *bōs* 'to be/dwelling' had /ɔː/. Yet *bōs* is a frequent element in place-names where it is spontaneously shortened in the English forms. Were George's view valid, we might expect to find spellings of place-names in which *bos* < *bōs* appears as **bas*. No such forms are attested.

7.06 The spelling <oy>

George does not dispute that <ui> (e.g. in *cuit* 'wood', *guit* 'blood') in Old Cornish represented a diphthong, yet he asserts that <oy> in Middle Cornish *coys* 'wood' and *goys* 'blood' represents the monophthong /oː/. It is certain, however, as we have seen that <oy> does represent a diphthong in native words, *moy* 'more' *oy* 'egg', *roy* 'give!' (see above), and in borrowings, *joy* 'joy', *voys* 'voice', *oynment* 'ointment', etc. Just how likely is it that the Cornish scribes used <oy> for /oː/, /ɔː/ and /oi/, if there was no historical relationship between the phonemes and all three were phonetically distinct?

The following is surely more likely: that <oy>, continuing <ui> was originally a diphthong but that it later monopthongized and fell together with /oː/ from other sources. Thereafter, starting with PA, but most notably in BM onwards, <oy> was used to represent /oː/ irrespective of origin.

7.07 The date of *[oː] > [uː]

In PSRC George suggested that [oː] became [uː] "*c.* 1625". In many cases his [oː] would have been the reflex of Old Cornish *ui* (Welsh *wy*) in *los* 'grey', *scos* 'shield', *scoth* 'shoulder', *bos* 'food', for example. If George's suggestion were valid, we would have to assume that [ui] in OCV (*c.* 1125) was first lowered to [oi] and monophthongized to [oː] before the earliest surviving Middle Cornish texts (*c.* 1350) and then was raised again in the early seventeenth century to [uː], i.e. [ui] > [oiː] > [oː] > [uː]. Although such a development, i.e. lowering > monophthonization > raising, is possible, one wonders whether it is likely.

That, however, is not all. I have pointed out that in two Middle Cornish texts, PC and RD, *ō* appears on occasion as <ou>. George is aware of this and has written elsewhere: "The occasional use of <ou> in Middle Cornish also suggests a more close realization." This is certainly correct and indeed <ou> in Middle Cornish can only mean [uː]. Yet PC and RD date from the mid- to late fourteenth century. For George's view to be valid, one would have to assume that the shift [ui] > [oiː] > [oː] > [uː] had all taken place between *c.* 1125 and *c.* 1375. This is difficult to credit.

I believe that <ou> spellings in PC and RD are dialectal and indeed I have suggested elsewhere and for two quite separate reasons that these two plays show clear signs of western dialect. George himself is aware of the occasional spellings with <ou> in Middle Cornish, but he believes that they are indicative of Middle Cornish in general, since he denies that we have any knowledge of Cornish dialects. This entails a difficulty, however. If [oː] has already become [uː] in the two plays PC and RD and if there is no discernible dialect in Middle Cornish, we would surely expect to find [oː] written sporadically as <ou> (for [uː]) in every text. TH is as long as the three plays of the *Ordinalia* (OM, PC and RD) put together, yet not once does TH write the reflex of Old Cornish *ui/oi* as <ou>. Indeed <ou> for <o> is a feature unique to PC and RD (and to the brief sixteenth-century dialogue from Borde—which, in my view, is also western).

7.08 Old Cornish *ui* > Late Cornish *ō*

There is a further problem with HTLO, since a number of words which ought, according to George, to have *ū* in Late Cornish, in fact have *ō*. The etyma in question include Middle Cornish *cor* 'wax' (Welsh *cwyr*), Late Cornish *kōr*; Middle Cornish *con* 'supper' (Welsh *cwyn*), Late Cornish *kōn*; Middle Cornish *whor* 'sister' (Welsh *chwaer* < **chwoir*), Late Cornish *hōr*; Middle Cornish *don* 'to carry' (Welsh *dwyn*), Late Cornish *dōn*; Middle Cornish *oan* 'lamb' (Welsh *oen*), Late Cornish *ōn*. In all these the Late Cornish reflex of George's shift [oː] > [uː] is unexpectedly *ō*. George suggests that the following *r* or *n* may have lowered the preceding vowel.

It is quite common in languages for following *r* to lower the preceding vowel. Good examples would be English *clerk, sergeant, varsity* (< *university*), *Berkshire*, etc. Following nasals on the other hand do not as a rule lower a preceding vowel. Rather they tend to raise it. Think for example of the way that *man* is *men* in many English dialects and *men* is *min*. In London, where I grew up, *engine* is regularly pronounced *ingine*. Think also of the following nasal in many Irish dialects which raises [oː] to [uː], for example in *i gcónaí, móin, Domhnach, ainneoin, bonn, fonn*, etc.

The second difficulty is as follows. If one accepts HTLO, not only are the six etyma with o + *r/n* anomalous but so is the word for 'naked'. In Middle Cornish this is *noth* (Welsh *noeth*) and were George's hypothesis correct, it should appear in Late Cornish as **nūth*. The attested Late Cornish forms are Lhuyd's *noath* (AB: 101a) and Rowe's *en hoath* (< *yn nōth*) at RC 23: 169 and 170.

GEORGE'S TWO LONG O VOWELS

Clearly the reflex of Old Cornish *ui* could be *ō* in Late Cornish even when no "liquid or nasal" was involved

The word *bloth* 'years of life' is also relevant here. In Middle Cornish this is *blōth* (cf. Welsh *blwydd*) and in Late Cornish one would expect forms with [uː]. This is indeed attested. Bodinar's letter, our last piece of traditional Cornish, has *bluth vee* 'my years' and *pager egance blouth* 'eighty years old' (Loth 1900: 228). Yet Nicholas Boson writes *canz bloath coth* '100 years old' and *wheeath bloah* [sic] *coth* 'six years old' (BF: 27), where <oa> can hardly mean anything but [oː]. It would appear then that Late Cornish had two forms of the word *bloth*: *blouth* and *bloath*. George's suggestion that *ō* became *ū* in Late Cornish (and indeed sporadically as early as the fourteenth century) does not explain these two forms which occur contemporaneously with each other in Late Cornish. I suggest that *blouth* with [uː] and *bloath* with [oː] are dialectal variants. That both variants occur in the mouths of different speakers in Late Cornish is not unexpected. George does not mention either *noath* nor *bloath*. Another example of his passing over in silence what he is unable to explain [AD}

7.09 The problem of *ō* 'he was' and *lō* 'spoon'

The Middle Cornish word for 'he, she was' is *ō* and corresponds with Welsh *oedd* and Breton *oa*. The Common Celtic from which all three derive was something like **esāt* and were HTLO valid one would expect *ō* in Cornish to have /oː/ rather than /ɔː/. Yet it is clear from the texts that the vowel of *ō* 'was' rhymes with the reflex of *ō* by lengthening. It is for this reason than George spells the word <o> rather than <oe> in Kernowek Kemyn. The word for 'spoon' occurs in Middle Cornish as *lo*. The word is exactly parallel with Welsh *llwy* and one might expect by HTLO that the word should have /oː/ rather than /ɔː/. Yet in Kernowek Kemyn George spells the word as <lo>, not *<loe>. According to George Primitive Cornish *ui* and *oi* gave /ɔː/ finally (PSRC: 125); he therefore spells *ō* (Welsh *oedd*) and *lo* (Welsh *llwy*) with <o>.

This explanation is open to question, however. If Welsh *oedd* corresponds to Cornish *ō* and Welsh *llwy* 'spoon' corresponds to Cornish *lō* and in both cases /ɔː/ < *ui/oi* is a function of the vowel's position in absolute final, then Cornish *oy* 'egg' (cf. Welsh *wy*) and Cornish *moy* 'more' (Welsh *mwy*) with Old Cornish *ui* in final position, are unexplained. If George's explanation were valid, these two would appear as **ō* 'egg' and **mō* 'more'. Neither is attested. George does not mention either *oy* 'egg' or *moy* 'more' in KKC21 [AD].

It is perplexing that George should suggest that final position could lower /oː/ > /ɔː/. In absolute final position long vowels would surely have been pronounced if anything with greater vigour than elsewhere and might in consequence be expected to be raised rather than lowered. This is surely the reason for the spelling <wy> 'egg' at BM 3593.

7.10 *ōf* 'I am'

"Liquids and nasals" and "final position" may (or may not) in George's view explain or partially explain some exceptions to his general rule that Old Cornish *ui/oi* gave Middle Cornish /oː/ and Late Cornish /uː/. Neither of them can explain *oy* 'egg' or *moy* 'more'. Moreover Late Cornish *nōth* and the Late Cornish alternation *blūth/bloath* appear not to conform to any of George's exceptions. Further HTLO cannot explain the simple and common etymon *of* 'I am'. The Welsh for 'I am' is *wyf*, and in Middle Cornish by all George's criteria the word should have /oː/—and thus in Kernowek Kemyn ought to be spelt *<oev>. It is apparent, however, from the rhymes in the texts that *ōf* 'I am' has the same vowel as *bos* 'to be', *mos* 'to go', etc. In consequence Kernowek Kemyn spells it <ov>. Does this not violate HTLO?

7.11 My understanding of the question

Before setting out very briefly my own understanding of the question of long *o* in Middle Cornish, I must here make a confession of past error. In *Cornish Today* I followed George and assumed that the earliest Middle Cornish did indeed have two long *o*-vowels, one open and one closed, but that by the time of our earliest Middle Cornish texts these two phonemes were falling or had fallen together. I was mistaken. Having studied the question more thoroughly since, I realize that Middle Cornish never had anything but one long *o*-vowel [oː] and this remained unchanged until the death of the language in the eighteenth century. Words with [oː] by lengthening always contained this vowel. When the reflex of Old Cornish *ui* monophthongized (at some time during the ?later fourteenth century), the resulting vowel fell together with [oː]. As a result in standard Middle Cornish *bos* 'to be' and *bos* 'food' were homophones, as were *ros* 'he gave' and *ros* 'net', *mos* 'to go' and *mos* 'table', etc. I assume that the vowel in question was close to cardinal 7.

Middle Cornish [oː] by monophthongization is the reflex of what in OCV is written either <ui> or <oi>. The distribution of these graphs is not completely etymological, since some words which have *wy* in Welsh have *oi* in OCV (e.g. *coir* 'wax'), while others which have *oe* in Welsh are spelt with *ui* (e.g. *cuit* 'wood'). Jackson assumes that in Cornish and Breton [oi] and [ɔi] fell together early as [oi]. This is what is meant by <ui> or <oi> in OCV. I take /ui/ in stressed long syllables to be [uui], i.e. a dimoric *u* followed by [i] or [j].

There can be little doubt that the monophthongization of /ui/ is a direct consequence of the Prosodic Shift. The shift meant that stressed Cornish vowels and diphthongs lost length but gained in intensity. Trimoric vowels lost one mora to become dimoric, whereas dimoric ones became unimoric. /ui/ was a trimoric diphthong and could be represented as [uui]. The Prosodic Shift reduced this trimoric diphthong in different ways according to whether the vocalic cluster stood before a consonant or was in absolute final position. In the first case [buuidz] 'food' (note that I have partially assibilated the final consonant) probably developed as [booⁱdz] with a lower vowel (if the vowel

GEORGE'S TWO LONG *O* VOWELS

was not already at this height) and a reduced [i]. This then simplified to [boo^{i}z] (written <boys>). As the Prosodic Shift gradually worked itself out, [boo^{i}z] lost a full mora to become [booz] (frequently written <bos>). The final stage *bos* was by the fifteenth century homophonous with *bos* 'to be'. Since, however, the earlier written form of *bos* 'food' was Old Cornish *buit* or *boit* and early Middle Cornish *boys* (our [boo^{i}z]), the vowel continued to be written in Middle Cornish as <oy> even after monophthongization had taken place. <oy> in the minds of scribes was associated with the long vowel [o:], as distinct from the corresponding short vowel. In the texts <boys> is written to represent both *bos* 'food' < *boys* and *bos* 'to be'—which had never had a diphthong. On the other hand <bos> is also used to represent both *bos* 'to be' (which never had a diphthong) and *bos* 'food' which was originally *boys*.

7.12 Confusion of <o> and <oy> in the texts

Here from the texts are some unetymological spellings of the words for 'food' and 'to be'.

A **bos** 'food' (etymologically **boys**; cf. Welsh **bwyd**)

dyvotter ru'm kymmer hag awel **bos** OM 365-56
ynno **bos** *thy'm the welas* OM 378
hag y[*n*] **bos** *theugh ordenys* OM 1218
thy'm devythys awel the **vos** PC 46
bos *pask thy'nny hep lettye* PC 618
bos *pask thy'nny ordyne* PC 623
gueyteugh dygtye **bos** *ynny* PC 639
the thygh[*t*]*ye* **bos** PC 651
dybry **bos** *pask omma ef a vyn* PC 671-72
aga **bos** *a vyth parys* PC 695
nans yv **bos** *soper parys* PC 701
keffrys dybry hagh eve war ow **bos** *yn uhelder* PC 812-13
kyns bos ['to be'] *prys bos* [two words identical!] PC 2784
megys gans an **bos** TH 41
ow kyge ew verely **bos** TH 51a
bos *y very corfe eff* TH 52
Ple ma ow **bos**? BK 36
mar synsough **bos** BK 1826
ow kyg ew verely **bos** SA 61.

B **boys** 'to be' (etymologically **bos**; cf. Welsh **bod**)

kyns ys **boys** *colyek clewys* PA 49b
na **boys** *yn y gowe3as* PA 110b
Own **boys** *crist mab du an neff* PA 122a [contrast *rag own bos* ['to be'] *megys* PA 206a]
trest ambus **boys** *acordys* BM 494
pronter **boys** *me a garsa* BM 522

TOWARDS AUTHENTIC CORNISH

ny vyn **boys** *covsis mas a crist* BM 789-90
heb **boys** *marov* BM 878
boys *lethys avel carov* BM 881
gase ny vyn **boys** *kefys* BM 1026
ena ermet purguir **boys** BM 1133
ov **boys** *ov powes* BM 1188
ov **boys** *fecycyen connek* BM 1421
mara kyll a **boys** *kefys* BM 1503
Ny dal dotho **boys** *goys best* [*bos* 'be' and *goys* 'blood' spelt with same vowel] BM 1506
may hallons **boys** *dewogys* BM 1556
in delma y hyl **boys** BM 1603
omgolhough in age goys / sav nefre mar mynnogh **boys** BM 1642-43 [*goys* 'blood' and *bos* 'to be' rhyme]
boys *lethys am govys vy* BM 1655
[cf. *boys* 'food' *ha dewes* BM 1673]
agys **boys** *mar pytethays* BM 1678
rag the **voys** *in dysgregyans* BM 1764
pyv ylly an rema **boys** BM 1797
boys *crystyan menna* BM 1817
ha **boys** *selwys* BM 2041
drefen y **voys** *sur heb mar* BM 2286
my ny won the **voys** *genys* BM 2449
the **voys** *crystyen* BM 2517
may wothaffsen **boys** *lethys* BM 2634
ov **boys** *in beys* BM 2648
the **voys** *revler* BM 2718
nynsyv y voth **boys** *kelys* BM 2745
y fensen ov **boys** BM 2864
boys *sensis detha* BM 2954
meryasek y **voys** *sacrys* BM 3020
drefen ov **boys** *anhethek* BM 3072
y **voys** *treas* BM 3520
kyn **boys** *dylyfrys* BM 3551
[cf. *deves na boys* 'food' BM 3578; *boys* 'food' *na dewes* BM 3603]
confort thum cervons dyson **boys** *y carsen* 3651-52
ov **boys** *heb y clowes* BM 3708
me a greys **boys** *grueys forth lan* BM 3715
hagis **boys** *wy the vlamya* BM 3743
the **voys** *socrys genogh why* BM 3820
[*boys eleth* 'food of angels' BM 3886; *boys neff* 'food of heaven' BM 3893]
da yv **boys** *fur* BM 3909
[*dewes han boys* 'food' BM 3929 rhymes with *moys* 'to go']
[*debre boys* 'food' rhymes with *droys* 'foot' BM 3984]
rag the **voys** *y servont len* BM 4061
[*dewes ha boys* 'food' BM 4243]
ny a yl **boys** *morethek* BM 4313
gans ancov y **voys** *tuchys* BM 4423
[*boys eleth* 'food of angels' BM 4464]

GEORGE'S TWO LONG O VOWELS

ny a gottha thyn **bois** *inflammyes* TH 3
may halla an raunson ma **bois** *perfect* TH 15a
ny yll **bois** *coveys, na ny yll kantyll bos* ['to be'] *annowys* TH 17a ['to be' spelt <bois> and <bos> in same line]
ny a res thyn **bois** *da* TH 26a
an yocke a crist the **vois** *wheg hay sawe the vos scaffe* TH 28 ['to be' with lenited initial spelt <vois> and <vos> together!]
fatell ylla **bois** TH 57.

Here from the two sixteenth-century texts TH and SA are the spellings of some *bōs*-words and *boys*-words compared:

mos 'to go' (cf. Breton *mont*): *mos* TH 6, 10a; *mois* TH 1, 6, 13a, 17a, 25a
moys 'table' (cf. Welsh *mwys*): *mois* TH 54

ros 'gave' (cf. Welsh *rhoddi*) : *ros* TH 36, 40, 42a, 45a
roys 'net' (cf. Welsh *rhwyd*): *roois* TH 34; *ros* TH 34

coth 'old' (cf. Breton *kozh*): *coth* TH 6a, 27 x 3, 27a, SA 59a; *coith* TH 27, 28a, 52a; *coyth* TH 38a; *coeth* SA 64
coyth 'falls, behoves' (cf. Welsh *cwydd*): *coth* TH 7a, 20a, 29a x 2, 32, 32a, 34 x 4

nos 'night' (cf. Welsh *nos*, Breton *noz*): *nois* TH 52
oys 'age' (cf. Welsh *oed*): *oys* TH 15, 28, 42; *ois* TH 17a.

Note also that *Bewnans Ke* rhymes *lader eth* **oys** [Kernowek Kemyn <os>] 'thou art a robber' BK 103 with *abarth o'm* **coys** [Kernowek Kemyn <koes>] 'within my wood' BK 105.

I (like Nance, Jenner and Smith) find it impossible to believe that by the period of our written texts *bos* 'to be' and *boys* 'food', *moys* 'table' and *mos* 'to go', *roys* 'net' and *ros* 'gave', *coyth* 'falls' and *coth* 'old', *oys* 'age' and *nos* 'night' had anything other than the same vowel.

7.13 <oy> in place-names

The shift of /d/ > /s/ is itself a result of the anglicization of Cornish phonology. Early Middle English lacked the fortis ~ lenis opposition of the Celtic languages. In consequence when English speaking Cornishmen were re-Celticized in the twelfth century, they replaced the opposition fortis ~ lenis with one of obstruence ~ affrication. Thus *Ta:d* with fortis *T* and lenis *d* was replaced by *ta:dz* with unmarked *t* and an affricated *d* > *dz*.

The Prosodic Shift is also part of the same process and appears to have worked itself out slightly later. I assume that [kuuid] 'wood' (which is exactly parallel with [buuid] 'food') developed as [kooⁱdz] > [kooⁱz] > [kooz] during the thirteenth and fourteenth centuries, that is to say at precisely the time when Cornish literature was beginning to flourish. It is for that reason, I believe, that *coys* for [ko:z] and similar spellings are so prevalent in some texts.

TOWARDS AUTHENTIC CORNISH

The stage *coys* [kooⁱz] is survives in modern in place-names, for example *Engoyse* < *?an coys* (Wendron); *Burgois* < *bargoys* (St Issey); *Tucoyse* < *tu coys* (Constantine); *Tucoyse* (*St Ewe*); *Pencoys* (Wendron) and *Pencoys* near Four Lanes. Note also *Devichoys* in Mylor. This was originally *Kylcoys* 'ridge-wood', then later *Tevyscoys* 'cultivated wood, plantation' (Weatherhill: 34);. The spelling of these names seems to represent the pronunciation at the time when they were borrowed into English, i.e. at some time during the period *c.* 1250-1450. In which case we have further evidence against HTLO. When these names were borrowed into English, Middle Cornish according to George had /oː/ in the word 'wood'. How does he explain these forms in -*coys*, i.e with a diphthong? He does not even mention them [AD]

7.14 *ui* > *oy* in absolute final position

In absolute final position /ui/ developed differently from internally. The coda in such a position is rather more exposed and functions as word boundary rather than merely an element in a diphthong. I suggest therefore that the element [i] became semivocalic: [ooj]. In this case the loss by the Prosodic Shift was not of the final element in the diphthong, since that would have distorted the shape of the word too severely, but rather of the element preceding [j]. I assume therefore that *moy* /mooj/ 'more' and *oy* /ooj/ 'egg', for example, lost one mora internally rather than finally to become /moj/ <moy> and /oj/ <oy> respectively.

This suggested development would explain how the diphthongal *moy* and *oy* survived into Middle Cornish. *Lo* 'spoon' is a special case—the word is attested as far as I am aware in Middle Cornish only in the dog's name *Lonkylo* 'swallows his spoon' at BM 3226. We can assume that the regular plural form *loyow* 'spoons' has by false division given a new singular **lo*. When one remembers how common is the plural ending -*yow* (Welsh -*iau*, Breton -*ioù*), such a development is not unlikely.

Ō 'he was' is also a special case, because one would actually expect **oy*. We cannot posit analogy from the rest of the paradigm, since the imperfect of the short form of *bos* is *ēn*, *ēs*, *ō*, *ēn*, *eugh*, *ēns*. Perhaps *ō* is to be explained as a generalized from the regular *ova* 'he was' with suffixed pronoun; here *o* is internal and originally half-long: /ooⁱva/ > /oova/ <ova>.

7.15 *oy* in Middle English loanwords

We have already noticed that <oy> occurs not infrequently in Middle English loanwords, e.g. *joy, voys, noys* etc. Such words may have been borrowed after the Prosodic Shift had begun to operate, ?*c.* 1125. Even if they had been borrowed before the shift, they would have remained unaffected. The vowel of *joy* would have already been dimoric /oj/, not trimoric /ooj/ and would have been too short to reduce further. The same would also have been true of *voys* /vojs/.

GEORGE'S TWO LONG O VOWELS

In dissyllables, however, the Prosodic Shift does appear to have affected borrowed words. In *joynya 'to join' the first element is often reduced from a dimoric to a unimoric vowel and the whole is written *junnya*. Cf. the unimoric stressed syllable of *vodya* 'to go away' but the dimoric *voyd* 'be off!'.

7.16 *Of/yw* and *moy/moghhē*

The different development of [uui] as [oː] before consonants and [oj] in absolute auslaut is corroborated by two separate formations in Middle Cornish. The first is *ōf* 'I am' as against *yw* 'he is'. The Welsh equivalents are *wyf* and *yw* (Breton *eo*), where the latter is metathesized from *wy. The same metathesis had occurred in Cornish before *ui* could become *oy. As a result Old Cornish *uif* 'I am' >* *ooiv* > *oov* <of>, with the regular development of the vowel. But 'is' appears in Middle Cornish as *yw*. This derives from Old Cornish *iu, the metathesized form of *ui.

In Welsh 'more' is *mwy* but 'increase' is *mwy'hau*. In the first instance the diphthong is in absolute final position, in the second it is not. In Cornish therefore the equivalents of *mwy* and *mwyhau* ought according to our hypothesis to appear as *moy* and *moghhe*. This is indeed the case. Here are some examples from the texts:

    A. *moy* OM 170; BM 192, 4389; CW 52, 60, 134, 318, etc.
    B. *mohghaho* OM 297; *moghheen* BM 1265; *moghheys* BM 2402.

It would seem therefore from the preceding discussion that originally Cornish had /uui/ which developed as /oj/ in absolute auslaut and as /oo/ elsewhere. George's HTLO is mistaken and his two spellings <o> and <oe> are without foundation.

7.17 [uː] in Late Cornish

In Late Cornish the reflex of Old Cornish [ui] is in some cases (but by no means all) <û>. Since it seems unlikely a priori that *ui* has become [oː], only to become [uː] again, I assume that [uː] for [oː] is a dialectal and western phenomenon. The evidence of place-names is ambiguous but it does, *pace* George, seem to corroborate this view (see below). I assume that western Cornish was affected by the Prosodic Shift slightly later than the more easterly dialects. [uui] remained unlowered while [d] > [dz] simplified. In western Cornish [dz] was in some cases affected by the preceding yod and became [dʒ], cf. Lhuyd's Late Cornish *gûdzh* 'blood'. I would suggest that the combined effect of yod + /dʒ/ was enough to keep [uu] from lowering to [oo]. In western Cornish in consequence [uui] before the reflex of Old Cornish [d] monophthongized to [uu]. This appears on occasion in Middle Cornish texts of western provenance as <ou> and in Late Cornish as <û>, e.g, *kûz* 'wood', *lûz* 'grey', *bûz* 'food', *trûz* 'foot' and rarely in other etyma as well.

TOWARDS AUTHENTIC CORNISH

In this context one should note that the western toponym *Cargease* 'fort of the wood' (Ludgvan) appears in 1319 as *Cargoys* but in 1356 as *Caerguys* (PNWP: 44). That last spelling is suggestive of still unmonophthongized [uuⁱ].

7.18 <oy> and scribal tradition

TH always writes 'church' as <eglos> or <egglos>. 'To get' he most frequently writes <cafus>, though sporadic spellings with final <-as> occur (TH 11, 36) [there is even one early example of *cafes* at OM 391]. It is clear, however, that the unstressed vowel in *eglos* and in *cafus* was in both cases schwa. TH almost always writes 'hands' as *dewleff*, though he must have pronounced the word as *dewla*. Only once does he give himself away and write *dewla* (TH 52). TH writes the third plural ending + enclitic pronoun both as <onsy> and <ongy>, yet it is very likely that he invariably pronounced the ending as *-ongy*.

Even so, in the face of scribal tradition, it is clear from the examples of *bos* 'food' and *boys* 'to be' cited above, that such words in Middle Cornish are not, *pace* George, kept separate. The spellings of the two were hopelessly confused because they were pronounced the same way. Yet scribal convention operates here as well, since *bos* 'to be', which never contained a diphthong, is frequently written with one: <boys>.

If we look at the four main texts, the *Ordinalia* (OM, PC, RD), PA, BM and TH, we notice immediately that Middle Cornish had a distinct and consistent orthography. This I have discussed in greater detail at **3.03-06** above. There is considerable variation in it. PA and BM (and the *Charter Fragment*) have features in common. TH resembles the *Ordinalia* in not using yogh for [θ] and [ð], but resembles PA and BM in spelling 'God' as <du>. We know that Glasney, near Penryn in West Cornwall, was the nearest Cornwall had to a university in the medieval period. The conventions of Middle Cornish spelling, however, seem to reflect a dialect with [oː] rather than [uː], with <s> rather than<g> in *wose, kerense*, etc. I have long believed that standard Middle Cornish orthography arose in the century or so following the Norman Conquest and that its the bulk of the speakers who created it were from Mid-Cornwall (i.e. between Bodmin and Truro). The orthography, as in the case of Welsh and Breton, is in a continuous tradition from the Roman period and the earliest British glosses. Cornish spelling has been affected not only by sound changes unique to Cornish but also by Anglo-Saxon and Middle English practice—the latter based to some degree on French. This is the origin, for example, of <gh> for Old Cornish <ch> in words like <mogh> 'pig'.

George denies that Middle Cornish has any scribal tradition. This is one of his most serious errors. He seems to assume that Middle Cornish scribes wrote as they spoke and based their orthography on contemporary English. If George had studied, for example, the Irish texts written by scribes ignorant of traditional Gaelic orthography, he would see how erratic and unpredictable such spelling systems are. He would realize how regular, systematic and indeed conventional is the orthography of the Middle Cornish texts. He would

GEORGE'S TWO LONG O VOWELS

not then, I think, persist with his mistaken view that Cornish was without a scribal tradition.

Although George has little regard for scribal tradition, his main argument with respect to <o> and <oe> assumes such a tradition. George attempts to show that Cornish scribes tended to write */ɔː/ as <o> and */oː/ as <oy>, yet <oy> itself is a conventional spelling for /oː/. <oy> naturally suggests a diphthong and for the Middle Cornish scribes to have used it for a monophthong was historically conditioned. They wrote <oy> because the sound in question had originally been /ooⁱ/. When it developed into something else, they continued with their historic spelling. If George accepts that <oy> can mean /oː/, he accepts implicitly the strength of scribal convention. In which case, his table (Fig. 5.1) is inexplicable. He cites the relative number of occurrences of "<oe>-type" and "<o>-type" spellings in *troes* and *tros* words and asserts that the proportions reflect the two different pronunciations—without regard to scribal tradition. But writing <oy> for a long closed *o* implies scribal tradition.

We can put the illogicality of George's position another way. If Middle Cornish had no scribal tradition, as George apparently believes, then the scribes based their orthography on contemporary English spelling. Indeed this is what George says:

> I do not consider that there is any particular intrinsic merit in the orthography of Middle Cornish; it is only one of four different orthographic styles used to write down traditional Cornish, and in the final analysis it is based on contemporary English orthography (KKC21: 14).

If the spelling of the Middle Cornish scribes is based on English, one may legitimately ask why they spell [oː] as <oy>. In Middle English <oy>, <oi> represents a diphthong: *ioye* 'joy', *Noy* 'Noah', *boye* 'boy', *destroye* 'destroy', etc. It is not used as a way of writing [oː], which in Middle English is <o> or <oo>. If the Middle Cornish scribes wrote [oː] as <oy>, they did it because of the scribal conventions unique to Cornish. In which case one can reasonably assume that their tendency to some degree to keep the reflexes of [oː] and [oi] separate is itself the result of the same conventions. George's assumptions about the lack of scribal tradition in Middle Cornish are clearly at variance with his statistics. I would suggest that his statistics in this case are invalid.

7.19 The rhymes in PA and the *Ordinalia*

If George's discussion of the spellings of the phonemes /ɔː/ and /oː/ is somewhat unsatisfactory; so also, I believe, is his treatment of rhyme. In the first place one should again notice that George does not actually cite any of the spellings on which he bases his arguments. In the second place, we should be fully aware that he does not confine himself to the discussion of long stressed vowels rhyming with long stressed vowels. He has also included in his statistics rhymes of short and unstressed vowels. I have demonstrated at length and in detail two aspects of Cornish phonology that render much of George's argument invalid: first that there is no phonemic distinction in Middle Cornish between stressed short /o/ and stressed short /u/ (see CT § 4.4); second that in unstressed position short vowels have become schwa (see CT § 7.1-15). If a text for example rhymes *gos* 'blood' with *gallos* 'power', this is an eye-rhyme only and proves nothing about the status of the second vowel of *gallos*.

Perhaps George's greatest omission in this matter is that he nowhere even considers the question of the difference between author and scribe. This may, I fear, have led him astray. Both BM and CW have scribal colophons and we therefore know both when the texts were written and by whom. In the case of PA and the *Ordinalia* we have no certain evidence when either was composed, nor do we know who the authors were. Moreover, we cannot even say what length of time elapsed between the original composition and the manuscripts.

It has long been known that there is a connection between the narrative of Christ's passion in PC, the second play of the *Ordinalia*, and the devotional poem PA. I subscribe to the view that PA precedes PC, but this opinion has been hotly disputed by some commentators. As far as the three plays of the *Ordinalia*, OM, PC and RD on the one hand and PA on the other are concerned, it is my view that the language of PC and RD, as we have them, are more archaic than OM. The language of PA is remarkably advanced, but this is only at the level of the scribe's speech. At an earlier stratum PA has some very archaic features. It alone in Middle Cornish preserves the *t*-preterite in *pan gemert* 'when he took' (PA 3a) and is also the only Middle Cornish text to preserve the pluperfect as a pluperfect rather than merely as a conditional.

This is not the place to go into detail about the history of the texts of PA and the *Ordinalia*. It is likely that neither was composed much later than the beginning of the fifteenth century and it is probable that both are considerably older. It is also highly probable with both texts, that the language of the scribes is later and more advanced than that of the original authors.

The rhyme-schemes in both the Ordinalia and PA are presumably the work of the original authors and are unlikely to have been radically altered by the later scribes. The rhymes, then, are likely to date from a period when the Prosodic Shift was working itself out and when in consequence [oo^i] and [o:] were still different. By the time the texts came to be written in the surviving manuscripts, however, [o:] and [oo^i] have fallen together completely and it is only the rhyme-schemes which suggest to us that [o:] and [oo^i] were ever distinct. In the manuscripts outside rhymes they are only imperfectly differentiated if at all. This is certainly true for PA as far as *bos* 'to be' and *boys* 'food' are concerned (see above) and yet PA does not rhyme *bos*-words with *boys*-words.

In the case of PC and RD there is a complicating factor. These two plays to me show strong evidence of a westerly origin. In the first place both are more prone to use <g> rather than <s> as a reflex of Old Cornish [d]. In the second place both, unlike OM, exhibit *benneth* 'blessing', rather than *banneth*. *Benneth* I take to be the precursor of the pre-occluded form *bedneth* (which occurs in the work of the *secunda manus* in BM). Pre-occlusion is, in my view, a largely western phenonomen (see my article on the subject in *Studia Celtica* 32 (1998): 129-54).* I have also pointed out that PC and RD on occasion spell the reflex of Old Cornish [ui] as <ou> rather than as <oy> or <o>—and this I take to be yet another western feature. Examples include *scouth* 'shoulder' PC 658; *scouth* 'shoulder' rhyming with *gouth* 'falls' PC 2623-26; *glous* 'pain' PC 1147; *trous* 'foot' PC 1223; *bous* 'food' PC 688, RD 541. It would seem that in PC in particularly, but probably also in RD, in the author's dialect *boys* 'food', *scoyth* 'shoulder', etc. had developed as *bous* [buːz], *scouth* [skuːð], etc. Not astonishingly, the original author was not happy about rhyming [oː] with [uː]. The forms in PC with [uː] occur before [s] and [ð] only. PC rhymes *a wor* 'knows' (Welsh *gwyr*) and *mara kor* 'if he knows how' with *mor* 'sea' at 386-92.

7.20 The rhymes in BM

The first few pages of BM are in a different hand from the rest of the play and the dialect of the scribe of this portion differs from the remaining part in being more westerly. I shall say something about this early section in a moment. As is clear from the scribal colophon, the bulk of BM was written by Dominus Rad. Ton i.e. Radulphus (or Richardus) Ton in the year 1504. He may well have been the author also. By this period the shift of [ooⁱ] > [oː] is complete and the author has no reluctance in rhyming *bos*-words with *boys*-words. Here are some examples with the *boys*-words are in bold (some of these rhymes have been quoted above):

> *me a vyn mois* 'I will go'—*y **woys*** 'his blood' 130-31
> *erbyn the voth* 'against thy will'—*ny **goth*** 'behoves not' 584-85
> *age **goys*** 'their blood'—*y hyl boys* 'can be' 1599-1603
> *age **goys*** 'their blood'—*mar mynnogh bos* 'if you wish to be' 1642-43
> *mar kyl boys* 'if it can be'—*yowynk ha **loys*** 'young and grey' 2168-71
> ***inhoth*** 'naked'—*poth* 'rot' 3064-66
> *kyn moys* 'before going'—*han **boys*** 'and the food' 3926-29
> *ov toys* 'coming', *moys* 'to go'—*anel **poys*** 'heavy breath' 4091-94
> *creseff y voys* 'I believe it to be'—*yonk na **loys*** 'young or grey' 4415-18
> *ov toys* 'coming'—*yonk ha **loys*** 'young and grey' 4476-78

George is prevented from allowing that these words all rhyme, because Kernowek Kemyn spells them differently and Kernowek Kemyn must be defended. In consequence George is compelled to engage in special pleading. He says:

---

* Now reprinted in WORC, pp. 65–92.

Now, it was evidently more important to Radulphus Ton, the author of Beunans Meriasek, to indicate that certain vowels were long, than to spell them differently because their quality was different. So he wrote *moys* for 'a table' and *moys* for 'to go', because they both contain a long vowel. It does not mean that the quality of the vowel was the same in each word. The statistics for the other plays show that the two vowels **were** different in quality (KKC21: 31) [SP].

What precisely does George mean here? Is he saying that Ton differed from other Cornish writers of verse in his approach to prosody? Is there any *evidence* that Ton was in significant ways unlike his predecessors in the matter of rhymes? Perhaps George means merely that Ton wished to show length rather than quality and that the quality was still important to him even though he did not always show it. In which case, one might legitimately ask why Ton rhymes vowels which in George's view do not rhyme.

George even goes so far as to criticize me for using evidence from BM. In his discussion of "<o>-type" and "<oe>-type" rhymes George says:

> It is a bit naughty of Dr Williams to use *Beunans Meriasek*, because the way its author spells words is different from the methods used in other plays (KKC21: 29).

George says "other plays". Perhaps he has forgotten that PA is a poem to be read, not a play to be performed. But that is a quibble. There is no evidence of any kind to suggest that BM spells Cornish differently from other texts. But even if there were any such evidence, it is remarkable that George should criticize a fellow investigator for using any evidence. If, as George suggests, BM really were different from other texts, one would have thought that the evidence it provided would be of particular value.

Let us return to our argument. We can assume that George means quantity was more important to Ton than quality. If that were so, then we should expect to find Ton rhyming long with long and short with short, but not long with short or short with long. Let us look at a random selection of Ton's rhymes from the second part of the play (well away from the portion by the *secunda manus*). I will underline the long syllables and will print the short ones in bold.

    b<u>ey</u>s—treylys (2514-16)
    grefijs—b<u>ey</u>s (2522-23)
    men**eth**—fr<u>eth</u> (2533-34)
    b<u>ey</u>s—genys (2569-71)
    vercy—dr<u>y</u> (261-18)
    ov t<u>o</u>n—bohosog**yon** (2638-41)
    r<u>ey</u>s—sensys (2663-65)
    dr<u>e</u>—neffre (2676-77)
    servys—pr<u>ey</u>s (2678-81)
    aleme—a v<u>e</u> (2689-91)
    av<u>ey</u>s—dewesys (2700-03)

GEORGE'S TWO LONG O VOWELS

pur thyog**e**l—in l**e**l (2702-02)
worthy—owh**y** (2704-05).

It would be tedious to continue. It is apparent to me that the author of BM does not really care at all about vocalic length in his rhymes.

There are two competing hypotheses to explain the *o*-rhymes in BM listed above: A) Nance's and mine; B) George's. They might be summarized as follows:

A By the time of BM *mos/moys* 'to go', *dos/doys* 'to come' and *bos/boys* 'to be' have the same vowel as *goys* 'blood', *loys* 'grey' and *boys* 'food'. Because the two sets of words rhyme perfectly, the writer not only rhymes them with each other but spells them identically as well. This involves his spelling *moys*, *doys* and *boys* 'to be' with <oy>, even though none of them ever contained a diphthong.

B Although *moys* 'to go', *boys* 'to be', *doys* 'to come' are made to rhyme with *goys* 'blood', *loys* 'grey' and *boys* 'food', the two sets of words have different vowels, *moys*, *doys* and *boys* 'to be' being pronounced with /ɔ:/ while *goys*, *loys* and *boys* 'food' have /o:/. The poet rhymes these two sets of words with each other because, unlike other writers of Cornish verse, he regards vowel length as more important than vowel quality— even though he rhymes unstressed short vowels with stressed long ones *passim*. The spelling of *goys*, *loys* and *boys* 'food' represents /o:/, since the vowel in these etyma was originally a diphthong /ui/ (sometimes written <oi>). The spelling <oy> in *moys*, *boys* 'to be' and *doys* represents /ɔ:/, which has never been anything but a simple vowel, rather than a diphthong. The reason that the author writes the two phonemically distinct vowels /o:/ and /ɔ:/ identically as though they were both diphthongs is that, unlike all other writers of Middle Cornish verse, he believes vocalic length to be of more importance than vocalic quality— even though, for example, he never once troubles to write the long high front vowel /e:/ in *beth* 'will be, be!' as *beyth to show length.

The reasonable person would choose A) as the more cogent hypothesis. George, however, is compelled to put B) forward, since Kernowek Kemyn spells *mos, dos* and *bos* 'to be' differently form *goes* 'blood', *loes* 'grey' and *boes* 'food' and Kernowek Kemyn must be defended at all costs. I suggest that George's argument here about the special character of BM spelling is a most unconvincing exercise in special pleading [SP].

7.21 The earlier portion of BM

The earlier portion of BM is clearly by a different scribe from Ton himself. The dialect of the secunda manus seems to be different from Ton's in a number of ways. He uses <3> for [ð] where Ton does not. He writes *cawas* 'to get' where Ton has *cafus*. He has *byth* 'will be' where Ton has *beth*. Most significantly he has the only examples of pre-occlusion in the entire play, for he writes *bedneth* at lines 198, 224 and 225. I have attempted to show elsewhere that *benneth* > *bedneth* is a western form contrasting with the more easterly *banneth*.

Although the *secunda manus* is probably later than Ton himself, he is less likely to rhyme *bos*-words with *boys*-words. My explanation is that his dialect is different. The *secunda manus* pronounces the vowel of the *boys*-words as [uː] and for him, therefore, they do not rhyme with *bos*-words at all.

7.22 George's working methods
One does not, I think, need to be a statistician to realize that George's statistics in his Fig. 5.1 are open to question. He attempts to show that two sets of graphemes mean different vowel units. At no point does he actually prove (or indeed try to prove) that these two vowel units are [oː] and [ɔː] rather than some other opposition. The possibility that the common spelling <oy> might conceivably mean [oi] he does not consider. Taking little account of the vagaries of scribal practice, George shows to his own satisfaction that */ɔː/ and /oː/ are spelt differently. On the basis of that unproven assumption, he proceeds to show that */ɔː/ and /oː/ are separate in rhymes as well. He does not allow the possibility that scribes and authors are different and that early rhymes may be at variance with later spellings.

Mícheál Ó Searcóid, read an unpublished article of George's on this question in which George uses exactly the same statistics as here in KKC21. Ó Searcóid is a professional mathematician, and he gives the following opinion of George's use of statistics:

> I must, therefore, on my understanding of the problem stated at the beginning of this note, conclude that the problem has been incorrectly transcribed into mathematics and that the calculations have no bearing whatsoever on the solution of the problem (Ó Searcóid 1996)

One does not, however, need to be a mathematician to realize that George's statistics in Fig. 5.1 are open to question.

7.23 George and dialect in Cornish
George asserts emphatically that there is no perceptible dialect in Cornish. This was not always his view. In April 1989 he gave a lecture in St Erth on dialect in Cornish as part of the 14th "Cornish Weekend". The event was reported in Welsh by Robat ap Tomos in *Carn* 66: 11, as follows:

> Rhan arbennig o ddiddorol o'r penwythnos i mi oedd sgwrs gan y Dr Ken George ynghylch tystiolaeth newydd sydd yn awgrymu bod rhai o'r gwahaniaethau rhwng Cernyweg Canol a Chernyweg Diweddar efallai yn

GEORGE'S TWO LONG O VOWELS

ganlyniad i wahaniaethau mewn tafodieithoedd ardaloedd gwahanol yn hytrach na newidiau yn yr iaith dros amser. Er enghraifft mae rhai geiriau a sillefir gydag 's' (sain 'z') gan fwyaf yn y llenyddiaeth Gernyweg Canol e.e. crysy 'credu', yn cael eu sillafu â 'j', 'g', 'gg' (sain 'j') yng Nghernyweg Diweddar. Y golwg traddodiadol yw bod y sain wedi newid rhwng y cyfnod canol (tua 1500) a'r cyfnod diweddar (tua 1700), ac esbonir hyn gan gyfeirio at enwau lleoedd lle mae'r 'j' yn y gorllewin pell yn ardal Penzance yn cyfateb i 's' yn yr un elfennau mewn enwau yn ardal Truro lle diflannodd yr iaith cyn i'r newid ddigwydd. Ond ar ôl archwilio dosbarthiad yr 's' a'r 'j' mewn dramâu unigol gwelwyd mewn ambell ddrama ma 'j' (neu lythyren gyfatebol) a ddefnyddid bron bob amser yn y geiriau hyn, ond 's' a geir yn gyffredinol yn y rhan fwyaf o ddramâu. Mae awgrym yma bod rhai o'r dramâu wedi cael eu hysgrifennu gan bobl oedd yn seinio'r iaith ychydig yn wahanol, pobl oedd yn siarad tafodiaith wahanol efallai. A phan gyplysir hyn â'r amrywio rhwng 's' a 'j' mewn elfennau cyfatebol rhai enwau lleoedd sydd yn rhannu gorllewin Cernyw yn ddwy; gwelir peth tystiolaeth o blaid tafodieithoedd daearyddol yn y Gernyweg gyda datblygiadau gwahanol o 'd' hanesyddol. Ategir hyn gan y ffaith nad ydyw patrwm dosbarthiad yr 's/j' mewn enwau lleoedd yn cyfateb yn hollol i batrwm diflaniad yr iaith e.e. credir bod yr iaith wedi marw ar Ynysoedd Syllan (Scilly) yng nghyfnod Cernyweg Canol ond ceir enwau lleoedd yno sydd yn cynnwys seiniau nodweddiadol o Gernyweg Diweddar, e.e. Pednathise, Pednbrose, Rosevear, Illiswilgig, Melledgan. Mae llawer iawn o ymchil i'w wneud yn y maes yma eto.

[To me a particularly interesting part of the week-end was a talk by Dr Ken George about new evidence that suggests that some of the differences between Middle Cornish and Late Cornish are perhaps as a result of variation in the dialects of different areas rather than changes in the language over time. For example some words that are spelt with 's' (pronounced 'z') for the most part in Middle Cornish literature, e.g. crysy 'believe', are spelt with 'j', 'g', 'gg' (pronounced 'j') in Late Cornish. The traditional view was that the sound had changed between the Middle period (c. 1500) and the Modern period (c. 1700), and this is explained by reference to the place-names where 'j' in the far west in the region of Penzance corresponds to 's' in the same elements in place-names in the Truro region, where the language disappeared before the change took place. But as a result of research on the distribution of 's' and 'j' in individual plays it was noticed that 'j' (or equivalent letter) was almost always used in these words, but 's' is found usually in the bulk of the plays. There is a suggestion here that some of the plays were written by people who spoke the language slightly differently, people who spoke a different dialect perhaps. And when this is linked with the variation between 's' and 'j' in equivalent place-names that divide western Cornwall in two parts, one sees a degree of evidence for geographical dialect in Cornish vis à vis the development of historic 'd'. This view is supported by the fact that the pattern of distribution of 's/j' in place-names does not correspond completely with the pattern of the disappearance of the language, e.g. it is believed that the language died out in Scilly in the Middle Cornish period but place-names are found there that contain distinctively Late Cornish sounds, for example, Pednathise, Pednbrose, Rosevear, Illiswilgig, Melledgan. There is much research to be done in this field.]

TOWARDS AUTHENTIC CORNISH

I was delighted to see George here espousing my unpublished work on dialect.

George has subsequently begun to assert that dialects did not exist in Cornish or at least we have no knowledge them. In consequence George now explains <s> and<g> in a way different from that of his talk in St Erth. He elucidated his current thinking in a short article in Kernowek Kemyn published in France (George 1992). He now seems to have changed his mind yet again. I discuss this question very briefly in chapter 15 below.

7.24 Dialect in Cornish

Starting entirely from first principles we can say a number of things about Cornish and dialect:

1) Cornish is a Brythonic language and like its sister languages, Breton and Welsh, was certain to have had dialects
2) Given that Cornwall is much smaller in area than either Wales or Brittany, the actual amount of dialect variation would have probably been less than in either of the sister countries
3) Cornwall is long from east to west but narrow from north to south. We would therefore expect that if dialects occurred, the isoglosses would tend to divide Cornwall across its length, rather than across its breadth
4) Cornwall is blessed with a very long coastline and the Cornish have always been great mariners. Sea-travel round Cornwall was in former times easier than travel by land. We would therefore expect to find that any east-west dialect features to be less than completely clear cut, for movement by sea would have tended to take western forms eastward and vice versa
5) Cornish is preserved for us in two chief sources, the medieval religious literature and the fragments of Late Cornish. The literary language probably arose among speakers in Mid-Cornwall. We might therefore expect to find that standard Middle Cornish differed from Late Cornish not only by being more archaic, but also by differences of dialect. We might also expect to find evidence of western dialect in certain Middle Cornish texts
6) We might expect also with judicious use of early forms of place-names to be able to discern some dialect features in Cornish
7) Isoglosses deduced from toponymy might also serve to localize some of our few surviving texts.

I have attempted to show that dialect did indeed exist in Cornish. In 1990 I put forward the thesis that in some words dialects west of Illogan/Camborne seem to some degree to prefer /dʒ/ to /z/. In my article on pre-occlusion I suggest that /ᵈn/ for /n:/ and /ᵇm/ for /m/ are uncommon east of Truro. I have noticed a few strays further east and I am sure there are others. Generally

GEORGE'S TWO LONG *O* VOWELS

speaking, however, it appears that pre-occlusion is very largely a western feature.

I also suggest that [uː] < Old Cornish [ui] before [s] < [d] is a western feature. It is impossible to say where the isogloss line should be drawn. Borde (first half of the sixteenth century) has two examples of *boues* 'food'—both misprinted *bones* (see Loth 1900) and he has examples of pre-occlusion as well (e.g. *me a vyden gewel* for *me a vyn gul* 'I will do'). The area of [uː] for [oː] is difficult to determine. Some of the evidence suggests that it was restricted. Other evidence suggests that it may have been widespread. Quite possibly [uː] for [oː] occurred in discrete areas.

7.25 The evidence of place-names

George makes much of the difference between the development of the *bos*-word *ros* 'promontory' and the *boys*-word *cos* 'wood' in Cornish toponyms. Indeed in Fig. 5.2 (KKC21: 34) he prints two maps dealing with the distribution of *coys* 'wood' names on the one hand and *ros, fos* and *gof* names on the other. As is usual with George, he cites no actual toponyms. We have therefore to take his isoglosses entirely on trust.

He points to the preponderance of -*coose*, -*goose* forms in toponyms containing *cos* against the frequency of -*rose* in toponyms containing *ros* and believes that this proves, if nothing else does, that the vowels of *cos* and of *ros* were different. While I believe that *cos* was indeed [kuːz] in western dialects, there is every evidence that in Mid-Cornwall *cos* was [koːz] and had exactly the same vowel as [roːz]. It seems to me that the place-name element *ros* may be rather unsuitable to George's purpose, since he seems not fully to have understood the implications of his maps.

Unlike George, I intend here to cite the actual toponymic evidence. He and I agree that *bos* 'dwelling' and *ros* 'promontory' have the same vowel. In which case one should expect them to behave similarly in place-names. In toponyms in which *bos* occurs initially followed by a second element, *bōs* is shortened to *bos* [bɔs], a change which has taken place inside English before the Great Vowel Shift. Here are some examples taken from CPNE: *Boscarne, Boscarn Boscawen Boskear Bosneives Boswinger Bosworgey Boswellick Bosulval, Bosliven Bosporthennis Bosigran Bossava Bosullow*. Here are some more from PNWP: *Bosanketh, Bosavern, Boscaswell, Boscathnoe, Boscobba, Boscobben, Boscreeg, Boscrowan, Bosfranken, Boskednan, Boskenna, Boskenwyn, Boskerris, Bostraze, Bosvine, Boswartha, Bosweddan*. There are no examples of initial **Bose*-.

When we come to look at place-names in *ros*, however, the picture is different. Names with *Ros*- are well attested: *Roscarrack, Roscarrock, Roscarnon, Roskear, Roskruge, Roskrow, Roscrowgey*. Much commoner, however, are names in *Rose*–: *Rosemaddock, Roselyon, Rosegothe, Roseworthy, Rosemodress, Rosemerryn, Rosemergy, Rosecadgehill, Rosenannon, Rosenithon, Rosecassa, Rosenun, Rosevallon, Rosevidney, Rosemorran, Rosemullion, Roselidden, Rosewin, Rosemelling, Roseglos,*

Rosecare, Rosemundy, Rosebenault, Rosemanowas. Rôspannel and *Rôskestal* belong here as well.

How are we to explain this difference in treatment of *bos* on the one hand and *ros* on the other? As soon as *bod* became *bos*, it and *ros* would have made a perfect rhyme. When the two elements were adopted in place-names in English, they ought to have behaved in exactly the same way—but they clearly do not. We thus have *Bosworgey* but *Rosemergy*, *Boskear* but *Rosecare*. Why are there no examples of **Bose-* and so many of *Rose-*?

The story of *Rose-* does not end there. *Rid* 'ford' > *rēs* is also a common element in Cornish toponyms. Yet not infrequently names that originally had *rid/res* have reshaped the first element to *Rose-*. Here are some examples from CPNE of toponyms originally containing *res*: *Rose-an-Grouse, Roseath, Rosecraddock, Rosecliston, Rosedown, Rosegarden, Roseladden, Rosesuggan, Rosevallen, Roseveth, Rosewall, Rosewin*. And we should probably include *Rôskennals*. These toponyms all contain *rid/res*, yet they appear in English with *Rose-* instead.

There are no examples of either *res* 'ford' or *ros* 'promontory' in any of the Middle Cornish texts. *Rid* 'ford' occurs in OCV but *ros* is known only in toponyms. *Cos* 'wood' was quite different. It is well attested in the literature at all periods, from *cuit* 'silva' in OCV (*c.* 1125) to *Kûz karna huîla* in "Jowan Chy an Horth" (JCH, *c.* 1680). We can be quite sure that as people abandoned Cornish, they remembered—probably for several generations—that *cos* meant 'wood'. The same speakers almost certainly were quite ignorant of the meaning of either *ros* or *res*. In consequence they did what was only natural, they replaced the unknown with the known. The unintelligible *ros* and *res* were assimilated to the English word *rose*. This may also explain why *Penroose* is pronounced *Penrose*.

The substitution of *Rose-* for both *Ros-* and *Res-* can be clearly seen by examining the earlier forms of toponyms. Though they are from a small area in West Cornwall, the earlier variants cited by Pool in PNWP are instructive in this respect. Here are some examples:

Roseangrouse: *Resincrous* 1375; *Reysangrous* 1520; *Roseangrowes* 1659; *Roseangrowse* 1725
Rosecadgehill: *Roscaswall* 1317; *Roskasewel* 1357; *Rescasewall* 1340; *Rescaswell/Rescadswell* 1630; *Rosecadgewell* 1736
Rosewall: *Redewall* 1246; *Ryswall* 1327; *Roswall* 1523
Roselucombe: *Rooselucombe* 1511 [NB <oo>]; *Roslucomb* 1522; *Roselucombe* 1550; *Roselucom* 1607
Rosemergy: *Renoumergy* 1342; *Rosmergi* 1356; *Rosemergy* 1519
Rosemorran: *Rosmoren* 1302; *Rosemorran* (Tithe Apportionment).

If unstressed *ros-* and *res-* with shortened vowels could be replaced in English by *Rose* by *Volksetymologie*, we can hardly be astonished to see that the long vowel of final long stressed *rōs* in toponyms like *Eglosrose, Trerose, Chyrose,*

GEORGE'S TWO LONG O VOWELS

Coldrose, etc. has also become *-rose*. What is more astonishing is that the expected development of *rōs* in English, i.e. *Roose*, occurs at all.

There are three examples of *Roose* (Laneast, Otterham and Treneglos). Note also *Eglarooze* in St Germans. These toponyms, borrowed into English before the English Great Vowel Shift in the fifteenth century, have developed exactly in the same way as names with *-coose*, *-goose* < *cōs*. Middle Cornish [oː] whether from Old Cornish [ui] or from Old Cornish [oː], was adopted before the mid-fifteenth century into English as [oː] and has, as expected, become [uː] as a result of the English Great Vowel Shift.

We have been discussing toponyms containing stressed *-ros* that now appear in English with *-rose*. I have no doubt, however, that if we examined the earlier English versions of names in *-rose*, we would find further examples of *-roose*/*-roos* rather than *-rose* (cf. *Rooselucombe* 1511 above). In East and Mid-Cornwall names in *-rose* have been English in many cases since the thirteenth and fourteenth centuries. These toponyms have now been English names longer than they were ever Cornish. The element *-rōs* in them has had a very long time to become assimilated to English *-rose*.

According to HTLO the vowel in *ros* 'promontory' would not have been [oː] but [ɔː]. This vowel (often spelt <oa> in English) did not become [uː] by the English Great Vowel Shift. We know this is the case, because Old English *rod* 'rood' became New English *rood*, but Old English *rád* 'road' became first Middle English *rood* [rɔːd] and then New English *road* [rowd]. Which means that the vowel in *ros* in place-names should not have undergone the shift to become [uː]. That is to say that the three instances of *Roos* and the name *Eglarooze* are inexplicable. George does not try to explain them himself. He merely observes that they occur in an area where 'wood' appears as *-quite* < *-cuit* in toponyms. This is not strictly speaking true, since *Coskallow Wood* occurs in the far east in the parish of South Hill. Even if it were true, it would be irrelevant. We cannot elucidate one form (*roos* < *rōs*) by reference to the development of an unrelated word with an entirely different phonology (*quite* < *cuit*). How *cuit* appears in the area of *Roos* is surely not material. The instances of [ruːz] in contemporary place-names requires explanation—without reference to other toponymic elements.

7.26 *Gof* 'smith' and *fos* 'wall' in place-names

Gof 'smith' has historic *ō* rather than *oy*. The place-name *Tregoiffe* < *tre gof* 'settlement of the smith' in the east of Cornwall spells the word with <oi>, which suggests Middle Cornish [oː], not George's */ɔː/. In Penwith at the other end of Cornwall *Trewoof* < *tre wof* 'settlement of the smith' is nowadays pronounced *Trove*. *Trove* is, of course, also an English word. The earlier forms of *Trewoof* cited by Pool include *Trewoeff* 1302, *Trewoyf* 1302, *Trewoef* 1348, *Trewoyeff* 1440 and *Trewoeff* 1668. These spellings would suggest [oː] rather than the */ɔː/ expected if HTLO were valid. I have no difficulty here, since I believe that Middle Cornish [oː] had arisen from both [ooⁱ] and [oː]. I wonder how

George would explain such early forms. Notice incidentally that the word for 'smith' is spelt <goyff> at PA 155a but as <goff> at PA 158a. Clearly the scribe of PA thought that the graphs <oy> and <o> were pronounced the same way in the word for 'smith'.

Fos 'wall' is also a *bos*-word and not infrequently appears in place-names as *-fose* or *vose*. There are examples of *-voose*, however, e.g. *Parn Voose* in Landewednack. The word also appears in the name *Foage* in Penwith. If one looks at the earlier forms cited by Pool (PNWP), however, one finds that the name was *Voos* in 1558 and *Boys* in 1567! Again I have no difficulty with these forms. I take both <oo> and <oy> to be graphs for /oː/. One would like to see the earlier examples of all the modern toponyms in *-gof* and *-fos* used by George. They might perhaps serve to nuance his conclusions.

7.27 New English [ɔː] and Cornish place-names

When in English, as a result of the Great Vowel Shift, [oː] became [uː], [ɔː] was raised to take its place before diphthongizing to [ow] (see below). The gap left by [ɔː] was filled *inter alia* by the reflex of [aː] before [l], e.g. *fall* [fɔːl], *call* [kɔːl], *hall* [hɔːl] and by the reflex of earlier [ow] before [xt], e.g. *bought* [bɔːt], *thought* [θɔːt], etc. The most frequent source of new [ɔː] was the reflex of earlier [aw], e.g. *haws* [hɔːz], *cause* [kɔːz], *brawn* [brɔːn], *yawn* [jɔːn], *daub* [dɔːb], *laud* [lɔːd], *fraud* [frɔːd], etc. <au>, <aw> are the commonest and most distinctive spellings for new [ɔː].

In Irish the high back *a* /ɑː/, written <á>, is frequently very close to /ɔː/ in those dialects that lack the phonemic opposition /ɔː/ ~ /oː/. When <á> is represented in English it is commonly written <au> or <aw>, e.g. in the toponymic elements *crockaun* 'hill' < *cnocán*, *illaun* 'island' < *oileán*, *faul* 'enclosure' < *fál* and *fauna* 'slope' < *fána* or in Irish survivals in Hiberno-English dialect, e.g. *claubar*, *clawber* 'mud' < *clábar*; *raumaish*, *rawmaish* 'nonsense' < *ráiméis*; *launa-vaula*, *launawalla* 'the full of the bag' < *lán a' mhála*.

If Cornish really had had /ɔː/ distinct from /oː/, it would have been very close indeed to English /ɔː/ < *au, aw*. We might therefore expect to find *bos*-words in place-names borrowed in the later period regularly spelt with <aw> and <au>, e.g. **rawse* 'headland', **gauve* 'smith', **fause* 'wall', etc. Such toponyms are not attested. The only vaguely comparable instance I can find is *Colvase* < **kylfos*, where the second element has been assimilated to English *vase* pronounced [vɔːz]. The general absence of toponyms with <aw>, <au> for Cornish /ɔː/ suggests that such a phoneme never existed.

7.28 *Coys*, *cos* in place-names

George's first map and his discussion divides Cornwall into two areas as far as the reflexes of Old Cornish *-cos* 'wood' are concerned. Approximately east of Bodmin *cuit* appears in English place-names appears as *–quite*. West of Bodmin his /koːz/ has everywhere become *-coose* or *-goose*.

GEORGE'S TWO LONG *O* VOWELS

In fact the picture is slightly more complicated than that. The *-cos* area and the *-quite* area seem to overlap somewhat. The name *Quoit* in St Columb major certainly appears to contain the element *cuit*. We have already noticed *Coskallow Wood* in the far east. In Mid- and West Cornwall alongside names in *-coose* and *-goose* we also find modern names in *-goys*. Although I have quoted them above, I will cite them again here: *Engoyse* < *?an coys* (Wendron); *Burgois* < *bargoys* (St Issey); *Tucoyse* < *tu coys* (Constantine); *Tucoyse* (St Ewe); *Devichoys* < *tevyscos* (St Mylor); *Pencoys* (Wendron) and *Pencoys* near Four Lanes. CPNE also cites the following now obsolete toponyms in *Coys-* from the sixteenth century: *Coiscuntell* 1556 (Wendron); *Coysbesek* 1527 (Ladock); *Coyseglase* 1550 (Creed); *Coyse Laydocke* 1547 (Ladock); *Coysynchase* 1560 (Kenwyn). Since by the sixteenth century *coys* 'wood' would have been [ko:z], it is likely both that these are fossilized forms and that some at least are already in English. George does not mention any of these names in *-coys, Coys-* at all and his silence suggests that he may have preferred not to notice them. This is perhaps another example of George's passing over in silence what he does not like or cannot explain [AD].

It seems also that George may not have given the rest of his own toponymic evidence sufficient thought, since it raises questions about HTLO that he does not appear to have recognized.

It is surely true that the quickest period of anglicization of Cornwall was the sixteenth century, the period of the Reformation and of increasing maritime activity in the West Country. It is thus likely that many place-names in Mid- and West Cornwall were adopted from Cornish into English in the years c. 1450-1625. The English Great Vowel Shift was probably accomplished during the first half of the fifteenth century. According to George's first formulation of HTLO (PSRC: 129) Middle Cornish /o:/ became /u:/ c. 1625. This means that the place-names adopted into English between 1450 (the Great Vowel Shift) and 1625 (George's raising of Cornish */o:/ > /u:/) would have contained the element *cōs* 'wood' pronounced [ko:z]. But English long [o:] had by this period become [u:]. Old [ɔ:] had risen to fill the gap, before diphthongizing into [ow]. The undiphthongized pronunciation survives in English dialect in England and in Ireland and America, for example in words like *goes, close* and *hose* This [o:] would undoubtedly have been the closest vowel in English to Middle Cornish [o:]. In which case, George's [ko:z] ought frequently to appear in toponyms in Mid- and West Cornwall as *-*cose, -*gose*. Such forms are unattested.

We can go further: **-cose* and **-gose* ought be the rule in parts of Cornwall rather than *-coose, -goose*. The two elements *-coose* and *-goose* that are common in toponyms and which form the basis of George's first map, show the effects of the English Great Vowel Shift of [o:] > [u:] which was probably complete by the first half of the fifteenth century. Yet until not very long before the shift the Cornish word for 'wood' was probably still *coys* with a diphthong (as is suggested by the toponyms in Mid-Cornwall with <oy> and <oi>). *Coys* would not have undergone the Great Vowel Shift, since [oi] was unaffected by it. Place-names adopted after *c.* 1450 but before *c.* 1625 (surely not an inconsiderable number) would have missed the English Great Vowel Shift and [oː] in them would have developed in English with exactly the same vowel as in English *goes, close* and *hose*. By George's HTLO *-coose,-goose* forms must all have been borrowed before the Great Vowel Shift, i.e. before *c.* 1450, otherwise they would not contain [uː] < [oː]. Yet until *c.* 1350 *coys* would have had a diphthong and indeed toponyms in *–cois/gois* occur in Mid- and West Cornwall. Where, then, do all the *-coose, -goose* names come from? HTLO can explain only those borrowed before the Great Vowel Shift.

One might argue that the vowel of [koːz] was so high as to be close to [uː]. By this argument [oː] would not have fallen together with surviving English long *o* in toponyms adopted into English after the Great Vowel Shift. But this involves a difficulty. Names with *-coose* and *-goose* have undergone the Great Vowel Shift, yet if [oː] was very close to [uː], it also should have undergone the Great Vowel Shift in English. In which case it ought to have diphthongized in English from [uː] > [au]; cf. Middle English *hous* [huːs] > Modern English *house* [haus]. Had *cōs* really been [kuːz] or very near it, we would expect in Mid-Cornwall in particular to find many names in **-gouse* and **-couse*. No such name is attested.

The Cornish etymon for 'wood' appears in English place-names as *-quite* (Old Cornish *cuit*), as *cut-* (Old Cornish *cuit*), as *-coys* (Middle Cornish *coys*) and as *kûz* (Late Cornish *kûz*). The commonest Middle Cornish spelling of the word is <cos>. Yet this form is nowhere attested in modern toponymy. George's <koes> appears only as *-goose* or *-coose*, i.e. showing the effects of the English Great Vowel Shift. Yet **-cose* is actually the expected form if 'wood' in West Cornwall were pronounced [koːz] (as George believes) and toponyms containing it had been adopted into English after *c.* 1450. Are we then to conclude that *Melangoose* near Helston, *Burncoose* in Gwennap and *Tregoose* in St Mawgan in Meneage, in Sithney and in Stithians and other *-coose, -goose* names in the west of Cornwall had all been adopted into English before AD 1450 at the latest? If so, they are at variance with the many Late Middle Cornish and Late Cornish names around them.

A high proportion of the toponyms in the far west of Cornwall were adopted into English in the Late Cornish period. George believes that the shift */oː/ > /uː/ occurred *c.* 1625. One might argue therefore that names like *Melangoose, Burncoose* and *Tregoose* in the west were not adopted into English until after 1625, i.e. after the change */oː/ > /uː/ had, according to George, occurred in Cornish. This is rather late but it is conceivable. It does present us with a problem, however. If the names in *-goose, -coose* in the far west, where Cornish survived longest, were adopted into English after 1625, the names in *-goose, -coose* in Mid-Cornwall must have been borrowed before 1450, since the vowel [uː] in these names can be explained only as a result of the the effects of the Great Vowel Shift, i.e. [oː] > [uː] where [uː] is spelt <oo>. Names in Mid-

GEORGE'S TWO LONG O VOWELS

Cornwall in -*coose*, -*goose* must clearly predate 1625, since Cornish had already died out there by the sixteenth century. They must have <oo> by the English Great Vowel Shift. They cannot have <oo> [u:] by the change */o:/ > /u:/ since that did not occur until "*c*. 1625" and such names were already in English before then; they could not have been adopted after "*c*. 1625" because by that time Cornish was dead where they occur. In West Cornwall names in -*coose*, *goose* by HTLO have <oo> by the change */o:/ > /u:/ "*c*. 1625". In order for George's explanation of -*coose*, -*goose* in Mid- and West Cornwall to be valid, we must believe that all names in -*coose*, -*goose* were adopted into English either before *c*. 1450 or after *c*. 1625—*but that none was adopted in the intervening years*. Is that really likely?

One might argue that the shift */o:/ > /u:/ was earlier than 1625 and indeed had occurred already by the medieval period. In which case, as has been suggested, we would expect to find that many -*coose*, -*coose* names with Cornish */o:/ > /u:/ had undergone the English Great Vowel Shift [u:] > [aw] and now contained the element *-*couse* or *-*gouse* with the diphthong [aw]. As noted above, not one such name is attested. Moreover an early date for the Cornish shift */o:/ > /u:/ leaves unexplained all the spellings of /o:/ as <o> in the later Middle Cornish texts, BM (1505), TH (*c*. 1555) and CW (1611). An alternative might be to suggest that many names in -*coose*, -*goose* have undergone analogical reshaping in English (cf. *ros*-/*res*- > *Rose*-). There is almost certainly something in this for some cases, but it would reduce considerably the value as evidence of place-names in –*coose*, -*goose*. Another alternative would be to suggest that -*cōs* was [ko:z] in Mid-Cornwall where it was borrowed before the Great Vowel Shift i.e. [o:] > [u:] in English, and that it was [ku:z] further west, where it was borrowed after. I believe this suggestion has much truth in it, though it is clearly not the whole picture. Unfortunately for George, such an explanation would require the admission of dialect in Cornish—something he is reluctant to do. To grant that there was discernible dialect in Cornish would mean abandoning HTLO and adopting my views. Unfortunately for George, that would admitting that Kernowek Kemyn was based on mistaken phonology.

7.29 The reflex of *cous* in toponyms and dialect in Cornish

George is emphatic in denying that there was discernible dialect in Cornish. Yet the treatment of *coys*- in toponyms tends to suggest that such a view may be a little over-hasty. In place-names after they have been adopted into English the reflex of *coys*- shortens to *cos*- when followed by a second element: *Cosskeyle*; *Coswinsawsin*; *Cosawes*; *Cossabnack*, etc. Such forms are clearly comparable with native English words like *gosling* < Middle English *gōsling* 'little goose', *gossamer* < *gōssommer* 'goose-summer, autumn—when cobwebs appear on bushes' and *gospel* < *gōdspel* 'good news, evangelium'. In all these native English words the first element originally had a long vowel and has been shortened before the Great Vowel Shift. Had the shortening occurred

79

after the shift of [oː] > [uː], one would find *gusling, *gussamer and *guspel; compare husband < Old Norse hūsbondi and hussy < OE hūswīf, where the first element has etymological [uː]. In Cornish toponymy, however, one finds occasional instances of coys- as Cus- in initial position: Cusgarne (Gwennap), Cusvey (Gwennap), Cusveorth (Kea) and Cuskayne Farm near Probus. This may suggest that in many places in the more westerly parts of Cornwall (and perhaps sporadically elsewhere) the reflex of coys 'wood' was not cōs [koːz], but cūz [kuːz] already before the English Great Vowel Shift, i.e. before c. 1450. Notice also moreover Coosebean in Carrick was Cusbyan c. 1400 (Weatherhill: 33). This form suggests that western [kuːz] had already shortened to [kuz] as the first element of a compound by about AD 1400. This means that [kuːz] already existed before 1400. Which is the same as saying that (pace George) [koːz] did not become [kuːz] in the seventeenth century; it was already [kuːz] at least three hundred years previously. Notice further that George fails to mention any of these place-names with initial Cus- [AD].

It should be remembered also in this context that place-names with <û> for George's /oː/ in monosyllables are also confined to the western part of Cornwall: Kus Scewes (Crowan), Carrick Lûz (St Keverne) and Carrag-Luz (Mullion).

As we have seen already, George himself allows that "the occasional use of <ou> in Middle Cornish also suggests a more close realization". Usually, according to George, cōs 'wood' is [koːz] but he seems to allow that it may occasionally have been /kuːz/. What is the difference between cōs and cūs, if not one of dialect? Kervella speaking of closed o (an O serr) in Modern Breton says En rannyezhoù a zo (Kernev-Izel dreist-holl) e vez distaget alïes evel OU "In certain dialects (Low Cornouaille in particular) it is often pronounced like OU [i.e. [uː]]" (YBB: 14). If the opposition /oː/ ~ /uː/ is dialectal in Breton, is it not also dialectal in Cornish?

7.30 A possible solution

My own view of the place-name evidence used by George would tentatively be as follows. When [d] had become [s] and [ooⁱ] had become [oː], ros and cos were homophones in Mid-Cornwall; but cos was *cous [kuːz] in the west and possibly in pockets elsewhere. Forms in -roos are the regular development of rōs. Over the last few hundred years rōs/roos has been largely assimilated to rose. Coys-names are early, i.e. before c. 1350. In Mid-Cornwall many cōs-names were borrowed early enough to undergo the English Great Vowel Shift and appear as –coose, -goose. In West Cornwall -coose, -goose forms were borrowed after the shift and their vowel is that of [kuːz], the western reflex of Old Cornish cuit. It is quite clear, nonetheless, that names in -coose, -goose have been subject to considerable standardization inside English. In part this is owing to words like goose, but more a function of the frequency of names in -cōs > coose. Once coose or goose had arisen in English, it affected neighbouring names until -coose, -goose became universal—or almost entirely so. Names in -coys were sufficiently different from -coose to be able to survive. Names in -cōs would

GEORGE'S TWO LONG O VOWELS

inevitably have succumbed to the more dominant -*coose*, A) < *cōs* by the Great Vowel Shift and B) < [kuːz] < *cuit* directly. This tentative explanation starts from the premise, which I regard as certain, namely that Middle Cornish had only one long *o*.

It should be noted in this context that the vowel of Middle Cornish *lōgh* 'lake' (a *bos*-word) appears as <oo> in toponyms adopted into English before the Great Vowel Shift, e.g. *Looe* (St Martin by Looe), *Landlooe* (Liskeard); and as <oe> in toponyms adopted after it, e.g. *Loe* (Feock; Sithney), *Nansloe* (Wendron). Notice further the following *bos*-words with <oo>: dialect *lizzamoo* 'hogweeed' < *les an mōgh*; *Croft Coothe* (field name in Gwennap) < *croft cōth*; *Carek-an-googe* (1660 St Stephen in Brannel) < *carrek an gōg*; etc.

7.31 Final remarks on George's maps

We are compelled, I think, to acknowledge that George may not fully have understood the problem inherent in the place-names he cites. Let us also not forget that names in -*rose* and -*vose* have a final /z/ whereas names in -*goose*, *coose* have a final /s/ (the final segment is on occasion written -*ce*, e.g. in *Stencooce*). *Coys/cos* would have had a final /z/ in Cornish as is apparent from Lhuyd's *kûz* and John Boson's *kooz* (BF: 43). The devoicing of -*coose* and -*goose* must have occurred in English and may well be connected with English words like *goose*, *loose*, etc.

7.32 Conclusion

Middle Cornish never contained two separate long vowels /oː/ and /ɔː/. The distinction made by Kernowek Kemyn between *troes* 'foot' and *tros* 'noise' is unjustified. The spelling <oe> is unhistorical. If George wished to use traditional spelling for 'wood', 'food', 'grey', etc. he would write <coys>, <boys>, <loys>, etc. Since, however, by the period of the manuscript of PA *boys* 'food' and *bos* 'to be' were pronounced the same way, there is nothing wrong with spelling them the same way i.e. <bos> as do both Unified Cornish and Unified Cornish Revised.

The view that <o> and <oe> represent two separate phonemes in Middle Cornish and that these were /ɔː/ and /oː/ is one of George's most important hypotheses. Among his strongest criticisms of my understanding of Middle Cornish phonology is my unwillingness to recognize the twofold opposition /ɔː/ <o> ~ /oː/ <oe>. I do indeed refuse to recognize any such distinction, simply because it never existed. Kernowek Kemyn is based on mistaken phonology.

CHAPTER 8
Long *a* in Middle Cornish *tas* 'father' (KKC21: 45-48)

8.00 Cornish long *a*

Jenner, Nance and Caradar all believed that Cornish long *a* for example in *tas* 'father' was pronounced [æ:] or even higher as [ɛ:]. When discussing the pronunciation recommended for /a:/ in Kernowek Kemyn George says:

> [a], which is the sound heard in the English dialect of east Cornwall, in words like *bat*. The vowel sound used in west Cornwall and in RP is [æ], which is slightly less open. When the vowel is half-long and long, the same sound should be extended appropriately in duration (SPRC: 117).

This is not at all clear, but it seems to mean that Cornish long *a* in *tas* is [a:] in Kernowek Kemyn and that the higher vowel [æ:] is not to be used.

In *Cornish Today* I set out my various reasons for believing that in Middle Cornish the long vowel in *tas* and similar words might have been [æ:] or even higher. Having read my arguments, George now appears to admit that I may be right to a very limited extent. He points out that the word *whath* 'yet, still' in the texts is written <wheth> rather than <whath> in 43 cases out of 179 and he says, "It may be that before [θ], /a:/ was realized as [æ:]" (KKC21: 48). Illogically he appears to deny that I am right in believing the vowel in *tas* 'father' to be [æ:]. In *Cornish Today* I did not mention <wheth> at all as evidence for a raised pronunciation of long *a*. I do agree, however, the frequently occurring form <wheth> corroborates my own views most satisfactorily.

The reasons I have for a raised pronunciation of long *a* that I set out in CT § 3.17 include the following:

1) spellings like <baal>, <graas>, <taal>, etc.
2) *fas* 'face' is spelt <feth> twice in PC
3) Lhuyd's *gest* 'bitch' corresponds to Welsh *gast*.
4) *haal* 'marsh' has the plural *hellow* at BM 3411
5) The place-names *Creeglaze*, *Polglaze*, etc. have a long raised vowel.

George dismisses 1) and ignores 3) and 4) [AD]. Although he omits to mention <feth> he does, to be fair, cite <wheth>. The only argument he attempts to deal with properly is 5). He is able to dismiss it simply by claiming that there were two pronunciations of any Cornish toponym, the English pronunciation and the Cornish version. He says:

LONG *A* IN MIDDLE CORNISH *TAS* 'FATHER'

I think it quite likely that the English speakers used ['glɛːz] while the Cornish speakers continued to use ['glaːz]

When challenged on this point by Dunbar, he answers:

> Why should English speakers have bothered to acquire the correct Cornish pronunciation? They rarely bothered anywhere else in the world. They don't bother today: we frequently hear such solecisms as ['lɪskaˑd] for *Liskeard* instead of [lɪsˈkard] (KKC21: 47).

When English speakers mispronounce Cornish names (or native names elsewhere in the world), the speakers are colonial administrators, visitors or blow-ins. When we talk about English and Cornish in medieval and Tudor Cornwall we are referring to bilingual or monoglot members of the same community—Cornishmen and Cornishwomen who spoke both Cornish and English or English only. Why any of them should have had two pronunciations of the same place-name I do not understand. In Ireland monoglot English speakers, especially with very local names, continue the Irish pronunciation (with marginal sound-substitution of consonants) for generations. George's argument that there were two pronunciations is *ad hoc* reasoning of a most unconvincing kind [SP], and has been invented solely to avoid admitting that Cornish long *a* was [æː] or [ɛː].

8.01 George's admission that /aː/ may have been raised

Illogically George now allows that /aː/ may have a high realization in the word *whath* 'still, yet' and ascribes it to the effect of the following [θ]. Yet there is no reason to believe that [θ] would have any special tendency to raise the preceding vowel. There is certainly some evidence that a following [s] raised the preceding vowel in Middle Cornish. If, then, [θ] raises preceding /aː/, by how much the more might one expect [s] to raise it: in which case *tas* 'father', *pras* 'meadow', *stras* 'low-lying land', *gas* 'leave!', *mas* 'good' and *glas* 'blue' should all be pronounced with [æː].

George admits that /aː/ may have a "high realization" before [θ], yet he seems to believe nonetheless that [æː] is not a suitable pronunciation for long /aː/. He says:

> Even if he [Williams] were right, the pronunciation [æː] would be unlikely to gain wide acceptance (KKC21: 48).

I do not understand what George means here. He admits that the vowel in *whath* may be at least as high as [æː], yet he denies that such a pronunciation would have been likely "to gain wide acceptance". I do not know whether he means in *whath* only, in similar words containing [θ] or in monosyllables with long *a* generally. If there was a pronunciation [æː] in some words, it must have become part of the phonetic inventory of Middle Cornish. George does not explain why it could not have been general. As far as can be ascertained there is only one block to the widespread use of [æː]: George's constant desire to defend Kernowek Kemyn against its detractors.

8.02 George's ulterior motive

George is anxious to discourage any pronunciation of the vowel as high as [æː] for /aː/ because he mistakenly believes that Middle Cornish had the long front vowel phonemes /iː/, */ɪː/, and /ɛː/. In consequence he thinks there would not have been enough room for <a> pronounced [æː] or [ɛː]. In fact Middle Cornish had only /iː/ and /eː/ and there is nothing against assuming a pronunciation for the vowel in *tas* 'father' anywhere between [aː] and [ɛː]. There is no doubt that this desire to keep the vocalic system of Kernowek Kemyn as credible as possible is what lies behind George's special pleading here:

> We have already seen, despite what Dr Williams believes, that Middle Cornish kept separate the three long front vowels /iː/, /ɪː/ and /ɛː/. In order to accommodate a fourth, /aː/, it minimises the risk of confusion if /aː/ is pronounced with as open a sound as possible, i.e. [aː].

Yet again George is engaging in special pleading. His argument seems to be as follows: Middle Cornish and therefore Kernowek Kemyn had three high front phonemes /iː/, */ɪː/, and /ɛː/. There was not room therefore for any further front vowel. There is evidence in Middle Cornish that in certain cases /aː/ was pronounced [æː]. Such a pronunciation could not have been widespread, because had it been so, there would have been too little room for the three higher "phonemes" /iː/, */ɪː/, and /ɛː/. This threefold set of phonemes is historically correct, because they are posited for Kernowek Kemyn and Kernowek Kemyn is a scientific system based on a computer analysis. George's argument is circular and I find it unconvincing.

The facts are different. Middle Cornish had only two high front vowels: /iː/ and /eː/ and in final position /iː/ had been replaced by a diphthong /əj/. Thus there is no need to discourage the use of [æː] and even [ɛː] in revived Cornish for the vowel in *tas, gas, pras,* etc. George's argument against such a pronunciation is a circular one based almost entirely on special pleading [SP]. The real problem that George encounters here is his belief that Middle Cornish had /ɪː/ separate from /iː/. It did not, although the distinction probably existed in Old Cornish. The disappearance of /ɪː/ as a separate phoneme was another result of the Prosodic Shift, which occurred before our earliest Middle Cornish texts. Reluctantly we must conclude that in the matter of /aː/ Kernowek Kemyn is based upon a mistaken phonology.

CHAPTER 9
Final long *i* (KKC21: 49-51); *te*/*ty* 'thou', *me*/*my* 'I' (KKC21: 51-53)

9.00 Final long *i*

Historical long /iː/ (written <y> in Middle Cornish) often appears in Late Cornish with a diphthong. Here are some examples:

chy 'house'
: ***Tshyi*** AB 55c; ***chei*** *a Horr* 'the House of the Ram' BF: 15; ***Tshei*** *an hor* 'the House of the Ram' BF: 16; *da* ***chei*** *Teeack* 'to a farmer's house' BF: 15; *dha* ***tshei*** *tiak* 'to a farmer's house' BF: 16; *en* ***chei*** 'in a house' BF: 16; *dha'n* ***tshei*** 'to the house' BF: 17; *ost an* ***tshei*** 'the host of the house' BF: 17 x 2; *en nessa* ***tshei*** 'in the next house' BF: 18; *hostez an* ***tshei*** 'the hostess of the house' BF: 18; *tal an* ***tshei*** 'the end wall of the house' BF: 18 x 2; *moas* ***Choy*** 'to go into the house' BF: 16; *Keou* ***Tshoy*** *Uun* 'hedges of Chywoon' BF: 17; *an Pobel-****choy*** 'the people of the house' BF: 27

cry 'cry'
: ***krei*** 'cry' BF: 17, 18

hy 'she, her'
: ***hei*** 'she' BF: 16, 19 x 2; ***hyi*** 'she' BF: 19

ky 'dog'
: ***Kei*** 'dog' AB: 46a

ny 'we, us'
: ***Nei*** 'we' AB: 100a; ***nei*** 'we' BF: 17 x 3; *barha* ***nei*** 'along with us' BF: 17; *abarhan* ***nei*** 'along with us' BF: 18; *dha* ***nei*** 'to us' BF: 18, 19 x 2

ry 'to give'
: *Dho* ***rei*** 'to give' AB: 54b

try 'three;
: ***trei*** *penz* 'three pounds' BF: 15 x 3, 16

why 'ye, you'
: ***Huei*** 'ye, you' AB: 177b; *dha* ***huei*** 'to you' (< *theugh why*) BF: 17; *tha goz guellaz* ***whey*** 'to see you' BF: 16; *ragoh* ***huei*** 'for you' (< *ragough why*) BF: 17.

It is possible that a diphthong is intended in the spelling ***trey*** *dyth wose y terry* 'three days after breaking it' PC 1315. The diphthongization of final long [iː] is certainly noticeable in the Middle Cornish period. Borde, for example, writes *Syrra*, ***tray*** *kans myledere* 'Sir, three hundred miles' (Loth 1900: 226), where *tray* is an early example of Late Cornish *trei*. Tregear writes ***whay*** *a yll gwelas eysy* 'you can see easily' TH 33a, where *whay* is an early example of Late Cornish *huei*, if it is not a misprint.

9.01 Final *y* in rhymes

The best evidence for the diphthongization of final [iː] in Middle Cornish is to be seen in rhymes. Historic [iː] not infrequently rhymes either with [oj] or [aj], and it would seem that [iː] itself is pronounced as some kind of diphthong, probably [əj]. I have collected the following rhymes from the texts:

A <y> rhyming with <oy>
ny 'we' ~ *ioy* 'joy' OM 555 & 558
ioy 'joy' ~ *deffry* 'indeed' OM 1374 & 1378
ioy 'joy' ~ *deffry* PC 1903 & 1906
th'y 'thither' ~ *ioy* 'joy' RD 185 & 186
ny 'we' ~ *ioy* 'joy' RD 1201 & 1202
ioy 'joy' ~ *genough why* 'with you' RD 1285 & 1286
deffry 'indeed' ~ *ioy* 'joy' RD 1431 & 1432
moy 'more' ~ *the thythyow thegy* 'thy days' (emphatic) RD 2036 & 2037
d'y 'thither' ~ *ioy* 'joy' RD 2415 & 2416
may ma hy 'where she is' ~ *moy* 'more' BM 4071 & 4072
moy 'more' ~ *the vee* 'to me' CW 60 & 62
moy 'more' ~ *menas me* 'except me' CW 134 & 135
oye 'egg' ~ *hy* 'she' CW 484 & 486
vry 'account' ~ *voye* 'more' CW 1353 & 1354
agen vyadge ny 'our attempt' ~ *oye* 'egg' CW 2064 & 2065.

B <y> rhyming with <ay>
by thys day 'by this day' ~ *bys d'y* 'thither' OM 2803 & 2806
fay 'faith' ~ *ahanes gy* 'of thee' BM 3515 & 3516
deffry 'indeed' ~ *pur gay* 'very gaily' CW 606 & 607.

C <y> rhyming with <ey>
dry 'to bring' ~ *fey* 'faith' PC 1993 & 1996.

One should also note the following stanza:

Del yw scrifys prest yma
adro ȝynny gans **otry**
mara kyll ȝeworth an da
ȝe weȝyll drok agan **dry**
folle yn ta y whela
ys del wra lyon y **pray**
drey den yn peyn a calla
neffre ny vnsa moy **ioy** (PA 21).

Here the rhyming words are *otry* 'outrage, violent attack', *dry* 'to bring', *pray* 'prey' and *ioy* 'joy'. There is no question, I think, that *dry* 'to bring' was considered to contain some kind of diphthong.

FINAL LONG I; TE/TY 'THOU', ME/MY 'I'

The following is also worth noting:

> noy mar lenwys ew an byes
> > lemyn a **sherewynsy**
>
> mayth ow dewathe devethys
> > vnna a gyke pub **huny**
>
> gans peagh pur wyre ew flayrys
> > ny allaf sparya na **moye**
>
> heb gwethill mernans a vear spyes
> > war pobell oll menas **tye**
>
> ha tha wreag ha tha flehys
> > han pythe a long the30 **gye** (CW 2244-53).

Note also *moy* 'more' rhyming with *rey* 'to give' PC 536 & 357, where *ry* 'to give' is spelt as a diphthong; cf. Lhuyd's *Dho rei* 'to give'. Remarkable also is *iuggys may fey* 'that thou mayst be judged' ~ *gueth os ys ky* 'thou art worse than a dog' RD 2023 & 2026, where both rhyming words have etymological [i:], but the first has been spelt <fey>, presumably to denote a diphthong.

On occasion *ioy* 'joy' and *moy* 'more' will actually rhyme with unstressed syllables, e.g. *owth egery* 'opening' ~ *moy* 'more' PC 2999 & 3001; *vercy* 'mercy' ~ *ioy* 'joy' RD 76 & 77; *vercy* 'mercy' ~ *ioye* CW 2075 & 2076; *moy* 'more' ~ *crygy* 'to believe' RD 1068 & 1069; *crygy* 'to believe' ~ *moy* 'more' RD 1088 & 1089; *fay* 'faith' ~ *eredy* 'indeed' BM 3552 & 3553; *eredy* 'indeed' ~ *ioy* 'joy' BM 4382 & 4385; *moy* 'more' ~ *ynny* 'in it' CW 1916 & 1917; *vercy* 'mercy' ~ *ioye* 'joy' CW 2075 & 2076. Compare both the stanza from CW quoted above and the following from the end of RD:

> hag yn ban the nef the'n **ioy**
> > ihesu a wruk yskynne
>
> worth an iaul ha'y **company**
> > rak a's guytho yn pup le
>
> ha'y vennath theugh pup **huny**
> > lemmyn ens pup war tu tre
>
> now menstrels pybygh **bysy**
> > may hyllyn mos the thonssye (RD 2639-2646).

Also of significance here is the Middle Cornish word for 'wolf'. It is spelt <blyth> BM 1104 and <blygh> CW 1149. Cf. the plural form <blythes> TH 19a x 2. One would have expected a diphthong in the root, since the Welsh cognate is *blaidd* and the Breton is *bleiz*. One suspects that the scribes wrote <blyth>, <blygh> because the final <th> was silent, and the word would naturally have been read as though containing [əi].

TOWARDS AUTHENTIC CORNISH

9.02 The same diphthong in Middle and Late Cornish
It seems to me certain that the diphthongal spellings like <tshei>, <choy>, <nei>, <rei> in Late Cornish and the rhymes in Middle Cornish have the same origin, namely that words like *chy, ny, ry, why* already had a diphthong in Middle Cornish. I ascribe the diphthong of *chy, ny, ry,* etc. to the Prosodic Shift. Before the shift these etyma contained /iː/ in absolute final position. We can analyse this as [iij] or [iˑj], that is to say a trimoric long vowel. The shift reduced the first element from half-long to short and in so doing untensed the nucleus: [iˑj] > [ij] > [ɪj]. In [ɪj], however, the nucleus and the coda were at different heights and the nucleus tended to move further away to give [əj]. It was this which gave an adequate rhyme with [aj] and [oj] in Middle Cornish and was spelt <ei> or <oy> in Late Cornish.

9.03 George's "explanation" for these rhymes
George is unwilling to admit that the Prosodic Shift has occurred in Middle Cornish, for to make such an admission would be the same as saying that Kernowek Kemyn is based on mistaken phonology. In order, therefore, to explain away the rhymes of the type *ny ~ joy, hy ~ oy,* he is compelled, as elsewhere, to rely on special pleading. He and Dunbar have the following exchange:

> K.G. The fact that words in /-ɔɪ/ and /-aɪ/ were sometimes rhymed with those in /iː/ does not mean that /iː/ had become /ɛɪ/.
> P.D. Dr Williams seems to think so.
> K.G. No, it means solely that in the absence of many true rhymes in /-ɔɪ/ or /-aɪ/, poets were forced to use imperfect rhymes in /iː/.
> P.D. Can you explain this further?
> K.G. Reference to fig. 9.1 shows that rhyming words in /-ɔɪ/ and /-aɪ/ are rather rare. They're floating about like free radicals, ready to join in a rhyme with any word that sounds reasonably close.
> P.D. That reminds me of some members of the Cornish language movement. So do you reject this criticism?
> K.G. I do not dispute that /iː/ in words like *ki* became a diphthong in Late Cornish; Lhuyd's spelling *kei* shows that. The dispute is again a question of when this change occurred (KKC21: 50).

9.04 George's "explanation" fails to convince
There is no evidence at all that the poets considered *my ~ joy* to be a "reasonably close" rhyme. To them such a rhyme was perfect, the two diphthongs being the same or very close. Moreover it is quite untrue that there were few rhymes for words like *joy, moy* and *fay, gay,* etc. The possible rhyming words are numerous. George lists *joy, moy, namoy, noy, Noy, oy, roy, ay, bay, fay, gay, gway, hay* 'enclosure', *cay,* and *pray. Noy* 'nephew' was not at the time of writing attested in Middle Cornish. It has subsequently appeared in BK where it is spelt <noe>. There a many further potential rhymes not listed by George.

FINAL LONG I; TE/TY 'THOU', ME/MY 'I'

We saw that English *by thys day* rhymed with *bys d'y* at OM 2803 & 2806. There are further words of English and French origin scattered through the texts that would have made better rhymes with *fay*, *gay* and *joy*, *moy* if the vowel in *chy*, *ny*, *dy* had really been [i:]. Here are some examples (my list is by no means exhaustive):

> *aray* OM 1967, BM 3461
> *assay 'attempts' (cf. *assy* < *assay* BM 3325)
> *bay 'bay tree' PC 261
> *be thys day* OM 2458
> *by godys day* OM 2223
> *delay* BK 1140
> *deray* OM 2224
> *doway* OM 484
> *eloy* PC 2955
> *hakney* OM 1966
> *hay* 'ho!' BK 902
> *lay* 'law' PC 936
> *palfray* 'palfrey' OM 1966
> *sley* 'cunning' (spelt <slegh> BK 2987)
> *wythovte nay* PC 987, *without nay* BM 3462
> *y pray* RD 1939
> *y say* BM 3370.

And we can be quite certain that if the poets had wished to find further rhymes for words in <ay> and <oy> they would have borrowed further items from English. George's explanation is not compelling

Notice that John Boson in the Pilchard song rhymes *chy* 'house' with *moy* 'more'. The relevant couplet from the Penzance manuscript reads:

> *Th'a Gweel Barcadoes en Kenifer* **Chey**
> *Gen Ganow leas. Hern, Hern—Holan* **Moy**

'To make bulks in every house
with many a voice, "Pilchards, pilchards—more salt"' (BF: 43).

The same couplet reads in the Tonkin manuscript B:

> *Tha Gweel baracodaoes en Kenifer* **Chy**
> *Gen Gannow leaz, Hern, Hern, Holan* **muy** (BF: 44).

The rhymes here are *chy* 'house' and *moy* 'more'. Precisely the same elements rhyme in *achy* 'within' (< *chy* 'house') and *moy* in *Beunans Meriasek*:

> *pan vo due ov stoff* **achy**
> *ware me a provy* **moy**

'when the stuff I have at home is finished
I will immediately provide more' (BM 1869-70).

TOWARDS AUTHENTIC CORNISH

I take Late Cornish *chey* ~ *moy* and *achy* ~ *moy* in BM to display exactly the same rhyme. The elements rhyme because in both Middle and Late Cornish the vowels are identical. If George were right, however, we would have to believe that the vowels in BM were "reaonably close" i.e. [iː] and [oj] but that in Late Cornish the rhyme was [əj] in both cases. Thus we would have to allow that the Late Cornish rhyme was better than the Middle Cornish one, even though Middle Cornish prosody was more highly regulated than the English-based free-for-all of John Boson's time. And in any case the principle of simplicity dispenses with this double explanation. The two rhymes are the same and therefore *achy* in BM contained a diphthong. In which case Middle Cornish final /iː/ was already [əj] in Middle Cornish.

9.05 George's uncertainty about the diphthongization of /iː/

George is not completely sure that /iː/ had not been diphthongized by the Middle Cornish period. The following exchange occurs between him and his pupil:

> K.G. Yes a few [i.e. exceptions]; one notable one is *tray* 'three' recorded by Andrew Borde, a non-Cornish speaker, in about 1543, which suggests that /iː/ had developed to a diphthong by that time.
> P.D. Is Dr Williams right then?
> K.G. We cannot tell. I think it unlikely. It is possible that historical /iː/ was realized as a diphthong in the fifteenth century, but the evidence presented by Dr Williams, viz. the existence of imperfect rhymes with /-ɔɪ/ and /-aɪ/ does not prove it. The spellings in Middle Cornish do not prove or disprove it (KKC21: 51).

This grudging concession on George's part is quite intelligible. In PSRC he suggested that "In stressed monosyllables [iː] took part in the Great Vowel Shift" (PSRC: 110). According to George final [iː] became [ɪi] by about 1525 and [əi] by about 1625. Moreover the vowel in *chy* 'house' went one stage further and developed as [ʌi], "as is shown by the spelling *choy*". The Great Vowel Shift alluded to by George refers to the English Great Vowel Shift, i.e. that group of related changes in the English vowel system that occurred during the course of the fifteenth century. I criticized George severely for suggesting that the phonemic system of Cornish could have taken part in a single aspect of a series of sound-changes in an unrelated language (CT § 13.8). George has clearly now accepted that my criticism was valid, but is still of the opinion that the sound change of Cornish [iː] > [əi] may have occurred before the Late Cornish period. Note incidentally that the change posited in PSRC by George [iː] > [ɪi] > [əi] is very similar to that suggested by me. The difference between us is that I ascribe the development to the Prosodic Shift—a wholly Cornish phenomenon.

At all events George now seems prepared to concede that by the fifteenth century final /iː/ may have been a diphthong, yet he does not appear to understand the consequences of such an admission. If by the fifteenth century final /iː/ was indeed a diphthong, the question arises why it had been diphthongized. The diphthongization of English [iː] by the Great Vowel Shift is an interesting parallel in an unrelated language. It can have no bearing on the development under discussion. As far as I can see the only possible explanation for the diphthongization of final long [iː] in Cornish, is that the long vowel had shortened and untensed: [iˑj] > [ɪj] > [əj]. But that is the same as admitting that the Prosodic Shift had already operated in Cornish, something which George emphatically denies. Either George does not understand the implications of his "possible" diphthongization, or he realises perfectly well but does not, publicly at least, admit the consequences [AD]. If long final /iː/ has indeed diphthongized by the Middle Cornish period, the Prosodic Shift is already a *fait accompli* and Kernowek Kemyn is based on mistaken phonology.

9.06 *my* 'I, me' and *ty* 'thou, thee' in Kernowek Kemyn
In *Cornish Today* I described /mɪː/ 'I, me' and /tɪː/ 'thou, thee' as "impossible" and I continue to find them completely incredible. My chief reason is that Middle Cornish did not have a long /ɪː/. No other Brythonic language contains the series /iː/, /ɪː/, and /eː/. Welsh has /iː/ and /eː/ but the phoneme represented in Welsh in monosyllables by <y> is a long central vowel /ɨː/, not comparable with Cornish */ɪː/, for the Welsh phoneme is not a front vowel at all. Moreover the Prosodic Shift has radically altered the phonology of Cornish and rendered it much less like Welsh and Breton. Thus to look to the sister languages for parallels is invalid. On theoretical grounds alone it is futile to expect three high front vowels in Middle Cornish.

George concluded that Middle Cornish had *my* /mɪː/ and *ty* /tɪː/ by his analysis of the spellings in the texts. The following exchange occurs between him and Dunbar:

> K.G. Fig. 9.2 confirms that the vowel in *my* (also its mutated from *vy*) and *ty* were
>   spelled in Middle Cornish as a mixture of <y> and <e>.
> P.D. I see that Dr Williams failed to find the two cases of *te* in BM.
> K.G. There are two choices here, either
>   (a) you take the spellings at their face-value, as Dr Williams has done, in
>   which case you have to postulate two different forms of *my* and *ty*: or
>   (b) you suppose that the mixture of <y> and <e> represent a vowel between
>   [iː] and [ɛː], such as [ɪː] (KKC21: 52).

George is prone to look at variant spellings and to assume that the variation <X> and <Y> means a sound midway between <X> and <Y>. My readers will remember how George noticed at the variation between <s> and <g/j> in the texts and assumed that the scribes meant something that was neither *s* nor *j*. In fact he erroneously concluded they meant */dj/ or */tj/. I, on the other hand, took the scribal evidence at face value and believing that <s> meant something like [s] and <g> or <j> something like English <g> in *gentle* or <j> in *joy*, I decided that the two phonemes in question were /s/ and /dʒ/. It seems that George, in spite of his unhappy experience with */dj/ and */tj/, still prefers the unlikely option (b) over the more probable option (a).

It might be admissible here to point out *en passant* how unlikely is George's proposition that an alternation of graphs indicates a sound that is not properly represented by either. A greater experience of historical linguistics and of the phonological analysis of texts in general would have argued against such unjustified conclusions. Indeed a greater experience of historical linguistics might well have prevented the development of Kernowek Kemyn in the first place. Medieval spelling systems tend not to be wholly phonemic, of course. Nonetheless, if Middle Cornish really had possessed a series of three separate long high front vowels /iː/, */ɪː/, and /eː/, it is very likely indeed that the Middle Cornish scribes would have tended, at least, to write them differently. Kernowek Kemyn spells this hypothetical series <i>, <y> and <e>, and it is very probable that Middle Cornish would have spelt them the same way, had the three phonemes existed. Since only two were part of the phonemic inventory of Middle Cornish /iː/ and /eː/, the scribes used only two separate graphs, <y> and <e>. In consequence any alternation in the distribution of these two graphs in Middle Cornish appears to mean a variation between /iː/ and /eː/ rather than some intermediate vowel.

That Middle Cornish should have had two forms of the personal pronouns *my* and *ty* is not remarkable. I assume that the two forms *me, te* and *my, ty* came about by differences in sentence stress. Low sentence stress would give the short forms [mə] and [tə], e.g. in, for example, *me a vyn, te a vyn*, whereas the forms with high stress would occur in pausa, e.g. *my ha ty* 'I and thou', i.e. [miː] and [tiː].

9.07 <tee> and <mee> in the texts

I have collected the following forms in the texts of the second person singular pronoun:

<tee> 'thou, thee'
<ty> CF x 2; OM *passim*; PC *passim*; RD *passim*; BM *passim*; CW x 41
<tee> SA 60a; CW 54, 914
<tye> CW 2251
<tî> AB: 252a
<chee> Kerew (RC 23: 180 x 2, 181 x 3, 187), BF: 16 x 2; <Chee> LAM: 242.

<te> 'thou, thee'
<te> PA *passim*; BK *passim*; TH x 26; SA 62a, 63 x 5; BM 1908, 2039; CW x 34
<ta> AB: 167b
<ti> AB: 252a
<te> BF: 41 x 2, 42 x 5
<che> Kerew (RC 23: 174, 182, 183 x 2, 187, 188 x 2, 195 x 2).

FINAL LONG I; TE/TY 'THOU', ME/MY 'I'

I do not know how George counts 10 examples of <te> in SA. It seems also that he has omitted the examples of <tee> in both SA and CW. Similarly he fails to mention the variant <tye> in CW [ID]. George also omits to mention in his discussion of the Late Cornish forms those variants that begin with <ch> [AD]. The assibilation of the initial [t] > [tʃ] is comparable with Middle Cornish *chy* < *ty*, and is probably old, though it was not shown in writing.

George wants us to believe (KKC21: 53) that Middle Cornish */tɪː/ and */mɪː/ became [tiː] and [miː] in Late Cornish. This is not credible. Not only was there no */ɪː/ in Middle Cornish, but there was no major shift from */ɪː/ > /iː/ between Middle Cornish and Late Cornish either. In fact the two variants <te> and <ty> in Middle Cornish persist in Late Cornish where they appear as <te>, <che> and <tî>, <chee> respectively. Something comparable happened with Middle Cornish <me> and <my>, which appear in Late Cornish as <mî>, <mee> (or with lenited initial <vee>), and <me>:

<mee>
mí AB: 57c; *ha mî ow mos* LAM 228; *Mî a glowas* LAM: 228; *mî a-droucias* LAM: 228; *mee rese mose* Bilbao MS; *mee resettias ow holan* Cornish Studies: Nine: 99; *vee* LAM: 244 x 3.
<me>
me a venja LAM: 224; *me ore* LAM: 224, 225; *Me a vedn* LAM: 228 x 2; *me reeg clowaz* LAM: 230; *me rig fanja* LAM: 238; *me rig desky* LAM: 244; *me ell* Bilbao MS.

Notice further that when discussing the personal pronouns in Cornish Lhuyd actually cites two different forms: *Mî* and *me* (AB: 244a). George fails to mention this [AD].

9.08 No diphthongization of *my/mee* or *ty/chee*

George quite rightly observes that in Late Cornish <mee> never appears as *<mei> nor <chee> as *<chei>. This is correct, but one has to remember that *chy* 'house' had already become *chei*, and that **mei* in speech would be indistinguishable from *moy* 'more'. I would suggest that in order to avoid confusion <chee>, <mee> remained undiphthongized. And we have an excellent parallel for this lack of diphthongization; both *ny* 'we' and *why* 'ye, you' often remain undiphthongized in Late Cornish as well. Here are some examples:

Late Cornish *ny* 'we' without diphthongization
Ny en gweel 'we ?will do' BF: 11
ny a wele an Teez younk 'we see the young people' BF: 25
tho ni an parah 'we are the flock' BF: 39
ro do ny 'give us' BF: 41
pecare terera ny gava 'as we forgive' BF: 41
buz gen guetha ny 'but preserve us' BF: 41
An Taz ny 'Our Father' BF: 45

TOWARDS AUTHENTIC CORNISH

*Ro dha **ni*** 'Give us' BF: 45
*bara **ny** peb Dydh* 'our daily bread' BF: 45
*Gava dha **ny** a gan Kam* 'Forgive us our trespasses' BF: 45
*erbyn **ny*** 'against us' BF: 45
*byz Gwitha **ny*** 'but keep us' BF: 45
***ni** el guelas* 'we can see' BF: 46
*en uz **ni*** 'in our age' BF: 46
*Garres ew **ni*** 'we are left' LAM: 240
***Ny** ol* 'we all' LAM: 242.

Late Cornish *whi* 'you' without diphthongization
*do **why*** 'to you' BF: 12
*ha **whi** el dendal gose bounas obba* 'and you can earn your living here' BF: 15
*deeaaw **why** deracta* 'come ye before him' BF: 39
*bethow **why** looan* 'be ye joyful' BF: 39
*Meero **why*** 'look!' BF: 44
***whye** ell evah* 'you can drink' LAM: 230
***Why** dalveha* 'you should' LAM: 230
*precara **why*** 'like you' LAM: 238
***Why** lader gweader* 'You thief of a weaver' LAM: 242
*comero **whye** weeth* 'you take care' LAM 244.

The real reason that George posits *my* 'I' and *ty* 'thou' with */ɪː/ where *hi* 'she', *ni* 'we', *hwi* 'you' and *i* 'they' in Kernowek Kemyn have /iː/ is that Modern Breton has *me, te* but *hi, ni, c'hwi* and *int*. This is no argument, since Cornish is not Breton. Middle Cornish never had */mɪː/ 'I, me' or */tɪː/ 'thou, thee'. Again we can see that Kernowek Kemyn is based on a mistaken phonology.

CHAPTER 10
Vocalic alternation: *y* in monosyllables ~ *e* in disyllables
(KKC21: 101-109)

10.00 The origin of the *y* ~ *e* alternation
In the transition from British to Primitive Welsh the reflex of British /u/ and /i/ were reduced to the neutral vowel schwa /ə/ immediately before the accent. Thus British *litanos* 'broad' in British became /ləˈdan/ in Primitive Welsh. Later when the accent shifted to the new penultimate syllable, the schwa received the stress and appears in Modern Welsh spelt as <y> but pronounced as /ə/: *llydan* 'broad'. In stressed position the reflex of British short /i/ appears in Welsh as /ɨ/ or /ɨː/, according to whether it occurred in a historically open or closed syllable. In either case in Modern Welsh orthography it is spelt as <y>. Thus Welsh has *bydd* 'will be' (third person singular) /bɨːð/ from British stressed /i/ in an open syllable, but *byddaf* 'I will be' /ˈbəðav/ from an originally unstressed /i/ that was reduced to schwa, before receiving the accent again when the accent shifted.

The alternation *y* ~ ə also occurs in Middle Cornish, where the result of stressed /i/ is either /ɪ/ or /iː/, whereas the unstressed vowel /ə/ gives /e/, for example in *ledan* 'broad' (Welsh *llydan*), *tevy* 'to grow' (Welsh *tyfu*), *eva* 'to drink' (Welsh *yfed*) and *enys* 'island' (Welsh *ynys*). This correspondence between Welsh *y* and Cornish *e* was first noticed by Lhuyd (AB: 19) in 1707. In Cornish therefore the Welsh alternation *y* ~ *y* appears as *y* ~ *e*, where *y* can either be long or short. In Cornish the vowel is long, for example, in *byth* 'will be, be!' alternating with *bethaf* 'I shall be', and in *gwyth* 'trees' alternating with *gwethen* 'tree'. It is short in *myn* 'he wishes' alternating with *mennaf* 'I wish'. As we shall see, in Middle Cornish the long /ɪː/ as a result of the Prosodic Shift disappears.

In CT § 3.6 I suggested that /ɪː/ in *byth* 'will be', *bys* 'world', *gwyth* 'trees', etc., became /eː/. This is certainly true, since the forms *beth* 'will be', *bes* 'world' and *gweth* 'trees' are all well attested. It seems, however, that alternative forms with long closed /iː/ were also found, e.g. *byth*, *bys* and *gwyth*. Indeed George observes that in *Cornish Today* I spell *gwedhen* 'tree' and *gwedh* 'trees' without any vocalic alternation and he remarks, "Evidently UCR is ignorant of the vocalic alternation *y* ~ *e*" (KKC21: 102). This is an understandable criticism and I deal with it in the next chapter. Vocalic alternation also affected words like *byw* 'alive' but *bewa* 'to live' and I discuss this matter in Chapter 12.

George himself appears not fully to understand vocalic alternation. His knowledge of Welsh is incomplete: "He [George] is fluent in Cornish, Breton, English and French and has a working knowledge of Welsh" (PSRC back cover). Moreover vocalic alternation has been analogically removed entirely from Breton. Because he does not appear fully to grasp the nature of vocalic alternation, George's section 16 of KKC21 which deals with this question is largely irrelevant. He discusses *myres, tryga, scryfa, y gyla* 'one another', and *whylas*, even though all these etyma have historic long /iː/ not /ɪː/, and have therefore no bearing on the matter in hand. Moreover my objection to Kernowek Kemyn in this matter concerns the disyllabic forms only. George's section 16, on the other hand, deal with monosyllables, about which we do not for the most part disagree. I have no quarrel with Kernowek Kemyn *bys* 'world' or *gyll* 'is able'. I object to the unhistoric and unjustified spellings **gwydhenn, *blydhen, *ynys*, etc. And these are what I intend to discuss below.

10.01 George's misconception
Before I explain why I am so very unhappy with Kernowek Kemyn about this aspect of its phonology, I should like to draw attention to another part of George's argument in this section. George mentions (Fig. 16.2) the etyma which he spells <mires>, <triga>, <skrifa>, <kila> (in *y gela* 'one another') and <hwilas> and shows the relative frequencies of spellings of them in Middle Cornish with both <e> and <y>. It is clear from George's table that the spellings with <e> in some of them are more numerous than those without. Dunbar makes just this point to George when he says:

> I can see that it is off-putting to find <e> used for a vowel which you maintain was [iˑ] in Middle Cornish. This appears to be a strong point in Dr Williams' favour, in *Cornish Today* § 4.2 he writes: "The common spellings like *trega, screfa, whela, merough*, etc. are by themselves sufficient evidence that Middle Cornish had only long and short vowels and that the three-fold distinction of long, half-long and short had disappeared from the language." Now what makes you so sure that <e> represented [iˑ] rather than the more obvious [e] as claimed by Dr Williams (KKC21: 104).

Dunbar is making a very telling point here. He asks George why he believes that <e> represents [iˑ], a half-long high front vowel. In fact, of course, there can be no answer, but George, anxious to vindicate Kernowek Kemyn, replies as follows:

> If we look at the forms of these words in Late Cornish {Fig. 16.3} [this is a mistake Fig. 16.3 deals exclusively with Middle Cornish], we see that they are spelled with <ee> or <i>, both of which mean [iː]. We have already noted other examples in Fig. 4.6. This indicates that the mid-length [iˑ] was maintained throughout Middle Cornish until the early seventeenth century, when it became lengthened to [iː] (KKC21: 104).

Dunbar then asks: "How does Dr Williams explain this evidence from Late Cornish?" and George replies:

VOCALIC ALTERNATION: *Y* IN MONOSYLLABLES ~ *E* IN DISYLLABLES

I don't think he does. How can he? Having stated that the [iˑ] in words like *mires* 'to look' has been shortened and lowered to [e] in Middle Cornish, there is no way in which it is going to be lengthened and tensed to [iː] in Late Cornish, The whole idea is crazy. He must be wrong (KKC21: 104).

When George says of the short and lowered vowel [e] or *myres, meras* 'to look' that "there is no way it is going to be lengthened and tensed to [iː]", he is, in my view, completely right. Indeed "the whole idea is crazy". I should remind my readers here that George cites just one example of *meero* 'look!' (plural) from Late Cornish (KKC21: 26). I have suggested at **5.09** this is an analogical form on the basis of the monosyllabic simplex *meer* 'look!' (singular). The verbs which he cites as having *[iː] < [iˑ] in Late Cornish in fact have [e] or [ɪ] and their stressed vowel is almost invariably short in them all. I have cited them before but I will cite them again:

1 *__mires__ 'look' in Late Cornish
meroyow: an dean yw devethez pocara ha onen anye RC 23: 185
ha, __mero__: elez neve theth ha droze thotha RC 23: 189
__mero__, elez neeve a desquethaz tha Joseph RC 23: 198
Ha Deu lavaras, __Mero__, ma res gennam do vy kanifer lushan gen haz BF: 53
ha __mero__, tho vo perth da BF: 53
dha __meraz__ rag an peth es moaz BF: 58.

2 *__triga__ 'dwell' in Late Cornish
ha garah Nazareth e theath ha __tregaz__ en Capernahum RC 23: 189
Habito…To dwell, to inhabit, to live in; to lodge Dho __trega__ AB: 64c
na huath __tregyez__ en an Ulaz-na mui vel padzhar miz AB: 222.

3 *__skrifa__ 'write' in Late Cornish
eth yw __screffez__ n'ara dean bewah dreath bara e honnen RC 23: 186
rag eth ew __screffez__ RC 23: 187
eth ew __screffez__ arta RC 23: 187
ryth ew __screffez__: che ra gorthi that arleth Deew RC 23: 188
rag andellma thewah __screffez__ gen an prophet RC 23: 195
Ma goz __screfa__ compaz BF: 46
Na Re'au gouas koler, rag __screfa__ vaze BF: 46
Scribo… To write… C[ornish] Dho __skrepha__ AB: 146c
Scriptus… Written… C[ornish] __Skrephys__ AB: 146c
veva __skrefyz__ arag AB: 222
dho __screfa__ ketella AB: 222
dho __skrefa__ neb 'ramatek AB: 222
Kernuak ha Godhalek __skrefyz__ arag AB: 222
a ryganz __skrefa__ ragov AB: 222
na ryg me na __skrepha__ bepprez AB: 223
__skrephyz__ muy po le AB: 223
nag ero huei a __skrefa__ an gerrio-ma AB: 223
tha __screfa__ do why LAM: 238

buz nagerra termen dem de **screffa** *du straft arta* LAM: 238
ha mouns **screffa** *inna warbedden ni* LAM: 238
Rag na algia ea clappia na **screffa** *Curnoack precarra why* LAM: 238
screfys *gans oleow horen* Keigwin
henwez Mean **scriffez** NG: 3
Scriffas, *Gomar mab Japhet vo en Beas* BF: 48

4 ***hwilas** 'seek' in Late Cornish
gworeuh **whellaz** *seere rag an flo younk* RC 23: 196
rag Herod vedn **whelaz** *an flo yonk rag e latha* RC 23: 198
rag ma Herod maraw eva **whellaz** *bownaz an flo you[n]k* RC 23: 200
mee a ved'n moze Da **whelaz** *weale da weele* BF: 15
ha reeg **whelaz** *ena weale da weele* BF: 15
Whelas *tees tha trehe kesow* ACB F f 2
Whelas *poble tha threhe ithen* ACB F f 2
Whelas *megouzion tha medge an isse* ACB F f 2
Whelas *colmurian tha kelme an isse* ACB F f 2
ez boaze **whelees** *car thurt an Tir* LAM: 226.

The only Late Cornish example of *kila 'mate' known to me is *ha an Sousenack nobla war e* **gilla** 'and the nobler English upon the other' from BF: 29, where the vowel is undoubtedly short. There is no hint here of George's putative lengthening of *[iˑ] > [iː].

10.02 These verbs did not contain */iˑ/ in Middle Cornish

It is quite apparent from these examples that in Late Cornish the five etyma *meras, trega, screfa, y gela* and *whelas* had a short vowel, most frequently written <e>. For George to claim that in these five words Middle Cornish [iˑ] was lengthened to Late Cornish [iː] is at variance with the evidence. Forms in [iː] do occur but they are marginal. The long vowel in the root, where it occurs in Late Cornish, can be ascribed to analogy with the monosyllabic simplex. The shortening of the vowel is already apparent in Middle Cornish and continues in Late Cornish. Such shortening was the result of the Prosodic Shift, which predates our earliest Middle Cornish texts. These etyma have short [ɪ] or [e] in Middle Cornish and the same short [ɪ] or [e] in Late Cornish. There was no lengthening of the vowel of these words between Middle and Late Cornish. Most importantly <e> was not used in Middle Cornish as a graph for [iˑ]. When the scribes wanted to write [ɪ] or [iː] they wrote <y>, or rarely, <i>.

Let us be completely clear what is involved here. Dimoric half-long [iˑ] would to English ears sound like long *i*. Indeed half-long *i* is classified as long by Breton grammarians. George appears to believe that this long *i* was regularly written <e> in Middle Cornish. His own pupil has doubts about the matter; it is moreover highly improbable that long *i* would have been spelt <e> by the medieval scribes. Yet George insists that [iˑ] is written <e>. If a person finds credible something that is inherently very unlikely, rational discussion

VOCALIC ALTERNATION: *Y* IN MONOSYLLABLES ~ *E* IN DISYLLABLES

becomes impossible. Since the deviser of Kernowek Kemyn holds such improbable views, it is not astonishing that the phonology of Kernowek Kemyn is very mistaken. It is also understandable that he should ignore the incontrovertible evidence for the mistaken basis of his system.

10.03 Blethen 'year'

The Cornish word *blethen* 'year' is not quite the same in origin as Welsh *blwyddyn* 'year'. *Blwyddyn* is from Proto-Celtic **bleidanī* (cf. Old Irish *bliadain*, Modern Irish *bliain*). Unlike the Welsh and Irish, which have the full grade of the root, Cornish has the zero grade, deriving as it does from a Celtic **blidanī*. This was stressed on the second syllable, and when by the period of Primitive Cornish the word was **bli'ðen*. The unstressed first syllable was then reduced to schwa: **blə'ðen*. When the accent shifted this gave *'ble·ðen*, and then by the Prosodic Shift the word became *'bleðən*, written <blethen>. There are, however, occasional spellings with <y>, which may reflect the historical stage *bli'ðen*. Or possibly they are the result of the raising effect of the following [ð]. I have collected the following examples from Middle and Late Cornish sources:

A **blythen**
yn **bly3en** *y a vye* PA 228c
dew vgens **blythen** *ha whe* PC 351
syth myl ha syth cans **blythen** RD 2494
ʒe lowenna rag **blythan** BM 243
dall y fueff lues **blythen** BM 4393
A trykkowgh bytte **vlythan** BK 1592.

B **blethen**
yn **blethen** *hyr* OM 2103
lues **blethen** *in bysma* BM 565
in **blethen** *ha moy in ta* BM 2821
lowar c. **blethan** *awosa* TH 13a
space a iii myll **blethan** TH 13a
iii gweith in **blethan** TH 27a
lyas **blethan** *tremenys* TH 40a
agy the cc **blethan** *wosa crist* TH 45
in dew[e]tha **blethan** *a reign an cruell Emperour* TH 47
pemp **blethan** *warnegans* TH 47
bys in dewetha **bletha[n]** TH 47
300 **blethan** *wosa crist* TH 49
nannsew myll **blethan** *ha moy* TH 49a
vi c. **blethan** *wosa crist* TH 51
viii **blethan** *wosa an ascencion* TH 52a
Mark x **blethan***, Luke xv* **blethan** TH 52a
an **vlethan** *i'n kensa deyth* BK 1881
try myl bowns i'n **vlethan** BK 2103
nang ew sure lyas **blethan** CW 1663

a pympe myell ha v cans **vlethan** CW 1894
nang ew ogas ha **blethan** CW 2466
rag trei penz an **vlethan** Gubber BF: 15
Ha pa thera duath an **vlethan** BF: 15
rag **vlethan** *moy* BF: 15
po thera duath an **vlethan** BF: 15
rag **blethan** *moy* BF: 16
ha pa thera duath an **vlethan** BF: 16
trei penz an **vledhan** *guber* BF: 16
pa thera diwadh an **vledhan** BF: 16
rag **bledhan** *moy* BF: 16
py **thera** *dhiuadh an* **vledhan** BF: 16
rag **bledhan** *moy* BF: 17
pa thera diuadh an **vledhan** BF: 17
Blethan *war* **blethan** *Gra Gorollien toas* BF: 43
Blethan war **blethan**, *Gwra Gorollion toaz* BF: 44
Kensa **blethan**, *byrla a' baye* ACB F f
Nessa **blethan**, *lull a' laye* ACB F f
Tridgya **blethan**, *comero ha doga* ACB F f
Peswarra **blethan**, *mollath Dew* ACB F f
Ry tha stener deck pens en **blethan** ACB F f 2
Ma douthack meese en **blethan** Bilbao MS
An **blethan** *ew douthack sithen ha do*[*ygens*] Bilbao MS
Quartan **blethan** *ew tarthack sithen* Bilbao MS
Hanter **blethan** *ew whe sithen warnig*[*ens*] Bilbao MS
Oll an **vlethan** *ew douthack sithen ha deusg*[*ens*] Bilbao MS
an kanzbledhan diuetha-ma AB: 223
an kanz ha'n hanter **bledhan**-*ma* AB: 223
adro an **Vledhan** *680* AB: 224
byz an **vledhan** *936* AB: 224
adro an **vledhan** *384* AB: 224
Seith **mledhan** *ne dhibryw vor-bozow* (Lhuyd) LAM 232
ca veca a **vlethan** *veth mar hir* (J. Tonkin) LAM: 226
En **Blethan** *a'n Deu Arlueth nei* 1710 (W. Gwavas) LAM: 238
do nisau **blethan** (O. Pender) LAM: 238.

The earlier spelling *blythen* is best explained as an archaism which reflects the Old Cornish form *bliþen*. The Middle and Late Cornish word for 'year' quite clearly is *blethen, blethan*. Revived Cornish wishing to show that the dental continuant is voiced should write <bledhen>.

10.04 *Enys* 'island'

The Cornish word for island is *enys*. This is from a Proto-Celtic form **inissa-* (cf. Irish *inis* 'island') < Indo-European **eni-stā* '(land) standing in the sea'. The British form **inissa*, after the loss of final syllables would have given **i'nis*, with the stress on the now final syllable. The initial unstressed syllable would have been reduced to schwa: **ə'nis*. When the accent shifted to the initial syllable, the

VOCALIC ALTERNATION: Y IN MONOSYLLABLES ~ E IN DISYLLABLES

schwa received full stress. In Welsh this gave *ynys* (where the first <y> represents stressed schwa), and Middle Cornish *enys*. In Middle and Late Cornish the only attested forms exhibit <e> in the first syllable. I have collected the following instances:

> *an* **enys** *hag arwennek* OM 2589
> *ha an Gwayne gun* **Enys** BF: 31
> *dhan* **Enez**-*ma* AB: 223
> *a'n* **Enez**-*ma* AB: 224
> *Tregeryon an* **Enez**-*ma* AB: 224
> *Rygollaz* **Enys** *Brethon y threvdaz* (Lhuyd) LAM: 232
> *Rhag pel tir Powys dhort Por-***Enaz** (Lhuyd) LAM: 234.

Enys is also a common element in toponyms. Padel cites *Ennis* (St Dennis, St Enoder, St Erme and Stithians), *Enniscaven* (St Dennis), *Ennis Morvah* (Constantine), *Ennisveor* (St Dennis 1632), *Ennys* (St Hilary), *Enys* (St Gluvias), *The Enys* (St Hilary, St Just in Penwith), *Enys Dodnan* (Sennen), *Enyshall* (Probus 1747), *Enys Head* (Ruan Minor), *Enysmannen* (Sancreed) and *Enys Vean* (Landewednack). He also cites some instances with <i> in the first syllable, *Ince* (St Stephen by Saltash), *Inisschawe* (Scilly *c.* 1540), *Innis* (Luxulyan), *Innis Pruen* (Mullion), *Ninnes* (St Allen, Lelant, Madron), *Ninnis* (Germoe, Gwennap, St Mewan) and *Ninniss Farm* (Kenwyn). These forms with <i> are all names in English and the pronunciation with [ɪ] has arisen inside English, where the following nasal has raised the short vowel. In Middle and Late Cornish the word for 'island' is always *enys* and in revived Cornish the word should be spelt <enys>.

10.05 *Dethyow* 'days'

The Primitive Cornish form was *$dɪːð$ and the plural would have been $dɪð'jow$. The unstressed syllable was reduced to schwa, giving *$dəð'jow$. Then, when the accent shifted, this would have given *$'deðjow$, written <dethyov> or <dethyow>.

> A **dythyow**
> *rak certan y tue* **dythyow** PC 2645
> *cot yv the* **thythyow** *the gy* RD 2037
> *me a vyn in ov* **dythyov** BM 2595
> *meryasek in ov* **dythyov** BM 2660
> *me a greys in ov* **dythyov** BM 4354
> *oll an* **dythyow** *agan bewnans* TH 41
> *ha* **dythyow** *da* BK 2193
> *In neb* **dythyow** *us ow tos* BK 2239
> *Ef a velyk an* **dythyow** BK 2316
> *in ow* **dythyow** *neffra lam* BK 2931
> *pan vo dewath theth* **dythyow** CW 1929.

B **dethyow**
en de3yow a vyth guelys PA 169b
*ny welys in ov **dethyov*** BM 1815
*thum gothfes in the **dethyov*** BM 1857
*den grassyes in y **dethyov*** BM 2226
*dremas o in y **dethyov*** BM 2237
*in ov **dethyov*** BM 2664
*te a yl in the **dethyov*** BM 2954
*in keth **dethyov** ma dywy* BM 2552
*pan vo dewath y **thethyow*** CW 1850
*chee ra moaz oll **dethyow** tha vowngas* RC 23: 180
*gen dewan chee ra debre notha oll **dethyow** tha vowngaz* RC 23: 182
*en **dethyow** Herod an matern* RC 23: 194
*mol de **dethyo** boz pel En tereath* BF: 42
*ha rag **dethiou** ha blethaniou* BF: 52
*el guz **Dethiow** beth pel vor an Tir* BF: 55.

It can be seen from the above lists that the forms with <e> are not the majority in Middle Cornish. Moreover plural forms with <y> in the stressed syllable are both early (in PC and RD) and late (in BK, TH and CW). I think we must conclude that the expected *dethyow* has been affected by the simplex *dyth* to give <dythyow> as a common spelling for the plural. We conclude, therefore, that there is no objection to <dydhyow> 'days' in Kernowek Kemyn.

10.06 *Prevyon* **'reptiles',** *preves* **'insects'**
The starting point here is the British word **prim-* 'reptile, worm'. This is attested as *prif* 'worm' in Old Cornish. The British word apparently had two plurals with different senses, the first being **primetes* 'worms, insects' and the second **primjones* 'reptiles, vermin'. Both would have been stressed on the penultimate syllable. With the loss of final syllables the two became **pri'med* and **prim'jon* respectively. In both cases the first, now unstressed, syllable was reduced to schwa: **prə'med and *prəm'jon*. When the accent shifted back to the penultimate syllable, the two items became **'preved* and **'prevyon*. In Middle Cornish these are *preves, prevas* and *prevyon* respectively.

****pryvyon, pryves**
*yn mysk **pryues*** RD 2011.

prevyon, preves
*ethyn bestes ha **prevyon*** OM 1160
*sesyogh thymmo an **prevyon*** BM 3526
*i'n preson in mysk **prevas*** BK 420
*gans **prevas** a bub sortowe* CW 111
*in myske oll **prevas** in bys* CW 497.

VOCALIC ALTERNATION: *Y* IN MONOSYLLABLES ~ *E* IN DISYLLABLES

The form *pryues* in RD may have been influenced by the simplex *pryf*. It is perhaps more likely tht the spelling with <y> is an archaism, reflecting the Old Cornish spelling **privet* 'worms, insects'. With *prevyon* one should also compare the word *anprevyon* 'vermin, miscreants', which occurs in BK:

> *Canhas, guarn an* **anprevion** 'Messenger, warn the miscreants' BK 3159.

With *preves* one should also compare *mylprevys* (for **mylpreves*), the plural of *mylpref* 'snake-charm' in BK:

> *Me, Pendrasys*
> *ew den descyn,*
> *gwerryor fers tyn,*
> *myghtern Egip* ***mylprevys***
>
> [I, Pendrasys,
> am a man with a plan,
> a warrior fiercely sharp,
> king of Egypt of the snake-charms] (BK: 2625-29).

It will be seen that *pryves* is weakly attested and **pryvyon* is not recorded at all. The two items in traditional Cornish are *preves*, *prevas* and *prevyon*. These should be used in the revived language. Kernowek Kemyn writes <pryves> and <pryvyon>. There is no warrant at all for the second of these.

10.07 *Gwethen* 'tree'

Gwethen, the Middle Cornish word for 'tree', derives from a British form **wi'dennā* (cf. Breton *gwezenn*, Old Irish *fid* 'wood'), with the stress on the second syllable. With the loss of final syllables this became **gwi'ðenn*, where the stress was on the final syllable. The unstressed first syllable was reduced to schwa to give Primitive Cornish **gwə'ðenn*. The accent shifted to the penultimate syllable to give Old Cornish **'gwe·ðenn*. The form in the Old Cornish Vocabulary is <guiden>, which is a fossilized spelling at the stage **gwi'ðenn*. The Prosodic Shift then gave Middle Cornish *'gweðən*, spelt <gwethen>. I have collected the following examples of the word from Middle and Late Cornish sources:

> *a'n* **wethen** *ha'y avalow* OM 176
> *na mos oges the'n* **wethen** OM 184
> *Stop an* **wethen** *trogha'a dor* OM 201
> *a vghaf war an* **wethen** OM 216
> *a'n* **wethen** *hag a'y vertv* OM 230
> *a'n* **wethen** *hep falladow* OM 240
> *ha tastye frut a'n* **wethen** OM 284
> *warnethy yma* **gvethen** OM 775
> *vn sarf in* **guethen** *yma* OM 797

TOWARDS AUTHENTIC CORNISH

ha myr gvel orth an **wethen** OM 800
yn **wethen** *me a welas* OM 804
ha warnythy vn **wethen** OM 837
an fut an **wethan** TH 2a
An **wethan** *a wothfes an da han drog* TH 2a
dybbry a bup **gwethan** TH 3a
an frut an **wethan** *vs in nes* TH 3a
an **wethan** *han barrow* TH 4a
the **wethan** *grappys* TH 39a
ha frutes war bub **gwethan** CW 365
an keth **gwethan** *ma* CW 372
an **wethan** *ma ew henwys* CW 375
gwethan *gothvas droke ha da* CW 376
in **wethan** *pur smoth* CW 536
pew ostashe es in **wethan** CW 548
es omma war an **wethan** CW 620
mes an **wethan** *defennys* CW 751
war an **weathan** *ven eal wheake* CW 759
orth y wellas in **weathan** CW 762
an eal ega in **wethan** CW 827
me a weall sure vn **gwethan** CW 1808
hona ew an keth **wethan** CW 1811
me a weall goodly **wethan** CW 1825
hag in tope an keth **wethan** CW 1834
ew an **wethan** *a vewnans* CW 1841
vn **gwethan** *woʒa henma* CW 1856
specyall vn **gwethan** *gloryes* CW 1899
nowe in toppe an **wethan** *deake* CW 1907
me a wellas **gwethan** *moy* CW 1916
a theth an **wethan** *defry* CW 1926
ew henwys **gwethan** *a vewnans* CW 1927
gwethan *a vyth pure precyous* CW 1935
a kenevrah **gwethan** *an Looar* RC 23: 175
Bez thorh an **gwethan** *e ez en Crease an Loar* RC 23: 175
tro an **wethan** *da rag booze* RC 23: 176
ha **gwethan** *tha voaze desyryes* RC 23: 176
a restah debre thort an **gwethan** RC 23: 179
hy a rose tha vy thor an **wethan** RC 23: 179
ha reege debre thor an **wethan** RC 23: 182
dore an **gwethan** *bownaz* RC 23: 184
an vor a'n **gwethan** *vownyaz* RC 23: 185
Meero why rag **Gwethan** *heer Tarthack Troos* BF: 43
Meero why rag **Gwethan** *heer Tarthack Trooz* BF: 44
ha **gwethan** *dri meas ffrueth* BF: 52
ha **gwethan** *drez meas frueth* BF: 52
ha kanifer **guethan** *menz es frueth* **guethan** *gen haz* BF: 53
Dew rygmeraz yn **whedhan** (Lhuyd) LAM: 234
Guedhan, *A tree* AB: 243a.

VOCALIC ALTERNATION: *Y* IN MONOSYLLABLES ~ *E* IN DISYLLABLES

The word in Middle and Late Cornish for 'tree' is clearly *gwethen, gwethan*. Revived Cornish, wishing to show that the dental continuant is voiced, should write <gwedhen>. Kernowek Kemyn spells it *<gwydhenn>.

10.08 Disyllabic forms of *bos* 'to be' in Kernowek Kemyn

Let us begin with the pre-form of *bethaf* 'I shall be'. In Primitive Cornish this would have been *$bi'ðaµ$, with the stress on the second syllable. The unstressed syllable was reduced to schwa: *$bə'ðav$. When the accent shifted this became *$'be·ðav$. After the Prosodic Shift this became $'beðaf$ or $'beða$, written <bethaf>. The development of the other disyllabic forms would have been similar. I have collected the following instances of all disyllabic forms of *bos* from the texts:

A **bythens**, etc.
*drethos y **fythyn** sylwys* PC 287
*dretho ef prynnys **bytheugh*** PC 767
bythens {KK -es} *kepar ha'n lyha* PC 794
***bythaf** bysy · sur war an dra* PC 1932
*the weth **vythons** the'n cronek* PC 2732
bythens {KK -es} *scon gurys* PC 2742
*pur wyr y **fythons** dampnys* PC 3093
*gans cryst y **fythyth** trygys* RD 3234
*gynen y **fythyth** tynnes* RD 2349.

B **bethens**, etc.
*ȝe ihesu **beȝens*** [KK -es] *grassys* PA 24d
*en box oll **beȝens*** [KK -es] *gwerthys* PA 36b
*yn nef ny **veȝyth*** {KK -y-} *tregis* PA 46c
*na **veȝough** temtijs dygnas* PA 52d
*mes **beȝens*** {KK -es} *guris ȝe vynnas* PA 55b
beȝens {KK -es} *kepar del vynny* PA 57d
*ha del **veȝaff*** {KK -y-} *hombronkis* PA 61d
*ol ow sor **beȝens*** {KK -es} *lowen* PA 113c
*ȝen mernans **beȝens*** {KK -es} *gurris* PA 126d
beȝens {KK -es} *ef yn crows gorris* PA 128a
beȝens {KK -es} *ef yn crows leȝys* PA 128d
*dreȝough why **beȝens*** {KK -es} *leȝys* PA 142c
*na **veȝens*** {KK -es} *clewys neffre* PA 148b
*ha warnan **beȝans*** {KK -es} *neffre* PA 149d
*ow ȝas whek **beȝens*** {KK -es} *gevys* PA 185c
beȝens {KK -es} *ȝe ves defendis* PA 188b
*ha **beȝens*** {KK -es} *ena gorris* PA 188c
*na **veȝough** dyscomfortis* PA 255a
***bethens** formyys orth ov brys* OM 8
bethens {KK -es} *ebron dreys pup tra* OM 21
*ytho **bethyth*** {KK -y-} *mylyges* OM 311
*gans pup na **vethaf*** {KK -y-} *lethys* OM 596
*Caym ny **vethyth*** {KK -y-} *yn della* OM 598

gans pek **bethens** {KK -es} *stanchvrys* OM 954
gans louan **bethens** {KK -es} *strothys* OM 1297
war the lergh **bethens** *revlys* OM 1434
fythys nefre ny **vethyth** {KK -y-} OM 1465
bethens *yn mes exilyys* OM 1576
omma ny **vethons** {KK -y-} *gesys* OM 1589
marow **vethons** {KK -y-} *kyns vyttyn* OM 1644
marow **vethyn** {KK -y-} *kettep pen* OM 1655
prest hep danger · {KK -y-} **vethaf** *parys* OM 1910
bethaf {KK -y-} *the mour* OM 2111
bethens *kyrhys* · *masons plente* OM 2262
bethens {KK -es} *gurys thyugh hep whethlow* OM 2560
yn bason **bethens** {KK -es} *gorrys* PC 842
pup vr parys thy'n **vethe** PC 918
bethens {KK -es} *gruys yn pup termyn* PC 1040
ynny hy **bethens** {KK -es} *taclyys* PC 2164
yn pren crous **bethens** {KK -es} *gorrys* PC 2374
bethens *tackys* PC 2518
bethens *an ebyl gorrys* PC 2574
hep kentrow byth ny **vethons** {KK -y-} PC 2698
quyk hep hokkye {KK -es} **bethens** *gurys* PC 2828
gon guyr y **fethaf** {KK -y-} *marow* RD 2030
betheugh *why fur* RD 2276
my ny **veʒaf** {KK -y-} *the well* BM 109
Ov lich kyng **bethugh** *mery* BM 292
ellas mar **pethen** {KK -y-} *schamys* BM 420
genogh why **bethens** {KK -es} *sesijs* BM 972
oma y **fetheth** {KK -y-} *cregys* BM 1242
costentyn **bethugh** *gena* BM 1460
why ny **vethugh** {KK -y-} *sav nefra* BM 1492
bethens *marov na sparyogh* BM 1614
Ser emperour **bethens** *lethys* BM 1637
ny a **vethe** *pur dyson* BM 2151
ellas mar **pethen** {KK -y-} *dampnys* BM 2159
bethugh *lowen* BM 2350
the larchya preysys **fethogh** {KK -y-} BM 2352
Ser ʒurle ny **vethugh** {KK -y-} *tollys* BM 2729
insol **bethugh** *glan ʒesseys* BM 2747
ser kyng na **vethugh** *dyswar* BM 3238
Cowethe na **vethen** *lent* BM 3245
ha na sparyovgh **bethens** *peys* BM 3299
benithe ny **vethen** {KK -y-} *vays* BM 3354
susten an neff **bethens** {KK -es} *reys* BM 3870
out drethy **bethen** {KK -y} *marov* BM 3945
benytha vays ny **vetha** {KK -y-} BM 4095
bethugh *sokyr an rena* BM 4262
bethugh *a cher* BM 4312
bethens {KK -es} *ov gol vy nefra* BM 4322
wolcum **vethugh** BM 4567

VOCALIC ALTERNATION: *Y* IN MONOSYLLABLES ~ *E* IN DISYLLABLES

an pith a ***vetha*** *gwrys syehar anotha* TH 6a
fatell ***vetha*** *onyn genys mes an stok han has a Eva* TH 13
bethow *ware rag dowt* TH 18
Bethow *ware a fals prophettys* TH 19a
rag mar ***pethans*** {KK -y} *gorys the vois* TH 25a
an tyrmyn cut a ***vethyn*** {KK -y-} *ny omma* TH 26
ny ***vethans*** *dysdaynys* TH 33a
kepar dell ***vethans*** *lymmyn* TH 33a
mas y a ***vetha*** *in tyrmyn na* TH 33a
an feithfull cristonnyan a ***vetha*** *rulyys* TH 37a
mar ***pethens*** {KK -y-}*consyddrys in ta* TH 43a
fatell ***vetha*** *an kithsam kyge na a* ***vetha*** *rys* TH 52
y gorfe eff y honyn a ***vetha*** *res* TH 52
an pith a ***vetha*** *dre an Jewes gorys then mernans* TH 53
Mar ***petha*** {KK -y} *ve lyftys in ban* TH 53a
bethyth {KK -y-} *marow* BK 259
mar ***petheth*** {KK -y-} *mettys i'n pow* BK 462
Bethans {KK -es} *mar freth del vynho* BK 558
na ny ***vethef*** {KK -y-} *hedre ven* BK 932
bethans *pur war!* BK 1262
bethough *pur glor* BK 1278
del ***vethin*** *dowr* BK 1298
Mara ***pethaf*** {KK -y-} *dywenhys* BK 1410
Ken fe emprour, ***bethans*** {KK -es} *war!* BK 1501
Bethans *pur glor* BK 1638
Bethans {KK -es} *por war!* BK 1739
Rag meth na ***vethens*** {KK -es} *gegys* BK 1844
e ***fethowgh*** {KK -y-} *why dybynnys* BK 2272
Bethough *gansa kyn pen mys!* BK 2372
te drog-den, ny ***vethyt***[*h*] {KK -y-} *gowr* BK 2961
mar ny ***vethaf*** {KK -y-} *curunys* BK 3095
ha ***bethough*** *war* BK 3261
ha nenna na ***vethogh*** {KK -y-} *troblis* SA 66a
them y ***fethow*** {KK -y-} *canhagowe* CW 67
rag ty ny ***vethys*** {KK -y-} *dowtyes* CW 523
me ne ***vethaf*** {KK -y-} *confethes* CW 532
y ***fethan*** *the well nefra* CW 890
ffystenowgh ***bethans*** *gweskes* CW 979
gans peb na ***vethaf*** {KK -y-} *lethys* CW 1176
cayme na ***vethys*** {KK -y-} *in della* CW 1178
ny ***vethis*** {KK -y-} *gans dean towches* CW 1183
mar ny ***vethaf*** {KK -y-} *ve prevys* CW 1449
gans peb a ***fethan*** *lethys* CW 1637
ny ***vethan*** *in keth della* CW 1640
bethans *gorrys in ye thyw fridg* CW 1854
cowetha ***bethowgh*** *parys* CW 2009
gans peyke ***bethance*** {KK -es} *stanche gwryes* CW 2259
mara ***pethowgh*** {KK -y-} *repentys* CW 2344
ragtha ***bethowgh*** *avysshes* CW 2367

arall **bethans** {KK -es} *delyverys* CW 2463
bethowh *ware na vo lethys* CW 2517
ha **bethez** {KK -y-} *enna terebah ve dry thez geere* RC 23: 198
Bethez {KK -y-} *gueskez duath, ken gueskel eneth* BF: 16
Bedhez {KK -y-} *guesgyz dhiueth, ken gueskal enueth* BF: 17
deeaaw why deracta ha **beatho** *looan* BF: 39
Ko oagoaze tha e drevon ha **bethow** *why looan* BF: 39
betho *lean gen haz* BF: 52
Betho *why fyrah nessa* ACB
Betho *fyr, ha heb drok* ACB
Bethes {KK -y-} *gwaz vaz, ha leal* ACB.

It is quite apparent from the above list that the stressed vowel in Middle and Late Cornish is [e] writtten <e>. A few forms in <y> of the imperative and future are attested in PC and RD. These are, I think, archaisms, where the <y> derives ultimately from the <i> of Old Cornish spellings like *<bidam> 'I shall be' and *<bident> 'let them be', etc. Nance apparently did not understand the nature of the *y* ~ *e* alternation in this verb and was led astray by the early spellings with <y>. Unified Cornish therefore has <e> everywhere except in the future which is *bydhaf, bydhyth, byth, bydhyn, bydhough, bydhons*. Nance probably believed that the third singular *byth* had influenced the rest of the paradigm. If so, he does not allow the second person singular imperative *byth* to influence the rest of the imperative paradigm, because that is *byth, bedhens, bedhen, bedheugh, bedhens* in Unified Cornish.

Kernowek Kemyn originally claimed to be an accurate form of the language based on a rigorous scientific analysis of the sources. It is remarkable therefore that Kernowek Kemyn posits [e] <e> in the past habitual *bedhen, bedhes, bedha*, etc., in the imperative (apart from the second singular) *bedhes, bedhen, bedhewgh, bedhens* but [ɪ] <y> in the future *bydhav, bydhydh, bydh, bydhon, bydhowgh, bydhons*. The stressed vowel in all these forms is exactly as in Unified Cornish. The variation between, for example, *bydhav* 'I will be' and *bedhewgh* 'be!' in Kernowek Kemyn corresponds to Unified Cornish *bydhaf* but *bedheugh*. As can be seen from the examples listed above, the distinction is without foundation in the traditional language. That Kernowek Kemyn follows Unified Cornish exactly here is remarkable. Kernowek Kemyn has the merit, according to Brown, "of greater accuracy than than [sic] the Unified system" (GMC2: v). It is remarkable that Kernowek Kemyn should so precisely here follow a system that is, according to the proponents of Kernowek Kemyn, very flawed.

Kernowek Kemyn, as we have seen, ignores vocalic alternation in *blydhen, *pryvyon, gwydhenn* and *ynys*. It also, as we shall see, ignores the same phenomenon in *byw* 'alive' ~ *bywnans* 'life', *bywa* 'to live', and even more remarkably in *klyw* 'hear' ~ *klywes* 'to hear'. It is difficult, therefore, to fathom why George settled upon the forms *bedhen, bedhes, bedha*, etc. in the imperfect, *bedhes, bedhen, bedhewgh, bedhens* in the imperative but *bydhav, bydhydh, bydhon,*

VOCALIC ALTERNATION: Y IN MONOSYLLABLES ~ E IN DISYLLABLES

bydhowgh, bydhons in the future. George originally claimed that Kernowek Kemyn was a scientifically designed phonology and orthography; moreover he criticized Nance for inconsistency. Why then did George not adopt a consistent stem *bydh-* in all these forms? Why does Kernowek Kemyn not prescribe **bydhen* 'let us be', **bydhewgh* 'be!' (plural) and *my a *vydha* 'I used to be'. It can hardly be because such forms are unattested, for George has often told us he has little respect for the orthography of the Middle Cornish texts. Indeed Kernowek Kemyn forms like **bywnans* 'life' and **klywes* 'to hear' are unattested anywhere in Cornish. All in all, I find the inconsistencies in Kernowek Kemyn perplexing.

10.09 The ending of the third singular imperative

Although we are discussing vocalic alternation rather than the desinences of the verb in Kernowek Kemyn, this does seem perhaps a suitable place to say something about the endings of the third singular imperative in Kernowek Kemyn. This synthetic imperative is commoner in *bos* 'to be' than in any other verb in Middle Cornish. By the sixteenth century it has been replaced by a periphrastic form, e.g. *gesow ny the vos war* 'let us beware' TH 9. In Kernowek Kemyn the recommended form of 'let him be' is *bedhes*. Brown says of the imperative: "In Modern Cornish [i.e. Kernowek Kemyn] has restored the use of the forms in *-es*. The 3p. in *-ens* has taken its place in many instances" (GMC2: § 182.3). In the case of **bedhes* 'let him be' it is not a question of "restoration" but of construction *de novo*. **Bedhes* is nowhere attested in Cornish.

10.10 Explanation of brackets in the list of disyllabic forms of *bos*

In order to remind my readers of the inauthentic spellings with <y> of the future in Kernowek Kemyn, I add {KK -y-} after forms of the future in the above list. Similarly to draw attention to the spurious third person singular imperative **bedhes* of Kernowek Kemyn, I add {KK -es} after the relevant occurrences.

10.11 Conclusions

George does not seem to understand the question of reduction of unstressed syllables and the accent shift. In consequence Kernowek Kemyn often exhibits <y> in disyllables and polysyllables, when <e> would have been authentic from the historical point of view. In the Middle and Late Cornish texts there is very little warrant for <y> in the stressed syllable of *blethen* 'year'; there is no support at all for <y> in *enys* or *gwethen*. Yet George spells the three etyma <blydhen>, *<gwydhenn> and *<ynys> respectively. Moreover Kernowek Kemyn's spellings <bedhen>, <bedhewgh>, for example, but <bydhav>, <bydhydh>, etc. are curiously incoherent. It would seem that in the matter of the vocalic alternation *y ~ e* Kernowek Kemyn is based on mistaken ideas of the phonology of Middle Cornish.

CHAPTER 11
The variation *gweth* ~ *gwyth, beth* ~ *byth, pref* ~ *pryf* (not in KKC21)

11.00 <gweth> ~ <gwyth>

In the previous chapter I examined some examples of <e> spellings in disyllabic words like *gwethen, blethen, bethaf* and *enys*. In this chapter I should like to say something about the development in Middle Cornish of the corresponding monosyllables. George points out in KKC21: 102 that I speak in *Cornish Today* of vocalic alternation in *gwethen* 'tree' ~ *gwyth* 'trees' but in UCR I spell the two items <gwedhen> and <gwedh> respectively. I had perfectly good reasons for doing so, and indeed I am not the first to spell such items thus. Jenner writes *gwêdh* 'trees', *gwêdhen* 'a tree' (HCL: 88), though he adds a circumflex to the vowel of both. Clearly Jenner believed that the long vowel of *gwedh* 'trees' analogically affected *gwedhen* as well. Similarly Jenner writes *bedh* 'be!' and *bedhough* 'be!' (plural) (HCL: 128); third singular *bedh* (*bydh*) 'he will be' and *bedhav* 'I will be' (HCL: 126).

Let us examine the question historically. Old Cornish *prif* 'worm' was probably pronounced [prɪːv], where the vowel was trimoric [prɪɪɪv] or [prɪˑɪv]. With the Prosodic Shift the vowel was reduced from three to two morae: [prɪɪv]. As a result, the nucleus was lowered slightly: [preɪv]. I assume that this then monophthongized to [preːv], in much the same way as <coys> [koˑiz] monophthongized to <cos> [koːz]. The monophthongized form [preːv] is attested in Middle Cornish as <pref> or <preff>. In exactly the same way Old Cornish *guid [gwɪːð] 'trees' became Middle Cornish [gweːð], written <gweth>.

11.01 *Beys* 'world', *beyth* 'be!', *deyth* 'day', etc.

The first stage of the development of the vowel is the lowering of [ɪː] to [eɪ], which is spelt <ey> in the Middle cornish texts. Let us start with the original forms *byth* 'be!', will be' (Welsh *bydd*), *bys* 'world' (Welsh *byd*), *dyth* 'day' (Welsh *dydd*), *fyth* 'faith' (Welsh *ffydd*), *gwyth* 'trees' (Welsh *gwydd*), *pryf* 'insect, vermin' (Welsh *pryf*) and *prys* 'time, meal' (Welsh *pryd*). I have collected the following examples with <ey> (the list is not exhaustive):

> **beys** 'world'
> *dre ov grath dalleth an* **beys** OM 6
> *a gertho war an nor***veys** OM 313
> *yn corf map den vyth yn* **beys** OM 926
> *yn ol an* **beys** *sav noe* OM 931
> *Noe mar luen yv an* **beys** OM 941
> *a gutho ol an nor* **veys** OM 982
> *myns den vs yn* **beys** *may fo* OM 983

110

THE VARIATION *GWETH ~ GWYTH, BETH ~ BYTH, PREF ~ PRYF*

mar ses dor segh war an **beys** OM 1100
cresseugh coullenweugh an **beys** OM 1161
trom dyal war ol an **beys** OM 1209
dre trom dyhal war an **beys** OM 1227
kyc gans gos bys worfen **beys** OM 1230
luen dyal war ol an **beys** OM 1233
ef yv arluth nef ha'n **beys** OM 1262
del yv arluth **beys** *ha nef* OM 1295
Awos den fyth war an **beys** OM 1340
gans tebeles war an **beys** OM 1466
hag a formyas nef ha'n **beys** OM 1507
lowene the flour an **beys** OM 1541
na theffo onan yn **beys** OM 1577
A dev lemyn guyn ov **beys** OM 1773
nep a'n gorthye guyn y **veys** OM 1938
ny gresaf awos an **beys** OM 2752
ol an **beys** *a ros thetha* OM 2832
ty yw sylwador a'n **beys** PC 304
ty yw arluth nef ha **beys** PC 412
pan wraf a'n **beys** *tremene* PC 430
nyn sus guel cusyl yn **beys** PC 2160
th'y lathe ken fyth yn **beys** PC 2168
an nyl a vynnyf yn **beys** PC 2186
nyn sues myghtern thy'n yn **beys** PC 2362
ena rewlys o an **beys** PC 2411
ef the wul bythqueth yn **beys** PC 2436
rak ny won yn **beys** *guel toul* PC 2920
ys dyweth ow map yn **beys** PC 2948
kynyuer dyaul vs yn **beys** PC 3062
a gollas pan eth a'n **beys** PC 3124
dres an **beys** *ol* RD 976
ihesu arluth nef ha **beys** RD 1151
pobel a'n **beys** RD 1185
an gokye den yn **beys** RD 1454
ha the'n **beys** *arte treylys* RD 1462
appeua marov an **beys** BM 646
hedre vo tecca an **beys** BK 3172
dowla tvs an **beis** SA 60
hag oll an bestas yn **beyse** CW 110
rag henna pobell an **beise** CW 2138
pur serten war oll an **beise** CW 2151
oll an **beise** *a vith bethys* CW 2315
oll an dorrow in **beys** *ma* CW 2321
a vyn dew buthy an **beise** CW 2330
kemmys pehas es in **beyse** CW 2335
awos destrowy an **beyse** CW 2388.

beyth 'be!, will be'
an pyth a thue gvelis **veyth** OM 854
myl vap mam a **veyth** *damneys* OM 314
pur vysy a **veyth** *thethe* OM 335
thy'so ef a **veyth** *besy* OM 405
dethy hy y **feyth** *gyfys* PC 529
a henna crous da y **feyth** PC 2550.

deyth 'day'
vn pres yn **geyth** *na peghy* PA 20c
An lor yn nos houl yn **geyth** OM 39
myns a defynno vn **geyth** OM 385
kefrys yn nos hag yn **geyth** OM 458
a versy yn **deyth** *dyweth* OM 742
arluth porth cof · yn **deyth** *dyweth* OM 1272
keffrys yn nos hag yn **geyth** OM 1516
a wra thethe **deyth** *ha nos* OM 1555
may fo rys vn **deyth** *a due* OM 1951
vn **deyth** *a thue yredy* PC 268
hep lorgh na scryp nos na **deyth** PC 914
ha **deyth** *brues theugh ef a thue* PC 1331
yn try **deyth** *ny'n threhafse* PC 1765
na nyl yn nos nag yn **geyth** PC 1881
ow benneth thy'so pup **deyth** PC 2549
me a'n te re'n **geyth** *hythew* PC 2684
drok pys of re'n **geyth** *hythew* PC 3089
yn certan the pen try **deyth** RD 45
na wylly **deyth** RD 57
kyns ys **deyth** *brus* RD 202
wose try **deyth** *ha hanter* RD 226
rak wheth byth ny thueth **deyth** *brues* RD 234
ha **deyth** *ha nos* RD 246
an trege **deyth** *dasuewe* RD 339
pan bostyas the pen try **deyth** RD 374
sur bys **deyth** *fyn* RD 416
hythew yv an trege **deyth** RD 681
en trege **deyth** *yv hythew* RD 691
vn **deyth** *vs ow tos goy* RD 1187
yn **geyth** *hythew* RD 1233
ha the pen try **deyth** *yn weth* RD 1277
hythew worthy'n yn **geyth** *splan* RD 1507
dev hugens **deyth** *dyuythys* RD 2437
an vlethan i'n kynsa **deyth** BK 1881.

feyth 'faith'
ihesu ru'm **feyth** *· a nazareth* PC 1117
my a'n te thy's war ow **feyth** PC 1469
my a'n te thy's war ow **feyth** PC 1756

THE VARIATION *GWETH* ~ *GWYTH*, *BETH* ~ *BYTH*, *PREF* ~ *PRYF*

ef a's dyllyrf war ow **feyth** PC 3072
me a'n mayl scon war ow **feyth** PC 3205
byth nynsyw rages rum **feyth** RD 1930
a uernona war ow **feyth** RD 2141
naneyll **feith**, *govenek, charite* TH 9
in **feith** *a crist* TH 16
an catholik **feyth** *only* TH 17
theworth an catholyk **feith** TH 18s
theworth an **feith** TH 18a
an catholyk **feith** TH 18a
vn **feith** *a crist* TH 31
an **feith** *a crist* TH 32
an **feith** *a russens y receva* TH 34
an discans han **feith** TH 34
len a **feith** TH 39
henew an **feith** TH 45a
ow buldya y **feith** 48a
faith *an tasow coth* SA 59a
dir **faith** *da ny* SA 61
Kemer **faith** *da* SA 63a.

gweyth 'trees'
may tefo **gveyth** *ha losow* OM 28
my a set ahugh a'n **gveyth** OM 37
may rug nef mor tyr ha **gveyth** OM 51.

preyf 'insect, vermin'
ha te **preif** *a wra cruppya* CW 912
honna o drog **preyf** *heb nam* CW 1919
nyng es beast na **preif** *in beyse* CW 2415.

preys 'time, meal'
ha lynneth benen pup **preys** OM 315
warnethe y tryg pup **preys** OM 1104
powes ny 'gys byth nep **preys** OM 1232
Yma an **preys** *ov nessa* BM 4269
orth harlutry prest pub **preys** CW 91
ow bosaf sertayn pub **preyse** CW 133
yn efarn yn tane pub **preyse** CW 459.

The graph <ey> in these instances I take to represent the first stage of the development of Old Cornish /ɪː/ to Middle Cornish /eː/. We will see in the next section that one also finds numerous examples in which the shift to [eː] appears complete.

TOWARDS AUTHENTIC CORNISH

11.02 *Bes* 'world', *beth* 'be!', *deth* 'day', etc.

Here are a selection of spellings with <e> (and Late Cornish <ea>), suggesting that the vowel is a simple long [e:]. The list is also by no means exhaustive.

bes 'world'
in nore ***ves*** SA 60a
Nag es travith a dale talves en ***Bes*** BF: 13
Scriffas, Gomar mab Japhet vo en ***Beas*** BF: 48
Ma Peath Hern pokar ol an ***Beaz*** BF: 43
Ma Peath Hern pokar ol an ***Bez*** BF: 44
Ha thera an ***bez*** *heb composter* BF: 51
oll an gwellasketh an ***beaze*** *ha'n worriance nonge* RC 23:188
Po rez deberra an ***bez*** ACB.

beth 'be!; will be'
yn meth an ioul te a ***feth*** PA 16c
Kyn fallens ol me a ***veth*** PA 49a
na porth ovn vyth na ***veth*** *trest* OM 1467
rag y ***feth*** *map yn bethlem* OM 1934
y ***feth*** *othom annethe* OM 1949
mara pewaf why a ***veth*** OM 2396
del ***veth*** *luen a bodrethes* OM 2714
ha ty a ***veth*** *prysonys* RD 70
ha ny a ***veth*** *the creffa* BM 331
ny a ***veth*** *scorne ol an pov* BM 368
te a ***veth*** *sur heb awer* BM 417
warbarth ny a ***veth*** *kellys* BM 605
a ***veth*** *gelwys an seson* BM 680
Tevdar me a ***veth*** *gelwys* BM 759
ny ***veth*** *ov les* BM 774
a vahum ny ***veth*** *sensys* BM 811
meryasek ***beth*** *avysyys* BM 840
ha the cothmen me a ***veth*** BM 894
wath coyl orthef ha ***beth*** *fuir* BM 905
crist mar ny ***veth*** *denehys* BM 974
neffra ny ***veth*** *da ow cher* BK 1036
Dremas ***beth*** *war pyth ylly* BM 1103
mar ***peth*** *in den bo benyn corruptys* TH 14
freth y ***feth*** *gweregys* BK 1846
Aragas y ***feth*** *lethys* BK 2702
mar ne ***veth*** *a dyhelhis* BK 2584
maria ***beth*** *ov socur* BM 3866
Syluester wek ***beth*** *lowen* BM 4031
Meryasek ***beth*** *lowen* BM 4343
pyw henna a ***veth*** *mar vold* CW 163
ha uelkom ti a ***uêdh*** BF: 17
ha uelkym ti a ***uêdh*** BF: 17.

THE VARIATION *GWETH ~ GWYTH, BETH ~ BYTH, PREF ~ PRYF*

deth 'day'
*in **geth** fovt in bugel* BM 2840
***deth** brus eff a thue purfeth* BM 4086
*nav re bue sur in vn **geth*** BM 4010
*pup **deth** a weske certen* BM 4444
*Ha mylwyth pur guir in **geth*** BM 4455
*may teffa an **Jeth** hag egery* TH 18
*hethow in **Jeth*** TH 37
*an **Jeth** o rag aga merite* TH 47
*pup **deth** vmma* SA 60
*in **geth** hythew* CW 2104
*ha an trugga **deth** Eau derauas arta* BF: 41
*wheha **deth** te ra guile whele* BF: 41
*bus an Sithas **deth** eu an Suil* BF: 41
*rag en wheha **deth** an Arlith guras nefe* BF: 42
*ha reg poaz an sithas **deth*** BF: 42
*reig guil an sithvas **deth** benigas* BF: 42
*Try termen en **death** meero why dotha* BF: 43
*Ha Deu gwres an golou **deth*** BF: 51
*do debarra **deth** vrt an noz* BF: 52
*Ha do moas dres an **deth*** BF: 52
*buz an sithaz **deth** eu zil benigas guz Arleth Deui* BF: 55
*ha pouesas an sithas **deth*** BF: 55
*Rag hedda an Arleth Benaz an sithas **deth** ha sonaz a* BF: 55
*Ro d[e]n hithou gun bara **deth** [de] **deth*** BF: 55
*an Tridzia **deth** E Thasurras* BF: 56.

feth 'faith'
*Cans den lethys war ow **feth*** BM 4009
*dre an **feth** a Jhesu* TH 7a.

gweth 'trees'
*owr hag arghans gwels ha **gweth*** PA 16b
*a thorr oll an **gweth** an Looar* RC 23: 175.

pref 'worm'
*han tebel el hager **bref*** PA 122c
*an falge dragon tebel **preff*** BM 4133
*orth an dragon **preff** an pla* BM 4173
*Gallas Lucifer droke **preve*** CW 335
*formya **preve** henwis serpent* CW 498
*a vghe beast na **preaf** yn bys* CW 502.

pres 'time, meal'
*vn **pres** yn geyth na peghy* PA 20c
*Tempus... Time, opportunity, season, leisure, &c.... C[ornish] **Prêz**, termen* AB: 161c.

As can be seen from the above list, some forms with <e> are poorly attested in Middle Cornish and are known mostly from the later language. Forms like *a uêdh* 'will be' in Lhuyd are excellent evidence that the vowel really was [e:] in at least some of these etyma. Tregear's *Jeth* 'day' also suggests that the vowel was pronounced with [e:].

11.03 Bys 'world', byth 'be!', dyth 'day', etc.
It is undeniable, nonetheless, that forms in <y> persist into Late Cornish. Here are some variants of the seven etyma that exhibit <y> or <i>.

bys 'world'
*yn **bys** ma rak dry ascor* OM 71
*a paynys in nor **bys** ma* OM 600
*the'n **bys** rag y cusyllye* OM 643
*ny dyf guels na flour yn **bys*** OM 711
*guyn ov **bys** kafus cummyas* OM 750
*ny yl taves den yn **bys*** OM 767
*ol an **bys** a fyth sylwys* OM 819
*lafur ha duwon a'n **bys*** OM 851
*yn **bys** ma nan geves par* PC 1578
*gothaf mernens yn **bys** ma* PC 1343
*my ny welaf ken yn **bys*** PC 1589
*arluth dres ol an **bys** ma* PC 1683
*ha sylwadur a'n **bys** ma* RD 480
*rak tus a'n **bys*** RD 740
*ef yv arluth nef ha **bys*** RD 803
*rak kerenge tus a'n **bys*** RD 833
*berth yn **bys** ma · onan a'y uos* RD 860
*omma in **bys** ma* TH 3
*the oll an **bys*** TH 7
*warbyn an **bys*** TH 7
*omma in **bys*** TH 7a, 20
*an creacion an **bys*** TH 14
*rag pehosow oll an **bys*** TH 16
*in oll an **bys*** TH 16a
*in sight an **bys*** TH 25a
*possessyon an **bys*** TH 28
*bys worfen an **bys*** TH 34a
*bys in gorfen an **bys*** TH 36a
*ow hothman a tra in **bys*** CW 579.

byth 'be!, will be'
*h'aga hynwyn y a **vyth*** OM 35
*gosteyth thy'mo y a **vyth*** OM 53
*moy drethof a **vyth** hynwys* OM 134
*tra ny **vyth** yn pow adro* OM 189
*ha nefre y **fyth** avey* OM 314

THE VARIATION *GWETH ~ GWYTH, BETH ~ BYTH, PREF ~ PRYF*

bysy ***vyth*** *the sostene* OM 398
arluth the voth a ***vyth*** *gvrys* OM 431
rag pup tra ol a ***fyth*** *da* OM 534
ty a ***vyth*** *genen nefre* OM 568
yn ioy na ***vyth*** *dywythys* PC 9
scon y gallos · a ***vyth*** *lehys* PC 21
henna a ***vyth*** *hep dyweth* PC 34
the vestry a ***vyth*** *leyhys* PC 143
why a ***vyth*** *aquyttys da* PC 310
del leueryth a ***vyth*** *gurys* PC 450
hy a ***vyth*** *pur wyr neffre* PC 552
worth ihesu pandra ***vyth*** *grueys* PC 568
aga bos a ***vyth*** *parys* PC 695
na ***vyth*** *na* ***vyth*** *yn awher* RD 1020
the pegh thy's a ***vyth*** *gefys* RD 1102
na gans dev ny ***vyth*** *trygys* RD 1110
thomas na ***vyth*** *dyscrygyk* RD 1369
mar ny ***vyth*** *an whethlow due* RD 1400
mar ***pith*** *den vith ioynys* TH 49
skon y ***fythe*** *gwrys der ow rase* CW 14
honna a ***vythe*** *ow skaval droose* CW 20
hag yny y ***fythe*** *gorrys* CW 25
a ***vyth*** *gorris thom service* CW 35
an kensa try a ***vithe*** *gwryes* CW 37
te a ***vyth*** *des arage vskys* CW 40
in second degre y ***fithe*** *gwryes* CW 51
ena ty a ***vyth*** *tregys* CW 246
why a ***vith*** *me a levar* CW 253
te a ***vyth*** *predar henna* CW 380.

dyth 'day'

yn secund ***dyth*** *y fynna* OM 17
yn kynsa ***dyth*** *myns vs grvrys* OM 20
yn pympes ***dyth*** *me a vyn* OM 41
hethyw yw an whefes ***dyth*** OM 49
may fe seythves ***dyth*** *hynwys* OM 144
hen yw ***dyth*** *a bowesva* OM 145
dew vgens ***dyth*** *my a as* OM 1027
yn tri ***dyth*** *y'n dreafse* PC 365
the pen try ***dyth*** *ha seuel* RD 958
dyth *brues y wregh ysethe* PC 814
bys in ***dith*** *hethew* TH 17
an present ***dith*** *ma* TH 34
bys in ***dith*** *hethow* TH 41a
In vn ***dith*** TH 47
Y a'n pren un ***gyth*** *a the* BK 2549
sure inter an ***gyth*** *han noos* CW 85
an tryssa ***dyth*** *me a wra* CW 92

*in pesera **dyth** bith gwryes* CW 100
*in pympas **dyth** orth ow breis* CW 106
*in whea **dyth** myns es formys* CW 413
*an **dyth** sure a bowesva* CW 416
*yeindre an **deeth*** RC 23: 178
*Try Termen an **Dyth**, meero why Dotha* BF: 44
*Ro dha ni hydhou bara ny peb **Dydh*** BF: 45.

fyth 'faith'
*yn certan y a dreyl **fyth*** OM 1817
*doro kenter er the **fyth*** PC 2746
*lauar th'ymmo er the **fyth*** PC 2028
*gueyteugh ol er agas **fyth*** RD 373
*leuereugh er agas **fyth*** RD 2027
*a phelyp lous os y'th **fyth*** RD 2379.

gwyth 'trees'
*ny ew **gwyth** crabbys* TH 9
*than **gwyth** sevall yn ban* CW 93
*a misk an **gweeth** an Looar* RC 23: 178.

pryf 'insect, reptile'
*an hagar-**Breeve** o moy foulze* RC 23: 174
*a lavarraz tha an hagar-**breeve*** RC 23: 175
*Ha an hagar-**breeve** a lavarraz* RC 23: 175
*an hagar-**breeve** a thullas ve* RC 23: 180
*a lavarras tha an hagar-**breeve*** RC 23: 180.

prys 'time, meal'
*koscough lemmyn mar sew **prys*** PA 61b
*yn **prys** hanter nos heb wow* PA 76c
*Nevngo deuethys an **prys*** PA 200a
*nanso **prys** gwespar yn wlas* PA 230a
*sur y vyllyk an **prys*** OM 338
*bynyges re bo an **prys*** OM 674
*a whythre warnas vn **prys*** OM 1414
*bynygys re bo an **prys*** OM 1979
*rag ol ov yenes pup **prys*** OM 2125
*yskyn yn ban marsyw **prys*** PC 222
*re bo gueres theugh pup **prys*** PC 224
*ow bennath thywhy pup **prys*** PC 308
*a thybry gynef vn **prys*** PC 456
*whet avar **prys** soper yv* PC 696
*lauar lemyn mar syv **prys*** PC 938
*yn guetha **prys** er y gv* PC 1130
*bynyges re bo an **prys*** RD 152, 455
*anken pup **prys*** RD 282
*gorthyans thotho ef pup **prys*** RD 802

THE VARIATION *GWETH ~ GWYTH, BETH ~ BYTH, PREF ~ PRYF*

ny thueth an **prys** RD 877
res thotha **prys** *merwell* TH 12
ha golarowe mere pub **pryes** CW 297
a soweth gwelas an **pryes** CW 1648
soweth an **pryes** CW 1659.

11.04 <ee> for [eː]

Some of the above spellings, particularly in the earlier texts, may simply be archaisms. Given that the vowel was in origin [ɪ] and was spelt <i> in Old Cornish, it is not improbable that <y> spellings reflect an earlier pronunciation. The two Late Cornish spellings *Dyth* and *Dydh* 'day' listed above are clearly taken from a written source, since Late Cornish invariably used *jorna* for 'day' in the singular. Late spellings like <preeve>, however, suggest that the vowel may well have been [iː]. This is not certain. Late Cornish often has <ee> when the vowel intended was clearly [eː]. I hve collected the following examples:

Middle Cornish	Late Cornish
cres 'peace'	*crees* BF: 8
res eth 'went'	*geeth* RC 23: 178, 198
ger 'word'	*geer* RC 23: 186
gwreg 'wife'	*wreeg, wreege* RC 23: 178, 181, 183
*hanter deg 'half of ten'	*hanter Deege* BF: 38
*ken poynt 'another point'	*keen point* BF:
nef 'heaven'	*neeve* RC 23: 184
ster 'star'	*steere* RC 23: 196
teg 'fair'	*teege* RC23: 187.

Notice moreover that Kerew writes both <gweth> and <gweeth> for 'trees' and we have examples in Nicholas Boson's writing for both <bes> 'world' and <bees> (BF: 8, 13).

11.05 Why *byth*, etc. did not always become *beth*, etc.

If, nonetheless, some of these etyma did exhibit [iː] in Middle and Late Cornish, it is likely that we are dealing here with dialectal (or even idiolectal) variants. [ɪ] > [eᴵ] > [eː] was the development in some forms of Cornish. In other dialects the nucleus probably did not lower and the coda particularly before [s] and [ð] was raised to [i]. This then pulled the vowel upwards to give [iː]: [ɪː] > [ɪi] > [ii], in consequence the final vowel was [iː], spelt <y>. This was rather similar to the development in western Cornish, where the reflex of Old Cornish /ui/ in *cuit* 'wood', etc. remained high before monophthongizing to give [uː] in *kuːz*, rather than lowering and then monophthongizing to give *koːz*.

The maintenance of a high vowel in *byth, gwyth, pryf* was probably also assisted by analogy. The variation of *trega ~ tryg*, where the disyllable has [e] and the monosyllable had [iː], was widespread in Cornish; and even imposed

119

itself unhistorically on *cresy ~ crys* and *pesy ~ pys*. It is not improbable therefore that the simple phonetic development *bethaf ~ beth, gwethen ~ gweth, prevyon ~ pref* was slowed or even halted by analogy, and the end result was *bethaf ~ byth, gwethen ~ gwyth* and *prevyon ~ pryf*.

George tells us that in Late Cornish /ɪː/ "was lowered and fused with the reflex of MidC /ɛ/, c. 1650." (PSRC: 112). This means, I assume, that George thinks Middle Cornish /ɪː/ appears in Late Cornish as [eː] <e>. George clearly has no explanation for Late Cornish forms containing [iː], etc. In fact, of course, there was no Middle Cornish /ɪː/. The vowel had already fallen together with either /eː/ as a result of the Prosodic Shift or with /iː/ for phonetic reasons or by analogy. If there were Late Cornish forms containing [iː], such items already existed in Middle Cornish. Kernowek Kemyn is based on a mistaken phonology.

CHAPTER 12
Bewnans 'life' and *clewes* 'to hear' (KKC21: 120-25)

12.00 George's defence of his spelling *<bywnans>

One of the least happy aspects of Kernowek Kemyn is the way it writes **bywnans* 'life', **klyw* 'hear!' and **klywes* 'to hear'. These three spellings are not attested anywhere at all in the traditional language. Indeed the spellings *<bywnans> and *<klywes> so astonished me when I saw them first in GKK, that I was moved to examine Kernowek Kemyn closely and thus to write *Cornish Today*.

George's opening defence of these spellings is remarkable. He says:

> The spelling <yw> for these words depends upon the following:
> (i) the roots *klyw-* and *byw-* each contain historical /ɪw/;
> (ii) <yw> is a reasonable grapheme to denote /ɪw/;
> (iii) the diphthongs in individual words within each set of words has not changed such as to invalidate the use of ɪw.
> Provided that these three assertions are correct, then we can be sure about the spellings in *Kernewek Kemmyn* (KKC21: 120).

The crucial portion here is (iii): "the diphthongs in individual words within each set of words has not changed such as to invalidate the use of /ɪw/." I think George here means that the original sound in the traditional language was /ɪw/, and if it can be shown that this had not changed too much away from /ɪw/ ("such as to invalidate the use of /ɪw/"), then there is nothing wrong with the spellings in Kernowek Kemyn. This is an astonishing statement. George is the inventor of a new spelling system for Cornish, based, he says, on his scientific analysis of the traditional language (see PSRC). In this analysis he claimed to have discovered various distinctions and oppositions that had escaped Jenner, Nance and Caradar. George's work purported to reveal for the first time half-length, geminate consonants, two long *o*'s and three high front vowels */ i ɪ e /*. Here in KKC21, however, he has abandoned any claim to scientific precision; if "the diphthong in individual words within each set of words" has remained fairly close to /ɪw/, then, he argues, we can continue to use unhistorical spellings like *<bywnans> and *<klywes>.

His expression "in individual words within each set of words" is also a fudge. He is referring to the distinction in the texts between *byw* 'alive', which is on occasion attested with <y> and *bewnans* 'life' which never has <y>. This is a question of *y ~ e* alternation, of which George appeared to be largely unaware when he devised Kernowek Kemyn. In order to justify his inauthentic spelling *<bywnans>, George tacitly lumps <byw> and

*<bywnans> together by speaking of "individual words" within "sets of words". This is special pleading [SP]. They may be related etyma, but historically their vowels are quite different. It is rather as though George were claiming that because *occurred* is related to *occur*, it should be spelt *occured.

12.01 George's diversionary use of Welsh and Breton

We can see that George is on rather weak ground here, because his next move is to set out in a table (Fig. 18.1) the spellings in the texts of *clew, clewes, bew* and *bewa* (NB not *bewnans*, which is written *<bywnans> in Kernowek Kemyn) together with their Welsh and Breton cognates. This is a diversion. We are dealing with Cornish, not Welsh nor Breton. Cornish is a separate language with its own particular history. How Welsh and Breton spell 'to hear' and 'to live' is at this point completely irrelevant—though it is George's practice, when he is in difficulties, to cite the Welsh and Breton forms. He does this again when discussing the diphthongs *yw* and *ew* in final position (see **13.00** below).

Rather than let George's arguments detain me, I shall at this point turn to the relevant words themselves and examine how they are attested in the texts.

12.02 *Byw/bew* 'alive', *bewa* 'to live' and *bewnans* 'life'

Old Cornish has *biu*, which I take to represent a dimoric vowel with a semi-vocalic coda: /bɪˑw/. With the operation of the Prosodic Shift this became [bɪw], where the vowel was shortened. Although there short stressed [ɪ] was phonemically distinct from [e], in the diphthong [ɪw], there is considerable hesitation in the texts We thus find *byw* 'alive' in Middle Cornish frequently written <bew>; indeed <bew> is commoner than <byw>. The disyllabic forms *bewa* 'to live' (and the other inflected forms), and *bewnans* already have /e/ here by the vocalic alternation *y ~ e* quite independently of the Prosodic Shift. I assume that the vowel in *bew* influences the vowel in *bewa* so that it remains <ew> in Middle Cornish. In *bewnans*, however, the following [w] rounds the mid-high front vowel to a rounded mid-high vowel. This process was probably already occurring in Middle Cornish. In Late Cornish we find instances of *bownans* for earlier *bewnans*. I have collected the following forms of the three words A) *byw* 'alive' and the monosyllabic third singular *bew* 'lives'; B) *bewa* 'to live' (and inflected forms); C) *bewnans*. My lists are as exhaustive as I can make them, though I have doubtless missed some instances.

12.03 *byw ~ bew* 'alive, lives'

1) **byw**
*y vos **byw** my ny gresaf* RD 904
***byw** yn poynt da* RD 1283
*saw an corf na **byw** a pe* RD 1657

BEWNANS 'LIFE' AND CLEWES 'TO HEAR'

*an keth corf na **byw** a pe* RD 1662
*benitha hedre ven **byv*** BM 354
*hedre ven **byv*** BM 1137
*gasa crystyen **byv** ny ven* BM 1327
*me as ornes in **fyv** dre* BM 1784
*mars ywe **byv** bo marov* BM 4352.

2) bew

*ty a **vew** bys may fy loys* OM 72
*rag ny **vew** moy es tryddyth* OM 829
*tus **vev** saw ny my a greys* OM 1152
*mara pethaf **bev** vlethen* OM 2385
*hedre veyn **bev** yn bys ma* OM 115
*hedre veyf **bew** yn bys ma* PC 1020
*guel vye y gase **bev*** PC 1590
*na corf dasserhy the **vew*** PC 3085
*ha lowenne a pe **bev*** PC 3158
*agan **bew** kyn kentreynnyn* RD 74
*ny **vew** dre ver lauarow* RD 986
*a ty iacob **bew** a pe* RD 1007
***bew** hedre ven* RD 1048
*yn **few** aban dassorghas* RD 1442
*ny fylleth hedre ven **bev*** BM 54
*ahanan ny **vev** vn den* BM 609
*ha gasa **bev** dyogel* BM 1661
*rag nyns us den **bew** a vith keffys* TH 10a
*ny ve nagonyn sawys **bew*** TH 39a
*an devotion aga huthmans ew **bew*** SA 66
***bew** hedre ve* BK 639
*hedre ve **bew** war an bys* BK 820
*a sof pottys oyow **bew*** BK 1134
*ny'th gas a'th **vew*** BK 2154
*gegys a'y **vew*** BK 2305
*us a'm ehan hethew **bew*** BK 2495
*hedre ven **bew*** BK 2586
*th'um arluth drys suel us **bew*** BK 2658
*drevon **bew** ow harenga* CW 847
*fetla wren omwetha **bew*** CW 1047
*haw hendas cayme whath en **bew*** CW 1280
*yn bys ma hadre von **bew*** CW 1458
*gans mabe den in bys ma **bew*** CW 1510.

12.04 *bywa* ~ *bewa* 'to live', etc.

1) bywa

*hedyr **vywy** hag harluʒes* CF 36
*vynytha hedre **vywy*** OM 243
*wheth ol **bywe** y a wra* OM 1877

*hedre **vywhy** PC 2930*
*ny'm bus **bywe** na fella RD 2210.*

2) **bewa**
*rag dre gleȝe a **veughe** PA 72b*
*caman na ylly **bewe** PA 204a*
*y woys **bewe** ny ylly PA 207b*
*bytqueth yn lan re **vewse** PA 204b*
*encressyens ha **bewens** pel OM 48*
*sperys [may] hylly **bewe** OM 62*
*troha ken pow the **vewe** OM 344*
*a yl den orto **bewe** OM 475*
*rag **bewe** orto certan OM 494*
*ny garse pelle **bewe** OM 738*
*onan vythol the **vewe** OM 1697*
*ny am byth cres the **vewe** OM 1714*
*nynsus **bewe** na fella OM 1703*
*nynsus **bewe** OM 1718*
*na'm bes **bewe** na fella OM 1884*
*my re **vewas** termyn hyr OM 2345*
*na fella my the **vewa** OM 2360*
*may hallons ynno **bewa** OM 2833*
*dre clethe nep a **vewo** PC 1158*
*a **vewhe** yn bewnans da PC 3110*
***bewe** pel a wruk yn beys RD 210*
*an trege deyth das**uewe** RD 339*
*y vos das**uewys** arte RD 345*
*kyn das**vewo** ny'n dregha RD 403*
*y wres yn ban das**fewe** RD 451*
*rak pup ol a gar **bewe** RD 600*
*ha das**uewe** RD 982*
*ny yl an corf na **bewe** RD 1121*
*ny gresyn ty the **vewe** RD 1549*
***bewe** pel ny elte gy BM 430*
*byteweth reys yv **bewa** BM 1480*
*ha me a ra mar **pewaff** BM 1864*
*ov **pewe** tek hag onest BM 2006*
*bys venary mar **pewa** BM 2124*
***bewe** pel ny eltegy BM 2570*
*numbus **bewa** BM 2632*
*hedre **vevhen** benythe BM 2816*
*solladeth y re **vewas** BM 2940*
*ha lor pegans the **vewa** BM 4292*
*y halse **bewe** defry BM 4466*
*Ny'th ues **bewa** nafella BK 69*
*i'n bys ma ny **vewans** pel BK 1444*
*Na **vewans** pel, re'n Passyon! BK 1445*
*rag **bewa** ha bos marow BK 1467*
*rag bos maraw ha **bewa** BK 1850*

BEWNANS 'LIFE' AND CLEWES 'TO HEAR'

*mar myn **bewa** in dan nef* BK 2259
*ny ra **bewa** omma mas termyn cut* TH 7
*in re na a **vewas** in law a nature* TH 14
*vgy ow tebell **vewa*** TH 16a
*han gela the **vewa** compys* TH 17
*gansa eff the **vewa*** TH 21a
*ha tus ow **pewa** compis* TH 26a
*han re esa ow **pewa** in tyrmyn coth* TH 27
*may hallan ny **bewa** ha trega in charite* TH 30
*supposya y honyn the **vewa** neffra* TH 40
*may alsans **bewa** ha plesya du* TH 40
*neb a rug **bewa** in tyrmyn sepherinus* TH 47a
*pana peldar a ruga **bewa** ena* TH 47a
*sperys may hallas **bewa*** CW 348
*tha greys an bys tha **vewa*** CW 974
*tha vyns a **vewa** in byes* CW 991
*y a wressa prest **bewa*** CW 997
*tha **vewa** omma neffra* CW 1011
*in chast gwren ny kes**vewa*** CW 1314
***bewa** in kethe order na* CW 1319
*yn cosow mannaf **bewa*** CW 1362
*nym bes pur suer ew **bewa*** CW 1439
*ha pegans lower tha **vewa*** CW 1476
*yma ef prest ow **pewa*** CW 1482
*avell beast prest ow **pewa*** CW 1521
*nymbes **bewa** na fella* CW 1571
***bewa** yth esaf pub eare* CW 1667
*nym beas **bewa** na fella* CW 1966
*tha **vewa** omma vdn spyes* CW 1969
*in keth order a **vewa*** CW 2062
*yma thyma tha **vewa*** CW 2236.

12.05 **bywnans ~ bewnans ~ bownans* 'life'

1) **bywnans; cf. *<bywnans> in Kernowek Kemyn
There are no examples in Cornish.

2) bewnans
*nyn geuas ol y **vewnans*** PA 12a
*am **bewnans** del yw scrifys* PA 73b
*crist an **bewnans** na sawye* PA 103a
***bewnans** Ihesus dre goyntis* PA 125a
*agan **bewnans** may fen sur* PA 191d
*war beyn kylly an **bewnans*** PA 241a
*an **bewnans** ny re gollas* PA 246c
*ha'n **bewnans** pan y'n kylly* OM 63
*rag governye ow **bewnans*** OM 89
*a'm **bewnens** my th'y bysy* OM 701

rag hyr lour ev ov **bewnans** OM 848
spyrys a **vewnans** *ynno* OM 985
spyrys a **vewnans** *ynno* OM 1090
a **vevnans** *ry dethe gura* OM 1834
a'm **bevnans** *sur yn bys ma* OM 1886
byth nyn jeves ol **bewnes** PC 65
the **vevnans** *y tasserhy* PC 1747
y **vevnens** *nynsus guythe* PC 2445
savye **bewnens** *tus erel* PC 2876
a vewhe yn **bewnans** *da* PC 3110
yn **bevnans** *gulan dywethe* PC 3215
y tasserghy the **vewnans** RD 375
the **vewnans** *y tassorghas* RD 516
the **vewnans** *ef the seuel* RD 590
the **veunans** *yn pur deffry* RD 784
bewnans *neffre ioy hep cas* RD 1585
sawye ow **bewnans** *certan* RD 1963
pup den ol yn **bewnans** *da* RD 2446
ham **bevnans** *vy yv henna* BM 117
bys benitha an **bevnans** BM 389
me an car in ov **bewnans** BM 483
y methe bue the **vevnans** BM 792
mar tur na pel ov **bevnans** BM 1163
benithe in the **vevneyns** BM 1467
squyth off omma am **bevnans** BM 1685
helma yv **bevnans** *nobyl* BM 2023
lemen prest sav ov **bevnans** BM 2126
bevnans *meryasek yma* BM 2500
ov **bevnans** *oma gedya* BM 2541
bevnans *ryel a feth sur* BM 2818
Arluth gays thym ov **bevnans** BM 2358
sav a vo in **bevnans** *da* BM 3662
meryasek in ov **bevnans** BM 3850
thage **bevnans** *bones dreys* BM 4114
bevnans *meryasek certan* BM 4550
an happy han felicite **bewnans** TH 4
aga pehosow haga drog **bewnans** TH 6a
ny a ledyas agan **bewnans** *in pehosow* TH 10
then stat an **bewnans** *heb deweth* TH 12
han **bewnans** *heb deweth* TH 13a
an **bewnans** *heb deweth* TH 14
Inweth teball **vewnans** *a thora dampnacion* TH 16a
attaynya an **bewnans** *heb deweth* TH 17
kemeras an dewas a **vewnans** TH 19
an entring thyn **bewnans** *heb deweth* TH 19
a ra avaylya then **bewnans** *eternall* TH 20
thin **bewnans** *heb deweth* TH 20
kyn fo y **vewnans** *vith mar detestabyll* TH 21
gans oll agan **bewnans** TH 21

BEWNANS 'LIFE' AND CLEWES 'TO HEAR'

Gans oll agan **bewnans** TH 21
hagan hooll **bewnans** *res thy servia eff* TH 21a
an lyvely fyntan a **vewnans** TH 22
aga theball **bewnans** TH 23
y **vewnans***, y conversacion* TH 23a
thyn dyscans a crist han **bewnans** TH 24
ha treweythow aga **bewnans** TH 24a
dyrectya agan **bewnans** TH 26
in present ha mortall **bewnans** *ma* TH 26
ny an gevith ganso eff eternall **bewnans** TH 26
henna ew an **bewnans** *heb deweth* TH 26
pana perfeccion a **vewnans** TH 26a
Pysell defferans a **bewnans** TH 27
nyns es mar stroyt **bewnans** TH 27a
na pith an bys, na **bewnans** *here* TH 28
merow war agys **bewnans** TH 28a
ha pecevia gas **bewnans** TH 28a
amendia aga lewde **bewnans** TH 29a
Ha wosa agan **bewnans** *omma in bys* TH 35
nynsevith eff **bewna[n]s** TH 40
oll an dythyow agan **bewnans** TH 41
mer a benegyttar a **bewnans** TH 41
Te ew mab an du a **vewnans** TH 44
grace in **bewnans** *ma* TH 51
ha the obtaynia an **bewnans** *heb deweth* TH 51
a vanna ve ry rag Ehas **bewnans** *thyn bys* TH 51a
rag an **bewnans** *a oll an bys* TH 52
sevys a vernans the **bewnans** TH 53
Ema genas ge girreow **bewnans** *heb dewath* SA 63
henna ew **bewnans** *heb dewath* SA 63a
bewnans *heb dewath, mith S. Austen* SA 66
Christ ew ow **bewnans** *ha'm boys* BK 427
a'th **vewnans** *may fy ge suer* BK 576
bewnans *moy suer* BK 764
a'gen **bewnans** *awherak* BK 2336
A'gys **bewnans** *mars ough ker* BK 2446
in e **vewnans** BK 2910
seyl a theyg **bewnans** *hogan* CW 99
han **bewnans** *pan an kelly* CW 349
ew an wethan a **vewnans** CW 1841
ew henwys gwethan a **vewnans** CW 1927
theth **vewnans** *gans ow spera* CW 1994
ow **bewnans** *tha gameras* CW 2000
sperys a **vewnans** *vnna* CW 2457.

3) **bownans**
whi el dendal gose **bounans** *obba* BF: 15
ha huei el dendel 'gyz **bounaz** *ybma* BF: 16

*ha an **Bounance** rag Neveravenitha* BF: 41
*ha **Bounaz** heb diuadh* BF: 46
*guayans gen **bounas*** BF: 52
*an taklou ez dothan **bounaz*** BF: 52
*ha dres kanifer tra es **bounas** ha guaya var an aor* BF: 53
*menz bos **bounas** eta* BF: 53
*ha **Bownas** heb duath* BF: 56
*Ha senzhia ol guz dethiow **Bownans** da* BF: 60
*oll dethyow tha **vowngas*** RC 23: 180
*oll dethyow tha **vowngaz*** RC 23: 182
*komeraz weeth dore an gwethan **bownaz*** RC 23: 184
*tha gweetha an vor a'n gwethan **vownyaz*** RC 23: 185
W[elsh] *Byuyd*, Life; Corn[ish] ***Bounaz*** AB: 13c
VITA... C[ornish] ***Bounaz*** AB: 298a
*eva whellaz **bownaz** an flo you[n]k* RC 23: 200
*ha gweel a **vownans** mear a heaze* LAM: 226
***Bounaz** heb Diueth* LAM: 238.

12.06 Discussion of *bew, bewa, bewnans*

Notice incidentally that in his Fig. 18.3 George says one example of *byw-* in polysyllables occurs in MC (my PA). He is mistaken. He means to say, I think, that one example occurs in the *Charter Fragment*. There are no examples in PA [ID]. Of the five disyllabic forms of *bewa* 'to live' in the list above that exhibit *y*, three are variants of the phrase *hedre vywhy* 'while you live', the second person singular of the present subjunctive. The final *-y* has almost certainly affected the root vowel by vowel harmony. The other two examples are variants of *bewa* 'to live', where the vowel has been influenced by monosyllabic *byw* 'alive'; the vowel *y* is not unexpected. Overall there are 5 examples with <yw> out of 80, i.e. 6.25% of the total. This is hardly a satisfactory proportion to form the basis of the spelling of the word, yet Kernowek Kemyn writes <bywa>, etc.

The figures with regard to *bewnans* are even less satisfactory from the point of view of Kernowek Kemyn. I have collected 101 examples of *bewnans* spelt with <e> and no examples at all with <y>. Kernowek Kemyn spells the word *<bywnans>. Given that there is no warrant whatever for this form anywhere in surviving Cornish, the spelling is regrettable.

12.07 George's defence of his spelling *<bywnans>

It is quite obvious that George, when he devised his orthography, was unaware of the existence of vocalic alternation. When I complained to him by letter about his newly-devised spelling <Bywnans Meryadjek>, in a personal communication dated 26 September 1987, he wrote that there was nothing wrong with <byw>, it was so written in Welsh and therefore <bywnans> in Kernowek Kemyn was justified (see **2.04** above).

BEWNANS 'LIFE' AND CLEWES 'TO HEAR'

George did not realize that I was objecting to <y> in *bywnans*. I had no problem with <byw>, because such a form is attested and <y> in the word is the historical spelling. George may not have understood that I was referring to the alternation *y* ~ *e*, with *y* in the monosyllable and *e* in the disyllable. Now that he realises that such an alternation was indeed a feature of Cornish, and that he has settled on a form without any warrant in the texts, he attempts to defend himself by saying that *y* ~ *e* alternation presupposes the Prosodic Shift (KKC21: 122). It does nothing of the sort. Vocalic alternation is everywhere apparent in Welsh, where there has been no Prosodic Shift. In fact vocalic alternation must have been a feature of Old Cornish (it was probably not shown in the orthography), although the shift had not occurred by the Old Cornish period. George is either mistaken here [ID], or possibly he is attempting to distract attention, in order to avoid admitting that his *bywnans* is not Cornish.

George correctly observes that the form *bownans* is nowhere attested in Middle Cornish; and he quotes me in *Cornish Today* where I make the same point. George continues by saying of *bownans* "It is almost irrelevant" (KKC21: 123). I do not understand what exactly George means by "almost irrelevant"; as far as I can see, something is either relevant or it is not. In this present case, however, *bownans* seems to me to be of the greatest significance. *Bownans* does not appear in writing until the seventeenth century, but the pronunciation was certainly in place before that. *Bewnans* became *bownans* in Middle Cornish, for the same reason that *clewes* became *clowes* and *dewthek* became *dowthek*, i.e. because the following [w] rounded the adjacent unrounded [e] to [o]. This rounding is similar to the phenomenon seen, for example, in Indo-European **swepnos* > Latin *somnus* 'sleep' or Indo-European **swesor* > Latin *soror* 'sister', where a contiguous [w] has similarly rounded the vowel—which remained at the same height. Cornish [ew] has become [ow] in *bownans*, but had the word been **bywnans* it would have rounded at the same height and become **buwnans*. *Bownans* is highly relevant because it is further evidence that **bywnans* did not exist. There is a further point to notice with respect to the form *bownans*; see **12.13** below.

It is difficult here, I think, for anyone to deny that Kernowek Kemyn is based on mistaken phonology.

12.08 *clew/clow* 'hear!, hears', *clewes/clowes* 'to hear', etc.
I should like now to examine the existing monosyllabic and disyllabic forms of this verb as they are attested in the traditional language. The phonology in Cornish of the forms *clew* 'hears' and *clewes* 'to hear', *clewaf* 'I hear', etc. is not straightforward. The root vowel was originally /u/; cf. Old Irish *do-cluinethar* 'hears'. We are dealing here with the zero-grade of the Indo-European root **kleu-*. /u/ gave *y* ~ *y* alternation quite regularly in Welsh. In Cornish one might expect *e* ~ *o*, but there is also the question of the possible *i*-affection of *o* > *e* in some of the inflected forms. One thing, however, is certain: since the root

vowel was never /i/, *clyw, *clywes would not be expected in Cornish. I list here under three separate heads the variants of both *clew* and *clewes* as they occur:

12.09 *clyw, clew, clow* 'hear!, hears'

*clyw; cf. *<klyw> in Kernowek Kemyn
No examples are found in traditional Cornish.

clew
a thev a'n nef · clew agan lef OM 1389
a thev a nef · clew agan lef OM 1619
clew galow a'n bobyl ma OM 1832
a clew lemmyn agan lef RD 754
clew agan lef RD 774
cryst clew ov lef · pesaf y weth RD 837
ihesu map ras · clew ow dysyr RD 858
cryst clew of lef · lauar an vr RD 881
me a'th pys clew agan lef RD 2422.

clow
dar ny glov an plos iovden BM 778
Ha my a clov BM 2662
agen attent why a clov BM 2930
why a well haga glow TH 39
eff am clow ve TH 41a
Attend ha clow BK 267
a clow the lef BK 2774
Clow ow lef BK 2812
clow ve dell os benen vas BK 2817
Umma why a glow Christ SA 60
bo yn assentys te a glow CW 654
yea yea me a glow CW 654
te a glow keen nawothow CW 724
clow ge ow leaf CW 1426
me an clow prest ow carma CW 1580.

12.10 *clywes, clewes, clowes* 'to hear', etc.

*clywes, etc. Cf. *<klywes> in Kernowek Kemyn.
No examples are found in traditional Cornish.

clewes, etc.
oll y voth a ve clewys PA 9d
kyns ys boys colyek clewys PA 49b
may clewo leff ihesus whek PA 78d
suel a vynna y clewas PA 79b
ordh en keth re as clewas PA 80b

BEWNANS 'LIFE' AND CLEWES 'TO HEAR'

*Gans hemma ef a **clewas** PA 86*
*yn **clewsons** ow leuerell PA 91b*
*Oll ow cows why an **clewas** PA 95a*
*ganso mar callo **clewas** PA 109c*
*lauar crist pan vo **clewys** PA 109d*
*ha gow bras ganso **clewys** PA 120d*
*na veʒens **clewys** neffre PA 148b*
***clewys** a'n nyl tenewen OM 214*
*pan **clewfyf** vy an tan tyn OM 1351*
*na **clewas** ov voys a vy OM 1436*
*a **clewas** ol y voys ef OM 1487*
*ny vynnyth **clewas** dev ker OM 1523*
*lemyn **clewas** agan lef OM 2027*
*mar **clewvyth** agan guary OM 2134*
*newethow mere **clewes** PC 229*
***clewys** vyth agas desyr PC 309*
*an pryns may hyllyf **clewas** PC 554*
*may **clewas** lyes map bron PC 1256*
*y'n **clewys** ov leuerel PC 1314*
*me a'n **clewas** ov tyffen PC 1573*
*lyes trefeth y'n **clewys** PC 1724*
*a **cleufyth** ov voys yn tyr PC 2026*
*certan yn ta may **clewfo** PC 3063*
*pan **clewys** ow teryfas RD 504*
*ha war ow kyn a'n **clewas** RD 518*
*yn vr na y fyth **clewys** RD 572*
***clewas** y vones sevys RD 930*
*a cowyth me re **clewas** RD 1231*
*an guyryoneth kyn **clewyth** RD 1384*
*agas **clewas** o pur vth RD 1768*
*aga **clewas** RD 1518*
*euth y **clewas** RD 2128*
*pur vth o **clewas** an cry RD 2244*
*vthyk yw **clewas** y lef RD 2340*
*ioy yv gynef the **clewas** RD 2616*
*ay num **clewugh** ov kelwel BM 959.*

clowes, etc.
*ay cowyth ny **clowys** cows BM 191*
*inweth gul dethe **cloweys** BM 806*
*me re **glowes** ov map wek BM 527*
*fatel om**glowugh** omma BM 709*
*in ca[m]bron me re **gloways** BM 730*
*me re **glowes** an den na BM 802*
*pan **glowe** y vos scappys BM 1030*
*del **glowas** lues huny BM 1160*
*us mertherijs del **glowa** BM 1324*
*A serys **clowugh** ov leff BM 1890*

TOWARDS AUTHENTIC CORNISH

del *glowevy* sur myl pas BM 1957
mars yv guir a *glowys* covs BM 2120
ov styward a *glosugh* why BM 2221
Clowys arluth galosek BM 2224
ny *glowys* ken leferel BM 2238
del *glovsugh* ha nyns yv pel BM 2244
prag na *glowys* helma kyns BM 2252
me a *glowes* in 3e pov BM 2394
me re *glowes* galosek BM 2356
Me yv den na yl *clowas* BM 2636
del *glowys* y acontia BM 2765
sav eff ny vyn del *glowys* BM 2876
mur the gul del *glowys* vy BM 2895
del re *glowys* meryasek BM 3102
then guelfoys del *glowys* vy BM 3247
ha henna wy a *clowyth* BM 3318
in nos praga nam *clowyth* BM 3621
ov boys heb y *clowes* lel BM 3709
ny *glowys* gans den genys BM 3971
heb numbyr sul del *clowa* BM 3999
cans pas del *glowys* ha moy BM 4072
gans ihesu y feth *clowys* BM 4299
Ov crossyer me re *glowes* BM 4349
meryasek del *glowa* BM 4357
del *glowa* yv tremenis BM 4370
ny *glowys* den rum lovta BM 4417
why a *glowas* TH 4a
nessa why a *clowas* TH 4a
why a ra *clowas* TH 5
why a *clowas* pandra TH 10
why an *clowes* dyskys TH 21a
Why a *glowas* pana kerensa TH 30
ha mar na vyn nena *clowas* TH 31a
pub tra a ru ve *clowes* TH 35a
ha inweth a *glowas* y dyscans TH 38
a russogh the *glowes* TH 38a
agan pesadow a vith *clowys* TH 39a
tyrmyn nena may fons *clowys* TH 40a
fatell vyn eff agan *clowas* ny TH 41a
Neb a rella agys *clowes* why TH 41a
why a ra *clowas* omma TH 45
why a *clowith* moy TH 46
may ra an tryssa han pesowra aes ahanan ny y *glowas* TH 50a
whya a *clowas* TH 55
fatell ve *clowys* sownde a trompet TH 56a
ny russns *clowas* tomder vith TH 56a
a vynnas *clowas* ow lef BK 2
rag me re'th *clowas* ow ty BK 115
ha gas *clowas* reson da BK 151

BEWNANS 'LIFE' AND *CLEWES* 'TO HEAR'

gans Teuthar pan vo **clowys** BK 489
ny **glowis** *moy in neb tra* BK 516
na ny **glowa**' *byttyth fynn* BK 517
nu'm **cloweth** *neb ow kyny* BK 623
del **clowas** *ve, in neb gwlas* BK 854
ow clowas e lavarow BK 950
Pan **glowaf** *the lavaraw* BK 973
pan e'th **clowas** *ow kylwal* BK 1108
Dar, nu'm **clowyth** BK 1242
a wel corf ny **glowyr** *cous* BK 1272
A wel corf ny **glowyr** *cows* BK 1288
Tra re **glowys** *vackya* BK 1413
Clowas *kethtel* BK 1705
whath ny **glowys** *skovernow* BK 1917
a well corf ny **glowys** *cows* BK 1937
a wel corf ny **glowys** *cows* 1945
Dun the **glowas** *e reson* BK 2082
Pan y's **clowo** BK 2151
pan **glowsyn** *the vos serrys* BK 2612
aban **clowys** *kyns e gows* BK 3132
E coyth thew' bos **clowys** BK 3163
na **glowo** *agys dolors* BK 3262
Pan vo an dewetha gyrryw **clowis** SA 59
mas gwra **clowas** *dew o cowse* SA 62
elathe oll why a **glowas** CW 140
me a **glowas** *awartha* CW 758
neb a **glowses** *owe cana* CW 770
pan **glowa** *an nowethys* CW 1136
theth voice arluth a **glowaf** CW 1166
war tha **glowas** *in torn ma* CW1200
an nowothow pan **glowa** CW 1205
Me a **glowaz** *dro tho an Karack Mean* BF: 25
Me a **glowaz** *lever…* BF: 27
Ha an Gye a **glowhas** RC 23: 177
Pe reeg Herod an matern **clowaz** *hemma* RC 23: 194
Pe reg an gye **clowaz** *an matern* RC 23: 196
En Rama a ve **clowez** *olva* RC 23: 200
Ha me rig **clowaz** *an poble galarou* ACB
tha kanna vee gy el e **glowas** LAM: 224
Me rig scantlower **clowes** LAM: 244.

12.11 Discussion of *clew, clewes*

As I have already mentioned, the root of *clewes* actually exhibited /u/ rather than /i/; there was never /i/ in the stem. George appears unaware of the Celtic etymology of the word and repeatedly speaks about the original /ɪw/ in it. In this section of his book George also goes so far as to acknowledge that I may be right "in the narrow sense" [*sic*] about *clewes*. He adds "because Dr Williams may be right about this one root [*sic*], it does not mean that he is right

133

about the *w*-dipthongs in general" (KKC21: 124). *Clew, clewes* is a verb; the root is quite different matter. George's argument is again reseorting special pleading [SP]. Given that there are difficulties in understanding the development of the verb *clew, clewes*, it seems to me that revivalists have only one course open to them: to spell as the texts spell. To attempt to respell on the basis of one's own theories is surely asking for trouble. Moreover we are compelled to ask ourselves a simple question: if George on his own admission is mistaken about *clewes*, how can we be sure that he is right about everything else? I would remind my readers that Kernowek Kemyn in its first hypostasis wrote <gantjo> 'with him', <tji> 'house', <kerentja> 'love', <wodja> 'after' and <Meryadjek> 'Meryasek.' It was I that demonstrated the inauthenticity of /tj/ and /dj/. Now here also George admits I am right "in the narrow sense" about *clewes*. Since I have discovered two errors in Kernowek Kemyn, it seems odd that George should insist I am wrong about *everything* else.

For George to admit that he himself was mistaken about *clewes*, is at least a step in the right direction. Kernowek Kemyn, we were assured, was based on a rigorous scientific analysis of Cornish by means of computer. It is astonishing that such a scholarly enterprise should have made an elementary mistake, when merely reading the texts to see how they spelt would have prevented any error. Clearly Kernowek Kemyn—even by the inventor's own admission—is not as perfect as was originally canvassed.

12.12 The reason for George's error

To be fair to George there were good reasons for him to have come somewhat unstuck here. In the first place Welsh has *clyw, clywed* and George with his limited knowledge of comparative Celtic did not understand that *clywed* developed from **kluw-* rather than **kliw-*. In the second place, I suspect that Lhuyd's spellings led George astray on this matter. Lhuyd in his semi-phonetic alphabet often uses the graph <y> to render [o] in spoken Cornish. Here are some examples with <o> (<u>) variants from other sources:

Lhuyd's spelling with <y>	Spelling with <o> (<u>)
pylta guel 'considerably better' AB: 222	*polta gwel* BF: 31
anydha 'of it' AB: 222, 223	*anothe* RC 23: 182
Tybm 'hot' AB: 223	*Tubm* AB: 45c
kyḋaz 'fell' AB: 251a	*Kothaz* BF: 15
ybma 'here' AB: 251a x 2, 252a x 2	*obba* BF: 15
a uyraz 'put' AB: 251a	*woraz* BF: 16
a gyzyuaz 'listened' AB: 252a	*gazowas* 'to listen' LAM: 224
kympez 'straight, faithful' AB 253a	*cumpas* LAM:244.

Lhuyd also writes *ha e glyuaz* 'and he heard' AB: 252 and *a klyuaz* 'to hear' AB: 253a. I think it must have been those two examples of *klyuaz* with <y> in Lhuyd's version of *Jowan Chy an Horth* that led George to think that the word contained /ɪw/. George does not appear to have noticed Lhuyd's *ev a vendzha*

BEWNANS 'LIFE' AND CLEWES 'TO HEAR'

klouaz in the story as well. There is in any event no real excuse for adopting *<klywes> in Kernowek Kemyn, since the form is wholly unattested elsewhere in Middle and Late Cornish.

In my view taken together *<bywnans> and *<klywes> are quite enough to vitiate Kernowek Kemyn, even were it correct in most other respects—and, in my view, it is not correct in very much. Again I believe that the impartial observer is compelled to acknowledge that Kernowek Kemyn is based on a mistaken phonology.

12.13 *Kernowek* ~ *Kernewek*

George says that I have emended *Kernewek* to *Kernowek* (KKC21: 128), when in fact I have done no such thing. It is not possible to emend a spurious word and *Kernewek* is an invention. The first occurrence appears to be the form *Cernewek* in LCB: 54. The earliest attested form of the word for 'Cornish' is *Cornowok* from 1572 (well within the Middle Cornish period). The word in Late Cornish always has <ow> or <u> in the second syllable. I recommended <Kernowek>, rather than the revivalists' <Kernewek>, because the change <ew> to <ow> was the smallest alteration I could make in bringing the word to conform with the evidence. I have collected the following examples of 'Cornish' from various sources:

Cornowok Wakelin: 89
Carnoack BF: 25 x 3, 59
Curnooack BF: 25 x 2, 27, 28 x 2, 312
Curnoack BF: 31, LAM: 238
Kernuak BF: 46 x 3, Bilbao MS
Kornooack BF: 48
Kernooak BF: 48
Kernuack LAM: 224
Kernuak LAM: 234
Cornoack LAM: 244.

Both Middle Cornish variants like *clowes, clowys*, etc. and the form *Cornowok* from 1572 are further corroborative evidence (if such were needed) that the Prosodic Shift had already occurred by the Middle Cornish period. If the shift had not occurred, 'to hear' would have been *[kle·wes] and 'Cornish' would have been *[kerne·wek]. Similarly *bewnans* would have been *[be·wnans]. In all three etyma the half-long stressed syllable would have been too powerful to have been rounded by the following [w]. The mere fact that by the Tudor period at the latest 'to hear' in Cornish was *clowes*, 'Cornish' was *Cornowok* and 'life' was almost certainly *bownans*, indicates that the stressed syllable in them all was short. The Prosodic Shift was a *fait accompli* of long standing by the time of our Middle Cornish texts.

Let us look for a moment at the spellings of the following disyllabic and polysyllabic forms in Welsh, Breton, and Kernowek Kemyn:

TOWARDS AUTHENTIC CORNISH

Welsh	Breton	Kernowek Kemyn
bydoedd 'worlds'	*bedoù*	*bysow*
bywiog 'lively'	*bevus*	*bywek*
chwythu 'to blow'	*c'hwezhañ*	*hwytha*
celynnog 'holly grove'	*kelenneg*	*kelynnek*
clywed 'to hear'	*klevout*	*klywes*
cylchog 'circular'	*kelc'hiek*	*kylghyek*
cymysgu 'mingle'	*kemmeskañ*	*kemmyska*
gwlybwr 'liquid'	*glebor*	*glybor*
gwydden 'tree'	*gwezenn*	*gwydhenn*
gwyden 'withe'	*gwedenn*	*gwydenn*
gwynder 'whiteness'	*gwennder*	*gwynnder*
gwyntoedd 'winds'	*gwentoù*	*gwynsow*
gwyryf 'virgin'	*gwerc'hez*	*gwyrghes*
llymder 'keenness'	*lemmder*	*lymmder*
llymu 'to sharpen'	*lemmañ*	*lymma*
llysoedd 'courts'	*lezioù*	*lysyow*
meddygaeth 'medicine'	*mezegiezh*	*medhygieth*
meddyglyn 'mead'	*mezeglen*	*medhyglynn*
melynder 'yellowness'	*melender*	*melynder*
mynnu 'to wish'	*mennout*	*mynnes*
pryfed 'insects'	*prenved*	*pryves*
syched 'thirst'	*sec'hed*	*syghes*
tynder 'tension'	*tennder*	*tynnder*
ynyd 'shrovetide'	*ened*	*ynys*
ynys 'island'	*enez*	*ynys.*

In all these cases the penultimate syllable has <y> in Welsh pronounced [ə], <e> in Breton, and <y> in Kernowek Kemyn, pronounced [ɪ]. There is, however, a notable exception to this pattern:

| *Cernyweg* 'Cornish' | *kerneveg* | *Kernewek.* |

It is quite apparent here that the name *Kernewek* is inconsistent in Kernowek Kemyn from the etymological and orthographical point of view. If George's orthography were really as consistent as he claims it to be, he would spell the word <Kernywek>. Indeed it seems to me a pity that supporters of George's system do not regularly write *Kernywek Kemmyn*, because such a spelling would help to put greater distance between Kernowek Kemyn and less inauthentic varieties of revived Cornish.

12.14 *<gwiw> 'worthy' in Kernowek Kemyn

George believes that in Middle Cornish *gwyw* 'worthy' was pronounced /gwiːw/, i.e. that the vowel was long (i.e. dimoric) /iˑ/. In consequence Kernowek Kemyn spells the word <gwiw>. Unfortunately for George the attested forms do not bear out his understanding of the word. We have

BEWNANS 'LIFE' AND *CLEWES* 'TO HEAR'

examples of the word from the *Ordinalia* to BK, but the word disappears from the language in the sixteenth century, being replaced by *worthy*. The spellings in the texts appear in three different forms: 1) *gwyw*, 2) *gwew* and 3) *gwyf/gwef*. Here are the instances I have been able to collect:

1 gwyw

*yn trevyth y nyn gens **gyw*** 'in nothing were they able' PA 68d
*3e vos cregis te yw **gyw*** 'you are fit to be hanged' PA 129b
***guyw** yv yn len the servye* 'he is worthy to serve thee loyally' OM 2608
***guyw** yv prest servye yn ta* 'it is always worthwhile serving well' OM 2776
*dre the voth ken nag of **gvyw*** 'through your will though I am not worthy PC 481 [rhymes with *blew* 'hair']
*en tas dev roy thy'n bos **gwyw*** 'God the Father grant us to be worthy' PC 829 [rhymes with *hythyw* 'today']
*bos y seruont nagos **guyw*** 'that you are not worthy to be his servant' RD 1005 [rhymes with *yw* 'is']
*the vos yn dor nynsyw **guyw*** 'it is not worthy to be in the earth' RD 2317 [rhymes with *yw* 'is']
*nyng ew **guyw** the vorogath* 'is not worthy to ride' BK 929
*Lemmyn, Ke, ow mata **guyu*** 'Now, Kea, my worthy friend' BK 1150 [rhymes with *ew* 'is']
*th'e begy ken nyns of **guyw*** 'though I am not worthy to pray for him' BK 1493 [rhymes with *ew* 'is']
***Guyw** ew ow arluth heb flows* 'Without any trifling is my lord worthy' BK 1494
*ha **guyw** the wormoladow* 'and worthy to be praised' BK 1629
*a ve **guyw*** 'it was worthily' BK 2017 [rhymes with *ew* 'is'].

2 gwew

*Du ha den ow Arluth **guew*** 'God and man, my worthy Lord' BK 204 [rhymes with *ew* 'is']
*ha **guew** the wormoladow* 'and worthy to be praised' BK 835
*ef a vith ow mata **guew*** 'he will be my worthy friend' BK 893 [rhymes with *ew* 'is']
*ow arluth **guew*** 'my worthy lord' BK 1320 [rhymes with *sew* 'will follow']
***Guew** os the vlam* 'You are worthy of blame' BK 2205
*nyng ew **guew** the varogath* 'is not worthy to ride into battle' BK 3227.

3 gwyf

***gweff** yw 3e vones lezys* 'he is worthy to be killed' PA 95b
***gvyf** os the vos wolcummys* 'worthy art thou to be welcomed' BM 226
*maria **guyff** nynsen vy* 'Mary, worthy I was not' BM 3700.

The examples with <y> and <e> alike rhyme with words in [ɪw], i.e. *yw/ew* 'is', *hythyw* 'today' and *sew* 'will follow'. This in itself implies that the vowel was [ɪw] rather than [iˑw]. Moreover the form <guew> indicates clearly that the vowel is short and has been lowered from [ɪ] to [e]. These are two arguments to suggest that the Prosodic Shift has affected the word and that *gwyw* as early as the *Ordinalia* had a variant [gwew].

137

TOWARDS AUTHENTIC CORNISH

The spellings <gweff> and <guyff> in PA and BM contain a geminate final <ff>, which is perhaps sufficient to show that the vowel is short. The form <gweff>, like <guew> clearly has a short vowel that has been lowered to [e]. It is probable that *gweff/guyff* is a back-formation from a comparative **gwywha* > *gweffa* (cf. *ha me **gweffa** the vos punyshes* 'and I more worthy to be punished' CW 587). Alternatively *gweff/guyff* may simply be a form that has arisen before a following [h], e.g. **gwyw ha worthy* > *gwyf ha worthy*. Whichever explanation is correct, there can be little doubt that the vowel was short. Had *gwyw* really been */gwi·w/*, as George appears to believe, it the comparative would have been **gwifa*; the analogical simplex would have been **gwif* <guyf>. *Gweff* in PA, *guew* in BK and *gweffa* in CW show that the word had [e] rather than /i·/. We can be quite certain that the vowel in *gwyw* 'worthy' in Middle Cornish was short. Which is the same as saying that the Prosodic Shift had occurred. Kernowek Kemyn is based on mistaken phonology.

CHAPTER 13
Du 'black' and *Dew/Du* 'God' (KKC21: 110-19)

13.00 George's discussion of *iw, yw, ew*
George has a long section in his book on the vowels in the forms *lu, lliw, lyw* and *lew* and in it he discusses the two spellings for 'God' in Middle Cornish, i.e. <dew>, <dev> on the one hand and <du> on the other. I will below answer his discussion of the words *dew* 'God' and *du* 'black' and 'God'. I will not trouble to answer the rest of his chapter. This is for a number of reasons.

In the first place, I cannot understand it. His arguments are perhaps too subtle for me—or possibly just a trifle confused. In the second place, as far as I understand what George is saying, I object most strongly to his evidence (of this more below). In the third place, I notice that in Fig. 17.5 (three quarters of the whole page) George sets out the development of the four vocalic sequences /yː/, /iw/, /ɪw/, and /ew/ in Welsh and Breton. It is George's custom, whenever he is in difficulties, to invoke Welsh and Breton. But the two languages, as I have said above, are irrelevant. We are talking about the phonology of Cornish, a language with its unique and particular history. If George had paid less attention to Breton, Kernowek Kemyn might possibly have been closer to traditional Cornish.

Let me now explain what it is in his arguments that I found so troublesome. I will start with the least important.

13.01 First objections: *lew* 'lion'
In his arguments George cites the Cornish word *lew* 'lion'. *Lew*, however, is not a Cornish word at all. The word *leu* 'leo' [lion] is attested in OCV and Lhuyd quotes the word from Old Cornish (AB: 78a). Otherwise the word is unknown. In Middle Cornish the word for 'lion' is *lyon* (see **18.49** below). I dislike George's lexical purism in his dictionaries and much prefer using words that are actually attested in Cornish. I would therefore in revived Cornish use the attested Middle Cornish word *lyon* in preference to the hypothetical **lew*. In the present case, however, it is not a question of lexical preference, but of phonology. I am quite prepared to discuss words that occur in Cornish. I do not wish, however, to say anything about spurious words that are not part of the language and for which we have no evidence at all.

13.02 Second objection: George's misrepresentation of Welsh phonology
George informs us (Fig. 17.5, KKC21: 114) that Welsh has three diphthongs containing a high front vowel + w: /iw/, /ɪw/ and /ew/. This is simply not true. Northern Welsh has only two diphthongs of this kind: /iw/ and /ew/. The third diphthong which George gives as /ɪw/, for example, in *llyw* 'rudder'

does not contain /ɪ/, but /ɨ/. Welsh has two high front vowels /i/ and /e/. The diphthong in South Welsh in *llyw* is /iw/, i.e. it is exactly the same vowel as in *lliw* 'colour'. In North Welsh the diphthong is /ɨw/, that is to say, a high centralized vowel /ɨ/ followed by /w/. Indeed North Welsh developed the phoneme /ɨ/ because otherwise the high front region of the vowel system would have been overcrowded. Southern Welsh has conflated earlier /ɪ/ and /i/ as /i/, whereas Northern Welsh has maintained a threefold opposition of long high vowels by shifting the middle member of the series backward in the mouth. It has done so precisely because three high front phonemes are too many and any system which contains them is inherently unstable. Northern Welsh actually avoids the three-fold opposition which George ascribes to Cornish. There is therefore no Brythonic language which maintains the series /i /, /ɪ/, and /e/—apart, of course, from Kernowek Kemyn. It is regrettable enough, that George has imposed an improbable and unstable vocalic system onto Cornish. But to claim that the same improbable system exists in Welsh is disingenuous.

13.03 Third objection: George's misrepresentation of my views

In Fig. 17.6 (KKC21: 115) George sets out what he describes at "the fate of the four phonemes" i.e. his /y:/, /iw/, /ɪw/, and /ew/. I question whether it is correct to speak of diphthongs as phonemes, but I will leave that. What I object to here is that George implies that I believe that all four fell together. I have never said or written anything of the kind. In absolute final I do believe that /y:/ and /ɪw/ fell together as /ɪw/. I do not believe that Middle Cornish distinguished between historic short /i/ and short /ɪ/. Both in my view, were phonetically [ɪ]. I also believe that /ɪ/ and /e/ were not always kept separate. This accounts for the hesitation in spelling in the texts between *tryga* 'to dwell' and *trega*, for example, or *yw* 'is' and *ew*. There seems to me to have been a certain degree of variation between /ew/ and /ɪw/ finally; cf. *gwyw* and *guew*. How far this variation went, I do not know.

George also points out that the words *bew* 'alive', *Dew* 'God' and *pleu* 'parish' are written with long <êu> by Lhuyd. I am quite well aware of the long vowel in *plêu* and *Dêu*, etc. and indeed I refer to it both in *Cornish Today* and my article on pre-occlusion.

I believed when I wrote *Cornish Today*, that Middle Cornish had only two diphthongs /ɪw/ and /ew/, and that on occasion the distinction between them was not maintained. I was careful (*pace* George) not to say that all the diphthongs fell together. There were two diphthongs and they were sometimes confused:

> Kernowek Kemmyn posits three diphthongs /iw/, /ɪw/ and /ew/, when Middle Cornish had two only (or in some cases only one) (CT: §13.39).

This is still my opinion. There was in Middle Cornish no distinction between /iw/ and /ɪw/. There were at most two diphthongs. Moreover according to

DU 'BLACK' AND DEW/DU 'GOD'

George's Fig. 17.6 (KKC21: 117) Lhuyd spells *bêu* 'alive', *Dêu* 'God', *blêu* 'hair' and *têu* 'fat' in exactly the same way; but *bêu* and *Dêu* historically had *yw*, whereas *blêu* and *têu* had *ew*. This was precisely the point that I made in *Cornish Today*: in some cases there is only one spelling, and therefore one pronunciation, for the two diphthongs.

13.04 *Pyw/pew* 'who' (**piw* in Kernowek Kemyn)

In order to show that Kernowek Kemyn *<piw> 'who?', for example, had a different diphthong from, say, *Dew* 'God', George cites in Fig. 17.6 some of Lhuyd's spellings with <iu>, in particular *piu* 'who', *liu* 'colour' and *diu* 'black'. *Diu* was originally not a diphthong and is hardly relevant here; though it will be highly relevant in the next section. *Liu* 'colour' does not survive into Tudor Cornish because it is replaced by *color*, e.g.

> *orth agan payntia ny in mes in* **colors** 'painting us in colours' TH 7a
> **colorys** *cler lvn a whekter* 'bright colours full of delight' BK 1712-13.

The last attestation of *lyw* 'colour' known to me is *ha frutes teke aga lew* 'and fruits, fair their colours' at CW 1051. Here *lew* (Kernowek Kemyn *liw*) rhymes with *nag ew* 'is not' at CW 1049 (Kernowek Kemyn *nag yw*). Neither spelling nor rhyme is much support for George's view that the word contained [iˑw].

If we look at how the diphthong in *pyw* 'who' (*<piw> in Kernowek Kemyn) is attested in the Tudor and Late Cornish texts we find the following:

A **pyw** 'who?'
me a leuer **pyv** *ew hy* BM 307
pyv *ens y suer* BM 1791
pyv *ylly an rema boys* BM 1797
agen epscop thynny **pyv** *a ve* BM 2691
pyv *a veth epscop in lel* BM 2702
pyv *a vo epscop thynny* BM 2708
pyv *a vyn ken leferel* BM 2714
pyv *a vo epscop sacrys* BM 2869
Hov seris **pyv** *yv in tre* BM 3301
pyv *a ros dywhy lescyans* BM 3463
pyv *re duth thymo ome* BM 3678
pyv *an iovle revue oma* BM 3719
pyv *us oma devethys* BM 4039
pyw *a thysquethas thyso* CW 872
Piua *ar medh an dzhei?* BF: 18 (Lhuyd)
Pîu *a 'ryg an bad-ober?* BF: 18 (Lhuyd)
Piu *a 'ryg an bad-ober* BF: 18 (Lhuyd)
Re Farîa **piua** *glow vi* BF: 19 (Lhuyd)
Quis?... Who? which?... C[ornish] **Piua** AB: 135a (Lhuyd)
Piua? *Who?* AB: 244c (Lhuyd)
Piua *yu an dén-na Who is that man?* AB: 244c (Lhuyd).

B **pew** 'who?'
pew a yll gull glan TH 7
pew vs ahanow why TH 11
pew vs in agan mysk TH 28a
pew vs in agan misk TH 28a
pew ew an guyde han gouernar an eglos TH 36
Pew vsy ow cows TH 43a
So pew a leverough why TH 44
pew a rug hemma TH 57
Ne ren vry pew a's pewa BK 100
pew o e das? BK 209
saw pew ew ny attendys BK 214
Pew a vo… BK 663
Ny won i'n bys pew a'th feth BK 1198
dusquethas unwyth pew of BK 2068
ynweth ow gwelas pew uge ow despisea SA 59
Pew a laver an gallus SA 59
ny wraf vry warbyn pewa CW 430
pew ostashe es in wethan CW 548
pewa abell yw lethys CW 1248
pew osta lavar thymma CW 1593
pewa te yw cayne mab the adam CW 1601
pew athe wrug ge progowther CW 2346
mar nyz medra dheffa previ peu a 'ryg an bad-ober BF: 18 (Lhuyd)
Peua ez enna en bar' Deu BF: 19 (Lhuyd)
Pew vedna why gawas rag seera rag guz flo ACB.

Lhuyd is George's only evidence that <iw> and <ew> are kept separate. It is clear from the above examples, however, that Lhuyd writes both <piu> and <peu> for 'who?', i.e. that he does not distinguish the two. George in his Fig. 17.6 implies that Lhuyd keeps the two separate and that *piu* is Lhuyd's only form. It is also clear that the word for 'who?' in Middle and Late Cornish is either *pyw* or *pew*. Or to put it another way, in *pyw* 'who?' the diphthong is either *yw* [ɪw] or *ew* [ew]. This was exactly my point in *Cornish Today* and George would, I think, have great difficulty in disproving it from the examples in Lhuyd—to say nothing of the other examples in the above lists.

If 'who?' is either *pyw* [pɪw] or *pew* [pew], we are forced to conclude that the vowel is no longer /iˑw/ but /ɪw/—alternating with /ew/. That is the same as saying that the Prosodic Shift has already operated in Middle Cornish.

13.05 *Du* 'God' and the Prosodic Shift

A remarkable aspect of traditional Cornish orthography is that the word for 'God' is frequently written <du>. The word is so spelt in PA, BM and TH, where the *Ordinalia* and CW prefer to spell it <dev> or <dew>. There are exceptions in several texts, however. BK, with its mixed orthography, exhibits both spellings, though it shows a marked preference for <du> over <dew>. My explanation for the spelling <du> is simple. *Du* is the Cornish word for 'black',

DU 'BLACK' AND DEW/DU 'GOD'

which before the Prosodic Shift was presumably pronounced [dyː]. This we could interpret as a trimoric vowel /dy·y/. As a result of the shift, the nucleus was shortened from [y·] to [y]. As it shortened, the nucleus untensed slightly and thus lowered a little. What had been a simple long vowel, now became a diphthong, where the less tense nucleus was lower than the more tense coda. The two parts began then to differentiate themselves further, the nucleus unrounding and the coda unfronting. The outcome was [ɪu] or [ɪw]. The process here is somewhat similar to the development in contemporary English. Some speakers, for example, pronounce *afternoon* as [ɑːftə'nɪwn] rather than [ɑːftə'nuːn].

We know [ɪu] or [ɪw] was indeed the outcome of final /yː/, because Lhuyd tells us three times that the Cornish for 'black' is *diu* (AB: 44a s.v. *Ater*; AB: 99a s.v. *Niger*; AB: 295a s.v. *Niger*). We have corroboration in the stanza from RD. The jailer and his servant are attempting unsuccessfully to bury Pilate, but his body jumps out of the earth and terrifies them. The servant then says:

pur harth dun thotho wharre
gorryn ef yn beth arte
du yw y lyw
me a grys ynno y sef
mar syw abarth dev a nef
bo ken deaul yw

'Very courageously let us approach him soon.
Let us put him in the grave again.
Black is his colour.
I believe he will stay there
if he is on the side of God in heaven;
otherwise he is a devil' (RD 2099-2105).

The jailer and his servant are a commonplace in the medieval Cornish plays. The same two characters occur in BK. This is obviously a slapstick part of the action and the diction is intended to be humorous. I assume that the third line in the above stanza has a double internal rhyme: [dɪw ɪw ɪ lɪw]. This line is also evidence that *lyw* 'colour' (Kernowek Kemyn <liw>) also had a short vowel, rather than a half-long one. That *lyw* was pronounced [lɪw] is corroborated by *ha frutes teke aga lew* in CW, to which we have referred. Notice also that *lew* 'colour' in CW rhymes with *ew* 'is', just as *lyw* 'colour' rhymes with *yw* 'is' in the present passage in RD.

If *du* 'black' was pronounced [dɪw] after the Prosodic Shift, *dev, dew* 'God' (Welsh *Duw*) was similarly pronounced. As we have already seen Middle and Late Cornish do not distinguish *pyw* from *pew*, or *gwyw* from *guew*. In Middle Cornish <du> is a perfectly good spelling for God, pronounced [dɪw] or [dew]; indeed it is an excellent spelling for the scribes, because it is shorter than <dev> or <dew> and the word for 'God' is of very frequent occurrence.

13.06 Further etyma in <-u>, <-ew>

There are further monosyllables apart from *du* 'God' in Middle Cornish that are spelt with either a final <u> or <ev>, <ew>. Some contain historical *ew* others historical *u*. In those cases where the final was historically *-ew* I assume that the scribes found <u> an acceptable spelling. Where the word had etymological final *-u*, the spellings with <ew> suggest that the word was in fact pronounced with [ew] or [ɪw]. The etyma with historic *-ew* and *-u* include the following:

A
1) *gew* 'woe' (Welsh *gwae*)
2) *gew* 'spear' (Welsh *gwayw*)
3) *glew* 'sharp, keen' (Welsh *glew*)
4) *pyw/pew* 'who'. The diphthongal spellings in later Cornish of this word have been cited at **13.04** above.
5) *plew* 'parish' (Welsh *plwy*, Breton *plou* < Latin *plebe(em)*). The vowel in Old Cornish was <ui>. This by the Middle Cornish period has metathesized to **plyw/plew*; cf. *yw/ew* 'is' from earlier **wy* < **ui*.

B
1) *du* 'black' (Welsh *du*, Breton *du*)
2) *tru* 'sorrow; alas' (Welsh *tru* 'sad', Breton *truek* 'wretched')
3) *tu* 'side' (Welsh *tu*, Breton *tu*).

I now list from the texts the spelling variants of *dew* 'God' and of these further words in <ew>/<u>. My examples are not exhaustive.

'GOD'
dew
*Adam del of **dev** a ras* 'Adam, as I am God of grace' OM 73
*arloth **dev** a'n nef an tas* 'the Lord God of heaven, the Father' OM 105
*bones ov fegh moy yn ta es mercy **dew*** 'that my sin is assuredly greater than the grace of God' OM 591-92
*mar sos map **dev** awartha* 'if you are the son of God above' PC 60
*laver **dev** maga del wra* 'how the word of God nourishes' PC 71
*del yw guyr **thyw*** 'as he is true God' RD 1018
*gans **dew** omma* 'by God here' CW 159
*avel **dewe** sure heb parow* 'like God surely without peer' CW 186.
du
*yn tre **du** ha pehadur* 'between God and sinner' PA 8b
*mab **du** ha den yw kyffris* 'he is son of God and man as well' PA 8d
*rag ef o pur wyr map **du*** 'for he was very truly the son of God' RD 1248
*mers yv gans **du** plygadow* 'if it is pleasing to God' BM 14
*Benath **du** 3ys meryasek* 'God's blessing to you, Meriasek' BM 31
*dyl vyn **Du** a'th prennas ker* 'as God wishes who redeemed thee dearly' BK 22
*gans gras **Du**, war ow ena* 'with the grace of God, upon my soul' BK 60.

DU 'BLACK' AND *DEW*/*DU* 'GOD'

'BLACK'
diu
Corn[ish] *Mola **dhiu*** glossing *Black-bird* AB: 13c
Ater...Black, Dark...C[*ornish*] ***Diu*** AB: 44a
November C[*ornish*] *Mîz **diu*** AB: 100b
*Hor' **diu**, A black ram; Davaz **dhiu**, A black sheep* AB: 243c.
du
*shyndyys of gans cronek **dv*** 'I have been wounded by a black toad' OM 1778
***du** yw y lyw* 'black is his hue' RD 2101.

'WOE, PAIN'
gew
*saw the face my ny welaf sur er ov **gevw*** 'but thy face I do not see indeed to my sorrow' OM 588-89
*my an knouk ef er y **wev*** 'I will thump him for his pain' PC 2085
*Gas cres, rag den melygas os er the **weu*** 'Silence, for you are an accursed man to your detriment' BK 110-11
*than noer veys er agen **gew*** 'to the world for our pain' CW 1043.
gu
*pur wyr ef a'n gevyth **gv*** 'very truly he will have woe' PC 963
*yn guetha prys er y **gv*** 'unfortunately for his sorrow' PC 1130
*Te a 'vith **gv*** 'you will suffer woe' BK 326.

'SPEAR'
gew
***gew** a ve yn y ʒewle gans an eʒewon gorris* 'a spear had been put in his hands by the Jews' PA 217c
*en **gew** lym ef a bechye* 'the sharp spear he thrust' PA 218c
*me an gweall prest gans **gew*** 'I see him always with a spear' CW 1970.
gu
*gans **guv** the wane an gal* 'with a spear to pierce the scoundrel' PC 2917
*pan fo **guv** yn y thule* 'when there is a spear in his hands' PC 2922
*pan wylys gorre an **gu** yn golon dre'n tenewen* 'when I saw the spear put through the side into the heart' RD 1245-46
*hag a dretha gans ow **gu*** 'and go through them with my spear' BK 1480.

'SHARP'
glew
*ow bommyn yv marthys **glev*** 'my blows are remarkably painful' PC 2088
*curyn a spern lym ha **glev*** 'a crown of thorns sharp and keen' RD 2582.
glu
*hag aspy ahas ha **glv*** 'and spy bitterly and sharp' OM 2062
*y astevith peynys **glu*** 'they will have sharp pains' BM 765
*Theugh e tof ve **glu** ha lym* 'To you I come bitter and sharp' BK 3204.

TOWARDS AUTHENTIC CORNISH

'WHO'
pew
pyw a thysquethes thy'so 'who showed you?' OM 261
pyv henna my agas peys 'who is that, I beg you' PC 784
saw pyw a vyn leuerel 'but who will say?' RD 589
pew vs ahanow why 'who is there of you?' TH 11
pew o e das? 'who was his father?' BK 209.
pu
pu a woras yt colon cows yn delma worth iustis 'who put it in your heart to speak thus to a judge?' PA 81d
en grows pu elle ʒy don 'who would be able to carry the cross' PA 160c
ʒeworth an beth an meyn ma ʒynny pu an ommelys 'from the tomb this stone who removed it for us?' PA 253d
pu reg laule theese 'who told you?' RC 23: 179.

'PARISH'
plew
ha anya holl tre, bo holl plew, Ea, holl pow 'and disturb a whole town, or whole parish, yes, a whole country' TH 25a.
plu
an antecryst yn lyes plu 'the Antichrist in many parishes' RD 247
hag a wel the lyes plu 'and in the sight of many parishes' RD 2584
bysy vye ol an blu rak y wythe 'all the parish would have a job to guard him' RD 2105-06.

'PITY, WOE'
trew
my re'n collas quyt dretho may canaf trew 'I have lost quite by it so that I sing "alas"' PC 149-50
Pandra rama? Tru, treu, trew! 'What shall I do? Alas, alas, alas!' BK 1018
ogh ogh trew ny re behas 'Oh, oh, alas, we have sinned!' CW 852.
tru
tru a thu elhas elhas 'woe, o God, alas, alas!' PA 246b
ow mornyngh vyth ogh ha tru 'my lamentation will be "alas" and "woe"' RD 438
Pandra rama? Tru, treu, trew! 'What shall I do? Alas, alas, alas!' BK 1018
Gove rag spyt! Tru, a Thew 'Woe is me for pain! Pity, O God!' BK 3200.

'SIDE'
tew
gwayte ow gworria war bub tewe 'be careful to worship me upon every side' CW 49
domynashon yn tew ma 'Domination on this side' CW 56
me a gomannd war bup tew 'I command on every side' CW 138
ny gavaf omma neb tew 'I shall not find here on any side' CW 1045
sor dew ha trub[e]ll pub tew 'the wrath of God and trouble on every side' CW 1256.

DU 'BLACK' AND DEW/DU 'GOD'

tu
*ha'n mor a pup **tu** thethe* 'and the sea on all sides of them' OM 1689
*war **tu** dylarg daras yn* 'behind a narrow door' OM 961
*treys ha dyvlef a pup **tu*** 'feet and hands on all sides' PC 2937
ny allaf guelas an fu anotho ef yn nep tv 'I cannot see sight of him on any side' RD 741-42
*ow yskerans in pub **tu*** 'my enemies on every side' BK 2027.

Notice also *y a **drewe*** 'they kept on spitting' PA 196c but *me a **tru** sur vn clotte bras* 'I shall indeed spit a large clot' PC 1399.

I think any reasonable person would conclude that the variation in spelling here between <dew> and <du>, <gew> and <gu>, etc., is just that—a variation in spelling, and that the words themselves are the same, whichever spelling is used. We are to conclude therefore that *du* and *dew*, *gu* and *gew*, *tu* and *tew* are pronounced identically in Middle Cornish. This means that /y:/ and /ɪw/ have fallen together as /ɪw/. But /y:/ has fallen together with /ɪw/ only because of the Prosodic Shift, whose effects are seen in the earliest Middle Cornish.

13.07 Rhymes

Not only are words in final *-ew* and *-yw* spelt with <u>, they and words with original final *-u* rhyme together throughout the texts. Here are a handful of examples.

tu 'side' ~ *glv* 'sharp' OM 2061 & 2062
glev 'sharp' ~ *tru* 'alas' PC 2088 & 2089
a's pew 'owns' ~ *a'y tu* 'on his side' PC 2858 & 2859
guv 'spear' ~ *tu* 'side' RD 431 & 432
y thu 'his God' ~ *tu* 'side' BM 1914 & 1915
gu 'woe' ~ *trew* 'alas' BK 1015 & 1018
te ywe 'thou art' ~ *tewe* 'side' CW 48 & 49
dew 'God' ~ *tew* 'side' CW 138 & 139
tew 'side' ~ *bew* 'alive' CW 1256 & 1258.

Unstressed *-u* will also rhyme with words in *-ew* and *-yw*. This is exactly parallel with the phenomenon we noted at **9.01** above, when unstressed *-y* rhymes with *joy* 'joy' and *moy* 'more'. Presumably in order to make the rhyme, unstressed *-u* [y] had to be given an unnaturally emphatic and lengthened pronunciation *[y:]. This in turn, like other examples of original final [y:], was pronounced [ɪw]. The emphatic and lengthened pronunciation of unstressed vowels is comparable with a similar practice in English rhyme, when an unstressed final rhyming [i] is lengthened and given greater stress than normal, becoming [i:]. A good example occurs in the line in "Rudolf the Red-Nosed Reindeer" which says "You'll go down in historee" ['hɪstoˈriː].

Here are some examples of *-yw* and *-ew* words rhyming with final unstressed *-u* [y]:

virtu 'virtue' ~ *yw* 'is' ~ *lyw* 'colour' ~ *gyw* 'worthy' PA 68
Ihesu 'Jesus' ~ *gyw* 'worthy' ~ *du* 'God' ~ *yw* 'is' PA 129
Iheus 'Jesus' ~ *tu* 'side' ~ *lu* 'host' ~ *du* 'God' PA 163
jhesu 'Jesus' ~ *vertu* 'virtue' OM 2635 & 2636
ihesu 'Jesus' ~ *dev* 'God' PC 1693 & 1694
tru 'alas' ~ *ihesu* 'Jesus' ~ *vertu* 'virtue' ~ *tu* 'side' PC 2931-2938
ihesu 'Jesus' ~ *hythev* 'today' ~ *tu* 'side' ~ *fvu* 'view' RD 463-469
vertew 'virtue' ~ *dew* 'God' CW 8 & 11.

13.08 George's errors of fact

It seems to me that the evidence of the above spellings and rhymes is overwhelming. *Dew* 'God' and *du* 'black' are pronounced in exactly the same way and in consequence the Cornish scribes often wrote <du> for <dew> or <dev>. The same phonetic development explains spellings like <glv> 'sharp' for *glew*, <tew> 'side' for *tu*, <pu> 'who' for *pew* and <plu> 'parish' for *plew*. George, however, refuses to accept that this argument is true, for to do so would be to acknowledge that the Prosodic Shift was a *fait accompli* in Middle Cornish.

Before I discuss George's explanation for the spelling <du>, etc., I should like to point out two small errors on his part. George claims that *Stewart* and *Stuart* are two ways to write the same name—though I am not exactly sure what his point is here. He does not appear to realize that Stuart as the name of the royal house is not English, but French. It was adopted by Mary Queen of Scots in the French court, when she was married to Francis II (†1544). It is not therefore relevant in any discussion of variant spellings in English.

George makes a more important error of fact when discussing Middle Cornish orthography. He says we have only one example in Middle Cornish of <ew> to denote /y:/ i.e. *trew* at PC 150, where, he says, it is so written to give an eye-rhyme with *tergwyth hythew* at line 147. He is, I believe, mistaken here. George has overlooked *ogh ogh* **trew** *ny re behas* at CW 852, where the word is not required to rhyme with anything. Of course, George did not know about the remarkable line *Pandra rama? Tru,* **treu, trew***!* at BK 1018. I am astonished, however, that he should say that there is only one example of <ew> for original /y:/, when there are several examples of the graph so used in CW. At the risk of become tedious I will now list all those examples I can find in Middle Cornish of <ew> for etymological final /y:/; I put the historical spelling in square brackets after the reference.

The graph <ew> used for historical final /y:/ in Middle Cornish
[*George can find one example only*]
  may canaf **trew** PC 150 [tru]
  Tru, **treu, trew** BK 1018 [tru]

DU 'BLACK' AND DEW/DU 'GOD'

trew ny re behas CW 852 [tru]
war bub tewe CW 49 [tu]
yn tew ma CW 56 [tu]
war bub tew CW 138 [tu]
neb tew CW 1045 [tu]
pub tew CW 1256 [tu]
pub tew CW 1971 [tu]
war bub tew CW 2142 [tu].

Given that there are only two common etyma in Middle Cornish that had etymological final /y:/, ten examples of them spelt with <ew> is significant. It implies that /ew/, /ɪw/ and /y:/ are pronounced the same way in the language. Notice also the curious spelling <tw> 'side' at PC 52, where the word rhymes with *dew* 'God' at PC 49.

13.09 George's explanation of <du> for *dew*, etc.

It is quite apparent that *Dew* 'God' was pronounced the same way as *du* 'black' in Middle Cornish and *tu* 'side' was pronounced like *tew* 'fat'. In order to explain this away George relies, as often, on special pleading. The following exchange occurs between him and Dunbar

> **P.D.** What do you make of the argument invoking rhymes?
>
> **K.G.** In a word weak. In each of the four categories of words (i.e. /y:/, /iw/, /ɪw/ and /ɛw/ finally in stressed syllables), there were fewer than half a dozen words which could be used. The use of unstressed syllables helped a bit, but in general, the paucity of perfect rhymes forced the composers of the plays to use near-perfect ones instead. We have already seen the fact that two words were rhymed does not mean that the rhymes were perfect. The subject matter meant that *dew* 'God' and *ihesu* 'Jesu' frequently featured as rhyming words; they were rhymed with each other, but such rhymes were not perfect. Even so, if you analyse the rhymes, you find that whereas /y:/, /iw/, and /ɪw/ were fairly often rhymed, there was more reluctance to rhyme these with /ɛw/.
>
> **P.D** Do you agree with the second argument?
>
> **K.G.** I take issue with the word "identically". I would prefer to say that the pronunciation of /ɪw/ and /y:/ were so close that scribes were sometimes confused when writing the former.
>
> **P.D** But not the latter?
>
> **K.G.** No; a curious feature of the confusion is that it is only one way. <u> was sometimes used to denote /ɪw/; I can find only one example of <ew> being used to denote /y:/.
>
> **P.D.** Which is that?
>
> **K.G.** The line *may canaf trew* at PC. 150. Here *tru* 'alas' has been written *trew* in order to make an eye-rhyme with *hythew* 'today' three lines before (KKC21: 113).

TOWARDS AUTHENTIC CORNISH

There are, as we have seen, ten examples of <ew> for original /y:/ (Middle Cornish [ɪw]) in the texts. Note, however, George's special pleading: "the pronunciations of /ɪw/ and /y:/ were so close that scribes were sometimes confused when writing the former" [SP] and "a curious feature of the confusion is that it is only one way" [SP]. There was, of course, no confusion. The Middle Cornish scribes were not fools. They wrote <du> for *dew*, because *dew* and *du* 'black' were identical in pronunciation. The same is true for the pairs *gew/gu* 'woe', *gew/gu* 'spear', *glew/glu* 'keen', *pew/pu* 'who', *plew/plu* 'parish', *trew/tru* 'pity' and *tew/tu* 'side'. The spellings alternate, because the pronunciation is identical.

George seems to have forgotten that the argument he is questioning concerns rhymes. It is quite legitimate to claim, as George does, that some rhymes in Middle Cornish were imperfect or eye-rhymes. We have, unfortunately, no way of knowing which rhymes were perfect and which were not, without knowing the precise pronunciation of the rhyming words—and the pronunciation of the rhyming words is the matter in question. Rhyming words are only part of the argument. Rhymes are one thing; spelling is another. Poets can use merely adequate, rather than perfect, rhymes. When a scribe consistently writes etymon X as though it were etymon Y, there is a presumption that X and Y are identical in pronunciation. We, however, have eight pairs of etyma that have two attested spellings: *dew/du*, *gew/gu* 'woe', *gew/gu* 'spear', *glew/glu*, *pew/pu*, *plew/pu*, *trew/tru*, *tew/tu*. Moreover Lhuyd tells us that *du* 'black' is *diu*. It seems to me that we have a very strong case indeed that historic final /y:/ has fallen together with /ɪw/ as /ɪw/. That is the same as saying that the Prosodic Shift had affected the earliest Middle Cornish. Kernowek Kemyn is based on a mistaken phonology.

CHAPTER 14
Pre-occlusion (KKC21: 54-63)

14.00 Introductory remarks
I do not intend to answer George's discussion of pre-occlusion at length. This is for several reasons. First, I have published an article on the question in *Studia Celtica** and I have little to add to what I said there. Secondly George's approach to pre-occlusion was not part of my original criticism of Kernowek Kemyn. Since pre-occlusion is not actually written, it does not form part of the reworking of Cornish orthography undertaken by George. I cannot criticize what is not apparent. Kernowek Kemyn, is, however, inconsistent on the question of pre-occlusion and I shall discuss this briefly below.

My last reason for not wishing to answer George's analysis of pre-occlusion, is that it does not seem to merit an answer. In his Fig. 10.6 on page 61 George sets out what he believes to be my understanding of pre-occlusion. The sample words he uses are **kann* 'white', **kannav* 'I bleach', *kan* 'song' and *kanav* 'I sing'. Neither **kann* 'white' nor **kannav* 'I bleach' is attested in Middle Cornish. *Can* occurs once in Old Cornish, in the expression *bara can* 'panis albus' in OCV. **Canna* 'to bleach' is a spurious word based on Welsh and Breton cognates. I have never used either etymon in any of my discussion of pre-occlusion and I certainly am not inclined to do so. I am willing to discuss the phonology of Cornish as it is represented in the surviving texts. I will not engage in any discussion based on fictitious etyma.

It seems to me that George may not understand pre-occlusion entirely. Certainly I find his section dealing with the question difficult to follow. I believe that Kernowek Kemyn's approach to pre-occlusion is mistaken in both fact and theory. I will deal systematically with George's errors and incorrect data in the next section. Before I do so, I should like to summarize what I said in my article in *Studia Celtica* and which I see no reason to retract. I believe the following:

1   Pre-occlusion was a direct result of the Prosodic Shift, replacing as it did the opposition between unlenited/lenited sonant with an opposition based on intensity.
2   Western dialects of Cornish maintained a distinction between historic /n/ and /nː/ which was lost for the most part in more easterly dialects.
3   Easterly dialects *per contra* lowered vowels before original /nː/. This explains the opposition between *benneth/bedneth* ~ *banneth*.

---

*   Now reprinted in WORC, pp. 65–92.

4 The difference between the reflexes of /n/ and /nː/ was phonetically something like [n] and [ᵈn] and persisted through the Middle Cornish period.

5 When pre-occlusion finally came to be written in the sixteenth century it was as a result of a general lengthening of syllables, evidenced by Lhuyd's forms *plêau*, etc.

14.01 Parallels for Cornish pre-occlusion

We have an exact parallel for Cornish pre-occlusion in a very similar phenomenon in Manx. Manx, as I have suggested elsewhere, is a variety of Eastern Gaelic in the mouth of Norse speakers. As such it has replaced the traditional Gaelic opposition of lenited and unlenited sonants with an opposition based on intensity rather than duration—exactly as happened, I believe, in Cornish. Although Manx arose as a contact language in the tenth century, pre-occlusion was not shown in spelling until the nineteenth. Pre-occlusion in Manx is thus similar to Cornish and it arose for the same reason. Pre-occlusion of the Manx kind is unknown in the other Gaelic languages; similarly pre-occlusion of the Cornish variety is absent from Welsh and Breton. Manx pre-occlusion occurred as a Celtic language, Eastern Gaelic, in contact with a Germanic language, Old Norse, replaced Celtic features with non-Celtic ones. In the same way Cornish in contact with Late West Saxon (or Early Middle English) substituted an English opposition for a Brythonic one.

It is perhaps significant that Cornish pre-occlusion is strongest in the western parts of Cornwall, that is to say furthest from English influence. In the more easterly parts Cornish under the impact of English lost the distinction between /nː/ and /n/ earlier than in the west. In the east the distinction was lost entirely, because the other language, Early Middle English, was without it. In the west the distinction survived long enough to be transformed into a new opposition of vigour rather than quantity: inherited /nː/—/n/ yielded to more Anglicized /ᵈn/—/n/.

In fact I believe we may have another parallel for Cornish pre-occlusion that is significant in its way. The Gaelic languages originally distinguish the long sonants /N L/ from their short or lenited counterparts /n l/. Notice that I designate Gaelic unlenited -*l*- and -*n*- by the symbols <L> and <N>. Here I am following the conventions of Gaelic linguists. The distinction is preserved everywhere in Scotland and in the Northern Half of Ireland. In Munster, however, the two series have fallen together as /n/ and /l/. The Munster dialect of Irish usually provides us with the standard English forms of Gaelic personal names. Thus *Siobhán*, *Maeve* (< *Méabh*) and *Sive* (< *Sadhbh*) are all pronounced in the Munster fashion. The masculine name *Domhnall* is anglicized in Scotland with a long or unlenited /L/ and appears in English as *Donald*. In Ireland, on the other hand, the same name appears in its Munster guise as *Donal*. What has happened here is that Scottish English has by sound-substitution replaced [L] by [ld], the nearest that English speakers could get to

PRE-OCCLUSION

the Gaelic unlenited /ʟ/. The longer duration of the sound by comparison with unlenited /l/ is transformed in English into a combination of [l] + [d]. In Ireland on the other hand *Domhnall*, being pronounced [doːnəl], appears in English with a simple English [l]. I would suggest there is a comparison here with early medieval Cornwall. English-speaking Cornishmen as they relearnt Cornish brought English speech-habits into their Cornish. In parts of Cornwall /nː/ and /n/ fell together. Where /nː/ remained distinct from /n/, however, the distinction of length became instead one of intensity. Thus for /benːeθ/ Cornish speakers substituted /beᵈneθ/, where long /nː/ was replaced by the shorter but more intense /ᵈn/. This is comparable with the two English versions of the name *Domhnall*, i.e. *Donald* where /ʟ/ survived and *Donal* where it did not.

14.02 *Can* 'song', *canow* 'songs'

As I mentioned above, George's sample words to exemplify pre-occlusion are *can* 'song' and *canaf* 'I sing' together with **can* 'white' and **cannaf* 'I bleach'. *Can* 'song' according to George has a single consonant and a long vowel. Presumably in George's view the plural *canow* would have a single consonant and a half-long vowel. The plural is attested in the Pilchard Song where it is written with a single <n> in one manuscript and with <nn> in another:

> Ma **canow** vee wor Hern gen Cock ha Rooz BF: 45 (Gwavas MS)
> Ma **Conna** ve war Hern gen Cock, ha Rûz BF: 46 (Tonkin MS).

There can be now doubt that the spelling with <nn> indicates a short vowel. Interestingly the same plural occurs in the Middle Cornish text *Bewnans Ke*, where it is also spelt with <nn>:

> *Dun ow amors ha'm cuvyon,*
> *gans solas hag eglynnyon,*
> *ha merth ha melody whek.*
> *Th'agan palas gwel ew thyn*
> *revertya gans **cannow** tek*
> *ha predery, ren Austyn,*
> *a'gan gwayow.*

> [Come, my friends and my dear ones,
> with entertainment and verses,
> and mirth and sweet melody.
> It is better for us
> to return to our palace with sweet songs
> and to consider, by St Augustine,
> our moves] (BK: 2058-64).

Clearly the scribe of BK thought that *cannow* had a short stressed vowel, unlike George who believes the vowel was half-long. The spelling <cannow> in BK does not, of course, mean that the medial consonant was pre-occluded. It does, however, suggest that the vowel was short in Middle Cornish. This is yet further evidence that the Prosodic Shift was early. It is also evidence that George's views on pre-occlusion are unlikely to be correct.

14.03 *Alenna* 'thence'

The scribe of BK not infrequently writes <nh> for <nn>: e.g. *gwenhal* 'swallow' NK 1109, *e gonha* 'his neck' BK 1221, *the gonha* 'thy neck' BK 2162. He also writes

Me a vyn mos, re'n gwerhesow
mos thu'm sofran **alenha**

[I will go, by the holy virgins
to my sovereign thence] (BK: 1308-09).

George says "*alena* incorrectly spelt *alenna* by Nance; the etymology indicates <n>, and if it had contained /nn/, it would have become *aledna* in Late Cornish" (GKK: 28). It contains <nh> here in BK, which is the scribe's way of writing <nn>, and yet the word is not pre-occluded in Late Cornish. George erroneously assumes that in Middle Cornish a geminate <nn> is an indication of /n:/ and that such a phoneme will automatically be pre-occluded after a short stressed vowel. <nh> here in BK is the scribe's equivalent of <nn> and simply means that the preceding vowel is short. This is further evidence that the Prosodic Shift was early.

The scribe of BK writing c. 1570 has <alenha>, his equivalent of <alenna>. At BK 1114, however, he writes <alena>. It is apparent that the scribe, writing after pre-occlusion is indicated in spelling, does not hesitate to write either <alenha> or <alena>. He is not concerned that <alenha> may be taken as a pre-occluded spelling, because in his dialect pre-occlusion did not occur (see below).

14.04 *Taran* 'thunder'

Pryce gives *Yein kuer,* **tarednow***, ha golowas, er, reo, gwenz ha clehe, ha kezer* 'Cold weather, thunder, and lightning, snow, frost, wind and ice [sic], and hail' (opposite F f 2). Under *Tonitru[s]* Lhuyd gives the Cornish words **Tredna***, taran* (AB: 164c) and he also quotes the sentence *Patl yzhi o kylyui ha* **trenna** 'How it thunders and lightens!' (AB: 284a); cf. *dho* **tredna, trenna** 'to thunder' (Pryce). In GKK George has a note *s.v. taran*: "N.B. Pryce's pl. *tarednow* suggests /nn/, which fits with Lhuyd's *tredna*, but is incorrect etymologically." Probably George meant to say that the pre-occlusion in *tarednow* and *tredna* < *tarenna* is unexplained. One should not, I think, label as incorrect forms occurring in any natural language.

PRE-OCCLUSION

Our starting point here should be Pryce's *tarednow*. The historic form of this etymon is *taran*, with an expected plural *taranow 'claps of thunder'. As a result of the Prosodic Shift the unstressed syllable *-an* is reduced to schwa and the word was then thought to be *taren, a feminine noun in *-en* with a regular plural *tarennow. This is the origin of Pryce's *tarednow*. The analogical simplex *taren give rise to a verbal noun *tarenna 'thundering', which is the origin of Lhuyd's *tredna* 'tonitru[s]'. It is curious that George should dismiss *tarednow* as "etymologically incorrect". It is in fact perfectly intelligible as an analogical form and is also incidentally corroborative evidence that the Prosodic Shift was early. Had the shift not been much earlier than the period in which pre-occlusion was shown in writing, the unstressed syllable *-an* with etymological /n/ would not have been understood as *-en*, where the *n* was historically /n:/. The Prosodic Shift neutralized the difference between *-an* and *-en* < *enn* and thus rendered possible the development of the plural form *tarennow > *tarednow*.

The same analogical process works in the reverse direction also. John Boson writes *e gwraz an* **sterradnou** *aveth* 'and he made the stars also' (BF: 52). The basic form is *steren* 'star', a feminine noun with a collective *ster* and a plural *sterennow. The reduction of unstressed syllables gives rise to an analogical *steran*, written <sterran> by Lhuyd s.v. *Stella* 'star' (AB: 154b); cf. *steran, stearan* 'star' (RC 23: 194, 196, 197). Instead, then, of the etymological plural *sterennow, the word is provided with a new plural *sterannow, the origin of Boson's *sterradnou*.

Nicholas Boson writes *neb* **Blethanniau** *alebma* 'some years ago' (BF: 29) His relative, John Boson, writes *ha rag dethiou ha* **blethaniou** 'and for days and years' (BF: 52). The vowel in the suffix *-aniou* < *-ynyow* appears to have been reshaped on the basis of the singular *blethan*. This is comparable with *sterradnou* < *sterennow. Interestingly, the Bosons' *blethaniou, Blethanniau* do not exhibit the expected pre-occlusion. This may be because neither writer marked pre-occlusion in writing on every occasion. Given that they spelt in the English fashion with no scribal tradition to act as a restraining factor, this in itself is remarkable. It is to be noted, however, that there are further instances where Nicholas Boson might be expected to indicate pre-occlusion, but does not. Pryce writes *bargidnia*. Lhuyd has *varginiaz* twice (BF: 16) without pre-occlusion but writes *vargidniaz* (BF: 17) and *bargidnias* (AB: 111a). Nicholas Boson, however, writes *varginiaz* three times (BF: 15, 16) without any pre-occlusion at all. *Blythydnyow* 'years' with pre-occlusion is attested three times in CW (see below); it is apparent, therefore, that some dialects of Cornish did pre-occlude the *-n-* in this etymon. It seems possible, therefore, that the Bosons wrote *blethaniou, Blethanniau* rather than *blethadniou because they did not always write pre-occlusion when it occurred in their speech.

Both Nicholas and John Boson do pre-occlude in other etyma. Nicholas writes <gwadnhez> (BF: 25), <idden> (BF: 25), <Codna> (BF: 25) and <vedden> (BF: 25), for example, and John writes <lebbn> (B: 48), <Pedn> (BF:

48), <vedn> (BF: 48) and <dadn> (BF: 52). If, then, the Bosons do not pre-occlude -*n*- in *Blethanniau, blethaniou,* it is also possible that their dialect used a form of this word without pre-occlusion. This might suggest that pre-occlusion was a dialectal feature and that the Bosons' dialect was a mixed one.

14.05 Pre-occlusion not shown consistently in Kernowek Kemyn

Kernowek Kemyn is intended to be a largely phonemic spelling system, that is to say that the pronunciation of any word should be immediately apparent from the spelling. In GKK George tells us that [dn] is an acceptable way to pronounce <nn> "when stressed" (GKK: 22). Moreover he tells us that /nj/ became /dnj/ *c.* 1575 (PSRC: 194). Nowhere, however, in the books for learners of Kernowek Kemyn are we told that <ny> /nj/ may be pronounced with pre-occlusion after a stressed vowel. This means that Kernowek Kemyn contains spellings which imply a pronunciation without pre-occlusion, even though such pre-occlusion is attested in the traditional language. I give here a list of relevant words:

Kernowek Kemyn	Attested form
apronyow 'aprons'	*aprodnieo* Kerew (RC 23: 177)
bargenya 'to bargain'	*vargidniaz* BF: 17; *bargidnia* ACB (opposite F f 2)
blydhynyow 'years'	*vlethydnyow* CW 1862, 2404; *vlethydnyowe* CW 1915
brunyon 'groats, oatmeal'	*brudnyan* Bilbao MS
fortunyes 'fortunate'	*fortidniez* BF: 31
linyeth 'lineage'	*lydnyathe* CW 2097.

One would have thought that Kernowek Kemyn, aspiring to be phonemic, would have spelt these etyma and others like them with geminate <nn>. Or at the very least the handbooks of Kernowek Kemyn might have mentioned that it was permissible to pre-occlude <ny> after a stressed vowel. As it is, learners of Kernowek Kemyn have no way of knowing that in these words in traditional Cornish pre-occlusion actually occurs.

There is however a further flaw in Kernowek Kemyn here. Although George realizes that /nj/ became /n:j/ at some point in the history of Cornish, he does not seem to understand the full consequences of this change. George tells us that /nj/ became /dnj/ *c.* 1575. I dispute his dating, but will accept it for the sake of argument. When he tells us that /nj/ became /dnj/, George is really saying /j/ after a consonant functioned as another consonant, shortening the preceding vowel; and in the case of /n/ strengthened it, i.e. /V·nj/ > /Vn:j/ > /Vdnj/. Yet in GKK George gives the pronunciation of *studhya* 'to study' as ['sty·ðja], where the vowel is marked half-long. If the vowel in *studhya* is half-long, why are the stressed vowels in *apronyow, bargenya, blydhynyow, brunyon, fortunyes* and *linyeth* not half-long also? But pre-occlusion occurs only after a short vowel. How then does pre-occlusion occur

PRE-OCCLUSION

in these words? It looks as though George has not quite unravelled all aspects of pre-occlusion in Cornish.

14.06 Kernowek Kemyn <unn> 'one'

There are two words for 'one' in Middle Cornish. The first *onen* is used when counting and as a pronoun. The second is used as an adjective preceding the noun it qualifies: *vn dra* 'one thing' OM 76, *vn den* 'one man' OM 94, *vn dev* 'one God' OM 110, etc. In Late Cornish *un* is frequently pre-occluded. I have collected the following examples:

> *try person yn **idn** dewges* 'three persons in one deity' CW: 6
> *comprehendys in **vdn** dew* 'comprehended in one God' CW: 11
> *ty a gyef in yet **vdn** eall* 'you will find an angel at the gate' CW 1753
> *ioies nef in **vdn** rew* 'joys of heaven one by one' CW 2145
> *ny ve **udn** mabe dean sparys* 'not one human being was spared' CW 2539
> *ha na ve **idn** froth na mikan* 'and there was no rebuke or spite' BF: 19
> *Po the'ns Salles da, **idden** Mees worbar* 'When they are well salted together for a month' BF: 43
> *Path' ens salles dah, **idden** miz warbar* 'When they are well salted together for a month' BF: 44
> *na ell'am lavar **idn** gear da vorth'an* 'I cannot say a good word about them' BF: 46
> *Re a **ydn** dra ny dal traveeth* 'Too miuch of something is worse than nothing' ACB F f
> *Me rig scantlower clowes **eden** ger Sowsnack* 'I scarcely heard a word of English' LAM: 244.

The word *un* (< *oinos; cf. Latin *unus*) has a historically single final consonant. It seems that when *un* occurred before a following stressed syllable, the initial consonant combined across word-boundary to form a consonant cluster. This rendered the vowel of *un* short and the /n/ was strengthened to /nː/. This was then pre-occluded in dialects which exhibit pre-occlusion, and emerges as <dn> or <den> in the Late Cornish period. The /nː/ is then generalized to positions before a vowel, e.g. *vdn eall* CW 1753.

Kernowek Kemyn arbitrarily respells historic *un* as <unn> because it is pre-occluded before a following noun. This is inconsistent, inasmuch as the *n* of *bargenya* and *blydhynyow*, for example, are written in Kernowek Kemyn with <n> even though both are pre-occluded in the traditional language. If *un* is <unn>, one would for consistency's sake expect *<bargennya> and *<blydhynnyow>.

14.07 Pre-occlusion in Scilly

I have pointed out that pre-occlusion is attested in Scilly where Cornish died out much earlier than in Cornwall proper. George, quoting Thomas, claims that Cornish may have been spoken in Scilly by some people as late as 1600. We are not talking here about a few speakers of Cornish, but rather about

Cornish as the language of a community. If the language is not widely spoken, it does not find its way into local toponyms. The Cornish place-names with pre-occlusion in Scilly are clearly much earlier than 1600. I suggest that they may be a hundred or so years earlier.

In my article in *Studia Celtica* I listed all those instances of pre-occlusion in toponyms known to me. These cluster in west Cornwall and Scilly. I noted one instance each in Veryan, St Ewe and Perranzabuloe; all the others were west of Truro. I am quite sure that other examples of pre-occlusion are attested to the east of Truro. This does not vitiate my contention that pre-occlusion is largely a western feature. If there are more easterly examples of pre-occlusion which I have missed, there are many more western examples that I have not been able to cite through lack of documentation. The proportions remain the same. Pre-occlusion is for the most part a western feature. It is not exclusively western; no would one expect it to be. The shape of Cornwall and its long coastline mean that dialect mixing in Cornwall was inevitable.

14.08 *Benneth* ~ *Banneth* 'blessing'

In my article I suggested that the spellings <bedneth> and <banneth> might represent the spellings of the word in the area of pre-occlusion on the one hand and in the area without it on the other. My explanation was that in the area of no pre-occlusion /nː/ and /n/ fell together early. The Prosodic Shift shortened the vowel in *benen* 'woman', and in the area of no pre-occlusion the long /nː/ in *benneth* was simplified. In order to maintain a distinction therefore between *benneth* and *benen*, dialects in this area lowered the vowel before original /nː/. This meant that western pre-occluding dialects had *benneth* but more easterly ones without pre-occlusion had *banneth*. I suggested on other grounds that OM to be more easterly than the two plays PC and RD. In which case one might expect to find *banneth* in OM but *benneth* in PC and RD (which were, of course, written before pre-occlusion was marked in writing). The complementary distribution of *banneth* ~ *benneth* is remarkable in the plays:

A **banneth**
banneth OM 471, 472, 911, 1579, 1723, 1827, 1917, 1969, 2168, 2585; OM *banat* 726; *bannath* OM 2433; *benneth* OM 2265.

B **benneth**
benneth PC 265, 560, 706, 928, 947, 2549, RD 818, 823, 1556; *bennath* PC 308, 704, 1803, RD 1579, 1605, 1873, 2237, 2238; *vennath* RD 2643.

It is quite apparent that OM has <banneth> where PC, RD have <benneth>, and that we have here discovered a significant isogloss.

Beunans Meriasek was written by two hands. The *secunda manus* who wrote the first ten pages writes *beneth* BM 31; *benneth* BM 50, 53, 54, 201, 202 and *bennath* BM 63. Three times he writes *bedneth* with pre-occlusion BM 198, 224

PRE-OCCLUSION

and 225. The second scribe writes *banneth* at 506, 507, 533, 581, 1011, 2677, 3093, 3179, 3705, 3706, 4306, 4307, 4365, 4557 and 4559. There is no pre-occlusion in portion of the play written by the *prima manus* (Rad. Ton). *Bewnans Ke* is later than *Beunans Meriasek* and probably dates *c.* 1575. It is entirely without pre-occlusion and the word 'blessing' is spelt *bannath, vannath* at BK 651, 1567, 1575, 1583, 2897, 3048, 3055 and 3114.

William Jordan of Helston, the scribe of CW, exhibits pre-occlusion in his own dialect. But his spellings are superimposed upon the orthography of his exemplar. He writes the word for 'blessing' in two different ways:

A < **banneth**
bannath CW 105; *banneth* CW 1871.

B < **benneth**
bedna CW CW 1541.

I assume that *bedna* represented Jordan's own western dialect and that the spellings *bannath* and *banneth* without pre-occlusion were the spellings of his exemplar.

A further distinction is perceptible in CW with respect to pre-occlusion. The text has either *vydnaf 'I wish' with pre-occlusion or *manaff* without. The two variants occur in the text as follows:

A < ***mydnaf**
vidnaf CW 36; *vidna* CW 1154; *vydnaf* CW 1457.

B < **mannaf**
vannaf CW 134, 507, 648, 682, 1380, 1697, 2360; *manaf* CW 313, 471, 503; *mannaf* CW 314, 1362, 2231; *mannaff* CW 1697.

Given that the form with <a> in the root syllable is never pre-occluded in CW, it is likely that it resembles *banneth*, i.e. it was already in Jordan's easterly exemplar which did not show pre-occlusion. The pre-occluded form *mydnaf*, I assume, represents Jordan's own speech.

14.09 Lhuyd's *henna ~ hana* 'that one'
Lhuyd has a very significant example of pre-occlusion versus no pre-occlusion. Under *Is* 'He, the same, that, such an one' he cites the two Cornish forms: *hana* and *hedda* (AB: 73b). Here we have the pre-occluding form with <e> and the non-pre-occluding form with <a> and a single consonant. Clearly these two variants derive from [ˈhenːa> ˈhe^{d}nə] and [henːa] > [ˈhænə] > [ˈhanə] respectively, and are clearly dialectal variants.

George is quite aware of my arguments about *benneth ~ banneth, vydnaf ~ mannaf* and *hedda ~ hana*. Taken together they seem to me to be strong evidence that pre-occlusion did not occur in all dialects of Cornish and that opposition *benneth/bedneth* ~ *banneth* was a dialect isogloss. George does not attempt to disprove this view. He does not even mention it or any of my evidence [AD].

14.10 George's chronology

George tells us that final /dn/ became [dən] *c.* 1750 (PSRC: 195). Given that Cornish was virtually extinct by then, this is possibly rather late. On theoretical grounds alone one might perhaps not expect the language to undergo any change at all while it was in such a moribund state. We have, moreover, good evidence to suggest that George's chronology is not correct here. The first instance of [dən] < earlier /dn/ is recorded by Borde in 1542, over two hundred years before George's proposed date: *Syrra, me e **uyden** gewel ages commaundement why* (Loth 1900: 226). George has subsequently become aware of this passage in Borde because he mentions it in KKC21: 63. George has thus changed his mind about the chronology of pre-occlusion without telling us [AD].

George insists that pre-occlusion is related to date rather than to dialect. He believes, correctly enough, that if he once concedes that there was discernible dialect in Cornish as far as pre-occlusion is concerned, he will be opening the door to further admissions. In particular he is anxious not to admit that there was a dialectal difference in Middle Cornish between those that pronounced 'wood' as [koːz] and those who said [kuːz], for if he were to acknowledge such a thing, he would be admitting that the distinction made in Kernowek Kemyn between, for example, <bos> 'to be' and <boes> 'food' was without foundation. Dialect must therefore be repudiated at all costs.

Rejecting discernible dialect in Cornish presents George with something of a problem. There is no pre-occlusion in the body of *Beunans Meriasek*, which was written in 1504. There are three examples of pre-occlusion in the ten pages of the play, however, which may have been written slightly later. John Tregear on the other hand, although his homilies are by far the longest surviving Cornish text, does not exhibit any pre-occlusion at all, yet Tregear was probably writing *c.* 1558. In order to explain all this, George invents the following story:

> BM. was written down by Radulphus Ton in 1504, **before pre-occlusion occurred**. Its first ten pages, or 270 lines, were re-written by another hand at a later date, **perhaps c. 1540, by someone of the younger generation**. When Andrew Borde came to Cornwall in 1543, he recorded *my a vynn* 'I will' as *me euyden*, which is usually taken to indicate pre-occlusion. If this chronology is correct, **his informant is likely to have been aged less than 30**. On the other hand, **John Tregear is likely to have been comparatively old when he translated Bonner's homilies c. 1558, possibly in his fifties**. It all fits a variation in time, without any need for a variation in space (KKC21: 63).

Much of this is special pleading [SP]. I have put in bold type those portions of George's argument for which there is no evidence at all.

PRE-OCCLUSION

14.11 Arguments against George's chronology: *Beunans Meriasek*
George tells us that "BM. was written down by Radulphus Ton in 1504, before pre-occlusion occurred." In that case <nn> and <mm> in Ton's orthography ought to mean long consonants that were subsequently pre-occluded. Examples of <nn> and <mm> in BM include *prenna* BM 868, 2746, *prennas* BM 2521, *prennys* (ppt) BM 885, *ny ammont* BM 2055, 3352, 3624, *dynnyte* BM 3025, 3094 and *ingynnys* BM 3367, none of which would have been pre-occluded. Indeed Kernowek Kemyn spells them <prena>, <prenas>, <ny amont>, <dynyta> and <ynjinys> respectively with an ungeminate <n> or <m>. How, I wonder, does George square the lack of pre-occlusion with the geminate spelling in BM?

14.12 Arguments against George's chronology: *Bewnans Ke*
I also wonder how George is going to deal with the evidence of the recently discovered play *Bewnans Ke*. The manuscript on palaeographical grounds can be dated to the middle or second half of the sixteenth century, i.e. between 1550 and 1600, and probably towards the second half of that period. Several strata are visible in the orthography of the text, reflecting as they do the various stages in the textual transmission. Perhaps the most interesting aspects of spelling of BK are a series of features linking it with *Sacrament an Alter* [SA] and the *Creation of the World* [CW]. SA is in language considerably later than Tregear and CW has a colophon dating it to 1611.

The late features in *Bewnans Ke* include the following:

a) *gwyr* 'true' is spelt *gwyer* at BK 194, 230, 254, 343, 504, etc. The spelling *gwyer* is attested twice at SA 62a and at CW 1676 and CW 2432.

b) the word *mur* 'great' is spelt *meer* at BK 2923 and as *mear* in the compound *mearthysaysys* at BK 1227. The spelling *meer* is also attested at SA 60 and at CW 203; similarly *mear* occurs at CW 702, 899, 1343, 1414, 1656, 1779 and 1872 (cf. also *meare* at CW 205 and 711).

c) the plural ending *-ow* is often written *-aw* in BK, e.g. *dvwaw* BK 223, *thewaw* BK 918, *galaraw* BK 524, *gallaraw* BK 3288, *grasaw* BK 536, 1235, *lavaraw* BK 973, 1135, 3089, *paraw* BK 1136, *rasaw* BK 1159, 1233, *prasaw* BK 1160. The ending *-ow* in non-plural forms also appears occasionally as *-aw*, e.g. *maraw* BK 580, 955, 1850, 1978, 1986, 3149, 3251, 3299, *arghadaw* BK 726, *casadaw* BK 728, *peiadaw* BK 763, *garaw* BK 971, 1977, 3296, *hanaw* BK 3104. The spelling of historic *-ow* as *-aw* is attested in other late texts, e.g., *ganaw* 'mouth' SA 61, *canhasawe* 'messengers' CW 29, *levyaw* 'floods' CW 2165, *benaw* 'female' CW 2271, 2414 and *gorrawe* 'male' CW 2414; cf. also Nicholas Boson's *Letherau* 'letters' BF: 27, *Gunneaw* 'downs' BF: 27, *Blethanniau* 'years' BF: 29 and Thomas Boson's *gannaw* 'mouth' BF: 39 and *derggawe* 'doors' BF: 39. The spelling of unstressed *-ow* as <aw> does not appear until the late sixteenth century.

d) In SA *yma* 'is' is spelt *e ma*, e.g. at SA 59a x 4, 60a, 61 x 3, etc. In BK the word is most frequently spelt *ema*, for example, at BK 56, 156, 236, 271, 399, 499, 515, 566, 615, 799, etc. Similarly *yth yw* in SA is often *e thew, ethew*, for example at SA 61 x 2, 61a, 62 x 2, 63 x 2. The same spelling occurs at BK 437 and 717 (though *yth ew* occurs at BK 356.)

e) The Cornish word for 'two' is spelt *deaw* at BK 587 and 2045. This is a distinctively Late Cornish spelling, and occurs, for example at CW 1056 and 1234.

f) In SA *e* is often used for *y* 'his', for example at SA 59 x 12. In BK *e* is also frequently written for *y* 'his', e.g. BK 57, 121, 154, 197, 198, 199, 209, 215, 221, etc.

g) The Blessed Virgin Mary is referred to as *an worthyas ker marya* at BK 159. This is immediately reminiscent of *an worthias maria* at SA 61.

It is clear that the orthography of BK is closely related to that of SA and CW, both of which show evidence of pre-occlusion. Indeed the spelling of the play has a decidedly Late Cornish flavour. A probable date for BK would be *c.* 1575, although it may well be considerably later. Interestingly enough there is no hint of pre-occlusion anywhere in the 3,308 lines of *Bewnans Ke*. I have already suggested that there is evidence that the scribe's dialect lacked it. It is difficult, therefore, to maintain as George does, that pre-occlusion fits "a variation in time, without any need for a variation in space." If George's contention were correct we should certainly expect some evidence of pre-occlusion in *Bewnans Ke*. As it is, there is none at all. I would also repeat here what I have said above: the word for 'blessing' in BK is invariably *bannath, vannath*. This is precisely what I should expect for a dialect without pre-occlusion.

14.13 Conclusion

Kernowek Kemyn is inconsistent with regard to marking pre-occlusion in spelling. Moreover George's claim that the absence of pre-occlusion is a question of date rather than dialect is difficult to maintain. We must, I think, conclude that as far as pre-occlusion is concerned Kernowek Kemyn is based on a mistaken phonology.

CHAPTER 15
Pesy 'to pray' and *bohosek* 'poor' (KKC21: 68-82)

15.00 George's <tj> and <dj>

My readers will remember that George once believed that historical *d* and *t* in words like *peswar* 'four' and *kerensa* were in fact a palatalized *d* and *t* respectively. In consequence Kernowek Kemyn in its first hypostasis used the graphs <tj> and <dj>, e.g. <pedjwar> and <kerentja>. My readers will doubtless also remember that it was I who demonstrated that these "phonemes" had never existed in traditional Cornish and should be removed. I, like George, noticed the variation in the texts between *kerense* and *kerenge* and *wosa* and *woge* and naturally assumed, as did Jenner, Nance and Caradar, that there were two forms of such words, i.e. *kerensa* and *kerenja* and *wosa* and *woja*. George obtained a copy of my then unpublished article and removed <tj> and <dj> from his system. In the present work George devotes two whole sections to assibilation of *d* and *t* in Middle Cornish and he attempts throughout to show that I am in most respects mistaken.

This portion of George's book seems to me to show a little ingratitude. Had it not been for me, Kernowek Kemyn would still be writing, for example:

> Re**dj** yw a**dj**won yth eu**dj**i Ka**dj**ek whath yn keren**tj**a gen**tj**i. Pan yth vi an try**dj**a prys dh'y **tj**i hi, ny yllys kry**dj**i ow laga**dj**ow. My a glywas hana**dj**ow gallo**dj**ek ha pan viris der an a**dj**wa my a a**dj**wonas an den bogho**dj**ek adhirak an darra**dj**ow ow syn**tj**i hi diwleuv hag orth hi fy**dj**i dhe a**dj**a dhodho my**dj**i an ka**dj**wydh gwel**dj**ek kyns penn pe**dj**war dydh.

For George, who has been saved from this folly by me alone, to turn and attempt here to prove me largely mistaken, might possibly be described as impertinent—particularly when he includes a comic verse admitting his own error, but simultaneously disparaging me:

> 'Twas Nicholas Williams who looked at the case
> And showed that these graphemes no longer have place;
> And after re-reading his paper so long,
> I must now admit that he's right and I'm wrong;
> The rest of his paper was nonsense, I feel,
> But with TJ and DJ his notions were real:
> To existence these sounds never had any claim!
> I'm sometimes embarrassed and covered in shame
> To admit imperfection, and thereby lose face… (KKC21: 71).

Given that the article I wrote was entirely about <tj> and <dj>, I am hard pressed to explain what George means by the "rest of his paper was nonsense". It was clearly not too nonsensical to save him from serious error.

15.01 George's changing opinions on *s/j* alternation

The two sections of KKC21 which deal with this question are not completely clear to me and I shall not attempt to answer them in detail. Instead I shall let George speak for himself on the matter of the *s/j* alternation in Middle Cornish. George has at different times apparently held a number of conflicting views on the question. Let us examine them.

15.02 George's interpretation of *s/j* alternation: first version

In PSRC George believed that the consonant in *ganso* 'with him' and *kerensa* 'love' was a palatalized *t* which he wrote <tj>. Similarly he believed that the consonant in *peswar* 'four' and *esof* 'I am' was a palatalized *d* which he wrote <dj>. He says of <tj>:

> This sound does not exist in English, though a similar sound is sometimes hear in the word *tune*. It is apparently common in several less well-known languages, such as Danish and Serbo-Croat. It is a palatalized [t], and lies between [t] (as *t* in English *tap*) and [tʃ] (as *ch* in English *chap*). Try putting the [t] in *tap* before the [j] in *yap*, making *"tjap"*, and saying it quickly.
>
> There was no suitable grapheme for this alien sound; scribes usually used <s>, sometimes <g> (PSRC: 158).

Speaking of <dj> George says:

> This sound does not occur in English, though a similar sound is sometimes heard in the word *duke*. It is a palatalized [d], and lies between [d] (as *d* in English *dot*) and [dʒ] (as *j* in English *jot*). Try putting the [d] in *dot* before the [j] in *yacht*, making *"djot"*, and saying it quickly.
> ...
> Nance did not recognize this sound as a phoneme; he therefore spelled most words containing it with <s>, with the result that those [above] are mispronounced with [z] or [s]: a few words he spelled with <j>, which represents the normal development in LateC[ornish].
> ...
> Before the reader used to Unified Cornish becomes too outraged, let him study the following spellings from the texts which show clearly that the phoneme in these words was /dj/ and not /s/.
> (PSRC: 165-66).

It is remarkable that George was so sure of the exact phonetic detail of his two new "phonemes". He was after all describing the phonology of a language which had not been spoken for two hundred years. Incidentally, George's confidence about the exact phonetic nature of his fictitious */tj/ and */dj/ contrasts with his aporia in the face of *rag ~ carrek* (see **17.02** below).

PESY 'TO PRAY' AND BOHOSEK 'POOR'

15.03 George's interpretation of *s/j* alternation: second version

In 1987 I wrote an article on this question, which was published in 1990. In 1989 George obtained a copy of my unpublished article and having read it decided that /tj/ and /dj/ should be removed. He wrote:

> Nicholas Williams, in a brilliantly argued paper to be published later this year, has put forward strong arguments to show that the phonemes /tj/ and /dj/ never existed. Close examination of his evidence confirms this (but refutes other points in his paper). To everyone's relief, this will mean the disappearance of the corresponding graphemes <tj> and <dj>. This should remove the chief obstacle to adoption of Kernewek Kemmyn by the supporters of Unified Cornish. The practical effect will be that instead of <tj> and <dj>, either <s> or <j> will be used, in almost all cases as in Unified Cornish (*Carn* 68, Winter 1989/90: 16).

George describes my article on /tj/ and /dj/ as "brilliantly argued". When I wrote it, however, I thought I was only stating the obvious; my objections to George's hypothetical "phonemes" seemed to me wholly self-evident. George also speaks in the above passage of my "evidence", as though I had brought new facts to bear on the question. I lived at the time (as I still do) in Dublin, and the only evidence to which I had access were the Middle Cornish texts and Padel's book on place-name elements. I am sure George had much more evidence when he wrote PSRC.

My own view of the alternation was as follows. The *-d-* in Middle Cornish was first affricated to [dz]. This either simplified to [z], written <s> or in some varieties of Cornish it palatalized to [dʒ]. The dialects of Cornish which had [dʒ] were the more westerly ones. The dialects that preferred [z] were those of central Cornwall and were also the dialects that formed the standard language of the plays. This is why, I argued, the texts tend to show <s> in, say, *wosa* 'after', whereas more westerly ones had *woge*. Even in texts written by western scribes the standard written form tends to dominate and <g> forms are relatively uncommon.

George appears initially to have accepted this view of mine about possible dialect in Cornish, and he actually went so far as to give a paper in April 1989 in St Erth on dialect in Cornish as part of the 14th "Cornish Weekend" in which he expounded the views put forward by me in my article—which was at the time still unpublished. I have already cited an account of this event at **7.21** above. By 1992, however, George had changed his mind again.

15.04 George's interpretation of *s/j* alternation: third version

In an article in Kernowek Kemyn published in 1992 in France George set out his third interpretation of the alternation of *s/j* in Cornish. In this paper, basing his arguments on place-name evidence which he does not actually cite, George suggested that Old Cornish *-d-* became some special kind of *s* and that this special s became [dʒ] *c.* 1675. He writes:

TOWARDS AUTHENTIC CORNISH

Gwiw yw an delinyans pellder-termyn rag whithra tybyansow a'n par ma. Delinyans 7 a dhiskwa an chanjyow $d > s > dzh$ rag geryow avel *boghosek*, hag a's tevo [d] yn h.Kn. warlergh bogalenn boeslevys ha rag bogalenn heb poeslev.

Sowedh, ny yll an delinyans derivas travith a-dro dhe nas an son bo sonyow diskewdhys dre *s*. Testenn rag paper arall yw hemma. Mes y hyll disprevi tybyansow Williams a-dro dhe dermyn ha rannyethow y'n mater ma. An delinyans a dhiskwa yn kler bos an chanj $s > dzh$ onan diwedhes, c. 1675; ha ny hwarva marnas y'n howlsedhes drefenn na vedha Kernewek kewsys saw eno y'n termyn na

[The distance-time diagram is useful for examining hypotheses of this kind. Diagram 7 shows the changes $d > s > dzh$ for words like *boghosek* which had [d] in Old Cornish after a stressed vowel and before an unstressed vowel.

Unfortunately the diagram can tell us nothing about the nature of the sound or sounds indicated by *s*. That is a subject for another paper. But it can disprove Williams' ideas about chronology and dialects in this matter. The diagram shows clearly that the change $s > dzh$ is a late one, c. 1675; and it occurred only in the west because Cornish was spoken only there at that period] (George 1992: 66).

Notice first of all that George uses the expression *delinyans pellder-termyn* to translate the English 'distance-time diagram'. This, however, would more naturally mean 'diagram of the distance of time'. George should perhaps, therefore, have written **delinyans pellder ha termyn*.

In the table at the end of this article George refers to the assibilation of *-d-* and gives the spelling as a change from *-d-* to *-s-* and as far as the sound is concerned he gives "[d] > ?" c. 1300 and "? > [dʒ]" c. 1675. He believes that there were two stages in the development some 375 years apart, though he cannot say what the first stage was. He gives no convincing reason for his belief that there were two separate changes, with such a large lapse of time between them.

15.05 George's interpretation of *s/j* alternation: fourth version
In KKC21 George has now abandoned his question-marks and is quite certain of the phonetic nature of the sibilant produced from Old Cornish *-d-* "c. 1325" (KKC21: 81). He now claims that in words like *pysy/pygy* the sound was [dz] and that sometimes it palatalized to give [dʒ] and sometimes simplified to give [z]. It is for this reason that in Middle Cornish one finds both *pysy* with [z] and *pygy* with [dʒ]. This incidentally is exactly my view of the development of *pysy/pygy* and of similar words.

In consequence of all this, according to George <s> in Middle Cornish has two values. In words with original *s* it means [s] and in words with original *d* it means [z]. He also regrets that Kernowek Kemyn does not spell [z] as <z> where it is the reflex of Old Cornish *-d-* rather than, as at present, as <s>. He tells us that privately he has been using *taz* 'father' and *pryz* 'time' for some time.

PESY 'TO PRAY' AND BOHOSEK 'POOR'

George also believes, however, that in certain words the [dz] remained. This occurred, he says, in *bohosek*-type words, i.e. in words of more than two syllables, where the reflex of Old Cornish -*d*- occurred immediately after the accent and where the following unstressed vowel was other than [ɪ]. George writes of such words:

(a) The spelling change *d* > *s*, circa 1325 represents the sound-change [d] > [dz];
(b) The almost exclusive spelling <s> in Middle Cornish means [dz];
(c) The spelling change *s* > *dg* circa 1675, represents the sound-change [dz] > [dʒ];
(d) The reduction [dz] > [z] took place in English, not in Cornish (KKC21: 81).

15.06 George's four different views

We thus see that George has changed his opinion three times. In the first two cases quite radically. The third change of mind seems mostly to concern the nature of the sound arising in Middle Cornish from Old Cornish -*d*-. If I understand him correctly, this became [z] in *taz* 'father' and *pryz* 'time'. It is clear from his discussion that he believes the <s> in *pysy* 'to pray' to represent [z] < [dz] and the <g> in *pygy* to represent [dʒ]. He seems, then, to allow some small amount of dialectal variation. In *bohosek*, however, he seems to be saying that <s> meants [dz] until *c*. 1675, when it became [dʒ].

George claimed originally to have subjected the Middle Cornish texts to the most rigorous scrutiny by means of a computer database. As a result of that thorough examination George recommended <tj> and <dj> for Old Cornish -*t*- and -*d*-. Then he changed his mind and recommended <s> and <j>. Then he changed his mind again and suggested that the sound of assibilated Old Cornish -*d*- was in certain cases unknown. He is now proposing that <s> in such cases meant [z] or [dz] and that there was a different development for, say, *pysy*/*pygy* *[ˈprˑzi]/*[ˈprˑdʒi] 'to pray' and *bohosek* *[boˈxoˑdzek] 'poor'.

In spite of his database and his scientific analysis of the data, George has so far had some difficulty in making up his mind on this question. Who knows, he may change it yet again.

15.07 George's *bohosek*-type words

George seems to be claiming that the [dz] in the word for 'to pray', for example, simplified to [z] giving *pysy* or was palatalized to [dʒ] giving *pygy* ?after *c*. 1325 (George does not appear to give a date for palatalization). In *bohosek*, however, he says the [dz] remained and was not palatalized until *c*. 1675. I must say that I find this latest suggestion unconvincing. There are at least seven reasons for my scepticism:

1) In the first place, it is highly unlikely that the reflexes of the same origin (i.e. Old Cornish -*d*-) would remain different for so long.
2) In the second place, it is not credible that the scribes would write both sounds, i.e. [z], for example in *pysy*, and [dz], for example in *bohosek*, in exactly the same way, i.e. as <s>, even though they were different.
3) In the third place, it is difficult to believe that the palatalization of [dz] in *bohosek* > *bohogek* should have been identical with that of *pygy* but should have taken place over three hundred years later.
4) In the fourth place George's unique environment for the retention of intervocalic [dz] is not convincing. He says that the reflex of Old Cornish -*d*- was maintained as [dz] in "three-syllable words in which medial -*d*- in a stressed syllable was followed by a vowel other than /i/ or /ɪ/" (KKC21: 72). We are dealing here with the development of Old Cornish -*d*- after a stressed vowel and before a non-front-high vowel. The number of syllables before the stressed one is surely irrelevant. There is no phonetic or phonological reason for an unstressed syllable before the stressed syllable to have affected the outcome of original -*d*- immediately after the stress. The development of Old Cornish -*d*- in *bochodoc* 'poor' > Middle Cornish *bohosek* is identical with the development of -*d*- in Old Cornish **Cadoc* 'personal name' > Middle Cornish *Casek* (cf. *Ne ve the bar, re* **Gasak** *'Never was thy equal, by St Cadoc'* BK 1974). To insist that trisyllables differed in development from disyllables is special pleading [SP].
5) In the fifth place it is to be noticed that [dz] is by no means uncommon in English, e.g. in *adze, sudsy, Pudsey, fads, lads, bids, lids, beds, heads, gods, odds, scuds, spuds, foods, prudes, moods,* etc. There is no reason to suppose that any simplification of [dz] in *bohosek*-type words in place-names should have occurred in English. English speakers would have had no incentive to simplify [dz], since the consonant cluster presents them with no difficulties.
6) In the sixth place, given the ease with which Anglophones can pronounce the consonant cluster [dz], if it existed, it ought to have left traces in toponymy. The word *logosek* 'full of mice' is a *bohosek*-type word and it occurs in the place-name *Trelagossick* in Carrick. The word **gwybesek* 'gnat-infested' (cf. Old Cornish *guibeden* 'scinifes' [gnat]) is another *bohosek*-type word which occurs in the Kerrier place-name *Halabezack* < *Halwebesek* (1338) 'gnat-infested marsh'. If George were correct, both toponyms would have included the consonant cluster [dz] and one might legitimately expect the English forms to be something like **Trelagodzick* or **Trelagodsick* and **Halabedzack* or **Halabedsack* respectively. The complete absence of place-names containing <dz> and <ds> in English makes me very sceptical about this latest suggestion of George's.

7) In the seventh place, the texts themselves make one very doubtful about George's latest hypothesis. George alludes to the paucity of *bohosek*-type words in the literature exhibiting palatalization and points out that we have only two examples: ***gallogek*** 'mighty' RD 2376 and ***clevegow*** 'diseases' BM 1457. He is no longer correct, however. We now have three more examples, however, all from *Bewnans Ke*:

te pen boba ***lagajak*** BK 210
in dryngys dv ***marthojak*** BK 250
gwra indella ***lagajak*** BK 367.

Were we to find further texts, we would almost certainly find further examples. George's is using here an *argumentum ex silentio*. Given the limited extent of the surviving texts, this last point is not compelling.

Altogether I find George's latest views about the palatalization of /dz/ > /dʒ/ to be as unconvincing as his original /dj/ hypothesis. I would advise George to abandon this latest suggestion as soon as possible.

15.08 Reflections on the assibilation of Old Cornish -*d*-

George's first suggestion that Old Cornish -*t*- and -*d*- gave /tj/ and /dj/ was unconvincing. Indeed George spoke of one of his newly discovered "phonemes" as "alien", even though, according to his explanation, it was an integral part of the language. Given that George's explanation looked so bizarre when adopted into his orthography, it is remarkable that he did not consult other Celticists to canvass their opinions. He was apparently so convinced of his discovery of /tj/ and /dj/ that he clearly thought further consultation unnecessary.

There is an important point here. George, though he has done research on Cornish, is not a professional Celticist or even a professional linguist. His experience of historical linguistics when he wrote PSRC was limited. His work displays great confidence in his own conclusions. Such confidence is not always a reliable guide. It is especially to be distrusted, if one is also engaging in linguistic planning, which has general consequences. A more experienced investigator would not have suggested <tj> and <dj> for revived Cornish.

To be fair to George, the question of the assibilation of Old Cornish -*d*- to *s/g* is in many ways perplexing. It is also of course unique to Cornish. Nowhere else in the Brythonic languages is there anything comparable. Such a fact ought to have alerted him to the unique phonology of Cornish. Languages do not undergo such idiosyncratic changes as -*d*- > *s/g* in isolation. If this aspect of the phonology of Cornish was unusual, there was a very high probability that other aspects of the system were also unlike Welsh and Breton. The assibilation of *t* and *d* began in the Old Cornish period and was closely related to the Prosodic Shift. The shift meant a radical reshaping of Cornish phonology. The Brythonic languages and Breton in particular distinguish between lenis and fortis. English has no such opposition. When after the Norman Conquest Anglicized Cornishmen began to relearn Cornish they brought into their Cornish English speech habits. Among those speech habits was the tendency to substitute for the opposition fortis—lenis a new opposition of stop—affricate. It was this which gave rise to the progressive assibilation of *t* and *d*. The whole process was, I believe, complete by the beginning of the Middle Cornish period. George's suggested shift of *bohosek* > *bohogek c.* 1675 can be dismissed.

CHAPTER 16
Unstressed syllables (KKC21: 93)

16.00 Unstressed syllables and the Prosodic Shift
The Prosodic Shift meant the intensification of the stress ictus in Cornish. Stressed vowels were pronounced shorter than previously but with greater vigour. As a result unstressed syllables reduced in intensity and tended to become the neutral vowel schwa [ə]. There can be no doubt at all that this process was occurring in the Middle Cornish period, since we can see it not only in the spelling of unstressed syllables in the texts, but also in the consequences in the morphological system of the language. Let us look at spellings first.

16.01 Reduction of unstressed syllables to schwa in spelling
Because unstressed syllables are reduced to schwa we find a variety of different vowels in the unstressed syllable of the same etymon. Here are some examples (I ignore initial mutations in these lists):

'ONE'
onan PA 42c, 43b, 71b, 81a, 145b, 154c, 199a, OM 3, 12, 90, 736, 1192, 1561, 2658, 2665, 2683, PC 833, 837, 867, 1146, 1336, 1371, 1801, 2231, 2251, 2412, 2435, 2500, 2641, 2765, 2770, 2814, 2821, 2840, 2856, 3071, RD 408, 677, 860, 1667, BK 2018; *unan* CF
onen OM 57, 2099, 2308, PC 1235, BM 3545, 3801, SA 59
onon PA 25b, 89c, 124a, 124d, 137b, 138a, 141c, 163b, 181d, 187c, 235c, 242c, PC 772
onyn BK 136, 184, 190, 194, 203, 262, TH 4a, 8a x 2, CW 143, 343, 678, 1459, 2010, 2182.

'SELF'
honan PA 6a, OM 94, 1455, 2248, 2650, PC 87, 2001, 2285, 2642, 2877, 3082, 3226, RD 642, 701, 1250, 1638, 2042, 2065, 2073, 2459, 2569, BM 504, 2961
honen BM 1960, 1996, 4059, BK 466, SA 59; *hunnen* N. Boson x 3 (BF: 27, 31)
honon PA 25d, 37d, 81c, 89d, 101b, 101d, 160d, 161b, 169a, 187b, 256d, PC 545
honyn OM 345, BM 3641, BK 1436, 2750, TH 1, 1a x 3, 2 x 2, 5, 6 x 3, 7a, 8 x 5, 9 x 4, 9a x 4, 10 x 5, etc., SA 59, 59a, 61, 61a, 62, 64a x 3, 65, CW 476, 925, 975, 2212, 2468; *honnyn* BK 312.

'HEART'
colan OM 357, BM 940, 1003, 2277, SA 61a, 65a, TH 9a, 19a, 20a, 21 x 2, 23a, 26a, 28, 30 x 2, 54, BK 363, 587, 733, 949, 1076, 1435, 1587, 1703, 2229, 2277, 2317, 2339, 2383, 2347, 2391, 2405, 2556, 2616, 2646, 2682, 2979, 3026, 3159, 3218, 3287, CW 306, 1199, 1206, 1212, 1224, 1228, 1263, 1351, 1391, 1503, 1523, 1689, 1964, 1998, 2496; *collan* CW 284, 734, N Boson x 2 (BF: 27, 31)
colen PA 115c, OM 365, 428, BM 2049, 2408, 3585, 3589

TOWARDS AUTHENTIC CORNISH

colon PA 1a, 25c, 26d, 30a, 37a, 40d, 81d, 87a, 89b, 101a, 122c, 126d, 128c, 139a, 141d, 164b, 166c, 172b, 172d, 186c, 216d, 217d, 218d, 219a, 221b, 222c, 223a, 224b, 225b, 228b, 231d, 256c, OM 511, 527, 721, 1264, 1337, 1376, 1381, 1525, 1568, 1608, 1758, 1857, 1873, 2088, 2135, 2174, 2181, 2628, 2748, 2818, PC *passim*, RD *passim*, BM 297, 545, 683, 690, 1258, 2507, 2598, 2606, 2992, 3034, 3560, 3494, 3650, 3788, 4102, TH 15a
colyn BM 628, 1804.

'CERTAIN'
certan OM 14, 93, 489, 494, 501, 1103, 1313, 1321, 1344, 1488, 1540, 1561, 1692, 1696, 1759, 1817, 1839, 2207, 2234, etc.; PC 31, 49, 90, 155, 285, 442, 475, 527, 632, etc., RD 18, 45, 100, 120, 235, 396, 444, 534, 569, 665, 948, 1142, 1158, etc., BM 175, 244, 247, 260, 445, 1938, 2117, 2139, 2275, 2959, 3111, 3824, 4041, 4053, 4550, TH 16, 26a, 42a, BK 681, 707, 952, 2101; *sertan* TH 3, 37a, BK 192, 921, 1080, 1542, 1934, 1960, 2396, 2700, CW 5, 52, 1836
certen OM 918, 2334, PC 69, 567, BM 361, 660, 732, 748, 1006, 1080, 1241, 1536, 1542, 1551, 1610, 1622, 1693, 1700, 1786, 1899, 2034, 2066, 2067, 2073, 2195, 2246, 2260, 2325, 2342, 2376, 2384, 2503, 2552, 2716, 2901, 3100, 3158, 3241, 3252, 3625, 3649, 3664, 3691, 3903, 4032, 4079, 4245, 4305, 4344, 4392, 4420, 4426, 4444, 4521, 4528; *serten* CW 25, 95, 228, 281, 298, 357, 381, 387, 689, 1619, 2051, 2085, 2151, 2231, 2372
certyn BM 1744, 1806, 1955, 1966, 2337, 2515, 3459, 4452, 4471, SA 60
certain BK 943; *certayn* TH 17a, BK 1526, 1535; *sertayn* TH 48a, CW 133; *sertayne* CW 256, 652; *certeyn* BM 315, 2305, 2306, 3644, 3988.

'CHILDREN'
flehas OM 975, 1031, 1159, 1168, BM 1580, 1699, 1782, 3153, TH 10a; *fleghas* PC 1924, 2503
flehes OM 932, 1036, 1258, PC 2643, 2647, BM 2014, TH 7a, 22, 22a, 28, 28a, 42, 54a; fleghes PC 239, RD 162
flehis TH 23a x 2, 24, 26, 37, 37a, 41, SA 59, CW 1385
flehys OM 1623, 1552, BM 41, 94, 116, 183, 1119, 1507, 1589, 1593, 1604, 1634, 1667, 1674, 1676, 1692, 1705, 1778, 1837, 2676, 3150, 3192, 4542, TH 9, BK 1552, CW 653, 1035, 2210, 2227, 2252, 2374, 2540; *fleghys* PA 169a, 246c, OM 1553, 1575, 1588, 1611, 2834, PC 307, 432, 1939, 1945, 1950, 1964, 2201, TH 41.

'TO WAIT'
gortas BK 1330, 2766, TH 13a, 36, CW 960, 1996, 2117; *gurtas* TH 13a, 36, 36; gortays BM 2472
gortes OM 1718, BM 3117, 3655; *gurtes* TH 39a
gortos PA 164d, 250d, RD 2146, 2412, 2435.

'PEOPLE'
pobal OM 1843
pobel OM 1543, 1557, 1564, 1574, 1594, 1597, 1627, 1648, 1687, 1815, RD 1185, SA 59, 63a, 65a, 66, BK 2368; *pobell* BM 242, CW 1518, 2138, 2206, 2251, 2338, 2364, 2382
pobyl PA 89c, 89d, OM 1803, 1832, PC 447, RD 248, BM 1249, 1579, 2022, 2324, 2437, 2489, 2496, 4168; *pobyll* PA 6b, 67a, 97c, BM 1325, TH 1, 4, 4a, 7, 11, 11a,

UNSTRESSED SYLLABLES

13, 13a, 14 x 3, 18, 19a x 2, 20, etc., BK 1230, 2798; *pobil* PC 2004, BM 1154, 1172, 3998; *pobill* TH 1, 5, 5, 9, 22a, etc.

Some of these variant spellings are used in rhyme. Many, however, are not and it seems that we have in the above examples convincing evidence that by the time our Middle Cornish texts were written, unstressed syllables had fallen together as schwa. This is, of course, another way of saying that the Prosodic Shift had operated well before any of the above texts were written.

16.02 The third plural of the prepositional pronouns

The reduction of final -*o* to schwa as a result of the Prosodic Shift had repercussions in the prepositional pronouns. It became impossible to tell apart *ganso* 'with him/it' from *gansa* 'with them', *ragtho* 'for him/it' from *ragtha* 'for them' and *ynno* 'in him/it' from *ynna* 'in them'. In order to maintain the difference the third plural was recharacterized by the edition of the third plural verbal desinence -*ans*. The first written examples are from TH and SA where we find the following:

gansans
ny an Jevith agan reward gansans y 'we will have our reward with them' TH 22a
yth owhy citesens gansans an syns 'you are citizens with them, the saints' TH 33
in aga mysk y ha gansans y 'among them and with them' TH 49a.

ynnans
pana vveldar ha humylite esa ynnans y aga honyn 'what lowliness and humility is in them themselves' TH 6a
openly gothvethis ha gwelys ynans y 'openly known and seen in them' TH 14
an re na as tevas an spuris sans innans 'those who have the Holy Spirit in them' TH 38a
fatla ugy faith an tasow coth a vam egglys inans y 'how the faith of the ancient fathers of the church is in them' SA 59a.

ragthans
eff a rug oll an da a ylly thethans y ha ragthans y 'he did all the good he could to them and for them' TH 23
mas eff a pesys ragthans 'but he prayed for them' TH 23.

thewortans
ny rug eff omdenna y favore thewortans y 'he did not withdraw his favour from them' TH 23.

thethans
thethans y re bo oll honor ha glory 'to them be all honour and glory' TH 16
eff a rug oll an da a ylly thethans y 'he did all the good he could to them' TH 23
eff a ve promysiis thethans y ha thega successors 'he was promised to them and to their successors' TH 36a
Jhesus a leverys thethans y 'Jesus said to them' TH 43a

*in generally **thethans** y oll* 'generally to them all' TH 44a
*Whath eth ew gwrys satisfaction **thethans*** 'Still satisfaction is made to them' SA 64
*ha rag henna nyng ew **thethans** corf Dew* 'and therefore it is not the body of God to them' SA 65a.

intrethans
*ha eweth brassa conjunction **intrethans*** 'and also a greater conjunction between them' SA 65.

The use of this *-ans* in third person plural prepositional pronouns is general in Cornish thereafter. There is no reason for such recharacterization, were it not for the effects of the Prosodic Shift. It is noteworthy that no such recharacterization has occurred in Breton.

Although *-ans* appears first in Tregear, we can be quite sure that it was a feature of speech considerably earlier, but was not allowed in writing. I assume that *-ans* was already present in Cornish of the fifteenth century.

16.03 Final -*o* as <e> and <a>

The third person singular of the present subjunctive ends in -*o*. Because the vowel was being reduced to schwa, in the earliest Middle Cornish the scribes had difficulty with it and spelt it with <a> or <e>. Here are some examples from the *Ordinalia*:

-*o* as <-e>
*ha pan wryllyf tremene a'n bys ru'm **gorre** th'y wlas* 'and when I pass from the world, may he send me to his kingdom' OM 531-32
*re'm **gorre** the gosoleth* 'may he bring me to peace' OM 858
*re'n **sawye** arluth huhel* 'may a noble Lord save us' OM 1088
*erna'n **prenne** an guas na* 'until that fellow buy it' OM 2152
*re'th **ordene** ty ha'th wrek pan vy marow yn y cver* 'may he enrol thee and thy wife when thou shouldst die in his court' PC 685-86
*byth na **scapye*** 'may he never escape' PC 1888
*ha why dreheueugh y beyn may **farwe** an thew vylen* 'and do you lift up the other one so the two scoundrels may die' PC 2826-67
*hag y a wyth y vody na **potre** bys vynary* 'and they will keep his body so that it never decays' PC 3199-200
*nyns us gorryth na benen byth wel cusyl bys vycken a **lauarre*** 'there is neither male nor woman who would ever speak better counsel' RD 420-22
*teulyn grabel warnotho scherp ha dalgenne ynno byth na **schapye*** 'let us cast a grappling iron on him sharp and seize him so that he never escapes' RD 2268-70.

-*o* as <-a>
*leuerel thu'm arluth gura ihesu na **wrella** damnpnye* 'speak to my lord that he do not condemn Jesus' PC 1957-58
*kemmys na **greysa** goef* 'woe to as many as believe not' RD 176
*ny gyf methek a'n **sawya*** 'he will not find a doctor who may heal him' RD 1648.

UNSTRESSED SYLLABLES

16.04 George's view of unstressed syllables

George originally claimed that unstressed *a, e* and *o* were different in Middle Cornish and that unstressed *-e* in the texts represented schwa /ə/. Indeed he gives several examples of *-a* contrasting with [ə], for example:

ihesu pendra leuerta
an fleghys vs ow cane
yowynkes menogh a wra
yn yowynkneth mur notye (PSRC: 120).

Now he claims that final unstressed *-e* represents */ɛ/ and that it fell together with /a/ c. 1475 in the texts and c. 1500 in place-names (KKC21: 89-90). He also says that in closed syllables unstressed */ɛ/ became /a/ c. 1550 in the texts and c. 1525 in place-names (KKC21: 90). He also says that final unstressed *-o* became /a/ c. 1525 and final unstressed *o* in closed syllables became /a/ c. 1575. This is all special pleading [SP]. There is no evidence that unstressed *a, e* and *o* became anything other than schwa; there is, moreover, no evidence that the falling together was so late. Indeed, as we have already seen, the evidence indicates that unstressed short vowels were all schwa by the fifteenth century. Scribal tradition alone kept the syllables separate in writing. What is really curious, however, is that in PSRC George asserted that final unstressed <e> was schwa; now, however, he claims that final unstressed <e> was */ɛ/. Are the users of Kernowek Kemyn aware that their phonology has been changed?

George has an ulterior motive for claiming that these changes occurred at such a late date: Kernowek Kemyn is based on George's understanding of Cornish phonology c. 1500. Since, according to George, *-o* did not become *-a* until c. 1525 and *o* did not become *a* in unstressed closed syllables until c. 1575, it is quite legitimate for Kernowek Kemyn to write them differently.

For George even to have admitted that unstressed syllables were falling together marks some kind of advance. There is one question, however, which George does not answer. In fact he does not even ask it [AD]: why have unstressed *e* and *o* fallen together with *a*? What conceivable reason was there during the course of the sixteenth century for these vowels to cease to remain separate? There was, I believe, no reason at all. They had already fallen together as schwa much earlier. The scribes attempted to keep them separate but found the task beyond them. The reason that unstressed vowels fell together (a process which almost certainly started before the beginning of the fifteenth century) was the same as the cause of all the phonetic changes we have been discussing to date, i.e. the Prosodic Shift. George's reluctance to admit that the Prosodic Shift had occurred before our earliest Middle Cornish texts were written, involves him in much special pleading—none of which is very convincing.

16.05 Confusion of final -*e*, -*a* and -*o* in PA

Passion agan Arluth after the *Charter Fragment* is our oldest Middle Cornish text. The date of composition is not known. The earliest manuscript is fifteenth century. In PA the confusion between -*o* and -*e* and -*a* in the subjunctive is remarkable. It is similar indeed to the confusion noted above in the *Ordinalia*. Since, however, PA is our oldest continuous text, I should like to look at the confusion of unstressed -*e*, -*o* and -*a* in it in some detail. The first two lines of PA read:

> *Tays ha mab han sperys sans wy a bys a levn golon*
> *Re **wronte** ʒeugh gras ha whans ʒe wolsowas y basconn*

> [Father and Son and the Holy Spirit you pray with all your heart
> to grant unto you grace and desire to listen to his passion.] (PA 1ab).

In line b *Re wronte* is for the present subjunctive *Re wrontyo 'may he grant'. Stanza 72 reads as follows:

> *Gor ʒe gleʒe yn y goyn ʒe pedyr crist a yrghys*
> *rag dre gleʒe a **veughe** dre gleʒe y fyth leʒys*
> *dewʒek lygyon yn vn ro vye an nef danuenys*
> *ha moy a mynnen ʒymmo pesy ow ʒas pur barys*

> ["Put thy sword in its sheath," Christ to Peter commanded,
> "For who lives by sword by sword shall be killed.
> Twelve legions all at once would be sent from the heavens
> and more if I wished for myself very readily to beseech my Father."]

Note that there is no rhyme in the first hemistich. The clause *rag dre gleʒe a veughe* is for **rag dre gleʒe a vewho* 'for whoever shall live by sword'. The expected -*o* has been written as <e> because there is no difference in pronunciation between the two final vowels.

Stanza 77 reads as follows:

> *Tus crist ʒe ves a fyas pep ay du pur voreʒek*
> *saw pedyr crist a holyas abell avel vn ownek*
> *ʒe dyller an prins annas ene yʒ ese sethek*
> *orto ef y a sethas may **clewo** leff ihesus whek*

> [Christ's people fled away, everyone his own way very sorrowful,
> but Peter followed Christ at a distance like one afraid
> to the place of the prince Annas; there was a tribunal there.
> Upon it they sat, that he might hear the voice of sweet Jesus.]

In the last hemistich *clewo* is present subjunctive, but the sense requires the past subjunctive *clewa* 'that he might hear', rather than 'that he may hear'.

UNSTRESSED SYLLABLES

Stanza 109 reads:

Y eth bys yn herodes ha crist ganse fast kylmys
ef a gara crist gwelas rag kymmys y3 o praysys
*ganso mar **callo** clewas whelth nowyth a **vo** coyntis*
*mar **callo** trylye 3e hes lauar crist pan **vo** clewys*

[They went unto Herod with Christ with them bound fast;
he wished to see Christ for he had been so praised,
that he might hear from him a new story that might be strangeness,
that he might turn round Christ's utterance when it should be heard.]

Here present subjunctive *mar callo* 'if he can' is written twice, though the sense requires the past subjunctive *calla* 'if he could'. Notice also *a vo coyntis* for **a ve coyntis* and *pan vo clewys* for **pan ve clewys*. Present subjunctive *bo* and past subjunctive *be* remain phonetically separate because their vowels are stressed and do not therefore fall together. That the present subjunctive is used for past subjunctive twice here suggests that present subjunctive *bo* and past subjunctive *be* were regularly confused in speech. This can only be by analogy with other verbs in which the unstressed *-o* of the present subjunctive is confused with the unstressed *-a* of the past. The confusion of the two subjunctives of *bos* suggests that present and past subjunctive had long fallen together in other verbs (for phonetic reasons) and now *bos* is following suit by analogy. I would suggest that *bo* for *be* is indicative of a development *-o* > *-a* that is already well established.

The first two lines of stanza 139 read:

*Colon den a yll crakye a **vynha** prest predery*
an paynys bras an geve han dyspyth heb y dyly

[The heart of a man may break who may wish continually to consider
the great pains he had and the undeserved hostility.]

The main verb is present and the present subjunctive **a vynho* 'who may wish' would be expected. As it is, the scribe writes *a vynha* 'who might wish' in the past subjunctive.

The second half of stanza 144 reads:

gor3eby te ny vynsys a ny wo3as ow mestry
*bos 3ymmo may **fes** le3ys bo delyffris 3e wary*

[You did not wish to answer. Do you not know my authority,
that I have power that you be killed or set at liberty?]

The main verb *wo3as* 'you know' governs *bos 3ymmo may fes le3ys* 'that it is in my power that you be killed'. One would expect the present subjunctive *may*

177

TOWARDS AUTHENTIC CORNISH

fy 'that you be' but the scribe writes *may fes.* Clearly all persons of the present and past subjunctive are confused in all verbs including *bos,* even though the vowel in *bos* is stressed. Indeed it is highly significant here that we are dealing with the second person singular rather than the third person. The third person singular is the commonest form in the paradigm and it is the basis upon which the rest of the paradigm is based. At this point in PA not only has *be* 'he would be' taken the place of *bo* 'he may be', but *bes* 'thou might be' has replaced *by* 'thou mayst be'. The analogy is here at two removes. We can, I think, be quite sure that at the time the manuscript of PA the identity of final *-a* and *-o* had been a feature of spoken Cornish for several generations

Stanza 150 of PA reads:

Camen pylat pan welas na ylly crist delyffre
*mannan **geffo** ef sor bras ȝeworth ol an goweȝe*
rag henna ef a luggyas Ihesus ȝeȝe ȝy laȝe
the ves y a thelyffras barabas quyth mayȝ elle

[When Pilate saw that he could not in any way deliver Christ
without incurring great wrath from all the company,
therefore he determined to hand Jesus to them to kill.
They released Barabas free that he might go off unimpeded.]

Mannan geffo 'that he would not get' is present subjunctive, but one would expect the past **mannan geffa* (for *ma na'n geffa*) 'that he would not get'. Stanza 158 reads:

In meth gurek an goff ȝeȝe kentrow ȝewy why ny fyll
awos bos claff y ȝewle toche vyth gonys ef na yll
del won yn vn fystene me as gura ny strechyaff pell
*aban nag es a **wothfe** ȝeugh paris an **guerelle** gwell*

[The wife of the smith said to them, "Nails will not be lacking to you.
Since his hands are diseased, he can do no stroke of work.
I will make them as quickly as I know how; I shall not delay—
since there is no one who knows how—who may make them better for you."]

The verbs *wothfe* 'who may know' is in the past subjunctive when *wothfo* present subjunctive is the expected form. Similarly for *gurelle* (< **gurella*) 'would make' is past subjunctive, when the present **gurello* would be more natural.

The first two lines of stanza 225 read:

An goys na dagrennow try dre y ij lagas y ȝeth
*nyg o comfort na yly a **wrello** y holon hueth*

[From that blood three drops went into her eyes;
it was no comfort or salve that might make her heart glad.]

UNSTRESSED SYLLABLES

The verb *wrello* 'may make' is in the present subjunctive, but the past **wrella* 'might make' would have been the expected form.

It is quite clear from the confusion of present and past subjunctive in PA that the three final vowels *-a, -e* and *-o* have fallen together in Middle Cornish. Moreover the confusion of present subjunctive *bo* with past subjunctive *be* is by analogy with other verbs in which the final *-o/-a* confusion has been phonetically determined. It is certain therefore that the confusion of *-a* and *-o* was of sufficiently long standing by the time of PA for the confusion in the subjunctive tenses to have influenced the verb *bos* 'to be', not merely in the relevant third person singular, but as we have seen, in other persons as well. I take it as proven that *-o, -a* and *-e* had fallen together well before the date of PA. George's suggestion (KKC21: 90) that *-o* and *-a* remained separate until about 1525 cannot be sustained.

16.06 Rhyme in Cornish

In Brythonic prosody words rhymed with each other if they ended in similar vowel and consonant. It did not matter whether the rhyming syllable was stressed or unstressed. Thus in medieval Welsh *tad* rhymes with *cariad*, *cig* with *ewig* and *ol* with *nefol*. The same system obtains in Middle Breton where *plen* rhymes with *termen*, *bern* with *espern* and *quet* with *estimet*. The Prosodic Shift in Cornish reduced clear unstressed vowel to schwa, but the poets had inherited a prosody in which unstressed vowels rhymed with both stressed and unstressed syllables. This meant that in Middle Cornish the neutral vowel schwa could be written in a variety of ways to give an eye-rhyme with syllables of varying stressed vowels or with syllables that also contained schwa.

This is exemplified in the way, for example, *certan* 'certain' rhymes in Middle Cornish with monosyllables containing completely different vowels.

1 -an
arluth whek ny amount man
an pyt a wrussyugh certan OM 2791-92.

2 -en
Drog yv genef gruthyl den
precius haual thy'm certen OM 917-18.

3 -yn
mones deglos ny a vyn
thy anclethyes in certyn BM 4470-71.

George is unwilling to admit that these syllables rhyme perfectly, because to do so would be to acknowledge that the unstressed vowels are schwa. And to allow that, is the same as admitting that the Prosodic Shift has taken affect in Middle Cornish. In order to avoid such a damaging admission George devises his own rules for Cornish rhyme.

TOWARDS AUTHENTIC CORNISH

16.07 George's approach to rhyme in Cornish

George tells us that in Middle Cornish there were three kinds of rhyme: 1) perfect rhymes; 2) imperfect rhymes and 3) poor rhymes. He goes so far as to devise his own technical terms for the first two calling them in Kernowek Kemyn *rimyow perfydh* and *rimyow isperfydh* respectively. A "perfect rhyme", according to George, is one like *avan* 'above' rhyming with *splan* 'brilliant', where the rhyming syllable is in his view [aːn]. An "imperfect rhyme", according to George, is one like *splan* 'brilliant' rhyming with *glan* 'clean, pure', where the first is [splaːn] but the second [glaːn]. All the "perfect" and "imperfect rhymes" for a syllable when taken together form, according to George a "rhyming ensemble". For example, according to George, the following would form a "rhyming ensemble": final [i] in *ki* 'dog' and *pysi* 'to pray', final [ɪ] in *my* 'I' and *ty* 'thou', and the [ɔɪ] in loan-words like *joy* 'joy'.

"Poor rhymes", according to George, are rhymes like Latin *dominus* 'Lord' at OM 1953 which rhymes with *hunrvs* 'dream' in the next line. This latter is also spelt <hunros> and George tells us it has been spelt *hunrvs* at OM 1594 to give an eye-rhyme.

George also enunciates two fundamental rules in this prosody of his:

1. If two words are rhymed, it does not necessarily mean that the sounds in their final syllables are identical; unless the rhyme is poor, it means solely that they are sufficiently close as to form part of the same rhyming ensemble.

2 If two words in a stanza are contrasted in rhyme, it means that the sounds in their final syllables are not the same.

This second rule, George tells us, is much more powerful than the first.

The first thing to notice is that the notions of a "rhyming ensemble", "perfect" and "imperfect rhymes" and the Cornish terms used to describe them are entirely of George's own invention. Of George's own devising is the "powerful" second rule that if words are contrasted in rhyme, their final syllables are different. George has devised everything here with the sole object of proving that final syllables are different, that they have not fallen together and that the Prosodic Shift has not affected Cornish. Unfortunately for George none of his suggestions can be sustained.

The notion of "rhyming ensemble" depends upon there being both perfect and imperfect rhymes, since "perfect" and "imperfect rhymes" together form George's hypothetical "ensemble". Middle Cornish, according to George, has not experienced the Prosodic Shift. In this respect Middle Cornish resembles Middle and Modern Welsh and Middle and Modern Breton. We should, therefore, expect something comparable with George's "rhyming ensembles" in Welsh or Breton. Such a notion is unknown in either.

UNSTRESSED SYLLABLES

16.08 Rhyme in Welsh and Breton

In both languages a rhyme is either a perfect rhyme or it is not used. Welsh is wholly ignorant of "perfect" and "imperfect" rhymes. Welsh does have three different kinds of rhyme. The first variety is where a syllable, stressed or unstressed, containing the same vowel and consonant as another, rhymes with it. There is no consideration of length. The Welsh word *man* 'small' has a long vowel but it rhymes, for example, with *cusan* 'kiss' where the syllable is short:

> ac oed ym medw unoed m**an**
> och Iesu Grist, a chus**an**.

George would doubtless consider this one of his *"rimyow isperfydh"* but in Welsh it is a perfect rhyme. [For all aspects of Welsh rhyme see, for example, G. Williams (1954), Appendix A.]

In Welsh the other two kinds of rhyme are half-rhymes only. The first of these is known as *proest*. Here the consonant is the same but the vowel is different. The vowel must, however, be of the same length. Thus in English *mode* would half-rhyme with *speed*, but would not half-rhyme with *bid*. This is nothing like any of George's alleged *rimyow isperfydh*.

The second kind of half-rhyme is sometimes known as *odl wyddelig* 'Irish rhyme'. Here the rhyming vowel is the same but the consonants differ. Examples of *odl wyddelig* occur in the poem *Gododdin* and include such half-rhymes as *med ~ offer, esgar ~ haual* and *enwauc ~ gwirawt*. Again this is nothing like anything suggested by George. His "rhyming ensembles" are an *ad hoc* creation of his own.

In his edition of the late manuscript of *Christmas Hymns* (CH) in the Vannes dialect, Roparz Hemon draws attention to rhymes in the text that rhyme in Vannetais, but would not have rhymed in standard Middle Breton, for example, *esant ~ argant* (Middle Breton *ezont ~ argant*), *eu ~ maneieu* (Middle Breton *eu ~ meneziou*), *advocades ~ tres* (Middle Breton *aduocades ~ treus*) and *Virihés ~ tres* (Middle Breton *Guerches ~ treus*). Moreover he points out that the non-rhymes *man ~ absolven* (Middle Breton *man - absoluenn*), *fen ~ man* (Middle Breton *penn ~ man*), *man ~ grenen* (Middle Breton *man ~ greunenn*), are in fact rhymes, though they do not appear to be in the text and would not have rhymed in standard Middle Breton. In Vannetais, however, they rhyme perfectly, because the word *man* 'this' (Cornish *-ma*) is pronounced *men* in the dialect of Vannes. In Breton therefore *man* does not rhyme with *grenen* but Vannetais *men* does rhyme with *grenen*. This is radically different from the situation in Middle Cornish where *certan* in OM rhymes both with *man* 'not, nothing' and *den* 'man'. George's notions of perfect and imperfect rhymes can be dismissed.

16.09 George's "contrasting" rhymes

George's suggestion that words contrasting in rhyme have different final syllables is also difficult to sustain. Look at the following stanza from *Origo Mundi*:

> gallas moyses ha'y pobel
> mes a'm glas hy yv thewel
> yn pur wyr war ov **ene**
> me a vyn aga *sywe*
> ha warbarth age *lathe*
> kyns me the treyle the **tre** (OM 1627-32).

The rhyme scheme here is *aabccb*, and *sywe* rhymes with *lathe* and contrasts with *ene* and *tre*. Contrast that with the following stanza also from *Origo Mundi*:

> an sacryfys · the thev yv gurys
> dun ny the **dre**
> ow map ysac · scon dus yn rac
> gura ov **sywe** (OM 1391-94).

Here the short lines of four syllables rhyme *aabccb*. In this second stanza *sywe* rhymes with *dre* the lenited form of *tre*, whereas *tre* and *sywe* were contrasted in the first stanza quoted.

According to George's rhyming rules *tre* and *sywe* must have different vowels because they contrast with each other. But in the second stanza quoted, they rhyme with each other, suggesting that they were part of the same "rhyming ensemble".

Look at the following stanza in PA:

> Pan o y besadow **guris**
> zen dow3ek y *leuerys*
> koscough lemmyn mar sew **prys**
> powesough wy yv *grevijs*
> tus vs 3ym ow **tevones**
> yv gans ow thraytor *dyskis*
> fatel dons thov **hemeres**
> ha del ve3aff *hombronkis* (PA 61).

Here *guris* 'made, done' contrasts with the verb *leuerys* 'he said' and the past pariciples *grevijs* 'grieved', *dyskis* 'taught', and *hombronkis* 'led'. Compare that with the following stanza also from PA:

> Ena hy a ve **seuys**
> yn ban ynter benenas
> arluth hy a **leueris**

UNSTRESSED SYLLABLES

ow holon y ma genas
kepar ha te hy ʒew **guris**
yn anken worth ʒe welas
bytqueth den ny ***woʒevys***
payn ella ʒy golon nes (PA 172).

Here *guris* 'made, done' rhymes with *leueris* 'said' (exactly the same verbal form as in PA 61) and also with the past participles *seuys* 'stood' and *woʒevys* 'suffered'. In one stanza in PA *guris* contrasts with *leuerys* and the past participles in *-is/ijs*, in the second stanza it rhymes with *leueris* and the past participles. In the first case the rhymes contrast, in the second they appear to form part of the same "rhyming ensemble". George's views on rhyme in Cornish can be disregarded.

CHAPTER 17
Concluding remarks on *Kernewek Kemmyn*: Cornish for the Twenty-First Century

17.00 Voiceless sonants *lh* and *nh*

George is adamant that the spelling <lh> in the texts is just an "occcasional spelling" for <ll> and the same is true of <nh> for <nn> (KKC21: 66). I disagree. Look at the following:

> *kynth ellen vy prest **in hoth*** 'though I always go naked' BM 3064
> *an Gie oyah tel er angye **en hoath*** 'they knew they were naked' RC: 177
> *rag theram **en hoath*** 'because I am naked' RC 23: 178
> *pu reg laule theese tell estah **en hoath*** 'who told you were naked' RC 23: 179.

There is no scribal continuity between BM and the translation from Genesis by Wella Kerew. Moreover Kerew writes phonetically and both he and the scribe of BM write *yn noth* 'naked' with a voiceless [nh]. I find this highly suggestive and am not prepared to dismiss it as an "occasional spelling".

Look at the following:

> *hep garra thotha **telhar** veeth* 'without allowing it any room' BF: 25
> *Palatium... A Palace. C[ornish] **Telhar**, plas* AB: 111b.

Both Nicholas Boson in the first example and Lhuyd in the second wrote phonetically. I do not think we can dismiss *telhar* as simply an occasional spelling for *tellar, tyller* 'place'. I assume there was a variant [telhər] with a voiceless [lh]. The same sound [lh] was clearly intended in the following:

> *tru a thu **elhas** elhas* 'woe, O God, alas, alas!' PA 246b
> ***ethlays** gwef pan ove genys* 'alas, woe is me that I am born' CW 1040.

I do not believe George would suggest <thl> in *ethlays* was merely an "occasional spelling" for <ll>.

17.01 The diphthong *ow*

I do not here wish to deal at length with the change of *ow* > *aw* in both stressed and unstressed syllables, nor with the shift of *ei* > *ai*, both of which changes occurred during the Middle Cornish period. I disagree completely with George on these points and it would not be difficult to prove his view mistaken.

I will, however, deal with just one error of his. He says that the shift of *ew* > *ow* took place in the sixteenth century and it is for this reason that one finds it in UCR but not in Kernowek Kemyn (KKC21: 129). In fact the most frequent occurrences of *ow* from earlier *ew* are in the verbs *clowes* 'hear' < *clewes* (which

CONCLUDING REMARKS ON *KKC21*

Kernowek Kemyn wrongly spells *<klywes>) and *cowsel* 'speak' < *keusel*. BM often writes <ov> or <ow> in these words. Here are a very few examples:

ow/ov < ew in *Beunans Meriasek* in **clowes** 'hear' & **cowsel** 'speak'
pan **glowe** BM 1030; del **glowas** BM 1160; del **glowa** BM 1234; **clowugh** BM 1890; del **glowevy** BM 1957; del **glowys** BM 2120; a **glosugh** why BM 2222; del ny **glowys** 2238; **glovsugh** BM 2244; prag na **glowys** BM 2251; me a **glowes** BM 2394; me re **glowes** BM 2526; na yl **clowas** BM 2636; my a **clov** BM 2661.
del **govs** BM 1499; a **covsis** BM 1729; y a **covsis** BM 1792; neb a **covs** BM 2091; ny **govsy** BM 2239; **covsugh** BM 2534; kyn **covseff** BM 2555; **covsis** BM 2773; bethens **covsys** BM 2914; **covsugh** BM 2934; na **govsugh** BM 2956; pendra **govsugh** why BM 3125; **covsel** BM 3752; erna **govsen** BM 3985.

George surmises that Rad. Ton, the scribe of BM was of the older generation in 1504, when he wrote the play down (KKC21: 63; see **14.10** above). I do not know what age George believed Ton to have been, but let us assume he believes he was 40 years old at least. By this reckoning Ton would have learnt to write c. 1470—yet he invariably has *covsel* 'to speak' and *clowes* 'to hear'. This is also at variance with what George believes, since he tells us "The change from <ew> to <ow> appears to have taken place in the sixteenth century" (KKC21: 129).

In fact the shift *ew > ow* is much older than c. 1470, since there are numerous examples in *Pascon agan Arluth*. Here are a few of them:

y a **gowsys** PA 50d; 3en **dowzek** PA 61b; ny **gowsyn** PA 79d; 3e ben **dowlyn** PA 137a; war ben **dowlyn** PA 171c; a **gowsys** PA 188a; 3y ben **dowlyn** PA 220b.

If Kernowek Kemyn were really based upon the Cornish of c. 1500, it would write <kowsel> and <klowes>. As it is these items are spelt <kewsel> and *<klywes> respectively. Kernowek Kemyn has been constructed upon a faulty understanding of Cornish phonology.

17.02 *Rag* but *carrek*

I have suggested that in Middle Cornish when words ended in unstressed original *k*, e.g. *Meryasek* PN, *carrek* 'rock', *marhak* 'horseman' and so on, the <k> was pronounced [k]. When the historic *k* was after a stressed vowel, it was pronounced [g], e.g. in *rag* 'for', *wheg* 'sweet', *teg* 'beautiful' and *mog* 'smoke'. I suggested also that the same alternation occurred with *p/b*, e.g. *morrep* 'seashore' but *mab* 'son'. This alternation I ascribed to the differential treatment of the Brythonic lenes as a result of the Prosodic Shift. The lenis after a stressed and thus vigorous vowel was smeared by the voiced nature of the vowel and itself acquired voicing. The same was not true after an unstressed vowel, where the lenis remained unvoiced and fell together with /k/ or /p/ from other sources.

TOWARDS AUTHENTIC CORNISH

We see this alternation operating in place-names in Cornwall. One finds, for example, *Breage, Mabe, Chyvogue* (< *chy fog*), but *Dorminack, Arwenack, Vorrap,* etc.

George denies that the Prosodic Shift has occurred in Middle Cornish and he is uncertain about the pronunciation of final *g/k, b/p*. The following exchange occurs between George and Dunbar:

> K.G. Dr Williams believes that //-g// was pronounced [-g] in monosyllables and [-k] in polysyllables in all phonetic environments, whereas I think it more likely that the pronunciation depended on the following sounds.
> P.D. Is that important?
> K.G. Not in my view; it's a phonetic problem, and one which cannot be fully solved in the absence of traditional Cornish speakers (KKC21: 157).

George is right when he calls this matter "a phonetic problem" but then the whole phonology of Cornish is "a phonetic problem" and he originally claimed to have solved the question of the phonology better than anyone before him. His two works PSRC and KKC21 are entirely concerned with little but one "phonetic problem" after another. Why then does George dismiss the opposition *rag ~ carrek* as a "phonetic problem"? Why does he not explain this matter to his pupil and thus show that I am wrong? After all, I have, according to George, "made a hash" of most of Cornish phonology. When it comes to Cornish my "credibility is tending to zero". How does it happen that George is unable to explain this question, when I have a coherent and cogent explanation for it?

George has taken it upon himself single-handedly and without consulting other investigators (some of whom might even be more experienced than he) to set out the complete phonology of Middle Cornish. He has, moreover, arbitrarily rewritten the entire orthographical system of the language, ignoring the practices of the medieval scribes. This he could only have done if he believed that he understood the phonology of the language uniquely well. Indeed he implies that he knows better than the medieval scribes, for he says:

> It would be a poor show, with our vastly increased knowledge of the Celtic languages and of linguistics, if we could not improve on the spelling of Cornish used in the Middle Ages (KKC21: 142).

Yet in the earlier quotation he says the question of *g/k* cannot be solved in the absence of native speakers. If there are problems that cannot, then, be resolved, we should not attempt to recast wholesale the orthography of Cornish on the basis of our limited understanding. In which case the radical restructuring of revived Cornish in 1987 under the name of Kernowek Kemyn was a mistake.

CONCLUDING REMARKS ON *KKC21*

17.03 Conclusion

I have to date answered without much difficulty a number of points made by George in KKC21 in defence of Kernowek Kemyn. Indeed not one of George's refutations of my arguments can be sustained. To disprove any of George's counterclaims is easy, since Kernowek Kemyn is so completely mistaken both conception (i.e. a new and artificial orthography for a resuscitated language) and execution (i.e. George's fundamental error of ignoring effects of the Prosodic Shift on Middle Cornish). Because I have answered enough of George's points, I do not intend to spend any more time answering those that remain. It does not seem wise to me to spend any more time on George's defence of Kernowek Kemyn. The whole system is, in my view, a mistake and cannot be defended. This latest work of George's does nothing to convince me otherwise. I have already above quoted Mills' damning judgement of KKC21. Let me quote the relevant sentence again:

> To demonstrate individually that each of George's analyses is worng would take a very long time, simply because there are a lot of analyses and there is very little that could be said to be right about any of them (*Cornish Studies: Seven*: 201).

Instead of continuing to answer KKC21 point by point, I should like to devote the following chapters to a short examination of two basic handbooks of Kernowek Kemyn: 1) George's *Gerlyver Kernewek Kemmyn* and 2) Wella Brown's *Grammar of Modern Cornish* (i.e. Kernowek Kemyn).

CHAPTER 18
Problems with George's *Gerlyver Kernewek Kemmyn* (GKK)

18.00 The inaccuracy of George's GKK
In my objections to Kernowek Kemyn in *Cornish Today* I included one (C26) about GKK, in which I said "The database on which Kernowek Kemyn was constructed is defective; as a result GKK is replete with omissions and misinformation". George takes exception to this judgement and calls it a "calumny" (KKC21: 12). I have more recently published a review article of GKK in *Cornish Studies: Nine* (2001): 246-311 in which, among other things, I draw attention to the inaccuracy of many of George's "authentication codes". I list approximately 370 erroneous entries in GKK. My observation therefore that GKK was "replete with omissions and misinformation" was no exaggeration. I should like now to discuss some further errors and omissions in the dictionary. Neither the list of entries I have selected nor my discussion of them is in any way exhaustive.

18.01 *Abram* [Abram] 'Abraham'
GKK citing this personal name adds a note: "N.B. Shortened form of **Abraham**." I am not sure this is true. As is well known, there are two forms of the name: *Abram* and *Abraham*. We read at Genesis xvii 5: "No longer shall your name be Abram, but your name shall be Abraham." The same distinction between *Abram* and *Abraham* is to be found in the Latin of the Vulgate, the version of the bible with which the Cornish scribes would have been familiar.

18.02 *Afrika* [Afryca] 'Africa'
This toponym is attested in TH:

> *ha ny*[*n*]*s ens y mas parcell bean a* **aphrica** 'and they were only a small part of Africa' TH 32.

It is omitted from GKK, which is regrettable. A variant form is now attested in BK:

> *me, Mustenar, an tebal-gower of myghtern in* **Affrycans** 'I, Mustenar, the evil man, am king in Africa' BK 2654-56.

18.03 *argument* [argument] 'argument', **argyans* [argyans] 'argument'
Under the first of these GKK tells us to use *argyans* in preference. This is curious. The word *argyans* is nowhere attested in Cornish, whereas *argument* is: *ma na wothfo gorthyby vn reson thu'm* **argument** 'so that he will not be able to return any reason to my argument' PC 1660-61; *Na esyn usya* **argumentys** *mas usya exampels Christ* 'Let us not use arguments but use the examples of Christ'

PROBLEMS WITH GEORGE'S *GERLYVER KERNEWEK KEMMYN*

SA 61a. I find it odd that a lexicographer should recommend ignoring an attested word in favour of one that does not exist.

18.04 *arvorek* [arvorek] 'coastal'
GKK cites this word and says it is unattested, having been taken from Nance's 1938 dictionary. GKK does not seem to have noticed that Lhuyd uses the word with a capital letter ten times (AB: 222 x 4, 223 x 5, 224) to mean 'Armorican'.

18.05 *'aria* [re Varya] 'by our Lady, O heavens'
GKK cites this word, tells us it occurs once in Lhuyd and cites the dialect form *areea*. The word does indeed occur in Lhuyd but at least three times and in its etymological form, as well as a more reduced version. It is not clear to me from where George derives his *'aria*. I have collected the following instances from Lhuyd:

> *Rea reva, rea rea, rea suas* and *repharîa, O strange* AB: 249a
> *Re Varîa, By our Lady* AB: 249c
> *Re Farîa pîa glou vi með hyi* '"By our Lady, who do I hear?" said she' AB: 253a.

GKK does not cite the longer form either here, under *re* 'by' (in oaths) or under *Maria*.

18.06 *budhek* [budhek] 'victorious', **Budhik* 'Boudicea'
GKK tells us that the first of these is unattested being confined to the place-name. The place-name however is mentioned in OM: *my a re thyugh plu* **vuthek** *ha'n garrak ruen gans hy thyr* 'I will give thee the parish of Budock and Carrack Ruan with its land' OM. 2463-64. The compiler credits himself, K[en] J. G[eorge], with the name *Budhik* 'Boudicea'. This is presumably on the basis of Welsh *Buddug* 'Boudicea'. *Buddug* is a pre-existing word in Welsh meaning 'victorious' and has merely been used in Welsh as a translation for *Boadicea*. Lhuyd gives Br[itish] *Bydhig*, Rom[an] *Boadicea* AB: 9a. The name *Boudicea* itself is for **Boudika*, which in Cornish would have given **Buthek* with *a*-affection of the final syllable. Cf. Lhuyd's *Brethonek* < **Britonnika*. It does seem curious that GKK should invent for Cornish a feminine name *Budhik* with an obviously masculine ending.

18.07 *bythkweyth* [bythqueth] 'never'. See **nevra**

18.08 *dampnashyon* [dampnacyon] 'damnation'
GKK informs us that this word is well attested in Middle Cornish. I have collected the following examples:

> *byth na thovtyogh* ***dampnasconn*** BM 1184
> *rag dovt cafus* ***dampnasconn*** BM 1251

in state a **thampnacion** TH 3
hag in stat a eternall **dampnacion** TH 4
thean stat a **thampnacion** TH 5
pehosow, **dampnacion**, ha myrnans heb deweth TH 10
mas drockolleth, ha **dampnacion** TH 11a
mab den then stat a **thampnacion** TH 12
in stat a eternall **dampnacion** TH 12a
ow mois pelha ha pelha in **dampnacion** TH 13a
the avoydya eternal **damnacion** TH 14a
teball vewnans a thora **dampnacion** TH 16a
in stat a **dampnacion** TH 20
sawys theworth **dampnacion** TH 39a
owh eva y **dampnation** y honyn TH 51a
dry iudgement ha **dampnacion** TH 53a
Y a's tevith **dampnassyon** BK 1447
Du roy thymmo **dampnassyon** BK 3140.

After his entry George adds a note: "N.B. The modern replacement **dampnyans** is preferred." *Dampnyans* is unattested and bears after it the initials K[en] J. G[eorge]. The compiler is thus telling his readers to replace a well-attested word with one of his own devising. This might be considered less than the very best lexicographical practice.

18.09 *degrena* [deglena] 'tremble, shudder'
GKK's "authentication code" after this word indicates that it is attested once, according to the compiler. In fact it was attested three times and with the discovery of *Bewnans Ke* occurs four times:

> yma ow trys ha'm dule thyworthef ow **teglene** 'my feet and my hands are shivering off me' PC 1216-17
> mar ethuk yv the weles may **tyglyn** an tybeles pan y'n guellons kettep pen 'so frightful is he to look at that the evil ones will shudder when they all see him' PC 3046-48
> In rag degough ou banar may halla bos **dyglynnys** 'Carry my banner forward that he may be terrified' BK 2796-97
> eva thysa a **theglyn** mar uthicke pan wella hy theth fegure yn kethe delma 'Eve will shudder at you when she sees your appearance so frightful in that same way' CW 485-87.

The most serious aspect of this entry in GKK is that the compiler has arbitrarily changed the form from the attested *deglena* to *degrena* on the basis of the Welsh cognate. This George gives as *dygrunu*. There is no such word. The Welsh cognate is *dygrynu* 'tremble, quake'. It is quite illegitimate to respell a word on etymological grounds. The word in Cornish is *deglena*, and *deglena* is the way it should be entered here.

PROBLEMS WITH GEORGE'S *GERLYVER KERNEWEK KEMMYN*

18.10 *delatya* [delatya] 'delay'
This word is attested once in Lhuyd's version of "Jowan Chy an Horth". The compiler gives an etymology: "DE + E[nglish] *late* + -YA" which he ascribes to K[en] J. G[eorge]. The origin of *delatya* is the same as that of English *delay*. Compounds of Latin *fero* 'I bear' can either contain the present stem *fer-* or the supine stem *lat-*. Doublets are therefore not infrequent: *transfer/translate, refer/relate, offer/oblate, defer/delay*. Cornish *delatya* derives ultimately from Latin *dilatare* 'to put off, to delay'. It has nothing to do with the English word *late*, which is of Germanic origin.

18.11 delk [delk] 'necklace'
This word appears as *delc* 'monile' [necklace] in OCV. GKK does not suggest an etymology. I suspect it is an Irish borrowing. The Old Irish word *delc, delg* originally meant 'thorn'. It later acquired the meaning 'pin, fastening', and was used in particular of a brooch fastening a mantle on the breast. 'Brooch at the breast' > 'necklace' would have been an intelligible development.

18.12 *Densher* [Densher] 'Devonshire'
GKK correctly states that this word is attested once from Nicholas Boson, who speaks of *marrak en pedden West pow* **Densher** 'a knight in the west end of the county of Devonshire' (BF: 27). It would appear therefore that he spoke of *pow Densher* rather than *Densher* by itself. George adds a note: "N.B. Use **Dewnens**." *Dewnens* (q.v.) is George's respelling of Lhuyd's *Deunanz* 'Devon', itself based on Welsh *Dyfnaint*. Since *Densher* was known to and used by a native speaker of Cornish, whereas *Deunanz* is a Welshman's Cornicization of a Welsh toponym, George is sacrificing authenticity for purism when he recommends *Dewnens*; see also **18.14** below.

18.13 *departya* [departya] 'depart'
This word is attested once in TH. George adds the note: "N.B. Use **mos** (**dheves**)." This is less than perfect advice, since *mos dhe ves* 'depart' is virtually unknown in Cornish. In Middle Cornish *the ves* 'away' is used with *towlel* 'to throw', *kemeres* 'to take', *kerhes* 'to fetch' and *cotha* 'to fall'; it is only very rarely used with *mos* 'go' and indeed the only example of which I am aware is: *ke the ves ymskemenys* 'go away you accursed one' PC 141. In traditional Cornish 'to go away' is almost always *mos yn kerth*. Here are some examples:

> *ke yn kerth ov map evy* 'depart, O my son' OM 725
> *dvn yn kerth ow bruder whek* 'let us depart, my dear brother' PC 188
> *ke yn kerth ty ihesu plos* 'go away, you foul Jesus' PC 1671
> *dun yn kergh gans an prysnes* 'let us depart with the prisoners' PC 2289
> *eugh yn kerth god yeve yow wo* 'go ye away, God give you woe' PC 2590
> *ke yn kergh dywhans hep let* 'depart immediately without delay' RD 116
> *yn kerth gallas mes a'n beth* 'he has departed from out of the tomb' RD 532

*ow arluth **yn kerth** gallas* 'my Lord has gone away' RD 722
*dun **yn kergh** rak dout pystyk* 'let us go for fear of harm' RD 2305
*hag a'n beth **yn kergh** gyllys the'n nef deffry* 'and departed to heaven indeed from the tomb' RD 809-10
***Duen** ny **in kerth** gans mur a nerth* 'let us depart with great strength' BM 813-14
*ov envy **in kerth** galsons* 'my enemies have departed' BM 1067
***duen in kerth** scon cowetha* 'let us go quickly, comrades' BM 1201
*Out **duen in kerth** cowetha* 'Out! Let us go, comrades' BM 1306
*In sol matis **duen in kerth*** 'Up, mates, let us go' BM 1878
*meryasek in certan o thymo pur oges car **in kerth** galles* 'Meryasek who was a very close kinsman has departed' BM 1938-40
***duen in kerth** uskis lemen* 'let us now depart quickly' BM 2354
*mar nyns **eth in kerth** war nuk* 'if you do not depart immediately' BM 2409
*te **a in kerth** genen ny* 'you shall depart with us' BM 2968
***in kerth** galles tobesy* 'Tobesy has gone away' BM 3278
*An presnour **in kerth** galleys* 'The prisoner has departed' BM 3717
*an presner **in kerth** defry galles eff haneth in nos* 'the prisoner indeed, he has departed this very night' BM 3724-25
***In kerth** sur galles holma* 'this creature has surely gone' BM 4148
***Duen in kerth** in hanov du* 'let us depart in the name of God' BM 4485
*ow tos omma thyn bys haw **mos in kerth** alemma arta ny woryn pyscotter* 'coming here into the world and departing hence again, we know not how soon' TH 6a
*eff a clomder hag **a in kerth*** 'he withers and departs' TH 7
***Ke in kerth** ha lavar thotha y fowt intre te hag eff only* 'Depart and tell him his fault between you and him only' TH 31a
***kewgh in kerth** inweth gonʒa* 'depart also with him' CW 323
***ke yn ker** eva benyn vas* 'depart, Eve, my good woman' CW 712
*quicke **in ker** ke alemma* 'quick depart hence' CW 1208
***deen ny in kerth** kekeffres* 'let us also depart' CW 1383
*Pe reg angye clowaz an matern, **y eath caar*** 'when they heard the king, they departed' RC 23: 196
*ha angye **eath carr** tha pow go honnen vor arall* 'and they departed for their own country another way' RC 23: 197
*Ha po 'th o angye **gellez carr*** 'And when they had departed' RC 23: 198
*po 'rygo huei **moz ker*** 'when you went away' AB: 253a.

If one does not want to use *departya* 'depart', one should say *mos yn kerth* rather than *mos dhe ves*.

18.14 *Dewnens* [Dewnans] 'Devonshire'

GKK wrongly says that this word occurs once only in Lhuyd. There are three examples in AB: 224, where is is spelt <Deunanz>. *Deunanz* is almost certainly Lhuyd's Cornicization of Welsh *Dyfnaint*. Given that in Kernowek Kemyn 'life' is **bywnans* (cf. Welsh *bywyd*), I do not understand why this word is not spelt **Dywnens* in Kernowek Kemyn.

PROBLEMS WITH GEORGE'S *GERLYVER KERNEWEK KEMMYN*

18.15 *digolonn* [dyglon] 'faintheartedness; fainthearted'

The compiler has decided to spell this word <digolonn> to show the etymology, but he does not indicate the position of the stress. Readers of his dictionary might be forgiven for pronouncing the word with the stress incorrectly on the penultimate syllable: *[dɪˈgolon]. The verb *dyglon* is also apparently a verb with the sense 'despair, lose heart'. It is also quite clear that it is to be pronounced [ˈdɪglon] and indeed should be so spelt:

> *in nos na gymer* **dyglon** *me ath dylerff an preson* 'in the night there do not lose heart, I will free you from prison' BM 3674-75
>
> *Na* **thyglon**, *saw the oners, del os myghtern heb parow* 'Do not lose heart, saving your honour, as you are a king without peer' BK 2070-71.

There is no justification for **digolonn* in GKK.

18.16 *dowr* [dowr] 'water'

GKK gives 'water; urine' as the two possible senses of this word. The word has another common meaning in the texts:

> *a dystough mars ty a theg a neyl pen the* **dour** *cedron* 'unless immediately you carry one end to the river Cedron' OM 2814-15
>
> *war* **thour** *cedron may fo pons* 'so that there may be a bridge over the river Cedron' OM 2811
>
> *arluth yn trok a horn cref yn* **dour** *tyber ef a sef er y anfevs* 'lord in the stout iron coffin he will stay in the river Tiber for his misery' RD 2135-37
>
> *teuleugh ef yn trok a horn yn* **dour** *tyber yn nep corn may fo buthys* 'throw him in the iron coffin into the river Tiber in some place that he may be drowned' RD 2162-64
>
> *den dreys* **dour** *tyber nyns a yn certan na vo marow* 'no man passes over the river Tiber unless he be dead' RD 2214-15
>
> *yn* **dour** *tyber ef a fue yn geler horn gorrys dovn* 'he was put deep in the river Tiber in an iron coffin' RD 2319-20
>
> *An duk a'n gevith pur wyer rag e laver ol an tyr a* **Thowr** *Hombyr the Scotland* 'The duke will get indeed for all his labour the country from the river Humber to Scotland' BK 3236-38
>
> **Dour** *Connor* 'Connor River' CPNE: 262
>
> *Ha gen Hern lean moas vrt* **Dour** *Gwavas* 'And full of pilchards will come to Gwavas Lake' BF: 45.

There is no hint anywhere in GKK that *dowr* can have the sense 'river' or 'lake'.

18.17 *dug* [duk] 'duke'

George says that this word has been assimilated to Cornish phonetic type and has a voiced final. I believe he is mistaken. The word was borrowed from either English or French and the final consonant is [k] rather than [g]. This can be seen from the attested plural:

dukis ʒurlys marogyon 'dukes, earls, knights' BM 294

Pax nunc, prelyatores, prynsys, **dukys**, *marrogyon* 'Peace now, warriors, princes, dukes, knights' BK 2380-81.

It is also significant that the word *duk* rhymes with *belsebuk* at PC 1925 & 1926. *Dukys* is, I believe, to be pronounced ['dykɪz]. George's *dug, dugys* are not credible.

18.18 *eles* [eles] 'angels'

This is correctly given by GKK as the Late Cornish plural of *el* 'angel'. George's "authentication code", however, implies that the form is attested once only. This is incorrect:

> *Della e a hellaz mease an dean ha e oraze **elez** neeve* 'Thus he drove out the man and sent angels of heaven' RC 23: 184
> *E ra ry tha e **eelez** an pohar ahanesta et ago doola* 'He will set power over thee into the hands of his angels' RC 23: 187
> *mero,* **elez** *neve theth ha droze thotha* 'behold, angels of heaven came and brought him...' RC 23: 189
> *mero,* **elez** *neeve a desquethaz tha Joseph* 'behold, angels of heaven appeared to Joseph' RC 23: 198
> *Pe tho Herod maraw,* **elez** *neve theath tha Joseph en cuska en Egyp* 'When Herod was dead, angels of heaven came to Joseph asleep in Egypt' RC 23: 200.

This is further evidence that George's database is inaccurate.

18.19 *eksilia* [exylya] 'exile'

After this word George adds a note: "N.B. Use **divroa**." But *divroa* is nowhere attested whereas *exylya* occurs in the *Ordinalia*:

> *an venenes ha'n fleghys bethens yn mes **exilyys*** 'let the women and the children be exiled away' OM 1575-76.

There can surely be no justification for replacing the attested Middle Cornish word *exylya* with a modern coinage **dyvroa*.

18.20 **ekspedyent* [expedyent] 'expedient'

This word is attested twice in TH:

> *Rag yth ewa very **expedient*** 'For it is very expedient' TH 20a
> *So lymmyn yth ew **expedient*** 'But now it is expedient' TH 36.

George does not include it in GKK, presumably on purist grounds. The word is now, however, attested in BK:

> *leverough **expedient*** 'speak promptly' BK 2139.

Expedient has been part of the lexicon of Middle Cornish since the fifteenth century and should have been included in GKK.

PROBLEMS WITH GEORGE'S *GERLYVER KERNEWEK KEMMYN*

18.21 *Evrek* [Evrok] 'York'

Although GKK does not mention it, this word has been in use by revivalists since the nineteen-sixties at the latest. In *Kemysk Kernewek*: 43, for example, a letter of Caradar's is published that was written in March 1950 to *Dr Mish, Evrok Noweth, Statys Unys America* 'Dr Mish, New York, United States of America'. *Evrok* is based on Welsh *Efrog* and *Evrek* is George's own version of the same. George tells us that the toponym was Latinized as *Eburacum* and meant 'abounding in hogweed'. I think not. The Latin *Eburacum* 'York' is for British **Eburakon*. The root here is Celtic **ebur* 'yew' (*Taxus baccata*); cf. Old Irish *ibar* 'yew'. **Eburakon* means 'sacred yew-grove'. York was presumably an important pagan cultic site before it was Christianized. There were two roots for 'yew' in Celtic, **ebur-* and **iwo-*. The latter is seen, for example, in the name of the Christian centre *Iona*, which derives from a misreading of **Iuoua* 'place of yew trees'. The development of Welsh *efwr* to mean 'hogweed' (*Heracleum sphondylium*) occurred when **ebor-* 'yew' in Welsh was wholly replaced by **iwo-* 'yew'.

18.22 *fannya* [fannya] 'to fan'

George cites this word from PC 1271 and adds a note: "N.B. Use **gwynsella**." The verb **gwynsella*, however, not merely is not attested in the texts, it is not cited by George in GKK. He is thus recommending his readers to use a word unattested in traditional Cornish, which he does not consider important enought to include in his dictionary.

18.23 *fenten* [fenten] 'spring, source'

In his entry on this word George adds a note: "N.B. the first <e> in the sg. is by vowel harmony." On the contrary <e> in the first syllable is the expected vowel. We start with the Latin word *fontāna* which was borrowed into British as **funtāna*. This by the Late British period would have been *[fun'ta:n] with final stress. The unstressed first syllable was reduced to schwa, while the long /a:/ developed regularly as [œ:]; cf. Latin *caseus* 'cheese' > Cornish *cues*. When the accent shifted to the first syllable, the schwa appeared as [e] and the newly unstressed syllable appears as [e]. After the Prosodic Shift the unstressed syllable was reduced to schwa, spelt in the first instance as <e>. We thus find *fenten* in Middle Cornish, exactly as expected. I have collected the following examples from the texts:

> *fenten bryght avel arhans* OM 769
> *yn paradys fenten ras* OM 836
> *hag y res gover fenten* OM 1845
> *ke the fenten the eve* OM 2436
> *kergh a'n fenten thy'm dour cler* PC 650
> *Inweth an dour ov fenten* BM 1005
> *eff ew an fentan vs ow resak* TH 11

*an lyvely **fyntan** a vewnans* TH 22
*crist a rug agery an **fentan** ma arta* TH 22
*ha mes an kyth **fyntan** na* TH 41
*Attomma **fyntan** spryngys* BK 786
*bys u'n **fyntan** us reban* BK 798
***Fyntan** dek ema ryban* BK 799
*an **fentan** ma hag adro* BK 818.

It is clear that the consonant cluster [nt] had a tendency to raise the stressed vowel to [ɪ]. Notice also that the schwa in the unstressed syllable is in later texts written <a>. George's note about this word is, I believe, mistaken.

18.24 *fevyr*; see *terthenn*

18.25 *Germany* 'Germany'
GKK cites *Almayn* 'Germany' from RD, where the torturer says: *arluth ow tevos a spayn yth egen yn cres **almayn** orth vn prys ly* 'lord, coming from Spain we were at a meal in the middle of Germany' RD 2147-49. One does not return to Cornwall from Spain via central Germany. It is apparent that *Almayn* 'Germany' here is merely an exotic or distant location in the mind of the poet. 'Germany' as a real country is *Germany* in the texts and we now have two instances:

> *ran yn **Germany** a levery, omma yma crist, omma yma an egglos, ran in Bohem a leuery, omma yma crist, omma yma an egglos* 'some in Germany were saying, Here is Christ, here is the church; some in Bohemia were saying, Here is Christ, here is the church' TH 32
> *Me thanvanas deffry duk an Saxens, Chellery, the whelas myns a geffa a bagans in **Germany*** 'I sent indeed Childerich, the duke of the Saxons, to seek as many as he can find of pagans in Germany' BK 3229-32.

George omits *Germany* (?*Jermani*) from GKK, even though he must have known it from Treager.

18.26 *gos 'it is known'
George is not content to respell Middle Cornish according to his own understanding of the phonology, he also ventures to invent verbal forms. On the basis of Welsh *gwys* 'is known' and Middle Breton *gous* 'is known' he has created the Cornish form *gos 'is known'. Both the Welsh and Breton forms are archaic. The ordinary form is in literary Welsh *gwyddys* and in Modern Breton the form is *gouzer* or *gouezer*. The Cornish form *gos is, in my view, unjustified. Even Nance, who was given to completing poorly attested paradigms, does not venture to create such a form. He prefers *godhyr. The expression 'is known' in Cornish occurs in Tregear's Homilies, where it is rendered by a verbal adjective and the verb *bos*:

PROBLEMS WITH GEORGE'S *GERLYVER KERNEWEK KEMMYN*

maga ver dell yll bos gothvethis gans du **ew** *openly* **gothvethis** 'inasmuch as can be known by God is openly known' TH 14

yth **ew** *openly* **gothvethis** 'it is openly known' TH 36.

Yth yw godhvedhys should be the form used by revivalists.

18.27 *gwer* [gwer] 'husbands'

For some reason GKK includes this plural as a separate headword and entry (GKK: 128). *Gwer* 'husbands' is the plural of *gour* 'man, husband, adult male person' which has already been cited (GKK: 117), yet there is no cross-reference between the two entries. There is no "authentication code" s.v. *gour* for the plural *gwer* which is cited there. Under *gwer*, however, the dictionary indicates that the plural occurs 2-3 times and is confined to OCV and Lhuyd. This is incorrect, since *gwer* 'husbands' is attested in Middle Cornish: *S poull a commo[n]dias an* **gwer** *the cara aga gwregath* 'St Paul commanded the husbands to love their wives' TH 31.

This is further evidence of the inaccuracy of George's database.

18.28 *gweli* [gwely] 'bed'

In Kernowek Kemyn this word is *gweli* rather than *gwely* and George adds a note: "N.B. The final vowel changed from /ɪ/ to /i/." No evidence is given for this alleged shift. Welsh *gwely* and Breton *gwele* are both against it.

After the plural *gweliow* George's code indicates that the form is unattested. This is incorrect, since Lhuyd gives **Gueliau**, *Beds* (AB: 242c).

18.29 Gwydhel [Godhal] 'Irishman'; *Gwydhelek* [Godhalek] 'Irish'

GKK discusses the Cornish word for 'Irishman' s.v. **Goedhel** on page 112 and s.v. **Gwydhel** on page 130. There is no cross-referencing under *Goedhel*; *Gwydhel* is described as a "Secondary form of **Goedhel**". GKK cites *Gwydhelek* 'Gaelic language' on page 130, and says the word is unattested in traditional Cornish, having been taken from Nance's 1938 dictionary. George appears unaware of Lhuyd's *Godhalek* 'Irish language' AB: 222 x 2; (cf. GODHALEK, *Irish* Price following p. 2).

The following instances of the two forms of 'Irishman' are attested in traditional Cornish:

A
Robert **Wydel** (from 1327; see CPNE: 122)
Guidhili, *Irish-men* (AB: 242c).

B
Margaret En**gothall** (from 1538; see CPNE: 122)
yonk ha loys, **Gothal** *ha Scot!* 'young and grey, Irishman and Scot!' BK 259.

George spells Middle Cornish *Gothal*, **Gothall* as <Goedhel> with <oe>, presumably because Welsh has *wy* in *Gwyddel*, and Welsh *wy* corresponds to *oy/o* in Cornish (spelt *<oe> in Kernowek Kemyn). The root is **weid-* 'wild', of which the zero-grade **wid-* is seen in Old Irish *fid* 'wood' and Cornish *gwethen* 'tree'. A Celtic form **weidelo-* gives Old Cornish **gwui'ðel*, with the stress on the second syllable and written <guidel>. This form survives in the early Middle Cornish lenited spelling *Wydel* and in the plural form **Gwydhyly* (written <Guidhili> by Lhuyd), where the high front vowel is maintained in the first and second syllables by vowel harmony. While the first syllable of *guidel* was still unstressed, the [ui] was presumably reduced to *u/o* + schwa: **gwoə'ðel*, which became **gwo'ðel*. Then, after the accent shifted to the first syllable, the word appears as *[']gwoðel* > *'goðel*. The Prosodic Shift reduced the now unstressed *e*, which was in consequence written <a>. This final *'goðəl* is written <Gothal>.

Under the word *Goedhel* George says "The suffix -EL is the same as that in *medhel* (gpc [i.e. *Geiriadur Prifysgol Cymru*]), and is not -*al*, as written by Nance in this word and all its derivatives." In the light of *Engothall*, *Gothall* and Lhuyd's *Godhalek* this criticism of Nance is misplaced. The Prosodic Shift reduced the final syllable early to shwa, written <a>, and it is this which appears as <a> in *Godhalek*.

George's treatment of these etyma is both deficient and incorrect.

18.30 *gwel* [gwel] 'field'

George's suggested etymology for this word is *gwel* 'sight' with the transferred sense 'view over open field' > 'field'. This etymology has little to recommend it. George rejects Padel's suggestion that the word may be related to Welsh *gwaell* 'knitting-needle, skewer, splinter'. It appears, nonetheless, that some of the earliest forms of *gwel* were disyllabic, e.g. *Guaelmeynek* from 1366 (CPNE: 267); this makes Padell's suggested etymology quite likely. The semantic shift 'skewer > narrow field > field' would have been similar to the use of 'strip' in English.

18.31 *hedra* [hadre] 'while'

George spells this word <hedra>, presumably because Nance spelt it so. In fact, however, *<hedra> is nowhere attested. The forms in the texts are either A) *hedre, hadre* or B) *hedyr, hader, dirr*. I have collected the following examples:

A **hedre/hadre**
hedre vons y ov plentye PA 32c
bynytha **hedre** *vywy* OM 243
hedre *vy may fo anken* OM 276
hedre *vo yn the herwyth* OM 1464
hedre *vyns y yn ov gulas* OM 1503
hedre *vyyn ov predery* OM 2035

hedre vyugh byv yn bys ma OM 2349
hedre veyn bev yn bys ma PC 115
hedre vy yn beys gynen PC 730
hedre veyf byv yn certan PC 847
hedre vyma ov pygy PC 1013
hedre veyf bew yn bys ma PC 1020
hedre vywhy PC 2930
bew **hedre** *ven* RD 1048
hedre vo yn y gerghen RD 1865
hedre ve ygys golok RD 1915
rak **hedre** *vyugh ow pleghye* RD 1950
neffre yn dour **hedre** *vo* RD 2225
ny fylleth **hedre** *ven bev* BM 55
benitha **hedre** *ven byv* BM 354
hedre *ven byv* BM 1137
hedre *vevhen benythe* BM 2816
ha kysvew **hedre** *veny* BK 622
bew **hedre** *ve* BK 639
hedre *ve bew war an bys* BK 820
na ny vethef **hedre** *ven* BK 932
hedre *vo by in e le* BK 986
ow cul tronkys **hedre** *ve* BK 1086
hedre *ven ow cul tronkys* BK 1088
hedre *vema orth e geys* BK 1182
hedre *vo nef in e le* BK 1472
Hedre *vo bys in e le* BK 1536
Hedre *vo bys in e le* BK 1544
hedre *vo bys in e le* BK 1967
hedre *ven bew* BK 2586
hedre *vo tecca an beys* BK 3172
yn bys ma **hadre** *von bew* CW 1258
hadre *vo omma yn beys* CW 1400
hadre *von omma in byes* CW 1425
hadre *vone bew* CW 2109.

B **hedyr**
hedyr *vywy* CF 36
Hader *vo bys in e le* BK 1528
Dirr *ve an enef in kigg* SA 60a.

It seems virtually certain that the conjunction was stressed on the second syllable. I would also suggest that the form *hedyr / hader / dirr* was the origin of Late Cornish *tereba* 'until' < **hedyr bo*. I should also tentatively suggest that *hedre* in origin was Old Cornish *hid* 'length' + *dre / der* 'through'.

George has apparently noticed neither that there were two forms in the texts, nor that the second syllable was never written <a>, nor that the word was stressed on the second syllable. This is further evidence of the inadequacy of George's database.

18.32 ***herwydh*** **[herwyth] 'according to, in accordance with, on the authority of'**
In Middle Cornish this word has two meanings of which 'according to' is only one. I have collected the following examples of it in this sense:

> ***herwyth*** *y volungeth ef ov map certan y fyth gurys* 'according to his will, my son, certainly it shall be done' OM 1320-21
> *neb a vo yn moghya gre a vyth an brassa henwys* ***herwyth*** *nep a vo yn le* 'whoever will be in the greatest position will be called the greatest according to him who is in a lower one' PC 797-99
> *ol an bys ma rak iugge pup ol* ***herwyth*** *y ober* 'all this world to judge everyone according to his deeds' PC 815-16
> *ha* ***herwyth*** *agas laha ha concyans guregh y iuggye the'n mernans mar coth henna* 'and in accordance with their law and conscience judge him to death if that is suitable' PC 1978-80.

Herwyth is also a noun used with the preposition *yn*, where the whole phrase means 'close by to, among, about (of garments)'. I have collected the following examples:

> *In aga* ***herwyth*** *y3 ese vn marreg longis hynwys* 'near them there was a knight called Longinus' PA 217a
> *hedre vo yn the* ***herwyth*** *fythys nefre ny vethyth* 'while it is about you, you will never be conquered' OM 1464-65
> *rag mur y carsen defry guthel thymmo oratry in* ***herwith*** *chy maria* 'for greatly should I like to make myself an oratory close by the house of Mary' BM 639-40
> *pa nyns esa xii dewesys gans crist rag bos in y* ***hyrwyth*** 'or there were not twelve chosen by Christ to be around him' TH 34.

George appears to have missed this sense. He does not mention it under *herwydh*, nor does he give **yn herwydh* as a separate headword. George also appears not to have noticed that in Cornish the most frequent way of saying 'according to, in accordance with' is *warlergh*, not *herwyth*. George does, of course, cite *warlergh* (which he spells <war-lergh>), and he tells us the word means 'after' both of time and space. He does not mention its transferred sense 'according to', although such a meaning is common in the texts. I have collected the following examples:

> **warlergh** 'according to'
> *y a ruge a 3esympys oll* ***war lyrgh*** *y arhadow* 'they all immediately did according to his command' PA 247d
> *ol* ***war lergh*** *the gussullyow bys venytha my a wra* 'all according to you counsels I will always act' OM 2269-70
> *a tus vas why re welas fetel formyas dev an tas nef ha nor* ***war lergh*** *y vrys* 'good people, you have seen how God the Father created heaven and earth according to his will' OM 2825-27

PROBLEMS WITH GEORGE'S *GERLYVER KERNEWEK KEMMYN*

yn certan mara pyth gurys sur **warlergh** *an keth dev ma ny fyth ef neffre dyswrys* 'if indeed it is done verily according to this same two fellows, never will he be destroyed' PC 2451-53

warlergh *sen luk me an kyf lell thyugh in awell* 'I will find it truly according to St Luke for you in the gospel' BM 391-93

kowses **warlerth** *an maner an bobill* 'spoken in accordance with the manner of the common people' TH 1

the vos vvel ha myke **warlerth** *an examplys a dus tha* 'to be humble and meek in accordance with the examples of good people' TH 10

Walkyow ha gwandrow **warlyrth** *an spurys* 'Walk and go according to the Spirit' TH 16a

fatell res thyn scripture bos vnderstondyys **warlerth** *an generall menyng a egglos crist, So not* **warlerth** *an priveth interpretacion a then vith* 'how the scripture must be understood according to the general meaning of the church of Christ, but not according to the private interpretation of any man' TH 18

neb na garra y gyscristyan **warlyrth** *an kyth sort ma* 'whoever does not love his fellow Christian in accordance with this' TH 20a

ow framya thotha y honyn charite, **Warlerth** *y vynd hay appetyd y honyn* 'framing charity for himself according to his own mind and desire' TH 21

yth esans ow pewa **warlerth** *an letterall sens a la moyses* 'they were living according to the literal sense of the law of Moses' TH 26a

hen o aga oberow **warlerth** *aga mynd aga honyn heb auctorite na gothfos* 'that is their works according to their own mind without authority or knowledge' TH 33

fatell rug agan saviour Jhesus crist cowese the abosteleth **warlyrth** *an vaner ma* 'that our Saviour Jesus Christ spoke to his apostles according to this manner' TH 35a

na rellan ny **warlyrth** *agan fantasy agan honyn iudgia* 'that we should not according to our own fantasy judge' TH 37

warlyrth *an measure an lene oys a crist* 'according to the measure of the adulthood of Christ' TH 42.

The sense 'according to' should be added to George's entry s.v. *war-lergh*.

18.33 *howlsedhes* [howlsedhas] 'sunset'

The only meaning given by George for this word is 'sunset'. Under *west* 'west', however, he adds a note: "N.B. Useful 1-syll. alternative to **howlsedhes**." It is difficult to see, therefore, why he does not give the meaning 'west' under *howlsedhes* itself. George's "authentication code" s.v. *howlsedhes* indicates that the word is confined to a single instance in Lhuyd. This is incorrect. Pryce gives the following:

Po res dal an vor, na oren pan a tu, Thuryan, **houl Zethas**, *go Gleth, po Dihow* 'When you begin the road, we know not which direction, east, west, north or south' ACB (opposite F f).

Here *howlsedhas* clearly means 'west' rather than 'sunset'.

18.34 *Hwevrer* [Whevrel] 'February'
GKK's "authentication codes" indicate that this word is attested 2-3 times. I have collected the following examples:

> S[outh] W[elsh] Heuvror, Corn[ish] Huerval (& **Huevral**) The month of February AB: 7b
> W[elsh] Xuevror, The Month of February; C[ornish] **huevral** AB: 31c
> Februarius... The month of february. C[ornish] **Huevral** (cor. Huerval) AB: 59a
> **Huevral**, February ACB following T2
> Mîs-**Huevral** (February) i.e. Huevral, the whirling month ACB Ff2 verso
> Mîz-**Huevral** (DG 1827: 229).

Nowhere does the dictionary mention that *Hwevrer* is not attested in Cornish, the form being *Huevral* or *Huerval*. One should also notice that *Chwefrol* for *Chwefror* is a common Welsh variant of the word, which has undergone the same kind of dissimilation. GKK's omission here is astonishing.

18.35 *jorna* [jorna] 'day'
George gives *jornys* as the unattested plural of this word. He does not seem to have noticed that Williams cites the plural *jorniow* (LCB: 190) and cf. *rag termeniow, ha rag **journiow**, ha rag blethedniow* (Davies Gilbert 1827: 190).

18.36 *kann* [can] 'white'
George correctly states that this word is attested as an adjective in OCV. He also apparently believes that it appears twice as a noun meaning 'brightness' in Middle Cornish. He is not, I think, correct:

> del vyth gans the gorf prennys adam hag eva kefrys ha gorrys the nef gans **can** 'as Adam and Eve will be redeemed by thy body and brought to heaven with song' OM 2638-40
> neb ese aberth yn beth gans **can** ha mur a eleth the vewnans y tassorghas 'he who was within the tomb with song and many angels has risen to life' RD 514-6.

The context is similar in both instances. Adam and Eve are being brought into heaven and Christ is rising from the dead; the word *can* in both passages means 'song' and is a reference to the choirs of angels.

18.37 *kaptyvita* [captyvyta] 'captivity'
GKK appears to be somewhat arbitrary in its approach to borrowed abstracts in *-yta*. The dictionary includes *antikwita* 'antiquity', *chastyta* 'chastity', *cheryta* 'charity', *dynyta* 'dignity', *kontroversita* 'controversy', *nisyta* 'ignorance', *solempnyta* 'solemnity', *trynyta* 'trinity' and *universyta* 'university', some of which are in TH only. On the other hand it omits from TH *auctoryta* 'authority', *captyvyta* 'captivity', *commodyta* 'commodity', *curyosyta* 'curiosity', *humylyta* 'humility', *necessyta* 'necessity', *qualyta* 'quality', *quantyta* 'quality', *mortalyta*

PROBLEMS WITH GEORGE'S *GERLYVER KERNEWEK KEMMYN*

'mortality', *pluralyta* 'plurality', *supremyta* 'supremity', *unyta* 'unity', *vanyta* 'vanity' and *ynfyrmyta* 'infirmity'. *Captyvyta* seems to me to be a serious omission, since there is no other word in Cornish. **Gwasonyeth 'servitude' is an invented word, so for that matter is *kethneth 'slavery' and there is no abstract from *prysonya* 'to imprison'. I have collected the following instances of *captyvyta*:

> *theworth an miserabill stat ha **captiuite** a veny ynna towlys* 'from the miserable state and captivity into which we had been thrown' TH 10
>
> *rag raunsona mabden ha'y thelver thea ponow ha thea **captiuite*** 'to ransom mankind and deliver them from torments and from captivity' TH 15
>
> *na rewgh mas meras war an pow ha gwlasow ha war an bobyll vs in **captiuite** gans an turk bras* 'merely look at the country and kingdoms and at the people who are in the captivity of the Grand Turk' TH 49a.

The omission of *captyvyta* is regrettable.

18.38 **karnashyon* [carnacyon] 'incarnation'

This word, is used once by Tregear, but is not included by George in GKK neither does he give any word for 'incarnation' in the English-Cornish portion of his *Gerlyver Kres*, whereas Nance in his 1952 dictionary gives *yncarnasyon*. It is now apparent from *Bewnans Ke* that the word *carnacyon* was an integral part of the Middle Cornish lexicon and could refer to a person's carnal nature as well as to the incarnation of Christ. We now have two examples of the word, only one of which refers to the Incarnation:

> *ament ow **carnacyon**, Du ha den kepar del os* 'correct my fleshly nature, as thou art God and man' BK 38-39
>
> *An here gurtas a crist therag eff the thos the gemeras **carnacion** an wyrhes maria* 'The long waiting of Christ before he happened to receive incarnation of the Virgin Mary' TH 13a.

The omission of **karnashyon* from GKK is unfortunate.

18.39 *koltrebyn* [coltrebyn] 'candlestick'

This word is included in GKK and the code tells us it is taken from TH, but no meaning or etymology is given. *Coltrebyn* is in fact the Middle Cornish reflex of Old Cornish *cantulbren* 'candelabrum' [candlestick] and there should have been a cross-reference to *kantolbrenn* on page 153, or possibly *coltrebyn* could have been mentioned in the entry there. Since *coltrebyn* is the Middle Cornish form, I should have preferred to have seen it as the headword. Tregear uses the word once only, but the sense is quite clear: *na ny yll kantyll bos annowys ha gorys in dan busshell, mas war **coltrebyn** bo chandeler* 'nor can a candle be lit and put under a bushel, but upon a candlestick or chandelier' TH 17a.

18.40 *konkerrour* [conquerrour] 'conqueror'

The second <k> should be <kw> in Kernowek Kemyn. GKK tells us to use the word *trygher*, which occurs once: *ambosow orth **tryher** gureys annethe nynses laha* 'compacts made with a victor, there is no law with respect to them' OM 1235-36. *Conquerrour* is better attested, however:

> *Me yv empour ha governour **conquerrour** tyr* 'I am an emperor and governor, a conqueror of land' BM 930-32
> ***conquerour** off corff da in proff* 'a conqueror am I, a good body in proof' BM 2403-04
> *I say Arthur is my name, myghtern bras ha galosak ha **conquerrour*** 'I say Arthur is my name, a great and powerful king and a conqueror' BK 1399-1400.

My own advice to readers of this dictionary would be to ignore the compiler's recommendation and to use *conquerrour* (though in Kernowek Kemyn it should be *konkwerrour).

18.41 *konkerrya* [conquerrya] 'conquer'

The second <k> in this word should be <kw> in Kernowek Kemyn. GKK tells us to use *tryghi* 'be victorious' in preference to this word. *Tryghi* is unattested in traditional Cornish. *Conquerrya* is a borrowing, but it does have the merit of being a genuine Cornish word: *adam plos a thesefse warnan **conquerrye** neffre* 'foul Adam would have presumed to always dominate us' OM 908-09. It is also now attested in Bewnans Ke: *ha dyswul ha **conquerya** the yskerans der gras Christ* 'and to destroy and conquer your enemies by the grace of Christ' BK 1485-86.

18.42 *konkludya* [concludya] 'silence in argument'

GKK tells us to use *gorfenna* 'finish' in preference. This advice is perhaps not very sound. *Concludya* in the *Ordinalia* does not mean 'finish, conclude' but 'restrain, silence,' as can clearly be seen from the following instances:

> *me a wra by godys fo y **concludye** war vn lam* 'I shall by God's foe silence him in a trice' PC 1463-64
> *ny a thy a ver termyn agan dev wythoute fal hag a'n **conclud** an iaudyn* 'we will come very soon, we two without fail, and will silence the scoundrel' PC 1654-56
> *me a'n **conclud** yredy ma na wothfo gorthyby* 'I shall silence him indeed so he will not be able to answer' PC 1659-60
> *bysy vye thy's gothuos yn certan mur a scryptours mara mynnyth gorthyby hytheu **concludys** na vy* 'it would be necessary for you indeed to know much of the scriptures, if you wish to answer so that today you be not silenced' PC 1672-75
> *mar keus y vos **concludyys** nyn syv lemyn vn boba* 'if he says he has been silenced, he is nought but a fool' PC 1777-78.

PROBLEMS WITH GEORGE'S *GERLYVER KERNEWEK KEMMYN*

Concludya is exactly the right word in Cornish for 'silence in argument'. *Gorfenna* is not a synonym of *concludya*.

18.43 *konstryna* [constryna] 'force, constrain'
George cites this word form PC 1512 and adds a note: "N.B. Use **strothhe**." *Strothhe* is a modern invention, unattested in the traditional language. It is also not included by George in GKK. Again George is recommending the use of a word he does not consider worth putting in his own dictionary.

18.44 *kort* [cort] 'court'
George includes this word, and tells us that it occurs twice in BM. This is incorrect. The examples in BM are of a different word *cur*. George also adds a note "N.B. Use **lys** or **breuslys**." This is an astonishing recommendation, given that *cort* 'court' is attested, while *lys* is not. I know of the following examples of *cort* 'court':

> *Gweth oge ys **court** renner* 'You are worse than a court runner' BK 178
> *Ma tha ve treall en **cort** an Vaternes* 'I have a trial in the Queen's court' Bilbao Manuscript.

I can find no examples of *lys* in Middle or Late Cornish. It does, of course, occur in toponyms.

18.45 *kost* [cost] 'coast'
The "authentication code" after this word implies the word is not attested, which is not true. George adds a note "N.B. Use **arvor**." Although George's recommended **arvor* is nowhere attested, there are a number of instances of *cost*, plural *costys*:

> *py tyller yma moyses ha py **cost** yma trygys* 'where is Moses and in what region is he living' OM 1551-52
> *Jhesus a theth then **costes** a cesarye philippi* 'Jesus came to the regions of Caesarea Philippi' TH 43a
> *nena eff a gemeras owne a drega na fella in **cost** na* 'then he became afraid of dwelling any longer in that region' TH 46a
> *Pan nowothow, pan guestlow us genowgh why a'n **cost** west* 'What news, what pledges have you from the western region?' BK 222-23
> *Ke souyth ha north ha gura cry cref in pub **cost*** 'Go south and north and make a cry in every region' BK 2350-51.

It is apparent that *cost* does not mean 'coast' so much as 'region, district'. George's advice to use *arvor* instead of *cost* gives the wrong impression of the meaning of the word *cost*.

TOWARDS AUTHENTIC CORNISH

18.46 *kosyn* [cosyn] 'cousin'
This word occurs twice in PC:

> *wolcom cayphas re iouyn and yk annas me **cosyn*** 'welcome Caiaphas by Jovyn and also Annas my cousin' PC 1687-88
> *wel thow fare syr cayfas and yk me **cosyn** annas* 'well thou fare, Sir Caiaphas, and also my cousin Annas' PC 1805-06.

The word is absent from GKK, which is unfortunate, given that it was clearly part of the vocabulary of the author of PC. It is now well attested in *Bewnans Ke*:

> *E vanneth genas, **cosyn*** 'His blessing be with you, cousin' BK 651
> *Dun ahanan, **cosyn** ker* 'Let us go hence, dear cousin' BK 1099
> *Welcum, **cosin**, by my soul* 'Welcome, cousin, by my soul' BK 1346
> ***Cosyn** whek, dun ny warbarth* 'Sweet cousin, let us go together' BK 1373
> *ha prag e rug dyelha ow **cosyns** heb mur awher* 'and why he behaved vindictively to my cousins without much anxiety' BK 1838-39
> *Lavar the'th arluth, **cosyn*** 'Tell your lord, cousin' BK 2112
> *pag e fuldrys ow **cosyns*** 'why he murdered my cousins' BK 2286
> *Farwell, ru'm fer, ow **cosyn** whek* 'Farewell by my fair, my sweet cousin' BK 2892-93
> *Ow sockors da ha'm **cosyns*** 'My goodly allies and my cousins' BK 2818
> *Ow bannath genas, **cosyn*** 'My blessing with you, cousin' BK 3048
> *Welcum, **cosyn** Chellery* 'Welcome, cousin Childerich' BK 3245.

18.47 *kyng* [kyng] 'king'
GKK cites this English borrowing and adds a note "N.B. Use **myghtern**." It is unlikely that any Cornish speaker would use *kyng* as the ordinary word for 'king'. *Kyng* is used in titles and in addressing the monarch:

> *nessa ʒen myterne vhell **kyng** conany* 'nearest to the high sovereign, king Conany' BM 4-5
> *Ov lich **kyng** bethugh mery* 'My liege king, be merry' BM 292
> *ser **kyng** na vethugh dyswar* 'sir king, be not unaware' BM 3238
> *hail, **king** Moddreth in the thron* 'hail king Modred on thy throne' BK 3252.

More often kings are called *mytern*:

> ***mytern** alwar ha Pygys*
> ***mytern** margh ryel, kefrys*
> ***mytern** casvelyn gelwys*
>
> [King Alwar and Pygys
> royal king Mark as well,
> and he who is called king Casvelyn] BM: 2463-65.

PROBLEMS WITH GEORGE'S *GERLYVER KERNEWEK KEMMYN*

Kyng is part of the lexicon of Middle Cornish and may be used in titles. It would also be of use when in syllabic verse a monosyllable is required. George's note is misplaced.

18.48 *lewd* 'wicked'; *lewdnes* 'wickedness'

In Middle English *lewd* meant 'wicked, bad' rather than 'lascivious, lustful'. The word was borrowed into Cornish and is used once by Tregear, who uses *lewdnes* 'wickedness' once also. George omits both *lewd* and *lewdnes* from GKK, which is regrettable, since both are now attested in BK and it is obvious that they formed part of the Middle Cornish lexicon:

> **lewd** 'wicked'
> *ha dre rebukys amendia aga **lewde** bewnans* 'and by rebukes amend their wicked life' TH 30
> *Ow holan ew crackys quyt drefen why th'y lowenhe der **lewd** omthon* 'My heart is quite cracked because you gave him joy by wicked behaviour' BK 2341
> *The **leud** desyr a'm cuth por wyer* 'Your wicked desire afflicts me in very truth' BK 2952
> ***Leud** ema owth umbrevy mar goyth pan ra ankevy pryns mar ryall* 'She is proving wicked when she so quickly forgets such a royal prince' BK 3001-03.

> **lewdnes** 'wickedness'
> *Vn teball person a yll tenna lyas onyn arell the **lewdnes*** 'One evil person can lead many others to wickedness' TH 25a
> *The **leudnys** gas rag meth an bys* 'Give over your wickedness for the shame of the world' BK 2209-10.

18.49 *lion* [lyon] 'lion'

Under this word GKK says "N.B. Use **lew**." *Leu* occurs in the *Old Cornish Vocabulary* and is cited from there by Lhuyd. In Middle Cornish, however, the word for 'lion' is *lyon*, of which we now have three examples:

> *folle yn ta y whela · ys del wra **lyon** y pray* 'he more ravenously seeks than does a lion his prey' PA 21c
> *yma agys escar an teball el kepar ha **lyon** ow huga ow mos adro ow whelas rag agys devowrya* 'your enemy the devil is like a lion going round roaring seeking to devour you' TH 3a-4
> *Whath **luon** goyth in y ugo thys a ynclyn* 'Moreover a wild lion in his den bows down to you' BK 1777-79.

Lyon is a Middle Cornish word; **lew* is not, and cannot therefore be recommended.

18.50 *longya* [longya] 'belong'

The "authentication code" after this word in GKK indicates that the word is confined to two instances in TH. This is incorrect; the word occurs in CW:

> *han pythe a **long** the3o gye* 'and the possessions that belong to you' CW 2253.

This is further evidence that George's database is inaccurate.

18.51 *nevra* [nefra] '(n)ever'

It is a universal feature of the Celtic languages that there is one word for '(n)ever' A) referring to past time and B) another referring to the future. In Irish one says, for example:

> A
> *Níor chuala mé a leithéid de sheafóid **riamh*** 'I have never heard such nonsense'
> B
> *Ní dhéanfaidh mé dearmad air **go deo*** 'I shall never forget it'

and in Welsh one says:

> A
> *Ni chlywais i **erioed** y fath lol* 'I have never heard such nonsense'
> B
> *Nid anghofiaf i **byth** mohono* 'I shall never forget it'.

In Cornish '(n)ever' in the past is *bythqueth*, whereas '(n)ever' in the future is *nefra*, and the distinction was maintained between them until the death of the language at the end of the eighteenth century.

Although GKK appears unaware of this distinction, it is apparent from the texts, that it is an essential one in Cornish. *Nefra* is used with the future and with the present continuing into the future. It is also used with the conditional (future in the past) in unreal conditions. *Bythqueth* on the other hand is used with the past. If in Cornish one wants to say 'I never saw, I never did, he never came' one must say: *Ny welys vy **bythqueth**, ny wrug avy **bythqueth**, ny dhueth ef **bythqueth***. To use *nefra* in such cases would be incorrect. Here are some examples from the texts exemplifying the usage:

> A **nefra** (*refers to present and future time*)
> *rag henna gor3yn **neffra** ihesus neb agan pernas* 'therefore let us for ever worship Jesus who redeemed us' PA 5d
> *the vestry a vyth le3ys **neffre** war an enevow* 'your domination upon the souls will ever be diminished' PA 17
> *ha ny a grys 3e vestry hag ad syns mester **neffre*** 'and we will believe your power and consider you master for ever' PA 197c

PROBLEMS WITH GEORGE'S *GERLYVER KERNEWEK KEMMYN*

*na byth moy ken mam **neffre** es hyhy te na whela* 'nor any mother are you to seek other than her' PA 198d

***nefre** gustyth th'y gorty me a orden bos benen* 'I ordain that a woman should for ever be obedient to her husband' OM 295-96

*ha **nefre** y fyth avey yntre the lynneth the sy ha lynneth benen pup preys* 'and always there will be enmity between thy offspring and the offspring of woman' OM 314-16

*ef a'n gefyth yn dyweth an ioy na thyfyk **nefre*** 'he will have in the end the joy that never fails' OM 516-17

*ha kyrghough the dre an guas may hallo cane ellas **nefre** yn tewolgow tew* 'and fetch the fellow home that he may sing "alas" for ever in the thick darkness' OM 514-16

*yn nef agas enefow **neffre** a tryg hep ponow yn ioy na vyth dywythys* 'in heaven your souls will dwell forever without pain in the joy that shall never be ended' PC 7-9

*ha kyn fons y ol sclandrys **neffre** awos bos lethys my ny wraf the thyflase* 'and though they be all offended, never for fear of being killed, shall I turn away from you' PC 899-901

*vn wyth mar pyth den marow y spyrys **neffre** hep gow byth ny thue yn y vody* 'if a man dies at all his spirit never in truth will return to his body' PC 1748-50

*na ken ny scrifaf **neffre** awos dout bones lethys* 'nor will I write otherwise ever in spite of fear of death' PC 2805-06

*na gefyn war ow ene kyn fen **neffre** ow ponye* 'we will not find him upon my soul, were we running for ever' RD 549-50

*rak an torment a'n gefe ym colon yma **neffre*** 'for the torment he endured is in my heart for ever' RD 694-95

***neffre** the dre my nyns af ow arluth mar ny gafaf* 'never shall I return home if I do not find my lord' RD 811-12

***neffre** ef the thasserghy me ny fynnaf y grygy* 'that he will rise again never will I believe it' RD 1046-47

*welcumma den benary **nefre** ny ȝue yn ov chy* 'a more welcome man never will come into my house' BM 249-50

*dar soposia a reta den rych **nefra** mones then nef da ny yl* 'What, do you suppose that a rich man can never go to the good heaven?' BM 459-61

*the lee **nefra** war ov ena me an car in ov bevnans* 'the less upon my soul will I ever love him in my life' BM 481-83

*rag **nefre** nahen dewes nyns a om ganov defry* 'for never indeed shall any other drink enter my mouth' BM 656-57

*hen ew tra an par na a rella contenewa **neffra** heb deweth* 'that is something of the kind that will continue for ever without end' TH 2a

*Saw gyrryow du a worta rag **nefra** perpetually* 'but the words of God remain for ever perpetually' TH 7

*an egglos catholyk **neffra** ny vith ouercommys gans error* 'the catholic church will never be overcome by error' TH 17a

*na ny ra **neffra** fyllell, na decaya, na agys decevya* 'nor will it ever fail, or decay or deceive you' TH 34a

*an ena mab den, **neffra** sawis mase dir criggyans da* 'the soul of man, never saved but by firm faith' SA 60a

*ha **neffra** me a'th vynyk* 'and ever will I bless you' BK 791

209

erna vony unwerhys **neffra** *ny veth da ow cher* 'until we be reconciled never will my heart be content' BK 1035-36

Neffra *ny vyth ankevys* 'Never will it be forgotten' BK 1609

ny yl **neffra** *ow dyscuthy* 'he will never be able to discomfort me' BK 2184-85

rag ʒa oth tha bayne **nefra** *te a wra dyiskynya* 'for your pride to pain for ever you shall descend' CW 233-234

nefra *na gybmar dowte te a yll bos pur verry* 'never fear, you may be very merry' CW 691-92

nefra *ny the alena rag yth ew malegas bras* 'never will he come hence, for he is greatly cursed' CW 929-30

malegas **nefra** *re by hag oll an tyer a bewhy ew malegas yth ober* 'accursed may you ever be and all the land is accursed in thy deed' CW 1158-60

ne vedn e **nevra** *dos vez a gyndan* 'he will never get out of debt' AB: 230c

neb ny vith **nifre** *ganz ny ankevys* 'which will never be forgotten by us' Keigwin

Oll a poble en Porthia ha Maraz-jowan **nevra** *ni or dho ga Zingy* 'All the people in St Ives and Marazion will never be able to hold them' T. Tonkin

Ne vedn **nevera** *doas vas a tavas re hir* 'No good will ever come of a tongue that is too long' ACB.

B **bythqueth** (*refers exclusively to past time*)

pedyr te am nagh tergweth **bythqueth** *arluth na vef ʒys* 'Peter, you will deny me three times that I was ever lord to you' PA 50c

pedyr arta a gowsas **bythqueth** *me nyn aswonys* 'Peter again spoke: Never did I recognize him' PA 84d

may fyth torrow benegis **bythqueth** *na allas e ʒon* 'so that wombs will be blest that never could bear it' PA 169c

ny woʒevys den **bythqueth** *kymmys peynys ow pewe* 'no man living ever suffered so much pain' PA 223d

ny welys tekke rum fay **bythqueth** *aban vef genys* 'I never saw fairer upon my faith since I was born' OM 1730-31

rag ny glewsyug yn nep plas sawor an par ma **bythqueth** 'for you never perceived anywhere a fragrance of this kind' OM 1990-91

ellas vyth pan yu kyllys Abel whek ov map kerra na **bythqueth** *pan vef formys* 'alas ever that sweet Abel is dead, my dearest son, or that ever I was created' OM 614-16

bythqueth *na ve bom a won a rollo whaf mar gales* 'there never was a blow I know that would give such a hard thump' OM 2710-11

bythqueth *bay thy'm ny ryssys* 'never did you give me a kiss' PC 522

na fyllys a arluth da na fout **bythqueth** *ny gen bue* 'there was no lack, good lord, nor did we ever suffer need' PC 915-16

ny wruk an den ma **bythqueth** *war an bys ma drokoleth* 'this man never in this world did evil' PC 2903-04

ef a vyth sur anclethys yn le na fue den **bythqueth** 'he indeed will be entombed where no man ever was' PC 3134-35

an emperour ef sawse maga tek **bythqueth** *del fue kyn fe y cleues mar bras* 'it would heal the emperor as smooth as he ever was however great his disease' RD 1658-60

drok den a fue sur **bythqueth** *a wul drok ny'n gefe meth yn y thythow* 'he was ever an wicked man who did not blush to do evil in his life' RD 1782-84

PROBLEMS WITH GEORGE'S *GERLYVER KERNEWEK KEMMYN*

mar mynnyth oma latha flehys **bythqueth** *na pehes* 'if you wish now to kill children who never sinned' BM 1592-94

me a wyl lemen in tek **bythqueth** *ny welys clerra* 'I now see beautifully; never did I see more clearly' BM 2624-25

maria me reth cervyes thum gallus **bythqueth** *defry* 'Mary, I have ever served thee as was in my power' BM 3595-96

Bythqueth *ny vue vays in pov aban vys crystyan heb wov* 'Never has there been any good in the land since you became a Christian' BM 3968-69

Adam an kynsa den **bethqueth** *a ve* 'Adam the first man who ever was' TH 2a

hag in y ganow eff ny ve **bythqueth** *kyffys deceypt vith* 'and in his mouth was never found any deceit' TH 11

rag eff **bythqueth** *ny pehas* 'for he never sinned' TH 15a

bythqueth *whath ny fyllys thea tyrmyn an appostelath bys in dith hethew* 'never yet did she fail from the time of the apostles until the present day' TH 17

Pan bugell a ruge **bithquath** *maga e thevas gans e members e honyn?* 'What shepherd ever fed his sheep with his own limbs?' SA 59

ha tra na wharva **bythquath** *del clowas ve in neb gwlas* 'and something which has never happened, as I have heard, in any country' BK 853-54

Ny vef re goward **bythquath** *na ny vethaf hedre ven* 'I was never too cowardly, nor will I be as long as I live' BK 931-32

Gove **bythquath** *e welys!* 'Woe is me that I ever saw it' BK 1208

Bythquath *ny ve thewhy parow* 'Never was there your equal' BK 1256-57

soweth **bythqwathe** *bos formys* 'alas ever to have been created' CW 1265

rag **bythquwathe** *me nyn kerys* 'for never did I love him' CW 1289

bythqwathe *me nym beys moy dewan* 'never have I had greater sorrow' CW 1393

ha sure me ew an kensa **bythqwath** *whath a ve dew wreag* 'and certainly I am the first ever to have two wives' CW 1453-54

rag na rigga ve **beska** *gwellaz skreef Bretten Coth veeth* 'for I never saw any ancient British writing' BF: 27

Besca *Rig dane Roule en Gwalaze buz nag ew an Poble vaze* 'Never did a man rule in a kingdom where the people are no good' LAM: 224

ha the hethes tha Careesk maga sowe **besca** *ve pesk* 'and to reach Exeter as safe as ever was fish' LAM: 224

na riga vee **biscath** *gwellas lever Cornoack* 'I never saw a Cornish book' LAM: 244.

It is clear from the Late Cornish examples that the distinction between *nefra* (*nevra*) and *bythqueth* (*biscath, besca*) survived until the death of Cornish.

Nance, meticulous scholar that he was, indicates in his 1938 dictionary that *nefra* means 'never, for ever' with reference to the future only. GKK on the other hand appears unaware of this very Celtic distinction between *nefra* and *bythqueth*. In GKK both *bythkweyth* and *nevra* are glossed alike as 'ever' and nothing anywhere informs the user that there is a syntactical difference between them. It is not astonishing, therefore, to find that the compiler of GKK himself uses *nevra* incorrectly:

> *Wel,* **nevra** *ny leveris bos Kernewek Kemmyn fonemek yn tien* 'Well, I never said that Kernowek Kemyn was completely phonemic' (*An Gannas*, December 1995, 5).

211

18.52 *obayans* [obayans] 'obedience'

George's "authentication code" here makes it clear that **obayans* is not attested anywhere. In fact the only word for 'obedience' in Middle Cornish is Tregear's *obedyens*:

> dre **obediens** kylmys the seruya TH 5
> rag nag us **obedyens** res thyn minister TH 42a
> the trelya thega dew **obediens** TH 49a
> theworth an **obediens** an sea han stall a rome TH 49a.

Compare Tregear's *dysobedyens*:

> an fowt han **disobediens** TH 4a
> o **disobediens** bras warbyn du TH 4a
> dre an **disobediens** a vn den TH 4a
> oll kynda pehosow ha **disobediens** TH 5
> vnkyndenys ha **disobediens** TH 30a.

GKK does not mention *obedyens* and *dysobedyens*, even to advise against them.

18.53 *obedyent* 'obedient'

GKK omits *obedyens* 'obedience' and in the same way it ignores the corresponding adjective *obedyent*. This is well attested:

> An corfe a then nena o **obedient** then ena TH 2a
> han ena o holly **obedient** the thu TH 2a
> mar ten ny ha contynewa fleghys **obedyent** TH 41
> according then commondement a thu, **obedient** TH 48a
> ry ken gorthyp the Lucy ha bonas moy **obedient** BK 2140-41.

Although *obedyent* has been in Cornish since the fifteenth century, the compiler does not mention the word, even to warn his readers against using it.

18.54 *oyow* [oyow] 'eggs'

The "authentication code" in GKK implies that the plural *oyow* 'eggs' is not attested. In my article in *Cornish Studies: Nine* I pointed out that this was incorrect, since the plural *eyo* 'eggs' is attested in Borde. What I should have noticed and did not, is that Pryce in his vocabulary gives *oyow* 'eggs' and *oyow ethen* 'bird's eggs'. We thus have three examples of the plural *oyow* in Cornish (which according to George is unattested!). This is further evidence that George's database is inaccurate.

18.55 *oyeth* [oyeth] 'oyez!, attention!'

GKK cites this word and adds a note: "N.B. Use **klywewgh** in preference." This is poor advice at best. *Oyeth* is for *oyez*, in origin the second person plural imperative of the French verb *ouir* 'to hear' (< Latin *audire*). *Oyez*, the cry of the English town-crier, does not mean 'hear!, listen!' so much as 'attention please!', calling people to stop what they are doing and to listen. This is the sense of the three instances in Middle Cornish:

> **oyeth** *syglewyugh thy'm ol* 'Attention, all listen to me!' OM 2297
> **oyeth** *or* **oyeth** *yn weth syglewyugh bryntyn ha keth* 'Attention! Attention now; listen to me both noble and common!' OM 2419-20.

The advice to use the verb *clewes* 'to hear' in preference is without justification.

18.56 *parda, parde* 'by God'
This word is omitted from GKK although it is well attested in the texts:

> *ihesu* **parde** *a nazare an fals crystyon* 'Jesus by God the false Christian' PC 1111-12
> **parda** *ef a rug an Ena Immortal* 'Indeed he made the immortal soul' TH 2a
> *Ow! Me a wothya* **parda***!* 'Oh! I knew it, by God!' BK 351.

It should be in GKK.

18.57 *parkya* [parkya] 'enclose'
GKK gets this word from Nance's 1938 dictionary and George adds a note: "N.B. The meaning in CE38 [Nance's dictionary] was 'to enclose, to put in a field', which is adequately expressed by **kea**. Verbal nouns in -YA from English loan-words containing [a] do not usually suffer analogous [*leg.* analogical] vowel aff[ection]. For those purists who think that they should, **perkel** might be an acceptable alternative." In this note George appears to be making two points: 1) that *kea* is adequate to express the sense; 2) if one must use this word, perhaps the verbal noun ought to be **perkel*.

It is clear that the author of *Bewnans Ke* did not agree with either of George's two opinions, since BK uses *parkya* 'to enclose' on a number of occasions:

> *me ny govytya' nahen saw an myns tyer a* **barkyen** *ow cul tronkys hedre ve* 'I do not want anything other than as much land as I should enclose, while you are taking a bath' BK 1084-86
> *An mens tyrath a* **barkys** *hedre ven ow cul tronkys, me a ro thys perpetual* 'The amount of land that you would enclose, while I be taking a bath, I shall give you as a perpetual gift' BK 1087-89
> *ke ge duwans the* **barkya** 'go straight to enclose' BK 1152
> *Kyn* **parkys** *myns a wylly, te a'n pew heb falladow* 'Thou you enclose as much as you see, you will own it without fail' BK 1157-58
> *ny gresaf awos an bys bos maner thotho* **parkys** *a dyrath whath* 'I do not believe for all the world that he has enclosed for himself a manor of land yet' BK 1189-91.

The author of BK clearly thought *parkya* was different from *kea* and his verbal noun was *parkya*, not **perkel*. George's note can be dismissed.

18.58 *Penntorr* 'Torpoint'
GKK includes this Cornicization of the toponym 'Torpoint' and adds a note: "N.B. Torpoint never had a traditional Cor. name, being a relatively new town; the form **Penntorr** has found acceptability among Cor. speakers." I think George must mean: "*Penntorr* has found acceptance among Cornish speakers." It could hardly find acceptability, being fundamentally mistaken. *Torpoint* is a corruption of *Stertpoynt* (1608), where *Stert* is for Old English *steort* 'tail of land, promontory' to which the tautologous element *-point* has been added. If *Torpoint* is to be Cornicized at all it should probably be *An Stert*. *Penntorr* is a solecism and cannot be recommended.

18.59 *playnya* [playnya] 'plane'
The "authentication code" for this word in GKK indicates that the word is not attested, having been taken from Nance's *English-Cornish Dictionary* of 1952 (NECD). The word is attested, however:

> Rag henna fystyn ke gura gorhel a blankos **playnyys** 'Therefore hurry, go, make a ship of planed planks' OM 949-50
> rag henna, fysten, ke, gwra gorhell a planckes **playnyes** 'Therefore hurry, go, make a ship of planed planks' CW 2254-55.

The speech in CW is obviously based on its predecessor in OM. George's failure to notice either of these two attestations, is further evidence of the inaccuracy of his computer database.

18.60 *prokurya* [procurya] 'procure'
This word is attested once in Tregear's *Homilies*: *may halla eff bos lene a vercy the* **procuria** *mercy rag pehosow an bobyll* 'that he might be full of mercy to procure mercy for the sins of the people' TH 13. After his entry George adds a note: "N.B. Use **kavoes** or **gwaynya**." In English the word 'procure' has some technical senses, in particular 'to get for immoral purposes, to pimp'. If, God forbid, one were talking or writing about such matters in Cornish, *gwaynya* 'to win' would be quite wrong and *cafus* 'to get' (Kernowek Kemyn *kavoes*) not specific enough. From the linguistic point of view, I should rather say *Yth esa ow* **procurya** *mowysy rag horyans* 'He was procuring girls for prostitution' to *Yth esa ow* **cafus** *mowysy rag horyans*, which is less clear. I certainly would not say *Yth esa ow* **quaynya** *mowysy* 'He was winning girls' in such a context. George's note is quite out of place.

PROBLEMS WITH GEORGE'S *GERLYVER KERNEWEK KEMMYN*

18.61 *promys* [promys] 'promise'

GKK cites this word and gives *promysyow* as the plural. It adds a note: "N.B. The pl. *promysys* is also found, but use **ambos**." It is astonishing that the compiler, with his purist notions, does not urge us to use *dedhewadow* for 'promise', given that *ambos* also means 'contract'. In Middle Cornish *promys* is the ordinary word for 'promise' and there is no possible reason for not using it. I have collected the following examples of *promys*:

> Oll the **promes** hath teryov gueth y lemen avel kyns 'All thy promise and thy lands keep them now as before' BM 2594-95
> may halla an **promys** dre an feth a Jhesu crist bos res the oll an re na a lell greys 'that the promise through the faith of Jesus Christ might be given to all those who truly believe' TH 7a
> fatell ew an **promes** ny colynwys 'as our promise is fulfilled' TH 13
> Arta yma du ow kull an second **promys** 'Again God makes the second promise' TH 13
> oll an **promysyow** ma a thu ny vea colynwys in crist 'all these promises of God would not have been fulfilled in Christ' TH 13a
> dre reson du the wortas mar bell heb colynwel an **promyses** 'since God waited so long without fulfilling the promises' TH 13a
> ha then kythsam eglos ma crist a rug **promys** in xvi chapter a mathew 'and to this selfsame church Christ made a promise in the sixteenth chapter of Matthew' TH 17
> Thyn kythsam eglos ma eff a rug an **promys** arall 'To this selfsame church he made the other promise' TH 17
> ha ny an Jeva **promes** a brassa royow dell vouns y 'and we had promise of greater gifts than they had' TH 28
> hag eff an Jeva an thorne vhella han victuri, then **promysyow** a crist 'and he had the upper hand and the victory for the promises of Christ' TH 34
> Gans mere moy stroytya **promysyow** yma eff ow kull mencion then re a rella disobaya 'With much more stricter promises he mentions to those who would disobey' TH 37
> fatell rug agan savyor Crist omma in bys gull solem **promys** a vois 'that our Saviour Christ here in the world made a solemn promise of food' TH 51a
> eff a ros henna according the **promysses** 'he gave that according to his promises' TH 51a
> In **promes** eff a leverys fatell vynna eff ry thynny y gyge 'In promise he said that he would give us his flesh' TH 52
> Arta ow kull an **promes** 'Again making the promise' TH 52
> ha in performans ay **promes** eff a leueris 'and in performance of his promise he said' TH 52
> kepar dell rug eff cowse in **promys** gwrys a henna 'just as he spoke in the promise made of this' TH 54
> hay **bromas** o mar wheake 'and his promise was so sweet' CW 776
> ha'y **bromas** yth o largya 'and his promise was more generous' CW 780
> an **promas** me ny roof oye 'for the promise I will not give an egg' CW 1379
> saw whath wos an **promes** na mere yth esaf ow towtya 'but still notwithstanding that promise I fear greatly' CW 1539.

TOWARDS AUTHENTIC CORNISH

In the face of all these instances of *promys* in traditional Cornish, I do not understand how a lexicographer can possibly advise Cornish speakers against this word.

18.62 *promysya* [promysya] 'promise'

GKK tells us to use *ambosa* in preference to this word. *Ambosa* is attested once: *kepar ha del ambosas* 'exactly as he promised' RD 915. *Promysya* is attested at later date than the *Ordinalia* but we have many more examples:

> *a rug du **promysya** wosa an towle agan hyndasow* 'which God promised after the fall of our ancestors' TH 13
> *Eff a **promysyas** the viterne Dauid* 'He promised to King David' TH 13a
> *kepar dell rug crist **promysya** in xvi chapter a mathew* 'just as Christ promised in the sixteenth chapter of Matthew' TH 17
> *Rag crist a **promysyas** fatell vynna eff bos gans y egglos rag neffra* 'For Christ promised that he would be with his church for ever' TH 20
> *nena yma crist ow **promysya** ha ow assurya thyn, fatell vsy eff worth agan cara ny* 'then Christ promises and assures us that he loves us' TH 26
> *Pan o **promysys** thetha an payne rag tyrry an vhella degry a charity* 'When the penalty for breaking the highest degree of charity had been promised to them' TH 27
> *ha yth ew thynny **promysys** an punishment na rag tyrry an lyha degre a cherite* 'and that punishment is promised to us for breaking the least degree of charity' TH 27
> ***promysys** thynny vght an Jewys* 'promised to us above the Jews' TH 27a
> *han brassa royow **promysys*** 'and the greater gifts promised' TH 28
> *na victory warbyn agan gostly eskerens, ew **promysys*** 'nor victory against our spiritual enemies is promised' TH 28
> *an spuris a wrioneth han spuris a vnite **promysys** dre crist* 'the spirit of truth and the spirit of unity promised through Christ' TH 32
> *Whath yma S Agustyn in kythsame tellar na ow **promysya*** 'Moreover St Augustine in the very same place promises' TH 32a
> *kepar dell rug crist **promesya** in vaner ma* 'as Christ promised in this way' TH 36
> *in mar ver dell rug crist **promysya** an conforter* 'inasmuch as Christ promised the Comforter' TH 36
> *fatell ve an spuris sans **promvsiis** then appostlys* 'that the Holy Spirit was promised to the apostles' TH 36a
> *eff a ve **promysiis** thethans y ha thega successors* 'he was promised to them and to their successors' TH 36a
> *nyg usy eff mas ow **promysya** an auctorite ma thotheff* 'he promises this authority to him only' TH 44
> *pan ruga **promysya** the ry thetho an alwetho a wlas neff* 'when he promised to give him the keys of the kingdom of heaven' TH 44a
> *kepar dell rug eff nena **promysya*** 'as he promised then' TH 51a
> *neb a rug **promysya** indella dry y only mercy* 'who promised thus through his mercy only' TH 54a
> *hag y **promysyas** tha vee* 'and he promised to me' CW 889.

PROBLEMS WITH GEORGE'S *GERLYVER KERNEWEK KEMMYN*

In the light of all these examples, the advice in GKK to shun the word seems curiously misplaced.

18.63 *prosedya* [procedya] 'proceed'
George correctly points out that up till now this word was known from Tregear only and he adds a note: "N.B. Use **mos yn rag**." It should be noticed, however, that the word *procedya* is also in *Bewnans Ke*. We thus have the following five examples in traditional Cornish:

> *Whath rag* **procedia** *pelha rag descernya an creacion a then* 'to proceed further to discern the creation of man' TH 1a
> *mas* **procedia** *pella inna, ha tyrry charite* 'but to continue further in it and rupture charity' TH 28a
> *agan savyoure a rug* **procedya** *then tryssa degre a vncharitablynesse* 'our Saviour proceeded to the third degree of uncharitableness' TH 28a
> *So lymmyn rag* **procedya** *in rag the declaria an seconde tra* 'But now to proceed on to mention the second matter' TH 55a
> *mar quver e* **procedya** 'if one is going to proceed with it' BK 1414.

In view of all these examples, I should, unlike George, be very reluctant to tell my readers to avoid this word.

18.64 *proseshyon* [processyon] 'procession'
On page 22 of this dictionary the compiler that when <s> is proceded or followed by a vowel internally or finally, it may be pronounced half-voiced. This implies that in *proseshyon* the first <s> can be pronounced something like [z], even though it is etymologically <c> and should not be voiced. One would have expected **prosseshyon*, cf. *posseshyon* in Kernowek Kemyn.

George mentions correctly that the word is attested twice in *Beunans Meriasek* (BM 1861 & 4174) and he adds a note: "N.B. Use **keskerdh**." 'Procession' in English has some technical senses, however. In trinitarian theology, for example, one speaks of the procession of the Holy Spirit, the single procession being from the Father alone, as in the creed of the Eastern Church, and the double procession from the Father and the Son, as in the creed of the Western Church. Were one talking about the schism caused by the *Filioque* clause, for instance, and the single procession of the Spirit from the Father alone, *keskerdh* 'walking together' would be quite the wrong word; *an processyon unyk*, however, would be a perfect translation. George's note is out of place.

18.65 **prysydh* [prydyth] 'poet'
This word is attested as *pridit* 'poeta' in OCV. George compares the Welsh *prydydd* 'poet' and tells us in a note that his **prysydh* is updated from Old Cornish. It should be noted that both UC and UCR render Old Cornish *pridit* as *prydyth* and do not "update" it. This is wise, as it turns out, since the word

is now attested: *moun senior, an **prydyth** mort* BK 2497. This I take to be for *moun senior, re'n **prydyth** mort* 'my senior, by the dead poet', a reference to Virgil, who was revered in the medieval period. It would seem that the disyllable *prydyth* behaves similarly to *peder* 'four', *gweder* 'glass' and *Peder* 'Peter'; in such cases the presence of *r* in the next syllable prevents assibilation of -*d*-. Here the *r* in the same syllable appears to have had the same effect. In monosyllables the *r* does not prevent assibilation, however, *prys* 'time' < Old Cornish *prit*; cf. Welsh *pryd*. George has been overhasty in his rewriting of Old Cornish and has thus produced an inauthentic form.

18.66 *rekompens* [recompens] 'recompense'
GKK includes this word but gives it no "authentication code". The only instance I can find of the word is: *ha mar na gefyn ny equall **recompens** vith* 'and if we get no equal recompense' TH 24.

18.67 *reportya* [reportya] 'report'
GKK cites this word from Tregear and adds a note: "N.B. Use **derivas**." It is clear, however, that the word was part of the vocabulary of Cornish from the fifteenth century. We now have four instances:

> *Mar pe oll an epscobow an bys re an par na, kepar del esta se falsly ow **reportya** y the vos* 'If all the bishops of the world were some of this kind, as you falsely report them to be' TH 48
> *Du Jovyn ew dyawl pub ur, del ma ef ow **reportya*** 'The God Jovin is a devil, as he always asserts' BK 940-41
> *Ny yl tavas **reportya** i'n tor' ma mur a'th noe* 'Tongue cannot at the moment report much of your nephew' BK 3194a-96a
> *Ny yl tavas **reportya** i'n tur' ma myuns us yna* 'Tongue cannot at this moment report all that is there' BK 3194b-95b.

This word is well-established in Cornish and George's advice to use *deryvas* in preference is without justification.

18.68 *restya* [wrestya] 'wrest'
GKK cites this word from RD with the meaning 'rest'. The compiler adds a note: "N.B. Use **powes**." The passage in question reads:

> *ow stons a fue crous a pren*
> *kyns en myghtern den ha dev*
> *yn le basnet war ow fen*
> *curyn a spern lym ha glev*
> *ol ov ysyly yn ten*
> *hag a wel the lyes plu*
> *yn golon dre'n tenewen*
> *the **restye** syngys ow gu*

PROBLEMS WITH GEORGE'S *GERLYVER KERNEWEK KEMMYN*

'My stand was a cross of wood.
Before I was a king, man and God,
instead of a helmet upon my head
a crown of thorns sharp and keen,
all my limbs pulled tight
and in sight of many a parish
in the heart through the side
I felt my spear being twisted' (RD 2579-86).

The verb *restye* (which might perhaps have been better spelt <wrestye>) means 'wrest, twist, turn'. It is attested again in Tregear's Homilies:

> *Eff a attendias fatell vynna oll an heretikys gylwall thetha an auctorite an aposteleth, han prophettys, ha fatell vynsans y **wrestia** aga screffa, hen o aga oberow warlerth aga mynd aga honyn* 'He noticed how all the heretics wanted to invoke for themselves the authority of the apostles and the prophets, and that they would twist their writing, that is their works according to their own mind' TH 33.

Two things are clear: first, the word *restya* does not mean 'rest' and second, *powes* is no substitute. George's note can be disregarded.

18.69 *rond* [rond] 'round'

After his entry George adds a note: "N.B. Use also **kylghyek**." George claims s.v. *kylghyek* that the word is his own invention, following it with the letters K[en] J. G[eorge]. **Kylghyek* is a variant of **kelghek* 'circular' given by Nance in his 1952 dictionary. George also cites *krenn* 'round', which is attested in Lhuyd as *kren, kern* (AB: 141c). This George does not mention when he tells his readers to use **kelghyek* as well as *rond*.

Rond occurs as an adjective in the following:

> *iij bran vrays marthys **rond** age mellov* 'three large ravens with wondrous round limbs' BM 3407-08
> *Dzhuan genz e golhan, trohaz [der an tol] mez a kein gun an manah pis pyr **round*** 'John with his knife cut through the hole from the back of the monk's gown a completely round piece' AB: 252a.

It also occurs in the compound preposition *a-rond*:

> *a **wronnd** an dor stremys bras ov tewraga gans mur nel* 'around the earth streams pouring with great force' OM 1083-84.

And the root now occurs in an abstract noun:

> *Y'n howl yma **rowndenab** ha golow splan* 'In the sun there is roundness and brilliant light' BK 383-84.

Rond should be the word of choice to translate 'round, circular'.

TOWARDS AUTHENTIC CORNISH

18.70 **ronsona* [raunsona] 'ransom'
GKK cites the noun *raunson*, which it respells <ronson>. The word *raunsona* is missing from GKK, however, although it is attested:

> rag **raunsona** mab den hay thelver thea ponow ha thea captiuite 'to ransom mankind and to deliver them from pains and from captivity' TH 15.

The failure of GKK to cite *raunsona* is further evidence of the inaccuracy of George's database.

18.71 *Rysoghen* [Resohen] 'Oxford'
George says the Cornish form of this toponym is not attested. This is not strictly speaking true. Lhuyd writes: *en Levarva Kollek Iesu en* **Red Ousk** 'in the Library of Jesus College in Oxford' AB: 223. *Red Ousk* is Lhuyd's Cornicization of Welsh *Rhydychen*; whereas *Resoghen* was Nance's version. It is interesting that Lhuyd uses Old Cornish *red* 'ford' and also apparently believed that the second element was identical with *Usk*, Welsh *Wysg*, rather than *ychen* 'ox'. George does not mention Lhuyd's *Red Ousk*.

18.72 *salvashyon* [salvacyon] 'salvation'
After this word George adds a note: "N.B. Use **selwyans**." It is quite apparent that the Middle Cornish writers themselves did not always follow George's advice. I have collected the following instances of A) *selwyans* and B) *salvacyon* from the texts:

A **selwyans**
ha **sylwans** ȝen enevow PA 1d
ma'm bethen drethe **sylwans** OM 1958
gothfetheugh y's byth **sylwans** RD 1574
ha **sylwyans** the tus a'n bys RD 1711
the'n beys danvonas **sylwyans** RD 2611.

B **salvacyon**
arta y vones prennys the **saluascon** BM 885-86
peys men geffo **saluasconn** BM 1248
ihesu grond thyn **saluasconn** BM 1259
ihesu map a **saluasconn** BM 1757
the vap den rag **saluasconn** BM 3051
nyg es gweras na **salvacion** TH 10
fatell ugy agan **salvacion** ow tos dre crist only TH 10
oll daddar ha **salvacyon** TH 11a
y a vynsa optaynya **salvacion** TH 13a
rag optaynya eternall **salvacion** TH 13a
an bewnans heb deweth ha eternall **salvacion** TH 17
a pub tra oll necessary rag **salvacion** TH 17
ymowns sure in forth a **salvacion** TH 20
hag oll **saluacion** thethy aga honyn only TH 32.

There is no reason at all to proscribe *salvacyon* in revived Cornish.

PROBLEMS WITH GEORGE'S *GERLYVER KERNEWEK KEMMYN*

18.73 *savyour* [savyour] 'saviour'

Under *savyour* George adds a note: "N.B. All but one of the 91 examples are in TH." This is incorrect. One example is in BM, 16 in *Sacrament an Alter*—which is not the same text as TH, though the pagination is continuous throughout the manuscript. The scribe, subject-matter, orthography and (*pace* George) dialect of SA are different from those of TH. These are the instances of the word *savyour* outside Tregear's Homilies:

> *Ihesu yv agen savyur* BM 4226
> *agyn arluth han saviour* SA 59
> *o qvelas agen saviour Christ* SA 60a
> *ew agen saviour Iesus Christ* SA 60a
> *ha [e] vab ras agen saviour Iesus Christ* SA 60a
> *pan rug agen saviour Christ leverall* SA 61
> *An sacrament a corf & gois agen savior Jesus* SA 61a
> *pan ruge girreow agen saviour Christ dos warnotha* SA 62
> *Dir geir Dew, hagen saviour Iesus Christ* SA 63
> *kigg ha gois agen saviour Jesus Christ* SA 63
> *mas kigg ha gois agen Saviour Jesus Christ* SA 63a
> *a Corf ha gois agyn saviour Jesus Christ* SA 63a
> *megis gans corf ha gois agen saviour Christ* SA 63a
> *Rag kepare ew an Corf na Ivnys thagan saviour Christ* SA 65
> *thony Ivnis thagan Saviour Christ* SA 65
> *dibbry worthely kigg agen saviour Christ* SA 66
> *an presivs Corf han gois a gyn saviour Christ* SA 66.

After his entry on *savyour* George observes "the Cornish word is **Selwyas**." This is remarkable. Given that *savyour* is much more frequently attested than *selwyas*, *savyour* can hardly be denied the status of a Cornish word. What George must mean, I think, is that the more native word of the two is *selwyas*. He seems at this point to have forgotten the other native word, *selwador* 'saviour', to which he devotes an entry in his dictionary.

18.74 *selwador* [selwador] 'saviour'

Under this word George adds a note: "N.B. No reason for vowel aff[ection] here." He is clearly perplexed that the word is *selwador* rather than **salwador*. He has apparently forgotten *salvador* in CW; cf. the following list:

> *ha **sylwadur** an bys ma* RD 480
> *ihesu agan **sylwadur*** RD 800
> *ha **sylwadur** thy'n keffrys* RD 1152
> *ha **sylwadur** pup enef* RD 1733
> *athyow thu'm tas yth sef **sylwadur** beys* RD 2485-86
> ***selwadour** an crustunyon* BM 539
> *thum **selwadour*** BM 4320
> *ha **salvador** yn teffry* CW 1865.

The three agent nouns in *-ador, -adur* of frequent occurrence in traditional Cornish are *puscador* 'fisherman', *pehador* 'sinner', (whence *pehadures* 'sinful woman') and *selwador* 'saviour'. All three etyma are from Latin, from *piscator* 'fisherman', *peccator* 'sinner' and *salvator* 'saviour' respectively. The etymology of all three was apparent to Cornish speakers; they knew that *puscador* was connected with *puscas* 'fish', *pehador* 'sinner' was connected with *pehas* 'sins' and the *Selwador* 'Saviour' was believed to save (*selwel*) Christians. It is no wonder therefore that the reflex of Latin *salvator* in Middle Cornish was *selwador*. I do not understand George's difficulty.

18.75 *Skot* [Scot] 'Scot'

GKK gives *Alban* 'Scotland; Scot' and *Albanek* 'Scottish'. *Alban* is used by Lhuyd. *Albanek* is otherwise unattested. Lhuyd also has *Skot-Vrethonek* 'Scot-Brythonic' (i.e. Scottish Gaelic) AB: 222. The word *Scot* is now attested in Middle Cornish:

> *Yonk ha lys, Gothal ha* **Scot** 'Young and grey, Irishman and Scotsman' BK 1259
> *na Cornow na* **Scot** 'neither Cornishman nor Scot' BK 2487.

The Cornish name for 'Scotland' in *Bewnans Ke* is *Scotland* and is attested three times, at lines 1280, 3237 and 3284. George cannot be expected to have known the contents of BK. Nonetheless Lhuyd's adjectival *Skot* 'Scottish' is inexplicably wanting from GKK.

18.76 *sira wynn* [syra wyn] 'grandfather'

This item is included by George under *sira* 'father'. George tells us that the form *sira wyn* is attested once in Lhuyd. This is incorrect. Lhuyd cites it twice: **sira wydn** (AB: 3b), **sira widn** (AB: 44b). George also adds a note: "N.B. unexpected lenition." The lenition of *wydn, widn* is hardly unexpected to anyone familiar with the Brythonic languages.

It is not uncommon in both Welsh and Breton to lenite the following adjective with a masculine noun, if the collocation of noun + adjective is a fossilized phrase. In Breton one finds such expressions as *Yann vras* 'Big John', *vikel-vras* 'vicar general' (*Breton Grammar*: 16), *Paol gamm* 'Paul the cripple' and *Pipi goz* 'Old Peter' (HMB: 35-6). In Middle Welsh were found expressions like *Howel Uychan* 'Howel the Small', *Catwaladyr Undigeit* 'Cadwaladr the Blessed' (GMW: 19). In Modern Welsh one still hears *Hywel Dda* 'Hywel the Good' and *Dewi Wyn* 'Holy Dewi' (EGC: 47). In both Welsh and Breton it happens when nouns are in apposition, the second noun functions as an adjective and is often lenited, e.g. Welsh *Dafydd Frenin* 'King David' and *Ioan Fedyddiwr* 'John the Baptist' (EGC: 47) and in Breton *Sant Ian Vadezour* 'St John the Baptist' (HMB: 35).

Lenition occurred in such instances because the collocation was frequently used either in the vocative or the genitive, i.e. either addressing the person in question or speaking about something associated with him. *Hywel Dda* in the genitive would originally have been **Soweli Dagi* where the initial of the adjective was between vowels and therefore liable to lenition.

In Cornish there are a number of examples of lenition with the second noun of two nouns in apposition, e.g. *Robert Wydel* 'Robert the Irishman' from 1327 (CPNE: 122) and *Richard Wycher* 'Richard the Merchant' and *Baldwin Wycher* 'Baldwin the Merchant' both also from 1327 (CPNE: 120). The best examples are now:

> *Arthor Gornow, myghtern freth* 'Arthur the Cornishman, a truculent king' BK 2502
> *Gas ve hag Arthor Gornow, me a'n dorn gans ow dornow* 'Leave me with Arthur the Cornishman, I shall box him with my fists' BK 2650-51.

Syra wyn is comparable, since the expression is very much a fossilized phrase, which would have been used when addressing one's own grandfather. In fact it is likely that the original expression for 'grandfather' in Middle Cornish was **tas wyn* with similar lenition of the adjective (< **tate winne*) and that the lenition was carried over when *syra* replaced *tas* in everyday speech. At all events, the lenition in *syra wyn* is by no means unexpected.

18.77 *Sen Ostell* [Austol] 'St Austell'

After this toponym George adds a note: "N.B. The spelling, especially of the first syllable, is doubtful." By first syllable I assume George means the first syllable of *Ostell*. The spelling is doubtful only if one has to devise it; if one spells as the Cornish did, there is no problem. The toponym *St Austell* is one of many in Cornwall in which the English form bears the title *Saint* (*St*) but where the original Cornish form was without it. Place-names without Saint in them are common, e.g. *Burryan, Sennen, Paul, Gwithian, Gwinear, Kea* and *Sithney*. St Austell is a similar name in Cornish, for the toponym was *Austol* in the middle of the thirteenth-century. There is no justification for **Sen Ostell*.

18.78 *sompna* [sompna] 'summon'

GKK includes this word from Nance's 1938 dictionary. George, however, adds a note: "N.B. Appears unnecessary; **gelwel** may be used." I am not sure that 'to call' and 'to summon' are the same. One is summoned to appear in court, but called to the bar. The two have different connotations in English and one suspects that *sompna* and *gelwel* had similarly divergent uses in Cornish. The word *sompna* is now attested in the form *somona*:

> *prag y tevons heb den vith th'aga gonys saw rag own bos* **somonys** 'why do they grow with nobody to weed them, if not for fear of being summoned?' BK 2133-35.

It is obvious that *gelwys* would have been quite inadequate here. The author of BK clearly thought that *somona* was not unnecessary. George's note is out of place.

18.79 *spryngya* [spryngya] 'to spring'
This verb occurs five times in TH. For reasons of linguistic purity George has omitted this word from GKK. This is unfortunate, since the word is in *Bewnans Ke* and has clearly been in Cornish since the fifteenth century. We have the following instances:

> *an kythsame nature na a rug **speringia** ha dos thea Adam* 'the very same nature which sprang and came from Adam' TH 12a
> *nag ew an egglos tevys ha **springis** in ban a thewethas* 'that the church has not grown and sprung up recently' TH 34a
> *ha mes an kyth fyntan na y ra **spryngya** thynny ha innan ny mer a begyttar a bewnans* 'and from that same source much holiness of life will spring up for us and in us' TH 41
> *Na in tyller arell, na dre menes arell, ew heresy **springys** in man* 'Neither in another place, nor by other means, has heresy sprung up' TH 42a
> *Nens ew nahen cowse y bos hereses drehevys ha scismes **springes** ha tevys* 'There is no other cause that heresies have arisen and schisms have sprung and grown' TH 48a
> *A Christ, re be benegas! Atomma fyntan **spryngys!*** 'O Christ, be thou blessed! Behold a spring has burst forth!' BK: 778-89.

A lexicographer's function is to record what occurs in a language, not to censor it.

18.80 *sopposya* [supposya] 'suppose'
I am perplexed as to why Kernowek Kemyn spells this word with geminate <pp>. In pronunciation it must surely have a single [p]. UCR spells it <supposya> for etymological reasons; UCR does not seek to be phonemic.

After his entry on *sopposya* George adds a note: "N.B. Fairly common in MidC, but **tybi** and **desevos** are preferable." *Supposya* is much more frequently attested than either *tyby* or *desevos*. I have collected the following examples:

> *dar **soposia** a reta den rych nefra mones then neff da ny yl* 'what, do you imagine that a rich man can never enter blessed heaven?' BM 459-61
> *dar **seposia** prest a wreta omma settya orth emperour* 'what, do you presume here to oppose an emperor?' BM 2445-47
> *Rag henna yth ewa poynt bras a error the **supposya** na rug crist kemeras y gyge mes a gyge an wyrhes maria y vam* 'Therefore it is a major matter of error to suppose that Christ took his flesh only from the Virgin Mary his mother' TH 12a
> *tus a russa **supposia** mar teffa du aga suffra the vsya aga naturall powers y a vynsa optaynya salvacion in ta lovr* 'people would have assumed, if God had allowed

them to use their natural powers, they would have obtained salvation well enough' TH 13a

*whath eff a ra **supposia** inna y honyn y bos gonsa charite* 'yet he will believe that in himself he possesses charity' TH 21

*So an perverse nature a then, corruptys gans pegh ha destitud a gere Du ha grace, ow **supposia** fatell ewa warbyn reason, bos res the vabden cara y yskar* 'But the perverse nature of man, corrupted by sin and devoid of the word of God and grace, believing that it is contrary to reason, that human beings should be obliged to love their enemies' TH 23a

*eff a ra **supposia** y bosa saw re bos ragtha the gara y yskerens* 'he will imagine that it is too heavy a burden for him to love his enemies' TH 24

*ny cristonyan a res thyn **supposia** an yocke a crist the vois wheg* 'it is necessary for us Christians to believe that the yoke of Christ is sweet' TH 28

*Eff a worrebys fatell essa eff ow **supposya** nag esa in oll Athens onyn drys in ban in dan y lawis eff, a vynna purposia na predery the wull mar heynys de na mar vars pegh* 'He answered that he assumed that there was not in all Athens anyone brought up under his laws who would intend or contemplate committing such a heinous deed and such a great sin' TH 29

*me a rug **supposya** fatell o va da ha mytt rag may hallowgh vnderstondia vn tra arell a thadder* 'I thought that it was good and meet for you to understand one further thing of good' TH 30a

*Rag lymmyn a thewethas pub den sempill heb vnderstonding na skyans a re **supposia** fatell yllens y bos iudges in maters a contrauercite* 'For recently everybody simple without understanding or knowledge assumed that they could be judges in matters of controversy' TH 37

*kyn rella eff **supposya** y honyn the vewa neffra mar war na mar worthy* 'though he assume that he himself live never so circumspectly or worthily' TH 40

*na onyn ew consyddrys na **supposys** the vos in egglos* 'nor is one considered or assumed to be in the church' TH 42a

*persuadya colonow an bobill neb ew da ha feithfull the **supposya** fatell rug agan Savyour ry an auctorite na the Pedyr* 'to persuade the hearts of the people who are good and faithful to believe that our Saviour gave that authority to Peter' TH 45

*Ith esaff ow **supposya** na veva heb cowse bras an ii the suffra in vn dith* 'I assume that it was not without great discussion that the two suffered on the same day' TH 47

*Rag kerensa an dus, an pith esta ow **supposia** the brogath an la* 'For the sake of the people, that which you assume preaches the law' TH 48a

*Indella me a **sopos** may halla kees e borpos* 'Thus I assume, that he might enclose what he intended' BK 1219-20

*me a grys hag an **suppose** y fynses sche comparya lemyn genaf* 'I believe and assume that you would want to compare yourself now with me' CW 215-17

*y whon gwyre dew agen tas y sor thyn y teige pur vras me an **suppose*** 'I know truly that God our Father will greatly bear against us his anger, I assume it' CW 860-62

*me a **supposyas** eall neff yth ova denvenys thym* 'I assumed that an angel of heaven had been sent to me' CW 1020-21

*therama **suppoga** andelna tho an liha rag an Bretten ha an Curnowean* 'I assume thus at least for the Bretons and the Cornish' BF: 29.

TOWARDS AUTHENTIC CORNISH

At the beginning of GKK George writes a *Ragskrif* of which the final paragraph reads as follows:

> Lemmyn yma devedhys an prys dhe dhyllo an obereth yn tien. Hevlyna y to ha bos klerra dhymm, rag y dhyllo erbynn an prys, nag yw [sic] an hwithransow mar vunys dell vynnsen; kler yw ynwedh nag yw hemma marnas kynsa dyllans an Gerlyver, hag y'n blydhynyow a dheu, y fydh edhomm mires arta orto

> [The time has now come to publish the work in full. This year it was becoming more apparent to me, in order to publish it in time, that the research is not as detailed as I would have wished; it is also clear that this is only the first edition of the Dictionary, and in the years ahead, it will be necessary to look at it again] (GKK: 4)

George seems to ignore the required sequence of tenses with *nag yw* for *nag o* in the above paragraph. His sense, however, is clear enough. He believed that he had done insufficient research when he published GKK. This is indeed true as can be seen from elsewhere in this chapter. It is particularly true in George's entry on *sopposya*. George gives it one meaning only 'suppose', whereas it is apparent from the instances in the texts that *supposya* in Cornish can mean 'suppose, assume, imagine, believe, think, infer; presume, claim.' Indeed it seems that in spoken Cornish *me a suppos* or *me a'n suppos* was the usual way of saying 'I assume'. One thing is certain, neither *tyby* nor *desevos* is preferable to *supposya*. The three verbs have different semantic ranges and all are useful. George's note on *sopposya* can safely be ignored.

18.81 *tabel* [tabel] 'table'
GKK tells us that this word occurs once in TH. It does not. The word is attested once in *Sacrament an Alter*: *ha pana* **tabell** *esta ow setha* 'and at which table you are sitting' SA 59. The table here is the Lord's table, since the Eucharist is the subject of *Sacrament an Alter*.

18.82 *taraner* [tarenner] 'thunderer'
Taraner, rather than Nance's *tarenner*, is George's own invention. Nance's *tarenner* is the correct word in Cornish. As I pointed out at **14.04** Pryce gives *Yein kuer,* **tarednow***, ha golowas, er, reo, gwenz ha clehe, ha kezer* 'Cold weather, thunder, and lightning, snow, frost, wind and ice [sic], and hail' (opposite F f 2). Similarly s.v. *Tonitru*[s] Lhuyd gives the Cornish words **Tredna***, taran* (AB: 164c). It is quite apparent that as a result of the falling together of unstressed vowels, the Cornish word *taran* 'thunder' was reshaped as **taren*, plural **tarennow*, Pryce's *tarednow*. The verb 'to thunder' was in consequence *tarenna*, Lhuyd's verbal noun *tredna, trenna* 'thundering' (AB: 165c, 248a). The agent noun therefore would have been **tarenner*. George's *taraner* is badly formed, since it has an agent suffix wrongly added to the noun stem *taran-*, rather than to the verbal stem *tarenn-*. George's neologism is curious, given that he

PROBLEMS WITH GEORGE'S *GERLYVER KERNEWEK KEMMYN*

includes the verb *tarena* in GKK, where he says erroneously that it contains "unexpected vowel affection". There is no affection and the vowel is not unexpected. *Taraner* is poor Cornish.

18.83 *taves* [tavas] 'tongue, language'

The Unified Cornish word for 'tongue' is *tavas*; cf. Welsh *tafod*, Breton *teod*. This Kernowek Kemyn has arbitrarily changed to *taves*. I have collected the following examples from the texts:

A with <e>
*ny yl **taves** den yn bys y leuerel bynytha* OM 767-78.

B with <a>
*yntre y thyns ha'y **davas*** OM 826
*hag vsya in ta y **tavas*** TH 23a
*agan **tavas** ew ruth gans e gos* SA 60
*Te a levar, **tavas** pan* BK 261
*saw e **davas** a vyth hyr* BK 512
*Syrr the thewan, **tavas** pan!* BK 918
*gwryth ow **thavas** ew pur vans* BK 974
*benytha gans **tavas** kyk* BK 1273
*benytha gans **tavas** kyk* BK 1289
*Ny yl **tavas** reportya* BK 3194a
*Ny yl **tavas** reportya* BK 3194b
*Gun **Tavas** Carnoack* BF: 25
*Rag an **Tavaz** Sousenack* BF: 25
*tho guthva[s] meer en **Tavaz** Curnooack* BF: 29
*dismiggia gun **Tavaz** ny* BF: 29
*dro tho an **Tavaz** Curnooack* BF: 29
*rag tho gwetha ge **Tavaz*** BF: 31
*naha an dadn an **Tavaz** a Dama* BF: 31
*ha adzhan an **Tavaz** kernuak dha boz **Tavaz** koth* BF: 46
*na vedn an **Tavaz** ma* BF: 46
*Ha skienz lyk en **Tavaz** Pou gen ni* BF: 46
*Ha Dotha **Tavaz** Kornooack vo Res* BF: 48
*Lebbn duath **Tavaz** coth ny en Kernow* BF: 48
*En **tavaz** Kernooak Gelles* BF: 48
*Boz **Tavaz** Coth Kernow [eu] kelles* BF: 48
*Lingua... A tongue, a language... C[ornish] **Tavaz*** AB: 80a
*Linguax... Long-tongued, a blab... C[ornish] **Tavaz** re hir* AB: 80a
*Sermo... A speech, discourse, talk... C[ornish] **Tavaz*** AB: 149b
*Bedh dorn re ver, dhon **tavaz** re hir* AB: 251c
*Mez den heb **davas** a gollaz i dir* AB: 251c
*Ne vedn nevera doas vas a **tavas** re hir* ACB
*Bes den heb **tavaz** a gollas e dir* ACB.

TOWARDS AUTHENTIC CORNISH

In view of the overwhelming numerical superiority of *tavas* to *taves* in traditional Cornish, it is remarkable that George should have decided to spell this word <taves>. I do not understand on what grounds, etymological, phonetic or other, he has done so. The word for 'tongue, language' in revived Cornish should be *tavas*.

18.84 *temptashyon* [temptacyon] 'temptation'
After this word George adds a note: "N.B. Use **temptyans**." Under *temptyans* we learn that it is George's own invention, created to replace *temptacyon*. *Temptacyon* is well attested:

> *pyiadow a luen colon a wor the ves* **temptacion** 'prayer from an earnest heart drives away temptation' PC 24-25
> *ow tas ynn y wolowys re bo gueres theugh pup prys worth* **temptacyon** *a'n tebel* 'may my Father in his glory be assistance to you always against the tremptation of the evil one' PC 223-25
> *ha why gynef re drygas yn* **temptacyon** *yn pup le* 'and you have dwelt with me in temptation everywhere' PC 804-05
> *ha war ow tas fast pysough na entreugh yn* **temptacyon** 'and pray my Father constantly that you enter not into temptation' PC 1058-59
> *a kescolon ol pesough nag yllough yn* **temptacion** 'and all of one accord pray that you go not into temptation' PC 1076-77
> *iesu arlud my ad pys orth* **temtacyon** *dewolow* 'Jesus, Lord, I beseech thee against the temptation of devils' BM 144-45
> *ha thum guythe pup seson omma the orth* **temptasconn** 'and to keep me at all times from temptation' BM 3857-58
> *Indelma der an provocacion han* **temptacion** *an teball el* 'Thus through the provocation and temptation of the devil' TH 3a
> *avoydya y* **temtacions** *hay successions* 'to avoid his temptations and successions' TH 3a
> *der* **temptacon** *bras an iowle chasshes on a baradice* 'by the great temptation of the devil we have been chased from paradise' CW 1768-69.

Temptacyon has been in Cornish since the time of *Passio Christi* at least and is attested in four different texts. To attempt to replace it with a modern coinage is inadmissible.

18.85 *termys* [termys] 'terms'
GKK tells us this word occurs once in TH, i.e. at 18a. I have noticed two instances:

> *ha gwra avoydya talys nowith ha fanglys* **termys** *ha bostow a scyens fals* 'avoid new tales and fangled terms and boasts of false knowledge' TH 18a
> *ha gans very vylle* **termes** *ow Jestya gansa* 'and with very vile terms mocking it' TH 55a.

This is a further example of the inaccuracy of George's database.

PROBLEMS WITH GEORGE'S *GERLYVER KERNEWEK KEMMYN*

18.86 *terthenn* [terthen] 'tertian fever'

GKK gives this word and suggests it means 'fever, influenza, flu'. The compiler tells us that the word derives from Latin *tertiana* 'three-day ague'. *Terthen* does not mean 'influenza' but a much more serious condition. *Tertiana* and *tertian ague* were the medieval Latin and English terms respectively for malaria. Parasitic protozoa are injected into the victim by the malaria mosquito (*Anopheles* spp.). They are carried to the liver and other organs where they multiply without causing symptoms. After a variable incubation period the parasites return to the blood-stream where they invade the red blood-cells and multiply rapidly. The red cells are quickly destroyed and the parasites are then free to invade further red cells, at which point the patient suffers a violent fever. After a while, often a whole day, the symptoms vanish until the next batch of parasites is released. All types of malaria cause attacks of fever at more or less regular intervals and increasing anaemia. The violent fevers of malaria with one-day intervals between them led to the disease's being referred to as a *tertiana* or *tertian ague*, i.e. with a fever every third day.

The meaning given in GKK for *terthen* (< *tarthennov* 'tertian agues' of BM 1423) is not correct. Under *fevyr* 'fever' (< *febyr* BM 693), moreover, GKK tells us to use *terthen*. This is unsound advice. *Fevyr* means 'fever' (of whatever origin), *terthen* means 'tertian ague, malaria'. The two should not be confused.

18.87 *tevi* [tevy] 'grow'

George adds a note after this word: "N.B. This word is found only 7 times in trad. Cor. with the commonest spelling *tevy* (4 times); the cognates suggest that *tyvi* might be more correct." Given Welsh *tyfu* 'grow' I should certainly expect *tevy* in Cornish; besides, I am not sure what George means by "correct". I prefer to spell as the scribes did. I have collected the following examples of *tevy* 'to grow':

> *hag yn tyr gorhenmennaf may* **tefo** *gveyth ha losow* 'and in the land I command that trees and herbs should grow' OM 27-28
> *pup gvethen* **tefyns** *a'y saf ov ton hy frvt ha'y delyow* 'let every tree grow standing upright, bearing fruit and leaves' OM 29-30
> *War bup frut losow ha has a vo ynny hy* **tevys** 'Upon every fruit, herb and seed that grows in it' OM 77-8
> *spern ha spethes ov* **tevy** 'thorns and brambles growing' OM 275
> *ny* **dyf** *guels na flour yn bys* 'neither any grass nor flower grows' OM 742
> *ha'y branchys yn ban* **tyvys** 'and its branches grown upwards' OM 785
> *Anethe ty a wylfyth tyr gvethen* **tevys** *whare* 'From them you will see three trees growing soon' OM 827-28
> *gurythyoug ha* **tyvoug** *arte* 'take root and grow again' OM 1894
> *ote an gvel theragon glas ov* **tevy** 'behold the rods before us growing green' OM 1984-85
> *ha'n guella may wrons* **tevy** 'and the best where they may grow' OM 2034
> *Eff a* **deffe** *in ban kepar ha flowren* 'He grows up like a flower' TH 7

> *ny a well nag ew an egglos **tevys** ha springis in ban a thewethas* 'we see that the church did not grow and spring up recently' TH 34a
> *ha scismes springes ha **tevys*** 'and schisms sprung up and grown' TH 48a
> *Praga i'gas kerthow why e **tef** lynas in erbers heb gonys veth?* 'Why in your territories do nettles grow without being weeded out?' BK 2295-97
> *lower flowrys a bub ehan yn place ma yta **tevys*** 'behold, many flowers of every kind have grown in this place' CW 363-64
> *ha frutes war bub gwethan y **teyf** gwaf ha have keffrys* 'and fruits of every kind grow in winter and summer also' CW 365-66
> *yn plas ma yta **tevys*** 'in this place beold it has grown' CW 541
> *deaw vabe yma thym genys ha **tevys** yth yns tha dues* 'two sons have been born to me and they are grown to men' CW 1056-57
> *mabe thymo yma genys ha **tevys** tha boya brase* 'a son has been born to me and he is grown into a big boy' CW1395-96
> *hay thop pur vghall in ban bes yn neave ma ow **tevy*** 'and its very high top, it grows up into the heaven' CW 1826-27
> *hag y **teiff** an keth spruse na vn gwethan woʒa hemma* 'and there will grow from those same pips a tree after this' CW 1855-56
> *mes an spruse y fyth **tevys** gwethan a vyth pure precyous* 'out of the kernels will be grown a tree that will be very precious' CW 1934-35
> *Cresco...To grow or wax bigger, to increase. C[ornish] Dho **teva*** AB: 52b
> *Na sorren may **teffo** gueith ha Losou* 'Let us not be angry that trees and herbs should grow' Lhuyd's MSS.

George could not have known about the example above from BK, but he could have counted the examples from the other texts. George says the word is attested only seven times; I have counted 24 instances. There was apparently *y* ~ *e* alternation in the earliest Middle Cornish, e.g. *dyf* OM 74 ~ *tevy* OM 275. But this has been replaced by <e> throughout. George's suggestion "that *tyvi* might be more correct" can be dismissed.

18.88 *tochya* [tuchya] 'touch'
GKK glosses this word 'touch accidentally'. *Tuchya* in fact has at least four separate senses. The first is 'to touch accidentally'. I have found this one example:

> *ʒe droys worth meyn ʒe **dochye*** 'lest you touch your foot against a stone' PA 14c.

The second is 'to touch deliberately'. I have collected the following examples:

> *y **tuche** a uer termyn gans ov clethe me a wra* 'I will soon touch it with my sword' PC 2311-12
> *a vynyn ryth na **tuche** vy nes* 'O woman, do not touch me at all' RD 875
> *Saw vn kynda a frut an tas du a chargias mabden na rella myllya na **tuchia** worta* 'But one kind of fruit God the Father charged man that he should not meddle with or touch' TH 2

*du agan defennas na rellan **tuchia** na myllia gynsy* 'God forbade us to touch or interfere with it' TH 3

*Eff ew **touchis**, eff ew squardis gans dens, agan tavas ew ruth gans e gos* 'He is touched, he is torn by teeth, our tongue is red with his blood' SA 60

*Tee a ill percevia ...pa vanar a sort esta o quelas agen saviour Christ, bus e **dochya*** 'You can perceive [not only] how you see our Saviour Christ, but also touch him' SA 60a

*not only [e] **touchia**, bus e thibbry* 'not only touch him but eat him' SA 60a

*kepar dell wruck S Thomas **touchia** corfe Christ, indella ny a ra **touchia** christ in sacrament* 'just as St Thomas touched the body of Christ, so we touch Christ in the sacrament' SA 60a

*rag Christ ew the vos **touchis**, rag e vos eff keveris Dew ha deane* 'for Christ is to be touched, for he is both God and man' SA 60a

*ny **vethis** gans dean towches* 'thou shalt not be touched by any man' CW 1183

*why na ra debre anothe na na rewa e **thotcha** lez why a varaw* 'you shall not eat of it nor shall you touch it lest you die' RC 23: 175.

The third sense is 'to affect, to infect'; I have found these examples:

*gans mernans me yv **tuchys*** 'by death I have been touched' BM 4258

*warlergh henna leferis gans ancov y voys **tuchys*** 'after that he said he had been touched by death' BM 4422-23

*An kigg ew **touchis** gans dowla rag malla an nenaf bos golowis gans & spiris sans* 'the flesh is touched by hands that the soul may be illumined by the Holy Spirit' SA 60a.

The fourth, and by far the commonest sense is 'to touch on, to mention, to concern.' Indeed the expression *ow tuchya* or *tuchyng* is often used simply to mean 'concerning, about'. I have collected the following examples:

*An kensa tra vgy ow **tuchia** an creacion a mab den* 'The first thing which concerns the creation of mankind' TH 1

*ha rag **tuchia** an corffe a vab den yma an scripture ow leverell* 'and to mention the body of man the scripture says' TH 2

*rag **tuchia** an estate a'y originall innocenci* 'with respect to the estate of his original innocence' TH 3

*yma eff ow cowsse haw **tochia** thyn catholyk egglos* 'he speaks and deals with the Catholic church' TH 18a

*An re ma ew an very gyrryow agan savyoure ow **tochia** an kerensa agan kyscristian* 'These are the very words of our Saviour concerning the love of our fellow Christian' TH 22

*a[n] dus coyth aunciant ow **tochya** an primacie* 'the old ancient people concerning the primacy' TH 46

*Whath, rag **tochya** thyn gyrryow ma* 'Still, to deal with these words' TH 53

*goodly ha largy processe ow **tochia** thin sacrament ma* 'a goodly and copious passage concerning this sacrament' TH 53a

***Tuchia** an seconde* 'As far as the second is concerned' TH 55

> *lyas onyn athewethas a gothas in errours war aga oppynyon ow **tochya** an sacrament benegas an aulter* 'many recently have fallen into errors with their opinion concerning the blessed sacrament of the altar' TH 55a
>
> *why a wore lymmyn pandra ew an lell crygyans ow **tochia** thyn sacrament[t] an aulter* 'now you know what is the true faith concerning the sacrament of the altar' TH 58
>
> *Me a wor nyth es paraw **tochyng** thegar benenas* 'I know you have no equal with respect to kindly women' BK 1136-37
>
> *Ny worthebe' thotha **toching** the'n questions eral* 'I shall not answer him concerning the other questions' BK 2127-18
>
> *An trubut pan ve **tochys*** 'When the tribute was mentioned' BK 2262.

GKK gives only the first sense 'touch accidentally', which is by far the least common. This is astonishing when one understands from the "authentication code" in GKK that the compiler knew of between 10 and 31 examples of *tuchya* in the texts.

18.89 *tryghi* [tryhy] 'triumph, be victorious'

The "authentication codes" for this word imply that it occurs 4-9 times in Middle and Late Cornish. I have not been able to find any examples. In his 1938 dictionary Nance tells us that *tryghy* is based on Welsh and Breton, and was not therefore found in traditional Cornish. This is further evidence of the inaccuracy of George's database.

18.90 *vyktori* [vyctory] 'victory'

After this word George appends a note: "N.B. use **trygh**"; s.v. *trygh*, however, George's "authentication code" indicates that the word is nowhere attested. We have no proof, therefore, that the word was ever in Middle Cornish. *Vyctory* is the usual word for 'victory' in the texts:

> *ha'n **victory** eth gyne yn arvow ruth* 'and the victory was mine in bloody armour' RD 2521-22
>
> *gorthyans the crist caradov grontia dym an **vyctory*** 'worship to dear Christ for granting me the victory' BM 2497
>
> *na **victory** warbyn agan gostly eskerens* 'nor victory against our spiritual enemies' TH 28
>
> *ha **victory** warbyn an dywolow* 'and victory against the devils' TH 28
>
> *hag eff an Jeva an thorne vhella han **victuri*** 'he had the upper hand and the victory' TH 34
>
> *hethew ma'm byf an **victory*** 'that today I may have the victory' BK 2815.

There can be no justification for avoiding *vyctory* in favour of *trygh.

18.91 *warlyna* [warleny] 'last year'

After his entry George appends the note: "N.B. Nance did not properly understand the correspondences between Breton and Welsh when he wrote *warleny.*" On the contrary, Nance understood them perfectly well. Nance's *warleny* is correct; **warlyna* of Kernowek Kemyn is mistaken.

'Last year' is *erllyned* in Middle Welsh and *y llynedd* in Modern Welsh. In Breton the word is *warlene* < * *warlenez*. When Welsh has stressed *-y-* in polysyllables, Cornish as we have seen (**11.00**) has *-e-*. In this respect alone Nance's *warleny* is better than George's *warlyna*. Hamp has shown (*Études Celtiques* 17 (1980): 166) that the Proto-British word for 'last year' contained **-blidniji* < Celtic dative **-blidnijai*. This would have given *-i* in Welsh, Breton and Cornish. The Welsh and Breton forms have both been reshaped, by analogy with the nominative ending, seen, for example, in Welsh *blynedd* 'years' < **blidnijas*. The Cornish form *warleny* < Proto-British **are-blidniji* is correct. *Warlyna* is without foundation.

18.92 ydyot 'idiot'

This word is cited by Nance in his 1938 and his 1952 dictionaries. The word is also in Tregear: *worth y gilwall **idiot**, bo hanow vith arell a vo unkunda* 'calling him "idiot" or any other name that would be unkind' TH. The word is now attested in *Bewnans Ke* and was clearly part of the vocabulary of Middle Cornish.

> *Attend ha clow. Na vith **ydyot*** 'Attend and listen. Don't be a fool' BK 267-78.

Ydyot is not in GKK, but the dictionary does give *edyek* 'simpleton', and the etymology, ascribed to K[en] J G[eorge], tells us the word is a "corruption" of Modern English *idiot*. With respect to George, it has always been known that *edjack* was a form of the word *idiot*, indeed his English-Cornish dictionary of 1952 Nance gives '*ydyot* (‡*edyak*)' (cf. *Edyack* 'an idiot, a simple creature' ACB).

Several things are curious about George's treatment of this etymon. In the first place, it is not clear why he should cite the derivative *edyek* but not the original form *ydyot*. In the second place, I do not understand why he gives *edyek* rather than *edyak*. In the third place, the spelling of the consonant in George's *edyek* is perplexing. He admits that the word is from English and compares Cornish dialect *edjack*. One would therefore expect the word to be pronounced in Cornish as in English, but the word contains <dy> [dj] in Kernowek Kemyn, a consonant cluster which does not occur in the English word. *Edjack* is pronounced ['edʒək]. I do not, therefore, understand why George does not spell this word **<ejjek> or **<ejjak> in Kernowek Kemyn.

18.93 yeynell 'refrigerator'

The compiler ascribes this neologism to K[en] J. G[eorge], i.e. to himself, and adds a note: "N.B. *yeyner* is often heard, but the editor feels that there is a case for distinguishing an inanimate agent with a different suffix." George apparently believes that the inanimate suffix *-ell* is preferable to the animate suffix *-er* when referring to an inanimate agent; cf. *reknell* 'calculator' on page 270. The neologism *korrdonner* 'microwave oven' given on page 180, however, refers to an inanimate agent but carries the animate suffix -*er*, rather than -*ell*. Oddly enough, according to GKK, *korrdonner* is the invention of K[en] J. G[eorge].

18.94 *ynjin* [ynjyn] 'ingenious; engine'

This word, as GKK correctly states, derives from Middle English < Old French *engin*. the word *jynn*, as GKK also correctly states, is from Middle English and is an aphetic form of Old French *engin*. Given that the two words have an identical origin, I find it odd that the deviser of Kernowek Kemyn believes their phonology to be so different. In the first case we have /i/ followed by /n/ and in the second /ɪ/ followed by /n:/. The identical etymon could hardly have developed in such variant ways. It should be noticed also that the Middle Cornish scribes spell them similarly:

> *den fel mur yv hag* **yngyn** 'he is a very dangerous man and ingenious' PC 1886-87
> *Der the* **injynnys** *hath hus* 'through your devices and your magic' BM 3376
> *envyes ove war y bydn me a vyn towlall neb* **gyn** *the dulla mara callaf* 'I am envious against him; I will devise some stratagem to deceive him if I can' CW 440-42
> *rag henna whela neb* **jyn** *po an vyadg ny dale oye eva thysa a theglyn* 'therefore seek some device or the business will not be worth an egg; Eve will shudder at you' CW 483-85.

In the light of *injynnys* in BM it is also remarkable that GKK should suggest *jynnow as the plural of *jynn*. Nance more sensibly in his 1938 dictionary gives *jyn*, plural *jynnys*.

18.95 *yn kever* [yn kever] 'with respect to, concerning'

This compound preposition is much used in revived Cornish—often incorrectly, since in traditional Cornish it is never used with nouns, only with possessive adjectives. *Y'th kever* 'with respect to you' is good Cornish, **yn kever an tavas* 'concerning the language' is not (see **19.18**). Curiously *yn kever* appears to have been omitted from GKK; I can find it neither under *kever* nor *yn*.

This is further evidence of the inaccuracy of George's database.

CHAPTER 19
Problems with Brown's *Grammar of Modern Cornish*

19.00 Introduction
Wella Brown published the first edition of *A Grammar of Modern Cornish* (GMC1) in 1984. This first edition was in Nancean Unified Cornish. A second edition in Kernowek Kemyn appeared in January 1993. I should like now to devote some time to an analysis of this second edition of *A Grammar of Modern Cornish* which I shall refer to as GMC2.

The first thing one notices about GMC2 when compared with the first edition, is how inferior it is in format. GMC1 was properly typeset, whereas GMC2 looks like a rather spiky typescript. The whole is much less readable than the first edition and much harder to use. In the introduction to GMC2 Brown nails his colours firmly to the mast when he extols George's new pronunciation and spelling for revived Cornish. Brown says:

> In the introduction to the first edition of this grammar I anticipated that further research and the use of computer techniques would add to our knowledge of Middle Cornish and allow us to improve our modern language, particularly as to its phonology, the grammar and its vocabulary, expanded to meet modern needs, being adequately understood. This forecast has been fulfilled by the work of Dr Ken George whose doctoral thesis, 'A Phonological History of Cornish', Brest, 1984, followed by 'The Pronunciation and Spelling of Revived Cornish' 1986, provided for the first time a comprehensive evaluation of the sound system used in Cornish at any given stage and the evolution of those sounds from the age of the first written records to the time of the demise of the language at the end of the eighteenth century. An improved system of pronunciation and spelling having been thus described, the Cornish Language Board decided in 1987 to adopt it as representing a considerable advance (GMC2: v).

Brown's faith in Kernowek Kemyn is remarkable, given that the system has been dismissed by all professional Celticists who have scrutinized it. Brown continues by paying tribute to the pioneers of the revival and adds:

> The advances made in recent years in no way invalidate the achievements of those who laid the foundations of the revival and the changes now introduced are to be seen as a continuous development of all that they did (GMC2: vi).

Jenner, Nance and Caradar were meticulous scholars. They understood perfectly well that to resuscitate an extinct language meant treating the traditional sources with the greatest respect. Respelling could be allowed in some limited cases, but to recast the whole orthography of the revived language on the basis of a speculative and, as it turns out, largely erroneous phonology is a denial of the work of the pioneers. If Jenner, Nance and Caradar had lived to see Kernowek Kemyn, I have no doubt they would have been most unhappy with it.

Pool as a pupil of Nance believed, correctly in my view, that Kernowek Kemyn was a repudiation of all that Nance had attempted to achieve. Pool writes:

> For anyone to claim better knowledge of Cornish and of its needs than Morton Nance is monstrous. The Language Board in their folly and ingratitude have abandoned sixty years of devoted work by Nance and his followers, but nobody should feel the least obligation to follow them. Should they show any signs of repentance, or of willingness to compromise, then every effort should be made to encourage them; otherwise, our prime task is to emphasise publicly that the Board has cast aside the aims of its founders (Pool 1995: 10),

and

> Instead, we found that the Language Board, which as followers of Morton Nance we had founded to continue his work for Cornish, based on his Unified system, had fallen into the hands of his detractors and Unified's opponents. The work of sixty years of revival, led by a scholar and prophet of true learning and vision, and then continued by the Language Board, had been cast aside and replaced by the theories of a false prophet (Pool 1995: 7).

I am familiar with all the texts of Middle Cornish, PA, the *Ordinalia*, BM, TH, SA, CW and now BK, as well as the more fragmentary remains of Late Cornish, by Kerew, the Bosons, etc. Yet it seems to me that the language described in GMC2 is very unlike the traditional Cornish of the texts, quite apart from the spurious orthography in which GMC2 is written. Indeed I find the discrepancies between what we know of traditional Cornish and the morphology and syntax presented in GMC2 to be highly disturbing. It is to these discrepancies that I now turn.

PRONOUNS

19.01 *huny* 'one'

GMC2 correctly points out at § 72.1 that *huny* is used after *lyes* and *pup*: *lyes huny* 'many a one' and *pub huny* 'everybody'. Brown continues:

> The use of *huni* many be extended by putting an 'the' or a possessive adjective before it to contrast something with a thing or person already mentioned or known to the hearer: *Gwell yw genev an huni rudh* 'I prefer the red one' (as distinct from those of other colours); *An huni hir yw y vroder* 'The tall one is his brother' (not any of the others); *Ow huni o terrys* 'Mine was broken' (others were not) (GMC2: § 72.1).

This "extended" use of *huny*, recommended by Brown here, has been borrowed from Breton and is without warrant in the Cornish texts. Brown's advice ought, I think, to be ignored. If one wishes to express such notions in Cornish, one has to specify the noun in question: *Gwell yw genef an gon rudh* 'I prefer the red dress', *An maw hyr yw y vroder ef* 'The tall lad is his brother'. Notice also that in Brown's sentence **Ow huni o terrys* there is a further problem. In English one can stress 'mine' i.e. '*Mine* was broken.' Cornish is a Celtic language and the stressing of possessive adjectives in them all is inadmissible. One must therefore use an enclitic: *Ow dewros vy o terrys* 'My bicycle was broken'. Brown's discussion of *huny* is very unsatisfactory.

19.02 *Keniver* 'as many'

Brown is correct when he tells us that *kenyver* means 'as many, all (who)'. He does not however, mention that already in Middle Cornish it bears the sense 'as many as there are > everyone, every.' Here are some examples from Middle and Late Cornish:

> The orth crist y ruk pesy certen desyr eredy the **kenever** an gorthya 'From Christ he besought the desire readily for all who should worship him' BM 4427
> So **keneuer** a wothfa redya ha vnderstondia a yll gwellas 'But all who can read and understand may see' TH 32a
> tha **Canevar** den gwyrrian a vo desyrius e gowis 'to every righteous man who may desire to receive him' SA 60
> Lowena ha lun yehas thu'm arluth ha gormolys drys **kenevar** us genis 'Joy and full health to my lord and praise beyond all men born' BK 2677-79
> Kensa, vrt an hagar auall iggeva gweell do derevoll warneny **Keniffer** termen dr' erany moas durt pedden an wolas do sillan 'First, because of the storm that he makes rise upon us every time that we go from Land's End to Scilly'
> che na raze debre a **kenevrah** gwethan an Looar 'you are not to eat of every tree in the garden' RC 23: 174-45
> Quisque...Every man, every one...C[ornish] **Kyniver** uonan AB: 135a.

19.03 **Yn neb maner* 'somehow'

Under this heading (GMC2 § 72.7) Brown mentions *neb tu* 'somewhere', *neb plas* 'some place' and the compounds *nebtra*, *neppyth* 'something' and *nepprys* 'sometime'. He seems here (and at § 260) to have forgotten one of the commonest collocations with *neb*, namely **yn neb maner** 'somehow, in some way, anyhow, in any way':

> arluth ker thy'mmo gueres gans the weel **yn nep maner** 'dear Lord, help me somehow with your rods' OM 2005-06
> guytheugh why y ma na vons **yn nep maner** remmvys the gen tyller 'keep them so that they be not somehow removed' OM 2043-45
> ny sconnyaf **yn nep maner** a wul ol the voluneth 'I shall not refuse in anyway to do thy will' OM 1291-92
> na allons **yn nep maner** kafus ken the thyscrysy 'that they may not in any way find cause to disbelieve' OM 1825-26

*ny goth thy's temptie the thew **yn nep maner*** 'you ought not tempt your God in any way' PC 102-03

*mars oge cryst map dev ker ymsav scon **yn nep maner*** 'if you are Christ the son of dear God, save yourself in some way' PC 2891-92

*a peue den drok y gnas ny alse **yn nep maner** pur wyr cafus mar mur ras rak sawye tus dre vn ger* 'were he a man of evil nature he could not indeed in anyway get such great grace to heal people with a word' PC 2969-72

*ny'm gref peyn **yn nep maner** a wrello thy'm drok neffre* 'no pain afflicts me in any way that might ever do me harm' RD 497-98

*thywhy byth nys dysk neffre **yn nep maner*** 'he will not remove it from you ever at all in any way' RD 1951-52.

Brown's omission is regrettable.

19.04 *neppyth* 'something'

I have two observations to make about the word *neppyth*. In the first place it is probably stressed on the second syllable and the first vowel is reduced to schwa written <a>. In the second place *neppyth* can also means 'a little of, to some degree' rather than simply 'something'. Both these features of *neppyth* can be seen in the following examples:

*ty re fue **napyth** re dovnt moys the serry an turant* 'you have been somewhat too presumptious in going to anger the tyrant' BM 3570-71

*pan vons y ow mois the wull **nampith** a ober bras* 'when they are going to do somewhat of great work' TH 1

*bo **nampith** a throg ha gwan hanow arell* 'or something of another evil and bad name' TH 28a

*Gear Christ ill changia takclennow the **nappith** na ve travith derag dorn* 'Can the word of Christ not change things to something they was nothing before hand?' SA 61a.

Neither of these features is mentioned by Brown.

19.05 *pynag, pypynag* 'whatever, whatsoever'

Brown (§ 72.11) gives *pynag, pypynag* 'whatever, whatsoever' and *piwpynag* 'whosoever, whomsoever'. *Pyv penag* in traditional Cornish (Brown's *piwpynag*) is attested twice at RD 2383 and 2467. In the texts, however, the commonest indefinite pronoun is *pynag oll* which means both 'whoever' and 'whatever'. One also finds the variant *pynag* or *pypynag oll* with the same sense. Here are some examples:

*my a'n taluyth thyugh ru'm pen **py penagol** a sconyo* 'I shall repay you by my head whoever may object' OM 2387-89

***penag** a wryllyf amme henna yv ef ru'm laute* 'whomever I kiss, that man is he upon my word' PC 1084-85

***py penagol** a wharfo* 'whatever may happen' RD 671

***penag** a worthya ken du* 'whoever worships a different god' BM 764

PROBLEMS WITH BROWN'S *GRAMMAR OF MODERN CORNISH*

Rag **penagull** *a rella pregoth discans vith a vo contrary* 'For whoever should preach teaching that would be contrary' TH 19a

ha **penagull** *a ve diskys then bobyll contrari the henna* 'and whatever may be taught to the people contrary to that' TH 19a

Ha **penagull** *a cause an geffa den in contrary* 'And whatever of cause a man may have in the contrary' TH 21a

Rag **penagull** *ew henna na garra y vroder* 'For whoever is he who loves not his brother' TH 23a

penagull *a rella latha a vith in danger a Judgment* 'whoever kills shall be in danger of judgement' TH 27

penagoll *a vo angry gans y brother* 'whoever may be angry with his brother' TH 27

ha **penagull** *a rella tyrry an re na* 'and whoever should break these' TH 33a

Penagoll *a vo deberthys theworth an Catholicall egglos* 'Whoever may be separated from the Catholic church' TH 40

ha **penagull** *a rylly kylmy in bys omma* 'and whomever you may bind in the world here' TH 44

penagull *a rylly dygylmy omma in bys* 'whomever you may loose here in the world' TH 44

ha **penagull** *a rylly lowsya po kylmy in bys* 'and whomever you may loose or bind in the world' TH 44

oll an re ew feithfull (po lene a feth) **pennagill** *a vons y* 'all they are faithful (or full of faith), whoever they are' TH 48

Penagull *a rella receva anotha* 'Whoever should receive of it' TH 51a

Penagel *a'm sorr gans cam* 'Whoever angers me with a wrong' BK 1474

pennagel *ew na lavarra nag ew lucyfer worthy* 'whosoever it is that says Lucifer is not worthy' CW 179-80

ha **pennagle** *a wra henna plages y fetha ragtha* 'and whoever does that, he should have plagues for it' CW 1641-42.

One would not suspect for a moment from Brown's treatment, that *pynag oll* was the ordinary Cornish expression for 'whoever, whatever'.

Brown goes on to say that when *pypynag* is used adjectivally, the qualified noun comes between *py* and *pynag*, e.g. *py lyver pynag* 'whichever book'. This is not so. 'Whichever' as an adjective in traditional Cornish is again *pynag oll* and it comes before its noun:

ha naha **penagull** *dra a vo pregowthis thetha* 'and deny whatever may be preached to them' TH 19a

penagull *tra a rella eff pretendia* 'whatever he may claim' TH 23a

penagull *person a rella eff ha gora y thewleff warnotha* 'whichever person he might lay his hands on' TH 46a

penagoll *mean a vova gothvethis ha aswones* 'whatever means by which he might be known and recognized' TH 50a

pynag[e]ll *for yth e an game* 'whichever way the game went' CW 811

pynagell *dean a weall henna hag a wrella tha latha* 'whichever man sees that and kills you' CW 1376-77.

Notice therefore that *pynag oll dra* and *pynag oll den, pynag oll person* are alternatives for *pynag oll* 'whatever, whoever'. Brown's treatment of the indefinite pronouns is very unsatisfactory

19.06 'how many?'
Brown suggests (§ 74.9) that the Cornish for 'how many' is *py lies, py seul* or *pes*. He seems to have forgotten *pana lyes* 'how many', since he does not mention it. It occurs three times in TH, however:

> **Pan a lyas** *gwethfas a ve gesys heb confort* 'How many widows have been left without support' TH 40a
> **pan lyas** *flogh omthevas a ve gesys heb confort na succur* 'how many orphan children have been left without support nor assistance' TH 40a
> **pan lyas** *testament ha blonogath an marow a ve tyrrys ha gesys heb collynwall* 'how many wills and desires of the deceased have been broken and left unfulfilled' TH 40a.

Brown's omission is regrettable.

19.07 *py eghenn* 'what kind of?'
Brown suggests that *pana* 'what kind of' is a derivative of *py* + *an* + *a* (§ 74.3). In view of the spelling <pahan> in *pahan cheyson a's bues why* PC 1970, I think this etymology is very unlikely. It is more probable, I think, that the word derives from *py ehen a* 'what kind of?' Brown also cites *py eghenn* 'what kind of' and also mentions *py kinda, py pan* and *py sort*. He does not, however, mention *pana vaner, pan vaner* 'what kind of', which is well attested:

> *ha the thisquethas pana dra ew an kythsame egglos ma,* **pana vaner** *a egglos ew hy* 'and to show what this same church is, what kind of church she is' TH 31
> *ha neb a vynna meras in y oberow a yll gwelas* **pan vaner** *marchant ova* 'and whoever wishes to look in his works can see what kind of character he was' TH 50a
> *may hallan ve attendya* **pan vanar** *lon yth ewa* 'that I may consider what kind of beast it is' CW 1568-69.

This is a remarkable omission.

ADVERBIALS
19.08 'how'
At § 77 Brown gives Kernowek Kemyn *fatell* 'how'. Increasingly in Middle Cornish *fatel* was used to introduce indirect speech. As a result it tended to be replaced by other expressions, *yn pan vaner* for example:

> *hag a wor* **yn pa vaner** 'and I know how' RD 526
> *Tee a ill percevia [...]* **pa vaner** *a sort esta o quelas agen Saviour Christ* 'You can perceive not only how you see our Saviour Christ' SA 60a
> *me a levar thys mar pleag* **yn pan vanar** *yn bema* 'I will tell thee, if it please thee, how I came by it' CW 755-56.

PROBLEMS WITH BROWN'S *GRAMMAR OF MODERN CORNISH*

Brown does not mention *yn pan vaner* and it would seem that he has not noticed it.

19.09 'how often, as often'
At § 259 Brown tells us that 'how often' is rendered in Cornish by *peskweyth, py lies gweyth, py lies treveth* or *py lies termyn*. *Pesquyth* is attested once, at CW 2502 where it means 'as often as': ***pesqwythe*** *mays gwella why hy* 'as often as you see it.' I am at the moment unable to find any example of *py lies gweyth / treveth / termyn* anywhere in traditional Cornish. In the only example of 'how often' I can find, the expression is translated *pan lowar torn*:

> *nyns o ef methek the confessia y pehosow,* **pan lowar turne** *a rug eff ernestly ha lamentably desyrya an mercy a thu* 'he was not ashamed to confess his sins, how often he earnestly and lamentably desired the mercy of God' TH 8a.

Brown does not seem to have noticed this.

19.10 *poken* 'or else'
At § 285 Brown tells us that the Cornish for 'or else' is *poken* or *boken*. He does not seem to have noticed another way of expression the same idea:

> *grua thegy crist ker gorthya* **ken maner** *kyllys os suir* 'do you worship beloved Christ, or else you are surely doomed' BM 901-02.

19.11 'how long'
At § 259.8 Brown tells us that the Cornish for 'how long' is either *pes termyn* or *pygemmys termyn*. I am unable to find any example of either in traditional Cornish. The only example of 'how long' with which I am familiar from the texts is *pana bellder*:

> *fatell rug pedyr dos the Rome, ha* **pana peldar** *a ruga bewa ena* 'how Peter came to Rome and how long he lived there' TH 47a.

Brown does not seem to have noticed this.

19.12 'always'
At § 259.7 Brown tells us that the Cornish for 'always' is *pup-prys*. This is true, but it is not the only way of expressing the idea:

> *beneges re bo an tas a vynnas dysquethes thy'n gvelynny a gemmys ras luen a vertu* **pup termyn** 'blessed be the Father who wished to show us rods of such grace, full of power always' OM 1745-48
> *gorthyys re bo dev an tas yn y ober* **pup termyn** 'blessed be God the Father in his work always' OM 2075-76

241

> *ha nep as tefo gallos a vyth gans yowynk ha los henwys tus vras* **pup termyn** 'and those who will have power will by young and old be called great people always' PC 788-90
>
> *rak the thescas tek dy'nny yv parys* **yn pup termyn** 'for your fair teaching is always ready for us' PC 818-19
>
> *bethens gruys* **yn pup termyn** 'may it always be done' PC 1040
>
> *rak y confort yv thy'mmo fest parys* **yn pup termyn** 'for his comfort is indeed ready for me always' PC 1052-53
>
> *yma thy'mmo hyreth tyn yn ow colon* **pup termyn** 'I always have bitter longing in my heart' RD 747-48
>
> *ha the henna me a vyn don dustuny* **pup termyn** 'and to that I will bear witness always' RD 1052-53
>
> *mercy pysaf* **pup termyn** *yn certan a luen golon* 'I pray for mercy certainly always with a full heart' RD 1157-58
>
> *myns may hyllen sur esyes ty a vyth* **yn pup termyn** 'as much as we can you will be eased always' BM 140-41
>
> *A dyves del redyn ny rych lour o* **in pup termen** 'as we read of Dives he was always rich' BM 446-47
>
> *mur yv ov rays* **pup termen** 'great is my grace always' BM 513
>
> *cryst roy dis* **in pup termyn** *omguythe prest in glander* 'may Christ grant you always to keep yourself in purity' BM 532-33
>
> *sav me a beys crist ihesus thagys socra* **pup termen** 'but I will beseech Christ Jesus to succour you always' BM 591-92
>
> *gallus an iovle* **pup termen** *dretho a veth confundijs* 'the power of the Devil will always be confounded thereby' BM 2032-33
>
> *the pup gruegh restorite myns may hallogh* **pub termen** 'to all make restitution as much as you can always' BM 2179-78
>
> *Gallus ha confort an tas re bo genen* **pup termen** 'May the power and comfort of the Father be with us always' BM 2735-36
>
> *E coyth thotha gothvas gras ha'y lunworthya* **pub termyn** 'One should offer him thanks and worship him always' BK 320-21
>
> *Gwayt ma'n gorthy* **pub termyn** 'Be sure to worship him always' BK 826
>
> *Parys on the'th unadow rag the servya* **pub termyn** 'We are ready according to your desire to serve you always' BK 2036-37.

Brown does not seem to mention (*yn*) *pub termyn* 'always' anywhere.

19.13 'at the one time'

Brown tells us (GMC2 § 258.1) that 'at the one time' is rendered in Cornish as *a'n eyl torn*. He does not seem to mention another way of expressing the same notion, i.e. 'the one time... at the other time':

> *fatell rug du thea dalleth an bys, lyas tyrmyn apperya the vabden,* **pare tyrmyn** *in vn sort, ha* **pare tyrmyn** *in sort arell* 'how God from the beginning of the world often appeared to mankind, at one time in one way and at another time in another way' TH 55.

PROBLEMS WITH BROWN'S *GRAMMAR OF MODERN CORNISH*

Given that this is a very useful expression and not otherwise attested, it is remarkable that Brown appears to have overlooked it.

19.14 'often'

Brown mentions *py lies gweyth* 'how often' (19.09), but he does not mention either A) *lyes gweyth* 'often' or B) *lyes termyn* 'often,' though both are attested in the texts:

A)
> *sav rak peder caradow **lyes guyth** me re bysys* 'but for dear Peter often have I prayed' PC 883-84
> *me a'n glewas dyougel **lyes guyth** ov leuerel an temple y wre terry* 'often I heard him say that he would destroy the temple' PC 1307-09
> ***lyes guyth** y wruk bostye* 'often did he boast' PC 2439
> *Maria me reth pesys rag ov map sur **lues guyth*** 'Mary, I have prayed to you often for my son' BM 3615-16
> *mes company **leas gwyth** a bub beast* 'but the company often of every beast' CW 1672-3.

B)
> *So **lyas tyrmyn** an froward nature a then a ra **lyas tyrmyn** predery a'n offencys* 'But often the froward nature of man will often think of the offences' TH 24
> *Whath kyn fe va **lyas tyrmyn** assays ha teball pynchis* 'Moreover though it was often under threat and in dire straits' TH 34
> *ha **lyas tyrmyn** ny a red in Aweyll* 'and often we read in the Gospel' TH 35a
> *Indella gans kepar reuerens yma S Augustyn **lyas tyrmyn** ow submyttya oll y Judgment eff* 'Thus with equal reverence St Augustine submits all his own judgement' TH 37a
> *fatell rug du thea dalleth an bys, **lyas tyrmyn** apperya the vabden* 'how God often from the beginning of the world appeared to mankind' TH 55.

It would seem that Brown has not noticed either expression.

19.15 'down'

At §§ 259.2-3 Brown gives the following expressions to translate 'down, downwards' in Cornish: *war-woeles* [*war woles*], *war-leur* [*war luer*], *yn nans*, *dhe'n leur* [*dhe'n luer*], *yn leur* [*yn luer*]. Curiously Brown does not seem to have noticed that by far the commonest way of expressing the notion 'downwards, down' in the Middle Cornish texts is *the'n dor*. Here are some examples:

> *ha ȝe dry **ȝen dor** gans meth* 'and to bring him down with shame' PA 97d
> *rag y thry **ȝen dor** gans meth* 'in order to bring him down with shame' PA 136b
> *yntre dew **ȝen dor** coȝys* 'in two pieces fallen down' PA 200c
> *toul an welen ol yn tyen **the'n dor** vskys* 'cast the rod completely down quickly' OM 1447-48
> *ha **the'n dor** scon a'n goras* 'and soon pulled him down' OM 2227
> *hethe **the'n dor** my a'd pys* 'hand it down, I beg you' OM 2521
> *bys may cothe hy **the'n dor*** 'that she may fall down' OM 2718

243

*terry **the'n dor** an temple* 'pull the temple down' PC 2441
*dyyskyn ha **the'n dor** ke* 'descend and go down' PC 100
*kyn fe dyswrys an temple **the'n dor** quyt* 'though the temple were completely pulled down' PC 344-45
***the'n dor** prag na ymwhelaf* 'why I do not fall down' PC 2594
*toul an grous **the'n dor** hep gow* 'throw the cross down without deceit' PC 2661
***the'n dor** an gos a cothas* 'the blood dripped down' RD 1119
*cothys **then doyr** attonsy* 'look at them fallen down' BM 1278
*deyskyn **then dor** mata* 'get down, mate' BM 1887
***then dour** gansa* 'down with them' BM 3528
*ow tenna **then dore** haw kemeras the ves an goth* 'pulling down and taking away the pride' TH 6
*ha tenna **then dore** an pryd* 'and pull down the pride' TH 6a
***then dore**, lost peacock (vel payon) prowt* 'down, proud peacock's (or payon's) tail!' TH 9
***then dore**, colonow prowt* 'down, proud hearts!' TH 9
***then dore**, brytyll prye ha dore* 'down, fragile clay and earth!' TH 9
*hag eff a putt **then dore** theth pen in dan y dros* 'and he will put down your head under his feet' TH 13
*ha nena ef a vith compellys the gotha **thyn dore** in corfe hag in ena therag du* 'and then he will be compelled to fall down in body and in soul before God' TH 30a
*Eff a thanvonas **then dore** an spuris sans* 'He sent down the Holy Spirit' TH 36
*the denna **thyn dore** an paell han kee ay vyne yard* 'to pull down the fence and the hedge of his vineyard' TH 40a
*pana abbys a vue twolys [sic] **then dore*** 'what abbeys were thrown down' TH 40a
*pana colyges, pana chauntreys a ve towlys **then dore*** 'what colleges, what chantries were thrown down' TH 40a
*gesow ny the gotha **thyn dore*** 'let us fall down' TH 40a
*y ben a ve treylys **thyn dore** in crowse* 'his head was turned downwards on the cross' TH 47
*pan rug du dos **thyn dore** thea nef* 'when God came down from heaven' TH 56a
***than doer** ganso mergh ha mawe* 'down with it, horse and rider' CW 294
*ha henna theth pedn ʒa gy **than doer** sure a wra croppya* 'and he will crush down your head surely' CW 916-17
*mo thosta maab Deew, towle tha honnen **doore*** 'if you are the son of God, throw yourself down' RC 23: 187
*mar minta poz cotha **an doer** ha gortha ve* 'if you will only fall down and worship me' RC 23: 188
*ha angye a cothaz **en doar** ha gorthaz tha eve* 'and they fell down and worshipped him' RC 23: 197
*Fatla gura ve agaz gorr why **en dowr*** 'How if I lay you down?' LAM: 228.

Brown makes no allusion anywhere to *dhe'n dor*. In view of the many examples in the texts, this is a remarkable, and indeed regrettable, omission.*

---

*   Brown's ignorance of *the'n dor* 'down' is remarkable, given that Nance cites *dhe'n dor* 'down' in both his *Cornish-English Dictionary* (1938: 41) and *s.v.* 'down, downwards' in his English-Cornish dictionary (1952: 53).

PROBLEMS WITH BROWN'S *GRAMMAR OF MODERN CORNISH*
PREPOSITIONS

19.16 *a'm govis vi* 'for my sake'

Brown tells us (§ 134) that *a-govis* is the usual way of expressing 'on account of, for the sake of.' I have been able to locate only the following examples of this compound preposition:

> *saw gvra vn dra **a'm govys*** 'but do one thing for my sake' OM 76
> *del russys moy **a'm govys*** 'as you have done more for my sake' OM 108
> *na gemerre den vith greff na duwen **am govys** vy* 'let no one be grieved or saddened on my account' BM 405-06
> *thywhy wy y fye cam boys lethys **am govys** vy* 'it would be wrong for you to be killed for may sake' BM 1654-55.

Brown gives a full paradigm, *a'm govis, *a'th wovis, *a'y wovis, *a'y govis, *a'gan govis, *a'gas govis, *a'ga govis*; all these except the first are hypothetical. We do not know which person apart from the first was ever employed in traditional Cornish, nor do we know whether the expression was used with a noun.

The customary way of rendering 'for the sake of, on account of' in Cornish is to use the phrase *rag kerensa*. I have collected the following examples:

> *dowr ha goys yn kemyskys weys crist **rag ʒe gerense*** 'water and blood mixed, the sweat of Christ for your sake' PA 58d
> *an paynys bras an geve han dyspyth heb y dylly hag ol **rag ʒe gerense*** 'the great pains he suffered and the undeserved contempt all for thy sake' PA 139b-c
> *certus **rag the gerense** syr vrry a fyth lethys* 'certainly for your sake Sir Uriah will be killed' OM 2123-24
> *ef a vyth hep falladow marow **rag the gerense*** 'he will without fail be dead for your sake' OM 2137-38
> *ny fue ragtho y honan yn gothefys ef certan mas **rak kerenge** map den* 'it was not for himself he suffered it indeed but for the sake of mankind' PC 3226-28
> *fatel fue cryst mertheryys **rak kerenge** tus a'n beys why a welas yn tyen* 'you have seen completely how Christ was martyred for the sake of the people of the world' PC 3220-23
> *mur a peyn a wothefys **rak kerenge** tus a'n bys* 'much pain he suffered for the sake of the people of the world' RD 832-34
> ***rag kerensa** an passyonn a porthes ihesu ragon pynys hyʒyw y fanna* 'for the sake of the passion which Jesus bore for us today I will fast' BM 122-24
> ***Rag kerense** crist an neff me a vyn agis pesy* 'For the sake of Christ of heaven, I will beseech you' BM 403-04
> ***rag kerense** an drensis na temptyogh vy the foly* 'for the sake of the Trinity do not tempt me to folly' BM 500-01
> *grua gueres dynny dyblans **rag kerense** ihesu ker* 'help us clearly for the sake of dear Jesus' BM 698-99
> *Me ath peys a luengolon ty the vynnes ov sawya **rag kerense** an passconn* 'I pray you with a full heart that you would heal me for the sake of the Passion' BM 2598-600

245

rag kerense crist map ras, myr thynny bohosogyon 'for the sake of Christ, son of grace, look at us, the poor' BM 2640-42

Na govsugh an dynyte *rag kerense* crist avan 'Speak not of the dignity for the sake of Christ above' BM 2956-57

Rag kerense an pasconn a thuk ihesu ragon ny 'For the sake of the Passion which Jesus bore for us' BM 2988-89

rag y gerense lemen agys pesy me a vyen epscop benytha na ven 'for his sake now I will beseech you that I should never be bishop' BM 2997-99

rag kerense an pasconn a porthes crist map guirhays 'for the sake of the Passion which Christ, a virgin's son, bore' BM 3032-33

Lemen *rag y gerense* regh thym queth rag ov huthe 'Now for his sake give me a garment to cover myself' BM 3040-41

rag kerense crist avan ny ages pesse certan gul gueres thyn dyogel 'for the sake of Christ above we would beseech you to help us indeed' BM 3110-12

Rag kerense arluth neff gueres dyn orth agen gref 'For the sake of the Lord of heaven, assist us in our trouble' BM 3128-29

rag kerense ihesu wek lauer dym a then grassyes 'for the sake of dear Jesus, speak to me, O gracious man' BM 4196-97

rag kerense an pasconn a porthes ihesu ragonn meryasek grua thym gueres 'for the sake of the Passion which Jesus bore for us, assist me, O Meriasek' BM 4208-10

ha *rag kerensa* agan saviour Jhesus crist 'and for the sake of our Saviour, Jesus Christ' TH 10a

rag y gerensa eff Du en tas ew lene pacifies 'for his sake God the Father is fully pacified' TH 10a

ha the forsakya pub tra oll in bys *rag kerensa* du 'and to forsake everything in the world for the sake of God' TH 21a

the gafus gyvyans *rag y gerensa* 'to obtain forgiveness for his sake' TH 24a

ny a gothyn gava thotha *rag kerensa* du 'we ought forgive him for God's sake' TH 24a

gava the bub den an trespas gwrys er aga[n] pyn *rag y gerensa* eff 'to forgive everyone the trespass done against us for his sake' TH 24a

the suffra myrnans *rag kerensa* y egglos 'to suffer death for the sake of his church' TH 31a

fatell rug an abosteleth a crist suffra myrnans *rag kerensa* crist 'that the apostles of Christ suffered death for Christ's sake' TH 36a

mars esta worth y wull *Rag kerensa* an dus 'if you do it for the sake of the people' TH 48

gothaf torment mayth ew own ha galarow thymmo *rag e gerensa* 'so that it is right for me to suffer torment and affliction for his sake' BK 430-32

Rag kerensa Marya ha'y Mab a'th pernas i'n pren saw ve a'n drog us o'm kyk 'For the sake of Mary and her son who redeemed thee on the tree heal me of this disease which is in my flesh' BK 788-90

rag tha garenga lemyn me a vyn gwyll paradice 'for your sake now I shall make paradise' CW 359-60.

Brown makes no mention of *rag kerensa* 'for the sake of, for the love of'. It is astonishing that a grammar book which is intended to be authoritative should be silent about such a well-attested and important expression.*

---

* Jenner gives *rag kerensa* 'for the sake of' (HCL: 150) and Nance cites *rag dha gerensa*

PROBLEMS WITH BROWN'S *GRAMMAR OF MODERN CORNISH*
19.17 *yn kyrghynn* 'about'
Explaining the use of the compound preposition *yn kyrghynn* [*yn kerhyn*] Brown says:

> The meaning is 'all around, on all sides of' and particularly as applied to clothing or covering of some sort, *an bows usi y'th kyrghynn* 'the coat which is around you'; *Gwisk dha dhillas y'th kyrghynn* 'Put on your clothes around you'; *Mayl lystenn yn kyrghynn y gonna bregh!* 'Wrap a bandage around his wrist!' The more general meaning of 'around' is co[n]veyed by *a-dro dhe* (GMC2 § 172).

I take from these remarks of Brown's that *adro dhe* 'about' is used in Cornish to mean 'around' in a general sense, whereas *yn kerhyn means* 'about' of clothes, garments, etc. Brown does not seem to have noticed that *adro (dhe)* is also frequently used of garments:

> *queth esa* **adro** *3030* 'there was a garment about him' PA 140c
> *hay bowys y honon gurris* **adro** *3030 hy a ve* 'and his own coat was put around him' PA 161b
> *vn queth tek hy a drylyas* **adro** *3030 desympys* 'a fair cloth she draped around him immediately' PA 177c
> **adro** *3y gorff y trylyas sendall rych yn luas pleg* 'around his corpse in many folds he wound costly sendal' PA 232c
> *a's guyskens athesempys* **adro thotho** *ef mar myn* 'let him put it on immediately if he will' PC 1788-89
> *hag a cach an cercot vras the ves vs* **adro thotho** 'and will snatch away the great surcout which is about him' PC 2074-75
> *otomma gynef hep fal queth ruth certan purpur pal the wyske* **adro thotho** 'behold here I have without fail red cloth certainly, a purple pall to put on around him' PC 2127-29
> *a dro th'y pen curyn spern* 'about his head a crown of thorns' PC 2934
> *An hevez* **adro** *y gein, The shirt on his back* AB: 250a
> *An lydrou* **adro***'z garro, The stockings on your legs* AB: 250a
> *An esgizou* **adro***'z treiz, The shoes on your feet* AB: 250a
> *An manak* **adro***'z dorn, The glove on your hand* AB: 250a.

If were to judge by Brown's grammar, one might be forgiven for believing that the above examples were poor Cornish, and yet such examples are numerous.

19.18 *yn kever* 'with respect to'
Brown tells us (§ 173.2) that *yn kever* is used with abstract ideas to mean 'concerning' and he gives the examples *Ny woer travydh yn kever an negys* 'he knows nothing concerning the message'; *yn kever an skrifenn ma* 'concerning this (piece) of [sic] writing'. This is incorrect in two ways. In the first place *yn kever* is never used in Cornish with a noun; it always requires a possessive

> 'for thy sake' (*Cornish-English Dictionary*: 89–90).

adjective. In the second place, *yn kever* means 'with respect to, regarding' rather than 'about'. *Yn kever* is not frequent in the texts. In fact I have been able to find only the following examples:

> *whet kerghough thy'mmo pilat* **yn y geuer** *del fuef badt* 'still fetch Pilate to me as I was lax regarding him' RD 1885-86
> *me a vyn pesy gevyans boys mar thyek* **yth keuer** 'I will beg forgiveness for being so lethargic regarding you' BM 3359-60
> *marya re buff re logh* **in the gever** 'Mary, I have been too slack with regard to thee' BM 3798-99
> *hag amyndya ef a ra* **y'th kevar** *del vo reson* 'and he will improve with regard to you as would be reasonable' BK 916-17
> *ev a dhelledzhaz an termen mal da va prev erra e ureg guitha kympez* **et i gever**: *erra po nag erra* 'he spun out the time so that he could prove whether his wife was keeping straight regarding him, was she or wasn't she' AB: 253a.

These five (one from the recently-discovered *Bewnans Ke*) are the only examples. They all allude to people and all are used with the possessive adjective. None means 'concerning'. Indeed traditional Cornish seems to have had no simple way of saying 'concerning, about'. In certain cases A) *a* 'from, of' was used. Later Cornish imitated English and used B) *adro the* 'about' to mean 'concerning, about'. In Middle Cornish the commonest way of expressing 'concerning, about' was C) to use the Cornish phrase *ow tuchya* 'touching, concerning' (*tuchya* 'to touch' < English *touch*) or even D) the English word *tuchyng* 'touching' itself. Here are examples of all four.

A **a** 'concerning, about'
Anotho *marth es preder worth y wythyes govynne* 'I thou art anxious concerning him, ask it of his keeper' OM 608-09
pur wyryoneth re geusys **ahanaf** *re'n geth hethev* 'about me you have spoken very truth by this day today' PC 1857-58
anotho *dygheth vye y wokyneth na age ha'y muscoghneth* 'it would be a pity about him were he not to leave his folly and his madness' PC 1988-90
ahanas *tra uyth ny'm dur kyn thos bysy* 'I shall in no way care about you, though you be persistent' RD 1059-60
me re glowes ov map wek **ahanes** *covs mur thadder* 'I have heard much good spoken about you, my dear son' BM 527-28
yma notijs sur ha covsis mur thadder **an** *keth den na* 'there is noted surely and much good spoken concerning that man' BM 2772-74.

B **adro the** 'concerning, about'
Nebbaz Gerriau **dro tho** *Carnoack* 'A Few Words about Cornish' BF: 25
gwellaz urt hemma **dro tho** *an Empack Angwin* 'see by this about the ?Empiric Angwin' BF: 25
ha meskeeges **dro tho** *Anko* 'and confused about *Anko*' BF: 25
Me a glowaz **dro tho** *an Karak Mean Omber* 'I heard about the rock Mean Omber' BF: 25

PROBLEMS WITH BROWN'S *GRAMMAR OF MODERN CORNISH*

Ma ko them cavaz tra an par ma en lever Arlyth an Menneth **dro tho** *e deskanz Latten* 'I remember finding something like this in Montaigne's book about his Latin education' BF: 29

ma lever vean rebbam **dro tho** *an Arlothas Curnow* 'there is a little book beside me about the Duchess of Cornwall' BF: 29

a orama **dro tho** *an Tavaz Curnooack* 'that I know about the Cornish language' BF: 29.

C **ow tuchya** (the) 'touching; concerning, about'

An re ma ew an very gyrryow agan savyoure **ow tochia** *an kerensa agan kyscristian* 'These are the very words of our Saviour concerning the love of our fellow Christian' TH 22

Omma ow ommyttya aucthors erall heb deweth, a dus coyth auncient **ow tochya** *an primacie* 'Here omitting other authors without end, of the ancient old people concerning the primacy' TH 46

ha largy processe **ow tochia** *thin sacrament ma* 'and wide process concerning this sacrament' TH 53a

war aga oppynyon **ow tochya** *an sacrament benegas an aulter* 'of their opinion concerning the blessed sacrament of the altar' TH 55a

pandra ew an lell crygyans **ow tochia** *thyn sacramen(t) an aulter* 'what is the true faith concerning the sacrament of the altar' TH 58.

D **tuchyng** 'touching; concerning, about'

Me a wor neth es paraw **tochyng** *thegar benenas* 'I know that you have no equal concerning kindly women' BK 1137

Ny worthebe thotha **toching** *then questons eral* 'I will not answer him concerning the other questions' BK 2128.

Expressions like Brown's **yn kever an negys* and **yn kever an scryven ma* are not Cornish and cannot be recommended.

NUMERALS

19.19 *dew/*diw* **'two'**

According to Brown (GMC2 § 96) the numeral 'two' has a masculine form *dew* and a feminine form *diw. Moreover he says that these two forms are prefixed to masculine and feminine nouns respectively to form the dual. This, according to Brown, means that 'two eyes' in Cornish is rendered *dewlagas* and 'two hands' *diwla. This is doubtful. It is likely that the masculine form *dew* and the feminine *dyw* were once distinguished in Cornish. By the period of the Middle Cornish texts, however, the Prosodic Shift meant that *dew* and *dyw* (*diw in Kernowek Kemyn) were no longer kept separate. That the two forms were no longer felt to be different is quite apparent from dual forms in the texts. Here for example, are some instances of *dewlagas* 'two eyes' (masculine, with *dew* in Kernowek Kemyn) and *dewla* 'hands' (feminine, with *diw in Kernowek Kemyn):

TOWARDS AUTHENTIC CORNISH

dewlagas 'two eyes'
y **ʒewlagas** PC 83b, 219c; *hay* **dewlagas** PA 224b; *th'y* **thewlagas** OM 2058; *ow* **dewlagas** PC 396; *ow* **devlagas** PC 410; *agan* **dewlagas** PC 1066; *the'th* **devlagas** PC 1193; *ha'y* **deylagas** PC 1395; *y* **theulagas** PC 1400; *the* **thevlagas** PC 2101; **devlagas** RD 54; *ow* **devlagas** RD 539; *ov* **devlagas** RD 617; *ow* **dewlagas** RD 791; **dewlaga[s]** CW 1647.

***diwla** '(two) hands'
ov **dywluef** OM 1346; *y'th* **dyvluef** PC 2174; **dyvlef** PC 2936; *a'y* **thywle** PC 3153; *yn* **thyvle** RD 1542; *ow* **dywle** RD 2590
Y **thewleff** PA 149a; *y* **ʒewleff** PA 178b; *om* **dewleff** PA 156c; *a'm* **dewluef** OM 1534; **devle** PC 474; *a* **thewleff** TH 8, 8a, 55a; **dewleff** TH 15a; *agan* **dewleff** TH 21a; *y* **thewleff** TH 46a; *in y* **thewla** TH 52; *y owne* **dewla** CW 1531; *a* **thewla** CW 2521 *ow* **dule** RD 2201; *Inter* **dula** BM 502; *gans y* **dule** BM 1315; *ha* **dula** BM 2603; *ha* **dule** BM 2991, 3035; **dula** *a Flehaz* BF: 31; *et ago* **doola** RC 23: 187
intyr **dowla** SA 60; *gans* **dowla** SA 60; **dowla** SA 61 x 2; *inter e* **thowla** SA 65; *inter* **dowla** SA 66.

Dewlagas is always written with <dew> or <dev>. It does not survive beyond the early Middle Cornish period however, being replaced by *lagasow*:

> *hagys* **lagasow** *a vith clerys* 'and your eyes will be opened' TH 3a
> *teg the sight y* **lagasow** 'beautiful in the sight of her eyes' TH 3a
> *ow dalhe* **lagasow** *an bobyll* 'blinding the eyes of the people' TH 19a
> *gans agan* **lagasow** 'with our eyes' TH 21a
> *therag agan* **lagasow** 'before our eyes' TH 42
> *gans aga* **lagasow** *kyge* 'with their bodily eyes' TH 56
> *nena agoz* **lagagow** *ra boz gerez* 'then your eyes will be opened' RC 23: 176
> *der o hi bleck tha'n* **lagagow** 'that it was pleasing to the eyes' RC 23: 176
> *Ha* **lagagow** *an Gie ve gerres* 'And their eyes were opened' RC 23: 177.

The forms *dewlef, dewla* survive, however, as the plural of *dorn* 'hand'. In the texts we have six examples with <yw>, <yv>, reflecting the original spelling But we have seen at **12.14** above that, <yw> and <ew> alternate as spellings, for example, in *gwyw/gwew* 'worthy', *byw/bew* 'alive', *pyw/pew* 'who'. We have also noted at **13.06** above that <u> is often used as a spelling for [ew] and [ɪw], e.g. *du* 'God', *pu* 'who', *gu* 'spear', etc. *Dywle, dewla* and *dula*, then, were clearly pronounced identically. It is quite apparent that the diphthong of *dewla* was [ew] where the first element was short. If the vowel had been half-long [iˑ] or [eˑ], it would not have rounded to [ow] in *dowla*. It is difficult, therefore, to maintain that in Middle Cornish the word for 'two hands, hands' was **diwla* with [ɪw] different from the diphthong in *dewlagas*, for example. Notice also 'two hands/fists' (*dewdhorn* in Kernowek Kemyn) occurs as *dywthorn* at RD 2596. Similarly 'two breasts' (**diwvron* in Kernowek Kemyn) occurs as *devra[n]* at CW 1837 and *defran* at CW 1910. In these instances the texts ignore any difference between *dew-* and *dyw-*. In a word, the distinction in GMC2 between

250

diw- and *dew-* is fictitious and should be dismissed. Nance was quite aware of the situation with respect to *dew-* and *dyw-*: in his 1938 dictionary s.v. *deu* he says "the texts confuse *deu-*, m. with *dyw-*, f."

19.20 The Cornish for 'second'

At § 93 Brown tells us that the Cornish for 'second' is *nessa*. This is not true. The Cornish word *nessa* is the comparative/superlative of *nes* 'near' and means 'next, nearest' as can be seen from the following examples:

> *honna yv y bous **nessa*** 'that is his undergarment' [i.e. next to the skin] RD 1096
> *meryasek ov goys **nesse*** 'Meriasek my nearest kin' BM 239
> *In ov **nesse** hevys ruen* 'In my undershirt of horsehair' BM 1968
> *indelle te a alse gul worschyp mur theth **nesse** ha boys selwys* 'thus you could do much good to your nearest and be saved' BM 2039-41
> *menogh y rer y pesy gans agen kerens **nessa*** 'often is he implored by our nearest kinsmen' BM 3440-41
> *Sow an **nessa** circumstance vs ow folya helma, ew moy surra proff* 'But the next circumstance which follows that is surer proof' TH 1
> ***Nessa** why a clowas an myschyw a theth the vabden dre begh* 'Next you heard of the mischief which came to mankind through sin' TH 4a
> *In **nessa** homely wosa helma why a ra clowas* 'In the next homily [the second] you will hear' TH 5
> ***nessa** eff the gemeras dynsys han substans aye gyge in wyrhes maria y vam* 'next that he took manhood and the substance of his flesh in the Virgin Mary his mother' TH 13a
> *na rella corruptia esylly glan erell a vo ow ionya **nessa** thotho* 'lest it corrupt other clean members joined closest to it' TH 25a
> *So in **nessa** Sermon ha homylye Ith off ve dre weras a thew purposys* 'But in the next sermon and homily [the eighth] I intend by the help of God' TH 35
> *So in **nessa** homelie why a clowith moy* 'But in the next [the ninth] homily you will hear more' TH 46
> *omma **nessa** thom throne ve an kensa try a vithe gwryes* 'Here next to my throne the first three shall be made' CW 37-8
> *prag y wrusta ye latha hag eve tha vrodar **nessa*** 'why did you kill him and he your nearest brother' CW 1677-78
> *ybma na vadna vi ostia bez en **nessa** tshei* 'here I will not lodge but in the next house' BF: 18
> *Kensa blethan, byrla a' baye; **Nessa** blethan, lull a' laye* 'First year, hug and kiss; next year lullaby' ACB F f.
> *Betho why fyrah **nessa*** 'Be wiser next time' ACB.

The penultimate example from Pryce involves a series, i.e. first year, next year, third year and fourth year. Although *nessa* means 'next' rather than 'second' in the series, it is not difficult to see how in such a context it could be taken to mean 'second'. This one item was probably what gave Nance the idea that *nessa* could mean 'second'; Brown and his fellow proponents of Kernowek Kemyn have followed him. It is apparent from the other examples, however, that *nessa* 'next' not infrequently refers to different ordinals. 'The next' may, as in the examples above, refer to the eighth or the ninth. *Nessa* does not mean 'second'. The Cornish for 'second' is *secund* as can be seen from the following examples:

> *yn **secund** dyth y fynna gruthyl ebron nef hynwys* 'on the second day I will make a firmament called heaven' OM 17-8
>
> *in meys est an viijves deth an **secund** feer sur a veth* 'in the month of August the eighth day the second fair will surely be' BM 2197-98
>
> *whi a ra vnderstondia an **second** chapter an lever a Moyses gylwys Genesis* 'you will understand from the second chaper of the book of Moses called Genesis' TH 1a
>
> *yth ew scriffes in **second** chapter in Genesis* 'it is written in the second chapter of Genesis' TH 2
>
> *y vn vab eff, an **second** person in dryngys* 'his only Son, the second person of the Trinity' TH 12a
>
> *mab du an **second** person in dryngys* 'the Son of God, the second person of the Trinity' TH 12a
>
> *yma Sent powle in **second** Chapter thyn hebrues ow leverell* 'St Paul says in the second chapter to the Hebrews' TH 13
>
> *an **second** person in dryngys du o ymmortall* 'the second person of the Trinity, God was immortal' TH 15
>
> *in Kynsa chapter in **second** pistyll* 'in the first chapter in the second epistle' TH 17a
>
> *ha in y tressa chapter the Thimothe in **second** pistill* 'and in his third chapter to Timothy in the second epistle' TH 18a
>
> *an brassa han kynsa commondement, han **second** ew havall the hemma* 'the greatest and the first commandment, and the second is like to it' TH 20a
>
> *in **second** chaptur in epistill scriffis thyn Galathians* 'in the second chapter of the epistle written to the Galatians' TH 29a
>
> *An **second** ew vniversalite, han tryssa ew unite* 'The second is universality, and the third is unity' TH 34a
>
> *dre an **second** ny a yll vnderstondya* 'by the second we can understand' TH 34a
>
> *han **second** circumstance the vos omma consyddrys* 'and the second circumstance to be considered here' TH 43
>
> *in y **seconde** Apologie directys ha danvenys then Emperour* 'in his second apologia, addressed and sent to the emperor' TH 46a
>
> *in xiiii chapter in **seconde** lever a Eusebius, ECCLESIASTICAL HISTORYE* 'in the fourth chapter of the second book of the *Ecclesiastical History* of Eusebius' TH 46a
>
> *Tuchia an **seconde**, kyn na vo travith nahene mas an generall cregians* 'As to the second, although it was nothing other than the general belief' TH 55
>
> *an kythsam **seconde** part ma* 'of this very same second part' TH 55
>
> *the declaria an **seconde** tra the vos consyddrys in sacrament benegas an aulter* 'to declare the second thing to be considered in the blessed sacrament of the altar' TH 55a
>
> *lebmyn yn **second** jorna gwraf broster a thesempys* 'now on the second day I make a firmament without delay' CW 80-1.

PROBLEMS WITH BROWN'S *GRAMMAR OF MODERN CORNISH*

George in GKK includes *sekond* 'second' but adds a note: "N.B. Use **nessa**." If one wishes to speak authentic Cornish this note should be ignored. Brown, however, does not even mention *secund* in his grammar. The basic handbooks of Kernowek Kemyn are unsatisfactory.

CONJUNCTIONS

19.21 *mes* 'but'

Brown tells us (GMC2 § 286) that *mes* is the Cornish for 'but' and that that *saw* means 'save, unless, except'. Brown does not seem to have noticed, that *saw* really means 'but' and is commoner than *mes*. Here are a very few examples from the texts

> *Tus crist ӡe ves a fyas pep ay du pur voreӡek* **saw** *pedyr crist a holyas abell avel vn ownek* 'Christ's people fled very sorrowful each in his own direction, but Peter followed Christ at a distance like one afraid' PA 77ab
>
> *ny gewsys ӡe blegadow* **saw** *war thu y a vynne dre envy leuerell gow* 'he did not speak to please but they wished for malice to speak falsehood against God' PA 90bc
>
> *my a genes the'n meneth* **saw** *kyns ys mos ov thas whek ro thy'm the vanneth perfeth* 'I will go with you to the mountain but before going, my dear father, give me your perfect blessing' OM 450-52
>
> *the lef arluth a glewaf* **saw** *the face my ny welaf* 'thy voice, O Lord, I hear but thy face I see not' OM 587-88
>
> *my a thy a thysempys* **saw** *pandra wrama govyn ny won na forth thu'm nygys* 'I will go there immediately, but what I am to ask or the way to my business I do not know' OM 697-99
>
> **Saw** *my a greys hy bos segh ha gurys noth ol rag an pegh* 'But I believe that it is dry and stripped all naked because of the sin' OM 757-78
>
> *an bos nos dywy a wra* **saw** *nyns ugy ov lesky* 'yonder bush is bright but it is not burning' OM 1397-98
>
> *den yw the pup theweles* **saw** *y ober hay thyskes pup ol a wra tremene* 'he is a man for the repentance of all but his work and teaching will all pass' PC 56-8
>
> *yma daggrow ow klybye the dreys rak evn kerenge* **saw** *me a's segh gans ow blew* 'tears are wetting your feet for sheer love, but I will dry them with my hair' PC 482-84
>
> *ny fynnaf y ry dywyth* **saw** *yn tokyn ov bos gulan a gous ihesu nazare me a wolgh scon ow dule* 'I will not give it twice, but as a token that I am clean of the blood of Jesus of Nazareth I will immediately wash my hands' PC 2496-99
>
> **saw** *pyw a vyn leuerel the vewnans ef the seuel* 'but who will say that he will rise to life?' RD 589-90
>
> *ny seuys nes* **saw** *yndella mara pe warbarth ol ny a vye marthys ates* 'he did not rise at all, but if it were thus, we all would be woundrously comforted' RD 1021-24
>
> **Saw** *thy'so y leuerys kepar del yw* 'But he related to you even as it is' RD 1394-95
>
> *ha pylat a'n dyallas* **saw** *an corf na byw a pe an emperour ef sawse* 'and Pilate executed him, but that body, were he alive, would heal the emperor' RD 1656-58

> *the ry nammur me num bus **sav** me a beys crist ihesus thagys socra pup termen* 'I haven't much to give but I will pray Christ Jesus to succour you always' BM 590-92
>
> *yma gena nowothov **sav** ny vethe sur heb mar y covsel thyugh gans ganov* 'I have news but I will not dare indeed to tell it you face to face' BM 768-70
>
> *eff hay lynnyeth o damnys **sav** an devgys a vynnays arta y vones prennys the saluascon* 'he and his lineage were damned but the Godhead wished again that he should be redeemed to salvation' BM 883-85
>
> ***sav** malbe dam a won vy gueres the cleves defry* 'but damn all do I know how to treat your disease' BM 1478-79
>
> ***sow** in creacion a vabden an tas a vsias solempnyty bras* 'but in the creation of mankind the Father used great solemnity' TH 1
>
> ***Sow** an nessa circumstance vs ow folya helma* 'But the next circumstance which follows this' TH 1
>
> ***Saw** vn kynda a frut an tas du a chargias mab den* 'But one kind of fruit the Father charged mankind' TH 2
>
> ***So** in mer ver dell ew an stat na kyllys* 'But in as much as that state was lost' TH 3
>
> ***Sowe** byth ware thymmo pub pryes an keth gwethan ma amma* 'But be thou careful for me always of this same tree here' CW 371-72
>
> *y a [thue] theth gorwmyn **saw** na bashe y war neb coore* 'they will come at your command but do not abash them at all' CW 401-02
>
> *marthys teke a vhe pub tra **saw** y skeans yw brvttall* 'marvellous fair above everything but her sense is fragile' CW 451-52
>
> ***Sow** an keth adam yw gwryes me a wore heb dowte in case* 'But the same Adam has been made, I know without doubt in the case' CW 461-62.

One would not guess for an instant from GMC2 that *saw* is the most frequent word for 'but' in traditional Cornish. In this respect the grammar is deficient.

19.22 'because'

At § 294 Brown gives the various ways of rendering 'because' in Cornish, i.e. *aban, awos, drefenn* and *rag*. He does not, however, mention the commonest way of saying 'because' in TH, namely *dre reson*. There are many examples:

> ***dre reson** y the Justyfia aga honyn dre aga contyrfett benegitter* 'because they justify themselves by their bogus sanctity' TH 9
>
> *Saw an dra ma ew strayng the ran an bobyll, **dre reson** du the wortas mar bell* 'But this matter is strange to some of the people, because God waited so long' TH 13a
>
> *rag henna yth esans y heb excusse, **dre reson** pan wothyans aswon du, ny rens y honora* 'therefore they were without excuse, because when they could recognize God, they did not honour him' TH 14
>
> ***dre reson** eff thegan dyluer ny vnwyth theworth pegh* 'because he once freed us from sin' TH 15a
>
> ***Dre reson** y bos an egglos An cyta vgy agan savyour ena ow menya* 'Because the church is the city which our Saviour means there' TH 17a
>
> ***dre reson** y bosow gwarnys therag dorne* 'because you were warned beforehand' TH 18
>
> *ha **dre reson** inweth y the gemeras warnetha an gothfos* 'and also because they took upon themselves the knowledge' TH 18a

PROBLEMS WITH BROWN'S *GRAMMAR OF MODERN CORNISH*

fatell rons y dos in crehyn devas, **dre reson** *y bosans y ow pretendya an gyrryow a thu* 'that they come in sheep skins because they lay claim to the words of God' TH 19a

ha **dre reson** *na ges fawt vith mar vras* 'and because there is no so great defect' TH 26a-27

gans moy payne dell rug an jewys, **dre reson** *ny the receva moy grace* 'with more pain than the Jews [had to], because we received more grace' TH 28

partly **dre reson** *y bos an payne an kythsame tressa degre ma tan yffarn* 'partly because the pain was of this same third degree of the fire of hell' TH 29

han ky[t]hsame egglos ma, **dre reson** *y bossy sanctifies* 'and this same church because she is sanctified' TH 31

hen ew the leverell an vnyuersall egglos, **dre reson** *nag ussy ow lurkya in cornettow* 'that is to say the universal church, because she does not lurk in corners' TH 31a

ha eplla is hemma **dre reson** *y bos S paule lynwys an Spuris-sans* 'and more able than that because St Paul was filled with the Holy Spirit' TH 33

dre reson *crist y honyn thy hevely the roois towlis in more* 'because Christ himself likens her to a net cast into the sea' TH 34

So **dre reson** *an reson y bos an mater ma settys in mes largely in Sacrament a penans* 'But because the reason that this matter is set out extensively in the sacrament of penance' TH 39-9a

a theth warnan ny **dre reson** *y bosen gyllys in mes thean chy a thu* 'which came upon us because we had left the house of God' TH 40a

ha **dre reson** *y vosa mar sure in feith, an egglos a ve buldys warnotha* 'and because he was so sure in faith, the church was built upon him' TH 45a

Inded Pedyr ew gylwys carrak **dre reson** *eff the vos an kensa a rug laya an fowndacion* 'Indeed Peter is called 'the Rock' because he was the first who laid the foundation' TH 45a

whath **dre reson** *y bosa gwrys dre an blonogeth a thu* 'still because she was made by the will of God' TH 50a

ny rug den vith dowtya **dre reson** *y bos du an gwrear anetha* 'nobody doubted because God was their creator' TH 57

ew gylwys dore, **dre reson** *y bosa gwrys a dore* 'who is called "earth" because he was made of earth' TH 57a.

Dre reson is similar in use to *drefenn* and it is astonishing that Brown does not anywhere allude to it.

19.23 *may hallo* 'in order that, so that'

Brown discusses final clauses (§ 349) and tells us they are introduced in Cornish by *may* or *rag may*. He does not seem to have noticed that in traditional Cornish the most frequent syntax to introduce final clauses involves *may hallen/-es/-a* 'that I/you/he, etc may' + verbal noun. This is common at all periods and in all texts. Here are a few examples:

yn meʒens y forth nyn ges **may hallo** *bos deflam guris* 'they said there is no way to make her blameless' PA 32d *golyough ha pesough ow 3as* **may hallough** *mos 3y aseth* 'watch and beseech my Father in order that you may go to his dwelling' PA 32c

ha me a ra the crist amme **may hallough** *y asswonvos* 'and I shall kiss Christ in order that you recognize him' PA 63d

ha kyrghough the dre an guas **may hallo** *cane ellas* 'and fetch the fellow home in order that he sing "alas!"' OM 514-15

my re gyrhas thy's the dre mab adam a fals huder **may hallo** *genen trege* 'I have fetched home Adam's son, the false deceiver in order that he may dwell with us' OM 564-66

th'y teller kyns ens arte noe gonys **may hallo** 'let it go to its former place in order that Noah may cultivate' OM 1095-96

hag y res gover fenten marth erhyth thotho hep fal **may hallo** *tus ha bestes ha myns a vynno eve* 'and if you order it without fail, a stream of a source will pour from it in order that man and beast and all who wish may drink' OM 1845-48

growetheugh ov arlut **may haller** *agas cuthe gans dylles rych del deguth* 'lie down my lord, so that you can be covered with rich clothes as is fitting' OM 1923-25

ha goryn ef yn y dron avel myghtern yn y se **may hallo** *bos kerenys kepar del fue thy'n yrhys* 'let us set him on his throne like a king on his seat in order that he be crowned as was commanded to us' OM 2372-75

dun ahanan th'y gerhas the dre certan **may hallo** *bos musurys* 'let's go to fetch it home in order to measure it' OM 2564-66

dev ker danvon thy'm an gras **may hallo** *henna sevel* 'dear God, send me the grace so that that one may stand' OM 2575

ol an beys a ros thetha **may hallons** *ynno bewa* 'he gave all the world to them so that they could live in it' OM 2832-33

kergh annas an pryns **may hyllyf** *clewas pyth yw an gusyl wella* 'fetch Annas the prince in order that I may hear what is the best counsel' PC 553-55

arluth yma dour tommys lour **may hallons** *bos golhys* 'lord, enough water is heated in order for them to be washed' PC 839-840

guyskys lemmyn nep cowyth **may hallo** *ef dysmygy mars yv map dev a vercy pyv a'n guyskys an barth kleth* 'let some companion strike him now in order that he can guess, if he is the son of God the merciful, who hit him on the left side' PC 1377-80

dun ganso er y anfus the pylat agan iustys **may hallo** *cafus y vrus* 'let us taken him for his misery to our justice Pilate in order that he get his judgement' PC 1501-03

may haller *ry yfle gras ha knoukye prest tys-ha-tas* 'that he may be given harsh treatment and be knocked hither and yon' PC 2076-77

me a gelm fast an losel **may hallo** *pup ol the wel dotho ef ry strekesow* 'I will bind the scoundrel fast in order everyone may all the better deal him strokes' PC 2078-80

rak ny wothas bos grontys thym gallos bras hethew **may hallaf** *dywys gallos am bues theth crousye ha gallos the'th tyllyfrye* 'for you do not know that I have been granted great power today so that I may choose the power I have to crucify you and the power to deliver you' PC 2181-85

drewhy yn rak dyssempys dismas iesmas baraban **may hallons** *bones brugys* 'bring forth immediately Dismas, Jesmas, Barabas, in order for them to be judged' PC 2232-34

PROBLEMS WITH BROWN'S *GRAMMAR OF MODERN CORNISH*

drewhy thy'm kettep onan **may haller** *aga iugge* 'bring me them all so that they can be judged' PC 2251-52

drou e thy'mmo the tackye a vgh y pen gans mur greys **may hallo** *pup y redye* 'bring it to me to pin above his head very quickly so that everyone may read it' PC 2807-09

ro thy'm kummeas me a'th pys a kymeres corf ihesu yv yn pren crous tremenys **may hallo** *bos anclethys* 'give me permission I beseech you to take the body of Jesus who died upon the cross in order to bury him' PC 3112-15

hetheugh thymmo ow klethe rak **may hyllyf** *y lathe kettoth ha'n ger* 'hand me my sword so that I can kill him without further ado' RD 1968-70

bys **may hallo** *bos iuggys ha dre lagha bos dampnys* 'so that he can be tried by law and condemned' RD 1980-81

eugh tenneugh a thysempys y goyl yn ban **may hallo** *mos gans an guyns* 'go, haul the sail up forthwith that she may sail with the wind' RD 2290-92

now menstrels pybygh bysy **may hyllyn** *mos the thonssye* 'now, minstrels, pipe vigorously that we may start to dance' RD 2640-41

3e scole lemmyn y worra me a vyn heb falladow dysky dader **may halla** 'to school now I will send him so that he learn goodness' BM 11-13

ihesu arluth cuff colyn the dyller da ru'm gedya gorthya crist ker **may hallen** 'may Lord Jesus, dear heart, guide me to a place so that I may worship beloved Christ' BM 628-30

soudoryan duen alemma **may hallen** *ganso rekna* 'soldiers, let us go hence so that we can deal with him' BM 799

Me a vyn moys then guylfoys ena ermet purguir boys **may hallen** *gorthya ov du* 'I will go to the wilderness and there be a hermit in order to worship my God' BM 1132-33

Pybugh menstrels colonnek **may hyllyn** *donsia dyson* 'Minstrels, pipe ye heartily that we may straightway dance' BM 2511-12

y vollys a veth screfys ha waree grueys dis parys **may hylly** *prest lafuria* 'his bulls will be written and got ready shortly for you so that you may at once travel' BM 2766-68

Lemen parusugh an beth in hanov crist del deleth **may hallen** *y anclethyas* 'Now prepare the tomb in the name of Christ, so that we may bury him' BM 4512

ha rag **may halla** *an raunson ma bois perfect, eff a suffras lyas kynde ha sorte a kammynseth* 'and in order that this ransom be perfect, he suffered many kinds and sorts of injustice' TH 15a

Hag in myske company an par na **may halla** *an gwyr bos progowthis* 'And among such company that the truth might be preached' TH 17a

the ry laude ha praise the oll an dus da rag aga oberow da **may hallans** *contynewa in dadder* 'to laud and praise all the good folk for their good deeds so that they may continue in goodness' TH 25

partly yth o rag **may halla** *an cristian bos mar war ha mar circumspect the wetha kerensa* 'it was partly so that the Christian might be so aware and so careful as to maintain charity' TH 29

yth ew gwris da aga rebukya, **may hallens** *bos methek ha kemeras sham aga fawtys* 'it is well done to rebuke them that they may be embarrassed and feel shame for their faults' TH 29a

ha **may hallan** *ny bewa ha trega in charite* 'and that we may live and remain in charity' TH 30 *me a rug supposya fatell ova da ha mytt rag* **may hallowgh** *vnderstondia vn tra arell a thadder* 'I assumed that it was good and meet that you might understand another one thing of goodness' TH 30a

neb a rug agan redemya, **may hallon** *ny neb an Jevas an vnderstonding ha perfect gothfas a thu pub vr thy honora* 'who redeemed us that we, who have the understanding and perfect knowledge of God, honour him always' TH 30a

hag eff a re thewhy conforter arell **may halla** *eff gortas genewhy rag neffra* 'and he will give you another comforter, to remain with you always' TH 36

me a vyn kemeras the veis an ke aw vyneyard, **may halla** *peryssya* 'I shall take away the fence of my vineyard that it may perish' TH 40

an kigg ew anoyntis, **may halla** *an nenaf bos consecratis* 'the flesh in anointed, in order that the soul be consecrated' SA 60a

an kigg ew selis, **may halla** *an nenaf bos defendis* 'the flesh is sealed, in order that the soul be protected' SA 60a

an kigg ew touchis gans dowla, **rag malla** *an nenaf bos golowis gans & spiris sans* 'the flesh is touched with hands, in order that the soul be enlightened by the Holy Spirit' SA 60a

& kigg ema ow tibbry corf ha eva gose agen arluth Iesus christ rag **may halla** *an nenaf bos mekys worth Dew golosake* 'the flesh eats the body and drinks the blood of our Lord Jesus Christ in order that the soul be nourished by Almighty God' SA 60a

an corf ema tibbry **rag malla** *an enef bos megys* 'the body eats that the soul may be nourished' SA 61

ha rag henna na ruk Christ gylwall participation, rag **malla** *ef signifia brossa mater ha eweth brassa conjunction intrethans* 'and did not Christ therefore call it participation, that he might indicate a greater matter and a greater conjunction between them?' SA 65

A wylta kyrwas enos del vynnas du whar ha dof orth an ewyow devethys gansa **may hallan** *gonys?* 'Do you see stags yonder as God wished gentle and tame come to their yokes so that I might plough with them?' BK 847-50

Indella me a sopos **may halla** *kees e borpos* 'Thus I suppose that he might enclose what he intended' BK 1219-20

In rag degough ou banar, **may halla** *bos dyglynnys* 'Carry forward my banner in order that he be frightened' BK 2796-97

dun the'n chamber, me a'th pys, **may hyllyn** *omacountya* 'let us go to the chamber, I beg you, in order for us to get to know each other' BK 2982-83

Ow amor, denvenough why etho warlerth arlythy **may hallowgh** *bos curunys* 'My love, send therefore for lords, in order for you to be crowned' BK 3012-14

hag a wheth yn [th]y body sperys **may hallas** *bewa* 'and will breathe into thy body a spirit, in order for you to live' CW 347-48

rag henna paynes pur vras yma ornes ragan ny **may hellyn** *kyny dretha* 'therefore great pains are ordained for us so that we will lament because of them' CW 1014-16

set ow seth the denewhan **may hallan** *tenna thotha* 'set my arrow aside order for me to shoot at it' CW 1554

lead vy quycke ewn besyn thotha **may hallan** *vy attendya pan vanar lon yth ewa* 'lead me quick to it so that I may consider what kind of animal it is' CW 1567-69

mynstrels growgh theny peba **may hallan** *warbarthe downssya* 'minstrels, pipe for us in order for us to dance' CW 2546-48

Malga e boaz composez a ve cowsez gen dean Deew Yzias 'that what was spoken by the man of God Isaiah might be fulfilled' RC 23: 189

dro geere tha ve arta, **m'ala** *ve moaze ha gortha thotha aweeth* 'bring me back word, so that I may go and worship him also' RC 23: 196

m'alga *boaz composez a ve cowsez gen Arleth neve der an prophet* 'that what the Lord of heaven spoke through the prophet might be fulfilled' RC 23: 198-99

ev a dhelledzhaz an termen **mal(dh)a** *va prev erra e wreg guitha kympez et i gever* 'he delayed the time in order to find out whether his wife was remaining faithful to him' BF: 18

Gura worry de Taz, ha de vam, **mol** *de dethyo boz pel En tereath* 'Honour thy father and thy mother that your days may be long in the land' BF: 42

mollogh *thy dythyow boz hyr yn tyr* 'that your days may be long in the land' ACB, two folios after E e verso

mal *de dythiow bethenz hyr war an tyr* 'that your days may be long in the land' ACB, two folios after E e verso.

The use of final *may hallo*, etc. is widely found in Cornish of all periods. It is remarkable that Brown nowhere alludes to it. His treatment of final clauses is in this respect defective.

VERBAL INFLECTION

19.24 Verbal paradigms in GMC2

The most striking point to notice about GMC2 is how complete are the verbal paradigms he cited in it. He gives full paradigms of each person and of the autonomous forms of all tenses, i.e. present/future, preterite, imperfect, pluperfect indicative and present/future and past subjunctive. He does not mention, however, that no verb (apart possibly from *bos* 'to be') is attested in all these forms. Traditional Cornish uses various verbs as auxiliaries, e.g. *bos* 'to be', *dos* 'to come', *gul* 'to do' and *mennas* 'to wish'. This practice should be imitated in the revived language. We should say, for example:

Yth esof orth hy hara 'I love her'

Na ve me dhe'th cara, ny vensen leverel henna dhys 'If I didn't love you, I wouldn't have told you that'

Mar tue hy ha leverel henna, ny vannaf y gresy 'If she says that, I won't believe it'

Mar teffa hy ha gul henna, ny wrussen gava dhedhy 'If she had done that, I wouldn't have forgiven her'

Me a wrug hy gweles 'I saw her'

Me a vensa hy gweles, na ve an golow dhe vos mar wan 'I would have seen her, had the light not been so faint'

Me a vyn govyn tra worthys 'I will ask you something'.

I discuss some of these formations below. Brown deals with the auxiliary verbs to some degree, but he does not make it clear just how widespread their use is in the traditional language. This is a serious defect in GMC2.

19.25 Pluperfect/Conditional

At § 180 Brown tells us that Middle Cornish had a pluperfect tense. This is true only for *Pascon agan Arluth*. The pluperfect is not found anywhere else. The attested examples of the pluperfect to be found in PA can be classified as A) examples of *byen* < *bos* 'to be'; B) examples of *dothyen* < *dos* 'to come'; C) examples of *gwrussen* < *gul* 'to do'; D) pluperfects of other verbs. Here are all the instances of the pluperfect in Middle Cornish:

A)
gans crist na **vye** *tregis* 'that he had not dwelt with Christ' PA 85d
bytqueth ef na **vye** *guell* 'that never had it been better' PA 91d
mar noyth genys del **vye** 'as naked as he had been born' PA 130a
praga dampnys re **bee** 'why he had been condemned' PA 187b
ef re **bea** *den a brys* 'he had been a worthy man' PA 217c
en deskyens del **vye** 'they told it as it had been' PA 248b.

B)
Then tyller crist re **dothye** 'Christ had come to the place' PA 33a
Then eʒewon pan **doʒye** 'when he had come to the Jews' PA 63a
Pan **doʒyans** *bys yn tyller* 'when they had come to the place' PA 65a
a dus fals y re **doʒye** 'from false people they had come' PA 90d
pan **doʒyans** *ʒy yntreʒe* 'when they had arrived there, among them' PA 176b
Then leuff arall pan **doʒyans** 'when they had come to the other hand' PA 180a.

C)
hag ol drok suel a **wresse** 'and all evil as much as he had done' PA 119d
lemyn an tol re **wrussens** 'except the hole they had made' PA 180d
rag an ober re **wresse** 'for the deed he had done' PA 220a.

D)
war an bys re **ʒewesse** 'whom he had chosen in the world' PA 41d
an ioul ynno re **drecse** 'the Devil had taken up residence in him' PA 47d
na bythqueth ef nan **quelse** 'nor ever had he seen him' PA 85d
a crist kepar del **welse** 'about Christ as she had seen' PA 123a
yn vrna del re **beghse** 'then as he had sinned' PA 86c
dreʒy adam may **beghse** 'through which adam had sinned' PA 152d
cleves vyth nyth **kemerse** 'no sickness had come upon you' PA 157d
rag an keth re ren **crowse** 'for the same people who had crucified him' PA 185c
a sensy marya crist del **arse** 'to keep Mary as Christ had commanded' PA 185c
yn lan re **vewse** 'in purity he had lived' PA 204b.

In a word there are only 25 examples of the pluperfect (as pluperfect, rather than conditional) in Cornish. Of these, six are from *bos* 'to be', six from *dos* 'to come', three from *gul* 'to do' and 10 from the verbs *gweles* 'to see', *peha* 'to sin', *bewa* 'to live', *erhy* 'to command', *kemeres* 'to take', *dewys* 'to choose' and *trega* 'to dwell' taken together. That is all. One certainly does not get the impression from GMC2 that the pluperfect is so poorly attested in the traditional language. Brown's treatment, therefore, is highly misleading and should be rewritten.

The pluperfect, as attested in PA, did not disappear in later texts, but was used as a conditional tense. It is noteworthy, however, that the conditional itself (originally pluperfect) is increasingly replaced by periphrastic forms with the auxiliaries A) *gul* 'to do' and B) *mennas* 'will; to wish'. Here are some examples:

A

*vn dra a won an gothfes a **russe** the **thythane*** 'one thing I know, which if thou knewest it would amuse thee' OM 151

*the'n nef **grusses** yskynne* 'thou wouldst ascend to heaven' OM 156

*awos travyth ny **wrussen** venytha the **gvhuthas*** 'for nothing would I ever denounce thee' OM 163-64

*pan clewfyf vy an tan tyn parhap y **wrussen fye*** 'whenever I feel the sharp fire, perhaps I would flee' OM 1351

*hag a cothfons yredy ny **wrussens** ov **dystrewy*** 'if indeed they knew they would not destroy me' PC 2776-77

*nena ny **russa** den vith **resak** in heresy, mas pub den a **russa glena*** 'the no one would run into heresy, but everybody would adhere' TH 19a

*Surly ny **russa** an egglos a crist **dos** then dishonor* 'Surely the church of Christ would not have come to the dishonour' TH 39

*mernans ny **wressans tastya*** 'they would not have tasted death' CW 995.

B

*ef a **vynse gul** deray hag a ros strokosow tyn* 'he would have broken the enemies ranks and gave cruel blows' OM 2224-25

*the **pygy** me a **vynse** na wrylly y dysyrye yn tor ma* 'I would beg thee that thou desire it not' RD 1932-33

*y a **vynsa optaynya** salvacion* 'they would have obtained salvation' TH 13a

*bo ken crist ny **vensa leverell*** 'otherwise Christ would not have said' TH 17a

*y a **vynsa stoppya** aga scovurnow* 'they would have blocked up their ears' TH 19

*Indelma an ii office a **vynsa bos** diligently executys* 'Thus the two functions would be diligently carried out' TH 25

*ny **vynsa** den vith **styrrya** na gwaya warbyn an colleges* 'no one would have stirred or moved against the colleges' TH 42a

*An kyth office ma ny **vynsa** pedyr **kemeras*** 'The same office Peter would not have accepted' TH 44a

*ny **vynsa** den vith **gwaya** na styrrya warbyn an bredereth* 'no man would have moved or stirred against the brotherhood' TH 48a

*an gwase a **vynsa leskye** agen esowe yn tevery* 'the fellow would have burnt our corn indeed' CW 1129-30

*sera tha radn an ryna ef a **vynsa disclosya** an distructyon* 'sir, to some of those he would have disclosed the distruction' CW 2356-57.

Brown mentions that the conditional is in form the same as the pluperfect, but nowhere does he indicate that the conditional is frequently rendered by periphrasis. Again Brown's treatment is incomplete and indeed misleading. It should be rewritten.

19.26 The second person singular of the present/future
Throughout GMC2 informs us that the desinence of the second person singular of the present/future is *-ydh*. This is not entirely true. In the first place the final continuant was almost certainly voiceless, i.e. the ending was [ɪθ] rather than [ɪð]. In the second place, Brown omits to mention that the desinence was being reshaped by analogy during the Middle Cornish period and not infrequently was <ys>. The monosyllabic *gwreth* 'thou dost, you do' similarly became *gwres*. The starting point for the analogous reformation were such second person singulars as *gothes* 'thou knowst' and *os* 'thou art', to say nothing of the other tenses where the second person singualar ended in /s/. Here are some examples from the texts of the second person of the present/future in <ys> and <s>:

> *So, ny **vynys** colynwall an la* 'But thou wilt not fulfill the law' TH 48a
> *rag ty ny **vethys** dowtyes* 'for thou shalt not be feared' CW 523
> *ny **vynnys** kola orthe da* 'thou wilt not hearken to good' CW 665
> *ny **vynnys** orthaf cola* 'thou wilt not hearken to me' CW 823
> *cayme na **vethys** indella* 'Cain, thou shalt not be thus' CW 1178
> *ny **vethis** gans dean towches* 'thou shalt not be touched by any man' CW 1183
> *Panna weale '**lesta*** (< *yllysta*) *geeal* 'what kind of work canst thou do?' BF: 15.

> *ganso pan **wres** comparya* 'when thou dost compare with him' CW 160
> *pan **wres** ortha vy settya* 'when thou dost attack me' CW 214
> *na **wres** na **wres**, na barth dowte* 'thou shalt not, thou shalt not, fear not' CW 218-19
> *orthaf vy pan **wres** settya* 'when thou dost attack me' CW 232
> *mara **gwrees** ow dyskevera* 'if thou dost expose me' CW 577.

This development is completely ignored by Brown.

19.27 mynnes [mennas] 'will' for future
Brown is aware that *mennas* is used as an auxiliary to express the future, but he seems to believe that there is always an element of volition with *mennas* that is absent with other future constructions. He tells us, therefore, that there is a distinction between *Ternos yth a ev tramor* 'He will go abroad in the morning' and *Ternos y fynn ev mos tramor* 'He will/intends to/is willing to go abroad tomorrow'. I would take issue with four aspects of Brown's second example here.

In the first place *ternos* does not mean 'tomorrow', but 'on the morrow, on the next day' in narrative, e.g. *En eȝewon ny vynne bos an laddron ow cregy **ternos** rag pasch o ȝeȝe* 'The Jews did not want the robbers to be hanging for the next day was Passover for them' PA 229ab. The word for 'tomorrow' in Cornish is *avorow*:

PROBLEMS WITH BROWN'S *GRAMMAR OF MODERN CORNISH*

auorou: cras [tomorrow] OCV
*guetyeugh bones **avorow** ov conys yn crys a'n dre* 'take care to be working tomorrow in the middle of the city' OM 2299-300
*hag a warn the vysterdens **avorow** thy's may teffens* 'and will warn your architects that they may come to you tomorrow' OM 2416-17
*ha tormentys yn garow kyns **avorow** hanter deth* 'and cruelly tormented before noon tomorrow' PC 721-22
*ha deug avar **avorow** my agas pys* 'and come early tomorrow, I beg you' PC 3239-40
*dewh a **vorowe** a dermyn* 'come early tomorrow' CW 2541
*Cras...To morrow; C[ornish] **y vuru** AB: 52a*
***Avoru** and †**avuru**, To morrow* AB: 249a.

In the second place *tramor* is an adjective (attested only in Lhuyd who spells it <tremor>) and should not be used as an adverb. 'To go abroad' means to go overseas and in traditional Cornish that is rendered by *mos dres mor*. Similarly 'to come from abroad, from overseas' is rendered *dos dres an mor*. Here are the attested examples of these expressions:

*A vreten sur then povma **dres en mor** me re dufa* 'I have come overseas from Brittany to this country' BM 649-50
***dres an mor** dy eff a thueth* 'he came thither from overseas' BM 2219
*ken fe rys thym mos **drys mor** [vor ms]* 'though I had to go overseas' BK 1448.

In the third place *y fynn ev* [*y fyn ef*] is hardly attested in the traditional language. The only example comparable with *y fynn ev mos* [*y fyn ef mos*] is *the vernans y fyn guelays* 'your death he will see' BM 2304. The ordinary and colloquial way of saying 'will go' with a person pronoun is PRON + *a vyn mos*. Because the bulk of Cornish literature is in the form of drama, the first person *me a vyn mos* 'I will go' is by far the most frequently attested. Here are some examples:

*mos the balas **my a vyn** OM 681*
*whare **my a vyn mones** OM 730*
***my a vyn mos** thyworthys OM 823*
***my a vyn mos** alema OM 1003*
***my a vyn** alemma mos OM 1035*
***me a vyn mos** the'n temple OM 1259*
***me a vyn mos** the vyras OM 1399*
*pur wyr **my a vyn mones** OM 1582*
***ny a vyn mos** the besy OM 1820*
*mos the blanse **my a vyn** OM 1887*
*mos the blanse **my a vyn** OM 2078*
*mos the vyres **my a vyn** OM 2437*
***my a vyn mos** th'y tempye PC 50*
***my a vyn mos** ow honan PC 87*
*ol **ny a vyn mos** er y byn PC 235*
***me a vyn** dyeskenne ha mos yn tempil ware PC 313-14*

263

me a vyn mos the'n tempel PC 355
me a vyn mos the vre PC 473
me a vyn mos the vyras PC 2965
mos the vyres me a vyn RD 685
me a vyn mos alemma RD 1238
me a vyn mones thu'm gulas RD 1580
me a vyn mos the vyras RD 1637
mos the wolhy ow dule a thesempes me a vyn omma yn dour RD 2202-04
3en chappell me a vyn mois BM 130
me a vyn mos the guandra BM 665
Me a vyn moys the verays BM 733
Me a vyn moys then guylfoys BM 1132
ny a vyn moys alemma BM 1322
Me a vyn moys thum guely BM 1683
me a vyn moys ahanan BM 2299
ny a vyn moys thage gore in lel forth BM 2330-31
me a vyn moys aleme BM 2689
me a vyn moys the pesy BM 3186
mos the[n] guelfos me a vyn BM 3213
rag ov map me a vyn moys BM 3590
moys me a vyn BM 3900
me a vyn mones uskys BM 4063
moys 3y veres me a vyn BM 4351
mos th'e warnya me a vyn BK 491
Me a vyn abarth an tas mos ahanan BK 1266-67
me a vyn mos gans mer grys BK 1283
Me a vyn mos heb gortas BK 1330
Me a vyn mos ahanan BK 2438
mos the'n batal me a vyn BK 2742
me a vyn mos heb fyllall CW 505
me a vyn mos tha wandra CW 538
mos then menythe me a vyn CW 1082
me a vyn mose thom sera CW 1184
me a vyn mos pur vskys CW 1294
me a vyn mos pur vskes CW 1467
me a vyn mos tha wandra CW 1488
me a vyn mos tha gutha CW 1543
moes alemma my a vydn gwella gallaf CW 1709-10
mos alema me a vyn en by and by CW 1758-59
me a vyn mos pur evall CW 1776
me a vyn mos alema CW 1877
me a vyn mos alemma CW 2397
mee a ved'n moze Da whelaz weale da weele BF: 15.

Cf. *ha **ef a vyn dos** the judgia oll an bobell* SA 59.

In the fourth place it is not true to say that *mynnes* [*mennas*] to form the future always implied volition. Here are some instances of the future with *mennas* where there is neither volition nor intention:

PROBLEMS WITH BROWN'S *GRAMMAR OF MODERN CORNISH*

*rag an lahys ȝynny es a **vyn** y dampnye porres* 'for the laws we have will comdemn him indeed' PA 32c

*then the'n myghtern the thysta an gyst na **vyn** dos the squyr* 'let us go to the king and testify that the beam will not fit the measurement' OM 2544

*mar **myn** ov descans servya* 'if my learning is sufficient' BM 524

*Ny **vedn** e nevra doz vez a gyndan* 'He'll never get out of debt' AB: 230c.

In the first three examples the subject is inanimate and cannot therefore have any intention or volition. In the last example from Lhuyd the debtor clearly wishes to get out of debt, since at that period (1707) he runs the risk of being sent to debtors' prison. His debts cannot be paid off, but that does not mean the debtor wishes to remain in debt.

The absence of volition with *mennas* as a future auxiliarly is also clear from TH. Look at the following examples:

*whath me **a vyn agys desyrya** why the vynnas* 'moreover I will want you to wish' TH 34

*So me **a vyn agys desyrrya** why, tus tha oll, the settia agys corfow hagys enevow hooll the thu galosek* 'But I will want you, all good people, to set your bodies and souls towards mighty God' TH 35

*me **a vyn agys desyrrya** why oll an lell cristonyyan* 'I will want you all, the faithful Christians' TH 38.

It is apparent in here that there is no implied intention in *a vyn*, since the volition is in the verbal noun *desyrya*. Tregear is not saying "I wish to want you all to...", but "I will (henceforth) want you to..." When Brown tells us that there *mennas* to express the future always implies volition, he is mistaken.

Brown's example should read *Ev a vynn mos dres mor avorow* [*Ef a vyn mos dres mor avorow*] 'he will go abroad tomorrow' and there is no implied intention in it. Brown's treatment of *mennas* as a future auxiliary is very unsatisfactory indeed.

19.28 Confusion of present subjunctive with past subjunctive

Historically the third person singular of the present subjunctive ended in *-o*. As a result of the Prosodic Shift, however, this vowel was early in Middle Cornish reduced to schwa, spelt <a>. It was difficult therefore to tell the third person present subjunctive from the same person in the past subjunctive, i.e. *may teffo* 'that he come' and *may teffa* 'that he should come' were not distinguishable. Furthermore the desinences of the plural for the same reason tended to fall together also, i.e. present subjunctive *clewyn, clewough, clewons* as a result of the weakening of unstressed syllables were identical with past subjunctive *clewen, cleweugh, clewens*. In consequence in all our Middle Cornish texts the past subjunctive has begun to replace the present subjunctive. This even happens to some extent with the verb *bos*, even though the third person singular present

265

subjunctive *bo* was quite distinct from the equivalent form of the past subjunctive *be* (see **16.03, 16.05** above).

Here are some examples from all texts of the use of the past subjunctive for the present subjunctive:

> *arluth nef roy thy'm gul da yn pup ober a **wrellyn*** 'Lord of heaven, give me to do well in all work that I may do' OM 444-45
> *bolungeth dew yv hemma bones gorrys an sprus ma pan **dremenna** an bys ma yn y anow* 'this is the will of God that these pips be put in his mouth whenever he depart from this world' OM 874-75
> *y offendye ny vynna kyn **fen** marow yn tor ma* 'I do not wish to offend him though I be dead at this time' OM 1330-31
> *popel ysral ny assaf na's **gorren** y thy whyl cref* 'I shall not leave the people of Israel without putting them to hard labour' OM 1489-90
> *y a vyth guythys calsa hedre **vyns** y yn ov gulas* 'they shall be worked hard as long as they be in my kingdom' OM 1502-03
> *ha me a wyth harth na **fe** den fyth ol sur anethe the wul the thev sacrifyth* 'and I shall see to it that no man at all of them indeed be bold enough to do sacrifice to God' OM 1517-19
> *orden the'th tus hy knoukye gans meyn na hethens nefre erna **varwa** eredy* 'order your men to smite her with stones, let them not stop until she die indeed' OM 2676-78
> *ol del vynny arluth ker my a wra yn pup tyller hedre **veyn** bev yn bys ma* 'I shall do, O dear Lord, all as you wish everywhere, as long as I shall live in this world' PC 113-15
> *my ny won kyn **fen** lethys* 'I know not though I be killed' PC 2536
> *ellas na **varwen** ynweth* 'alas that I do not also die' PC 2946
> *Me a vyn moys then guylfoys ena ermet purguir boys may **hallen** gorthya ov du* 'I will go to the wilderness to be there a hermit indeed, that I may worship my God' BM 1132-34.

This is an important aspect of the inflection of Middle Cornish. GMC2 is entirely silent on the matter and thus gives a false impression of the language.

19.29 *dov* 'I come'

Brown tells us (§ 206) that the first person singular is *dov*. This form is certainly attested in the texts:

> *re vahun y **tof** yn weth* 'by Mahound, I shall come also' RD 610
> *a thew ple **tof** na ple ythaf* 'O God, where shall I come or where shall I go' RD 1665.

Another form *duef* (?**deuv* in Kernowek Kemmyn) is also attested, however:

> *ha mar **tuff** thagis kerheys* 'and if I come to fetch you' BM 3365
> *mar **tema** (< tuema) disquethas theugh* 'and if I come and show you' SA 60
> *rag mar **tema** ha rowtya* 'for if I come and overpower' BK 1639
> *hag y **teaf** thewhy arta* 'and I shall come to you again' CW 1760.

Brown does not mention *tuef, tuema*, although it is well attested in the Middle Cornish texts.

19.30 *mynnav* 'I wish'
Brown tells us (§ 226) that the first person singular of *mynnes* [*mennas*] is *mynnav* [*mynnaf*]. This is only partially true, since A) *mennaf* and B) *mannaf* are more frequent in the texts than *mynnaf*:

A) **mennaf**
*thy'so ny **vennaf** cresy* OM 233
*yn della byth ny **vennaf*** OM 486
*my ny **vennaf** growethe* OM 624
***mennaf** yn scon* OM 1581
*ny **vennaf** onan sparye* OM 1644
*a nef **mennaf** yskynne* OM 1976
*er y byn **mennaf** mones* PC 232
*ow box **mennaf** the terry* PC 485
*me ny **vennaf** cafus le* PC 594
*ny **vennaf** pella lettye* PC 1612
*ny **vennaf** pel ymbreyse* PC 1677
*thywortheugh **mennaf** mones* RD 1134
*the'th fath ker **mennaf** amme* RD 1734.

B) **mannaf**
*y worʒeby ny **vannaff*** PA 155d
*thethe ganov **mannafi** amma* BM 64
*mones y **fannaf** lemmyn* BM 172
***manneff** uskyes* BM 1152
***Mannaff** gueles agys dour* BM 1440
***manneff** ry alesonov* BM 1829
*theth palys lemen **manaff** gans procescyon the gora* BM 1860
*Ny **vannef** y annye* BM 2054
*y **fannavy*** BM 2123
*ha thys y **fanaff** omry* BM 2127
*ny **vannaff** an dynyte* BM 2813
*the venitens **mannaff** moys* BM 2863
***mannaff** the weles gueres* BM 3106
*mones a **vanna** rygthy* BM 4016
*Lymmyn ny **vanna** ve namoy agys gylwell* TH 35a
*ny **vanna** agys vnya na fella* TH 46
*an foode a **vanna** ve ry rag Ehas* TH 51a
***mannaf** gref penys ha nawn* BK 428
*ny **vanna**' e vos kelys* BK 1886
*Na **vanna** heb the dolla* BK 2143
*ny **vannaf** orth eale na moy* CW 134
*sowe Eva **manaf** saya* CW 471
*yn henna **manaf** entra* CW 503
*me as rowle hy del **vannaf*** CW 507

*na **vannaf** tha theskyvra* CW 578
*genas ny **vannaf** flattra* CW 648
*na ny **vanaf** usya gowe* CW 649
*ye lesky ny **vannaf** ve* CW 1088
*ny **vannaf** bos controllys* CW 1125
*y dristya ny **vannaf** vye* CW 1380
*ny **vanaf** thaworth an tase* CW 1324
*theso ny **vannaf** gava* CW 1697
*me ny **vannaf** moy es kye* CW 2360
*ybma na **vadna** vi ostia* AB: 252a.

Brown mentions neither *mennaf* (*mennav) nor *mannaf* (*mannav). His treatment of this verb is therefore defective.

19.31 *y'm bues* 'I have'

This verb has undergone three developments in Middle Cornish: 1) confusion of persons; 2) recharacterization; 3) replacement by *bos* 'to be'. I will deal with these in turn.

1) Confusion of Persons

By this I mean that a form of *y'm bues* historically associated with one person, singular of plural, is used by other persons. The confusion is normally confined to forms associated with A) the third singular masculine or B) the third singular feminine. We thus get examples like the following:

A) 3rd singular masculine used with other persons
*rag an re ew claffe **an gevas** othom ay elyow* 'for those who are sick have need os his remedies' TH 8a
*an turkys, an Jewys, an Infideles, neb **nan Jevas** perfect crygyans* 'the Turks, the Jews, the infidels who have not perfect belief' TH 16a
*Han kythsam catholyk eglos ma **an gevas** an lell vnderstonding* 'And this same Catholic church has the true understanding' TH 17
*han re **an Jeffa** cure a enevow* 'and those who may have the cure of souls' TH 25
*ha ny **an Jevith** agan reward gansans y* 'and we will have our reward with them' TH 22a
*ny **an gevith** ganso eff eternall bewnans* 'we will have with him eternal life' TH 26
*han felicte bewnans **an geva** adam hag eva* 'and the felicity of life which Adam and Eve had' TH 4
*ha ny **an Jeva** promes a brassa royow* 'and we had a promise of greater gifts' TH 28
*why **an Jeva** sufficient declaracion anotha* 'you had enough declaration of it' TH 30a
*ow rome ve **na gevas** peare* 'my space, I who have no peer' CW 257
*ny **an gevyth** sure droke lam* 'we shall surely have misfortune' CW 806
*me **an gevyth** oll an blame* 'I shall have all the blame' CW 809.

B) 3rd singular feminine used with other persons
*neb **as tevas** spot vith a gras* 'whoever has any small amount of grace' TH 30a

PROBLEMS WITH BROWN'S *GRAMMAR OF MODERN CORNISH*

Rag henna why **as tevith** *sufficient instruccion* 'Therefore you will have sufficient instruction' TH 31a

ef **as tevyth** *vii plague moy* 'he will have seven more plagues' CW 1378.

2) Recharacterization

By this I mean that the third person singular verb is recharacterized for person by the addition of an enclitic emphatic personal suffix or by personal endings.

pur luen yma thy'm ow whans **a'm ben** *cowethes ordnys* 'very great is my desire that I should have have ordained for me a help-meet' OM 91-2

Nans yw lemmyn tremenes nep dewcans a vlethynnow **na'm buef** *the wruthyl genes* 'For some two hundred years I have had no dealing with you' OM 656-68

gueres ny **nag y'n beny** *bylyny gans pharow* 'help us that we suffer no villainy from Pharaoh' OM 1608-10

ef a yrhys thy'm kyrhas a mount tabor gueel a ras **ma'n bethen** *drethe sylwans* 'he ordered me to fetch from Mount Tabor rods of grace that we might have salvation through them' OM 1956-58

dyworto **ma'm boma** *gras mos the blanse my a vyn en gueel* 'that I may have grace from him I will go to plant the rods' OM 2077-79

deus mei miserere herweth the grath ha'th pyte **na'm byma** *peyn yn gorfen* 'have mercy upon me, O God, according to the grace and thy pity that I get no pain in the end' OM 2252-54

ny yl colon predyry an tekter **as betheugh why** 'heart cannot consider the enjoyment you will have' PC 32-3

rag ow thorment a the scon genogh **na'm byve** *tryge* 'for my torment will come soon so that I may not remain with you' PC 541-42

ha saw ny gynes ynweth **na'n beyn** *mar hager thyweth* 'and save us with thee that we get not such a horrible end' PC 2894-95

pesef agis bannothow **maym beva** *the well grays* 'I beseech your blessings that I may have the better grace' BM 47-8

byth **nys tufons** *guel bugel in age oys* 'never will they have a better pastor in their age' BM 2785-86

benytho arluth ath par pur thefry **nygyn bethen** 'never a lord equal to thee will we have' BM 4267-68

peseff rag an keth re na **mays tefons** *y luen ʒehes* 'I pray for those same people that they may have full healing' BM 4286-87

Pys the Vab ras hethew **ma'm byf** *an victory* 'Beseech thy gracious Son that today I may have the victory' BK 2815

me a levar thys mar pleag yn pan vanar **yn bema** 'I will tell you, if you please, how I got it' CW 756

kyn **nam boma** *lowena an chorle adam hag eva tha effarn y towns thymmo* 'though I may not have joy, the churl Adam and Eve will come to me to hell' CW 928

kemys gyrryow teake **am beff** 'so many sweet words had I' CW 1018

maym bome *grace woʒa hemma* 'that I may have grace after this' CW 1427.

269

TOWARDS AUTHENTIC CORNISH

3) Replacement of *y'm bues* by *bos* 'to be'

In many parts of the paradigm the verbal portion begins with *b-*. In the second person the person pronoun is *'th*. Not infrequently this pronominal form is assimilated with the initial *b > f* and thus disappears. Thus, for example, *te a'th fyth > te a fyth*, which latter is indistinguishable in writing from *te a fyth* 'thou shalt be'. In this way it comes about that the verb *bos* 'to be' is frequently used instead of *y'm bues* with the sense 'have, get'. Here are some examples.

> *yn mes alemma ty a hag **a fyth** marow vernens* 'out from here you shall go and will have mortal death' OM 83-4
> *ow bennath prest **ty a fyth*** 'my blessing you shall always have' OM 457
> *oll an bys ma **ty a fyth*** 'you shall have all this world' PC 128
> *oll an re ma **ty a fyth*** 'all these you shall have' PC 130
> *gallos warnaf **ny fyes** na fe y vos grantys thy's* 'you would not have power over me had it not been granted you' PC 2187-88
> *I a gollas an originall innocency stat **a vongy** in aga creasion* 'They lost the original innocence, a state they had when they were created' TH 4
> *kyn **fene** ken henwyn a honor ha dignite omma in bys* 'though we have further names of honour and dignity here in the world' TH 7a
> *pana rewarde a **vethow** why?* 'what reward will you have?' TH 22
> *pana comodite a **vethyn** ny dretha* 'what advantage we will have by it?' TH 22a
> *mar **pethans** y respect vith the thu* 'if they have any respect for God' TH 25a
> *whath kyn **na von** ny scriptur vith rag henna* 'even though we have no scripture for that' TH 37
> *na worship te ny **fethyth*** 'nor shall you have respect' BK 47
> *te a **vith** gu* 'you shall suffer wrong' BK 326
> *ha moyha pas **te a vith** dihogal* 'and a greater amount of land you shall certainly have' BK 1091
> *me ew an kensa bythqwath whath **a ve** dew wreag* 'I am the first moreover who ever had two wives' CW 1453-54
> *ha pennagle a wra henna plages **y fetha** ragtha* 'and whoever does that should have plagues for it' CW 1641-42
> *mar **pethama** kibmiez tho gweel Semblanz* 'if I have permission to make allusion' BF: 29
> *me **a vee** owne rag theram en hoath* 'I was afraid for I am naked' RC 23: 178.

All three developments of *y'm bues* are well attested and of great importance for the history of Cornish. No grammar of the language should pass over them in silence. Brown does not so much as mention any one them.

19.32 Reflexive verbs

Brown tells us at § 232 that verbs are rendered reflexive by the addition of the leniting prefix *om-*. This is certainly true. Brown omits to tell us, however, that from the earliest period this prefix is yielding to an analytical syntax of reflexivation by means of the pronoun *honen* 'self'. Here are some examples

PROBLEMS WITH BROWN'S *GRAMMAR OF MODERN CORNISH*

from the texts of A) reflexive *om-*; B) reflexive verbs with *honen*; C) mixed construction:

A reflexive/reciprocal **om-**
peb ʒe ves a **omdennas** 'everyone withdrew' PA 33d
mygtern neb a **omwrello** 'who should purport to be a king' PA 121d
ragon ny wor **omweʒe** 'he cannot protect himself from us' PA 194c
hag a **ymsensy** *den cref* 'and held himself to be a strong man' OM 2222
mar ny wreth **ymamendye** 'if you do not improve yourself' OM 1526
guel yv thy'n **ymassaya** 'it is better for me to try' PC 2302
ymsaw *scon a throkeleth* 'save yourself quickly from ill' PC 2866
ymthysquethas *ny vynna* 'I do not wish to show myself' RD 1496
crist roy dis in pup termyn **omguithe** *prest in glander* 'Christ grant you always to keep yourself in purity' BM 532-33
sevugh inban a tus vays fetel **omglowugh** *omma* 'stand up, good folk, how do you feel here?' BM 708-09
gwetyogh **omprevy** *manly* 'take care to prove yourselves manly' BM 1194
Tav gas thym the **ombrene** 'Silence, let me redeem myself' BM 1252
me a **omgemer** *ragogh* 'I will act as your sponsor' BM 1882
hag **omwetha** *theworto* 'and keep oneself from it' TH 3a
saw whath rys ew mos thotha hag **omthyvlamya** *orta* 'but yet I must go to him and excuse myself to him' BK 448-49
mes pub ere ow **omgwetha** *yn cossowe hag in bushes* 'but always hiding myself in woods and bushes' CW 1519-2.

B reflexive with **honen** 'self'
rag ny ny russyn ny **gull agan honyn** 'for we did not make ourselves' TH 1
yth esan **ow desyvya agan honyn** 'we deceive ourselves' TH 8
inweth nyng o mabden abyll the **weras y honyn** *in hemma* 'moreover mankind were not able to help themselves in this' TH 12-12a
hag anethe hy kemeras dynsys ha **Joynyas y honyn** *then dusys in vnite a person* 'and from her took humanity and joined himself to the Godhead in unity of person' TH 12a
mar lyas del ra **devydya aga honyn** *theworth an kysam egglos ma* 'as many as divide themselves from this same church' TH 17a
Hag indelma eff a **vsyas y honyn,** *ow exortya y yskerens* 'And in this way he conducted himself, exhorting his enemies' TH 22a
kyn rellens y **groundya aga honyn** *apparently war an scriptur benegas* 'although they base themselves apparently upon the sacred scripture' TH 32
onyn an chyff duty[s] ew the **preparya agan honyn** *the vos worthy* 'one of the chief duties is to prepare ourselves to be worthy' TH 51a
pan rellens **preparia aga honyn** *the thos* 'when they prepare themselves to come' TH 51a
ow ry thyn kusyll diligently rag **examyna ha trya agan honyn** 'diligently counselling us to examine and try ourselves' TH 54
ymowns **ow desyvya aga honyn** *ow myskemeras an significacion an ger ma* 'they deceive themselves, misunderstanding the meaning of this word' TH 57a

*mas **ow groundia aga honyn** war an gyrryow agan Savyour Jhesu crist* 'but basing themselves upon the words of our Saviour Jesus Christ' TH 57a

*ha dir sarchia & scripture eth esa **ow trylya ow honyn** then Arluth Christ* 'and by searching the scripture I turn myself toward Christ the Lord' SA 64a

***towle tha honnen** doore* 'throw thyself down' RC 23: 187

*dre vengama **gweel a hunnen** tho bose devethez drez Maur* 'that I would make myself to have come over the sea' BF: 31.

C mixed construction

*lemmyn **y honan** ny yl sur ymsawye* 'now he cannot indeed save himself' PC 2877-78

***y honan** yth ymwanas gans y gollan marthys scon* 'he stabbed himself with his knife wondrous quickly' RD 2065-66

*rak hacre mernans certan eys **emlathe y honan** ny gaffe den my a grys* 'for a more cruel death certainly than to kill himself no man could not find, I believe' RD 2072-74

*ny a gottha thyn **omry agan honyn** dhe wetha ha the colynwall y commondment eff* 'we should devote ourselves to keeping and fulfilling his commandment' TH 21a

*mas **omry aga honyn** ernystly the thu* 'but devote themselves earnestly to God' TH 23a

*ymons ow **homdenna aga honyn** theworth aucthorite an Epscop a rome* 'they withdraw themselves from the authority of the bishop of Rome' TH 50a

*rag **omsawya ow honyn** keffrys ow gwreak haw flehys an lester a vythe genyn der weras dew vskes gwryes* 'to save myself, also my wife and my children, the vessel will by the help of God soon made by us' CW 2373-76.

Brown omits all but type A from GMC2. It will be noted moreover that many of the verbs in A are not true reflexives, but are rather lexicalized verbs with a reflexive origin, e.g. *tenna* 'draw' ~ *omdenna* 'withdraw'; *clowes* 'hear, perceive' ~ *omglowes* 'feel (oneself)'; *gul* 'do, make' ~ *omwul* 'pretend to be, claim to be'; *kemeres* 'take' ~ *omgemeres* 'act as guarantor for'; *dysquethes* 'show (transitive)' ~ *omthysquethes* 'show oneself, appear'. Only true reflexives are to be found in section B.

Brown has also failed to notice, or perhaps he prefers not to mention, that *dysquethes* 'show' is used intransitively in the later language:

*e a vednyaz thoranze seer puna termin reeg an steere **disquethaz*** 'he asked them precisely when the star appeared' RC 23: 195-96

*elez neeve a **desquethaz** tha Joseph a ve hendrez* 'angels from heaven appeared to Joseph who was asleep' RC 23: 198.

It must, I think, be admitted that the treatment of reflexives in GMC2 is defective.

PROBLEMS WITH BROWN'S *GRAMMAR OF MODERN CORNISH*
SYNTAX

19.33 *Bos* 'to be' with the present participle
Brown discussing the present tense of verbs says at § 228.1 "By contrast, the present participle construction can only be translated by the English continuous present: *Yth esov owth oberi* 'I am working'." What Brown says is simply not true. In Middle Cornish *yth esof ow cul* can mean 'I do' as well as 'I am doing'. There are countless instances in the texts. Here are a very few examples:

> *in crist ihesu caradov* **yth eseff** *prest* **ov cresy** 'In beloved Jesus Christ I believe always' BM 833-34
> **Nyns esos ov attendya** *an laha del vye reys...* 'you do not consider how the law had to...' BM 848
> *in crist* **yma ov cresy** 'he believes in Christ' BM 971
> **yth eseff orth** *y care* 'I love him' BM 4023
> **Ima** *an profet Dauit in peswar vgans ha nownsag psalme* **ow exortya** *oll an bobyll the ry prayse hag honor the du* 'The prophet David in Psalm 99 exhorts all the people to give praise and honour to God' TH 1
> *Arluth* **esta ge ow Jugia** *mett the veras won onyn an parna* 'Lord, does thou judge me meet to look upon one like those?' TH 7
> *kepar del* **vgy** *an profett* **ow prononcia** 'as the prophet pronounces' TH 7a
> **yth esan ow desyvya** *agan honyn* 'we deceive ourselves' TH 8
> *fatell* **essan** *ny* **ow deservia** *le gyvyans theworth du* 'that we deserve less forgiveness from God' TH 24a
> *nena* **yma** *crist* **ow promysya** *ha* **ow assurya** *thyn, fatell vsy eff worth agan cara ny* 'then Christ promises and assures us that he loves us' TH 26
> *kyn nag* **esogh** *why* **ow consyddra** *an plag a behosow* 'though you do not consider the plague of sins' TH 40a
> *rag eth on ny megys gans an kethsam tra,* **vgy** *an elath* **ow gwelas** *ha* **ow trembla** 'for we are fed by the same thing which the angels see and tremble at' SA 59
> *rag neg yns abell the welas heb mere a own rag an golowder* **use ow tos** *thaworta* 'for they cannot see without great fear because of the brilliance that comes from him' SA 59
> *Indella* **emay** *Christ* **worth agyn maga** *ny, gans e gorf ay gos ef* 'Thus Christ feeds us with his body and his blood' SA 59
> *mas Christ, an mammath nyy, neg* **esee o gwell** *indella genan. Insted rag henna a boos ema ef agyn maga gans e kegg e honyn ha eweth insted e thewas,* **emay vrth agen maga** *gans e woos* 'but Christ did not deal thus with us. Therefore instead of food he feeds us with his own flesh and likewise instead of drink he feeds us with his blood' SA 59a
> **Ima** *lowarth onyn* **o bostia** 'Many a one boasts' SA 59
> *O markell ha blonogath da a thew disquethis theny* **ugy setha** *in gwlas neff* 'O miracle and good will of God shown to us that sits in the kingdom of heaven' SA 60
> *neg* **esa ow desquethas** *theugh elath nanyle arthelath* 'he does not show you angels nor archangels' SA 60a

*Tee a ill percevia pavaner a sort **esta o qvelas** agen saviour Christ* 'thou canst perceive in what kind of sort thou seest our Saviour Christ' SA 60a

*an kigg **yma causya** an ena the vos Iunys the dew & neff* 'the flesh causes the soul to be joined to the God of heaven' SA 60a

*indelma **ema ef o tisquethas** kepar a rug Iudas betraya e arluth dew* 'thus he shows just how Judas betrayed his Lord God' SA 61

***eth esan ny o recevia** dan an lell mystery kigg ay corf benegas* 'we receive under the true mystery the flesh of his blessed body' SA 61

***Ema ow leverall** Iudas a ruke tastia Corf an arluth* 'He says that Judas tasted the body of the Lord' SA 65a

*ema Chrisostom **ow scrifa** than philipians A remembrance a vea res thotha bos in keth sacrament na rag an marow* 'Chrysostom writes to the Philippians of the remembrance which should be in the same sacrament for the dead' SA 66

*yn defyth yn myske bestas **yma ef prest ow pewa*** 'in the desert among animals he lives continually' CW 1481-82

*mere **yth esaf ow towtya** y vedna ʒym ny vyn ef* 'I fear greatly he will not give me his blessing' CW 1540-82

*An planattis es awartha han steare inweth magata **ow poyntya mowns** pur efan* 'The planets that are on high and the stars also as well point very plainly' CW 2156

*urt an hagar auall **iggeva gweel** do derevoll warneny* 'because of the storms he make to rise against us' BF: 9

***Theram ry** do why an bele ma* 'I give you this ball' BF: 12

*ma eaue **gon maga*** 'he feeds us' BF: 39

***Thera ve crege** en Speres Zance* 'I believe in the Holy Spirit' BF: 41.

Brown's observation about the sense of such sentences is mistaken and should be ignored.

19.34 Conditional sentences

In Cornish the verb *dos* 'to come' is very often used as an auxiliary in conditional sentences. This is true both with real and unreal conditions. When expressing real conditions in future time in Cornish *mar(a)* is used with the future, where such exists as a separate tense, or with the present/future. In order to avoid the necessity of inflecting the verb and mutating its initial consonant after *mar(a)*, a periphrastic syntax emerged early in Middle Cornish. This involved using the verb *dos* 'to come', i.e. *mar tof/tuef (ha)* + verbal noun, *mar tue eff (ha)* + verbal noun, etc. This syntax is very common indeed in Middle Cornish. Here are a few examples:

***mar te** venions ha cothe war agan flehys yn fras* 'if vengeance falls greatly upon us and upon our children' PA 149cd

*myrugh **mar te** drehevell ay beynys ʒy delyffre* 'see whether he will arise to deliver him from his agony' PA 203c

***mar tue** nep guas ha laddre en gueel theworthyn pryve* 'if some fellow come and steal the rods from us surreptitiously' OM 2064-65

***mar tufe** ha datherghy mur a tus [a] wra crygy* 'if he rise again many people will believe' RD 7-8

PROBLEMS WITH BROWN'S *GRAMMAR OF MODERN CORNISH*

ha mar tuff thagis kerheys arta sur why a far guel 'And if I fetch you again, you will fare better' BM 3365-66

mara tuen ha debatya 'if we fight' BM 3476-77

ha mar te ha gull an dra 'and if he does the thing' TH 4

the vrassa ew y begh mar te ha gull an dra 'greater is his sin if he does the deed' TH 4a

mar te den ha receva royow bras theworth y gothman 'if a man receives great presents from his friend' TH 4a

mar te in byanby ha tyrry blonogath y soveran 'if by and by he violates his sovereign's wishes' TH 4a

Mar ten ny ha leverell nag ony pehadoryan 'If we say we are not sinners' TH 8

mar ten ha menegas agan pehosow 'if we confess our sins' TH 8

mar tene leverell na russyn peha 'if we say we have not sinned' TH 8

mar tene ny consyddra hag vnderstondya 'if we consider and understand' TH 10

mar ten ny in delma submyttya agan honyn 'if thus we submit ourselves' TH 11a

rag mar ten ny ha peha hay ankevy eff 'for if we sin and forget him' TH 15a

ha mar ten ny y folya ha sewya 'if we follow and adhere to it' TH 17a

mar ten ha kemeras wyth in ta bys may teffa an Jeth 'if we take good care until the day come' TH 18

mar teva ha folya henna 'if he follows that' TH 20

mar ten ny ha cara pub den heb exception 'if we love everyone without exception' TH 22a

So mar ten ha gull ken 'But if we do otherwise' TH 22a

Ha mar ten ny ha consyddra henna neb a rug agan offendia ny 'And if we consider him who offended us' TH 24a

mar te cherite requyria the predyry 'if charity requires us to think' TH 24a

Ha mar ten ny indelma dyrectya agan bewnans dre kerensa 'And if we thus direct our life by love' TH 26

lymmyn mar te cristonyan ha concevya anger in aga colonow 'now if Christians conceive anger in their hearts' TH 28a

Mar te the brother ha gull trespas war the byn 'If your brother trespasses against you' TH 31a

mar te ran ahanow why dowtya 'if some of you doubt' TH 32

Mar teugh why ha gurtas inno ve 'If you remain in me' TH 39a

mar ten ny ha gurtas in Catholik egglos 'if we remain in the Catholic church' TH 39a

fynally mar ten ny ha contynewa fleghys obedyent 'finally if we continue obedient children' TH 41

mar te an bys ha durya mar bell 'if the world lasts so long' TH 50a

Mar tene ny comparia an gyrryow cowsys gans crist 'If we compare the words spoke by Christ' TH 52

mar tema disquethas theugh certyn tacclow arall 'if I show you certain other things' SA 60

Mar tewhy demandea 'If you ask' SA 64

Mara tof ha tewelas, ny vyth mab den ou gwelas 'If I get angry, no man dare look at me' BK 1402-03

rag mar tema ha rowtya ha ferneuwhy ha stowtya 'for if I domineer and rage and brag' BK 1639-40.

19.35 Unreal conditions
In unreal conditions in Cornish one can use *a* + past subjunctive. It is common in TH, however, to use *mar teffen, mar teffa* + verbal noun. Here are some examples:

> Rag **mar teffa** *crist ha dos in dallath an bys* 'For if Christ had come at the beginning of the world' TH 13a
>
> **mar teffa** *du aga suffra the vsya aga natural powers* 'if God had allowed them to use their natural powers' TH 13a
>
> *fattla* **mar teffa** *ha contradicion ha varians chansya the vos drehevys war questyon bean?* 'what if contradiction and variation had chanced to arise upon a small question?' TH 19
>
> **Mar teffa** *den vith ha pregoth thyn kythsame barbarus nacions ma* 'If anyone had preached to these barbarous nations' TH 19
>
> **Mar teffa** *an epscobow han brontyryan in tyrmyn passis, inweth an dus leg, dysky ha practysya aga duty haga vocacyons* 'If in times past the bishops and the priests, and also the laity, had learned and practised their duty and vocations' TH 39
>
> **mar teffa** *an holl brodereth obeya according then commondmentys a thu, ny vynsa den vith styrrya na gwaya warbyn an colleges* 'if the entire brotherhood had obeyed according to the commandments of God, no man would have stirred or moved against the colleges' TH 42a.

It is apparent that *mar tue* and *mar teffa* are well established in Middle Cornish. Brown is completely silent about them both. His discussion of positive conditions is thus very unsatisfactory.

19.36 *na ve* 'had it not been for' in negative conditions
There is a further feature of unreal conditions which is not uncommon in the texts. In order to avoid having to inflect a verb in the protasis of a negative unreal condition, traditional Cornish uses the phrase *na ve* 'were it not for, had it not been for' + the verbal noun of the relevant verb. Here are some examples:

> **na ve bos** *fals an denma nyn drossen ny bys deso* 'had this man not been false, we would not have brought him to you' PA 99b
>
> *gallos warnaf ny fyes* **na fe y vos** *grantys thy's* 'you would not have power over me, if it had not been granted you' PC 2187-88
>
> **na ve y vose** *guir sans mar lues merkyl dyblans byth ny russe* 'were he not a true saint, he would not clearly have done so many miracles' BM 2051-53
>
> *Surely ny vynsan cresy an aweyll,* **na ve** *an Catholyk egglos* **the ry** *thym experiens* 'Surely I should not believe the gospel, if the Catholic church did not give me experience' TH 37a
>
> *An kyth office ma ny vynsa pedyr kemeras* **na ve** *crist* **the ry** *thotha an auctorite* 'This same office Peter would not have accepted, if Christ had not given him the authority' TH 44a
>
> *Me a thothya gans an ger,* **na ve ow maw thu'm lettya** 'I should have come at the very command, if my servant had not hindered me' BK 469-70
>
> **na vea me theth cara** *ny vynsan theth cossyllya* 'if I did not love you, I should not advise you' CW 669-70.

PROBLEMS WITH BROWN'S *GRAMMAR OF MODERN CORNISH*

There are examples of this syntax in six different texts, which suggests it was an integral part of the syntax of spoken Middle Cornish. There is no mention of it anywhere in GMC2.

19.37 Indirect statement

Brown deals with indirect statement under the heading "noun clauses" (§§ 335, 336). His treatment is less than completely clear, but he mentions both sentences of the kind *Lavar dhedha y fydhav gansa kyns na pell* 'Tell them I will be with them soon' and of the kind *Ev a lever Peder dhe gara lowartha* 'He says Peter loves gardening', *Gwir yw y vos klav* 'True it is that he is ill'. There are, however, two developments of these constructions that are attested in the texts.

In the first of them the pronominal subject appears as a possessive adjective before the verbal noun *bos* 'to be' (cf. *y vos klav* above) but the verbal noun itself is recharacterized by a personal ending:

> A) *my a leuerys thywhy **ow bosa** henna deffry* 'I told you that I was he indeed' PC 1119-20
> *podrethek am esely drefen purguir **ov bosa*** 'because I in very truth I am putrid in my limbs' BM 3061-62
> *ov sclandra mar mynnogh why ha leferel **ov bosa** omma cruel* 'if you will slander me and say that I am cruel here' BM 3747-49
> *tovlel a wrons warnavy bones an causer defry begythys rag **ov bosa*** 'they will cast it up to me that I am the cause indeed because I have been baptized' BM 4000-02
> *me a vyn may fo gwellys **ow bosaf** dew heb parow* 'I want it to be seen that I am God without peer' CW 78-9
> *cresowh **ow bosaf** prince creif* 'believe that I am a powerful prince' CW 116
> *why a wore yn ta henna **ow bosaf** gwell es an tase* 'you know that well, that I am better than the Father' CW 122-23
> *henna degowhe destynye **om bosof** prynce pur gloryous* 'of that bear witness that I am a most glorious prince' CW 126-67
> *why a yll warbarthe gwelas **ow bosaf** sertayn pub preyse* 'you can together see that I am always thus indeed' CW 132-33
> *splanna es an tase deffry henna cresowhe **om bosaf*** 'brighter than the Father indeed that do you believe—that I am' CW 224-25
> *me ham cowetha der gletha a vyn trea **ow bosaf** moy worthya agis an tase* 'I am my companions will by the sword prove that I am more worthy than the Father' CW 316-19
> *fensan **ow bosaf** marowe* 'I would that I were dead' CW 1264.

In the second the verbal noun *bos* is preceded by the particle *y*, which causes no mutation. The verbal noun may also be recharacterized by a suffixed pronoun or personal ending:

> B)
> *In nena an venyn a welas **y bos** an frut da the thybbry* 'Then the woman saw that the fruit was good to eat' TH 3a
> *wosa **y bosa** gwarnys* 'after he had been warned' TH 4

277

*remember **y bosta** dore, dore* 'remember that thou art earth, earth' TH 7a

*oll an re na vgy ow leverall **y bos** an catholyk egglos, egglos vnwothfos* 'all those who say that the Catholic church is a church of ignorance' TH 17a

*dre reson **y bosow** gwarnys theragdorne* 'because you have been warned beforehand' TH 18

*fatell rons y dos in crehyn devas, dre reson **y bosans** y ow pretendya an gyrryow a thu* 'that they come in skins of sheep, because they claim to have the words of God' TH 19a

*ny a yll gwelas ha disky **y bos** an egglos tra vhell ha excellent* 'we can see and can teach that the church is a noble and excellent thing' TH 31a-32

*ha eplla is hemma, dre reson **y bos** S paule lynwys an Spuris-sans* 'and more ably than this, since St Paul was filled with the Holy Spirit' TH 33

*why a yll in ta vnderstondia **y bosa** lell* 'you can well understand that it is genuine' TH 36

*So dre reson **y bos** an mater ma settys in mes largely* 'But because this matter is set out fully' TH 39-39a

*Oll an re ma sure, gans mere moy, a theth warnan ny dre reson **y bosan** gyllys in mes thean chy a thu* 'All these indeed, and many more, have come upon us because we have departed from the house of God' TH 40a

*So pew a leverough why **y bosama*** 'But who do you say that I am?' TH 43a

***y bosans** an successors, hennew an sewysy, a pedyr* 'that they are the successors, i.e. the followers, of Peter' TH 49

*whath dre reson **y bosa** gwrys dre an blonogeth a thu* 'moreover because he was made by the will of God' TH 50a

*ha ry grace the thu ragtha, rag **y bosa** an moyha precius Jewal* 'and to give thanks to God because it is the most precious jewel' TH 54a

*dre reson **y bosa** gwrys a dore* 'because he was made of earth' TH 57a

*yth falsa orth y favoure **y bosa** neb bucka nos* 'it would seem from his appearance that he is some goblin of the night' CW 1589

*me ny allaf convethas **y bosta** ge ow hendas* 'I cannot believe that you are my grandfather' CW 1609-10.

Jenner discusses A) briefly (HCL: 166). Discussion of both A) and B) together with examples are to be found in my *Clappya Kernowek* (Williams 1997: 75-7). Brown mentions neither.

Brown is also completely silent about the use of *del* and *fatel* to introduce indirect statement. Such syntax is attested from the earliest Middle Cornish to the later language (see Williams 2006f). It is nowhere mentioned by Brown.

These are all serious omissions and mean that Brown's discussion of indirect speech in Cornish is very defective.

19.38 'he lives' in Cornish

I take issue with Brown's *neb eus ow tryga gensi* 'someone who is living with her' at paragraph § 72.7. Brown also cites *Ev a dryga ena ugens blydhen* 'He lived there for twenty years' (GMC2 § 113). Neither is, in my view, correct Cornish. 'To live, to be living' in the sense of 'dwell, be resident' in Cornish is not expressed in Cornish by *bos ow trega* or *a dryg/a dryga*, as Brown seems to

PROBLEMS WITH BROWN'S *GRAMMAR OF MODERN CORNISH*

believe. Cornish uses *bos tregys* for 'to dwell, to be living'; this is a distinctively Celtic idiom and there are many examples of it in the texts:

> *byth na wrella compressa ow tus **vs trygys** ena* 'that he should never oppress my people who are living there' OM 1434-35
> *punscie y tus mar calas **vs trygys** agy the'th wlas* 'to punish his people so hard who are living in your kingdom' OM 1482-83
> *py tyller yma moyses ha py cost **yma trygys*** 'where is Moses and in what district does he live' OM 1551-52
> *the'n tyreth a thythwadow yw reys gans dev caradow thyn ena rag **bos trygys*** 'to the land of promise which is given by beloved God to us to dwell there' OM 1624-26
> *pan fy a'n bys tremenys gans cryst y **fythyth trygys** agy th'y clos* 'when you depart from the world you shall live with Christ within his court' PC 3232-34
> *mar ny'th wolhaf dre ow ras yn nef ny **vythyth trygys*** 'if I do not wash you by my grace, you shall not dwell in heaven' PC 857-58
> *nep na crys ny fyth sylwys na gans dev ny **vyth trygys*** 'who does not believe will not be saved nor will he dwell with God' RD 1109-10
> *en den-ma war ow ene gans ihesu a nazare yn certan a **fue trygys*** 'this man upon my soul lived indeed with Jesus of Nazareth' RD 1277-79
> *my a wor pur wyre yn ta py **ma** an mester **trygis*** 'I know very well where the master lives' BM 39-40
> ***yma tregys** in cambron den ov cul merclys dyson* 'there is a man living in Camborne doing miracles at once' BM 687-88
> *py **ma tregys*** 'where does he live?' BM 816
> *omma yth **ese tregys** avel hermyt in guelfos* 'here I live like a hermit in the wilderness' BM 1963-64
> ***tregys off** lemen heb wov berth in castel an dynas* 'I live now without a lie within the Castle-an-Dinas' BM 2209-10
> ***Tregys vue** yn lestevdar* 'He was dwelling in Les-Teader' BM 2284
> *Ihesu eff re thendelas in gluas neff **bones treges*** 'Jesus, he has deserved to live in the kingdom of heaven' BM 4337-78
> *then wlas **vgy** y vab Jhesus crist inhy **tregys*** 'to the kingdom in which his son Jesus Christ dwells' TH 11a
> *neb yma an spuris sans, hag a **vith triges** rag neffra* 'where the Holy Spirit is and will dwell for ever' TH 36a
> *ha neb a **ve** an prince an heynes, hen ew, Prince an Jewys, **tregys*** 'and where the prince of the heathens, that is, the prince of the Jews dwelt' TH 47a
> *py te a fyth edrega kyn **fes tregys** gans an Jowl* 'or you will be sorry for it though you live with the Devil' BK 44-45
> ***Yma tregys** in Kembra* 'He lives in Wales' BK 1292
> *ena te a **vyth tregys** ha myns assentyas genas* 'there you and as many as agreed with you shall live' CW 246-47
> *En Termen ez passiez **thera Trigaz** en St. Levan Dean ha Bennen en Tellar creiez chei a Horr* 'Once upon time there was living in St Levan a man and a woman in a place called Chy an Horth' BF: 15.

Expressions like **yth esof ow trega*, *ef a drega cannot be recommended.

279

TOWARDS AUTHENTIC CORNISH
LEXICON

19.39 *berr* 'short'

Brown uses the word *berr* [ber], but this word is not the usual word for 'short' in Middle Cornish, being attested only in such expressions as *a ver dermyn* 'shortly' (e.g. OM 2381) and *a ver spys* 'shortly' (e.g. OM 1540). The only place where *ber* is used as an ordinary adjective meaning 'short' is in Lhuyd's englyn *Bedh dorn rê **ver**, dhon tavaz rê hîr* 'The hand is wont to be too short for the too long tongue' (AB: 251c). This is probably an archaism. The ordinary word for 'short' in Middle Cornish is not *ber* but *cot*, as is clear from the following examples:

> *na vo hyrre es am syn na byth **cotta** war nep cor* 'that it be no longer than my mark nor any shorter in any way' OM 2511-12
> *re **got** o a gevelyn* 'it was too short by a cubit' OM 2520
> *lemyn re **got** ev a gevelyn da yn guyr* 'now it is too short by a good cubit truly' OM 2540-41
> *tres aral re **got** in guyr* 'another time too short truly' OM 2549
> ***cot** yv the thythyow thegy* 'short are your days' RD 2037
> *me a ra pur **cot** y guyns* 'I will render his wind very short' BM 2253
> *an lesson **cut** ma* 'this short lesson' TH 26
> *ha wosa an tyrmyn **cut** a vethyn ny omma* 'and after the short time we will be here' TH 26
> *in kyth same lesson bean **cut** ma* 'in this very same short lesson' TH 28a
> *an moar brase yn **cutt** termyn adro thom tyre a vyth dreys* 'the great sea will be brought round my land in a short time' CW 88-9
> *in **cutt** termyn ages negys cowsow y praya* 'in a short time tell your business, I pray' CW 592.

Brown should replace *berr* [ber]' 'short' with *kott* [cot] 'short'.

19.40 *bleujenn* 'flower'

Throughout GMC2 Brown uses the term *bleujenn* [blejenn] for 'flower'. This word is unattested anywhere in Middle Cornish, where the word for 'flower' is *flowr* or *flowren* and the plural is *flowrys*:

> *palm ha **floris** kekyffris er y byn degis a ve* 'palm and also flowers were carried to meet him' PA 29d
> *ny dyf guels na **flour** yn bys yn keth forth na may kyrthys* 'no grass nor any flower in the world grows in that same path where I walked' OM 712-13
> *A frut da ha **floures** tek menestrouthy ha can whek* 'Of good fruit and fair flowers, music and sweet song' OM 769-70
> *yma gynef **flowrys** tek yn onor thu'm arluth whek* 'I have beautiful flowers in honour of my sweet lord' PC 258-59
> *ow tos yn onor thy'mmo gans branchis **flourys** kefrys* 'coming in honour to me with branches, flowers also' PC 266-67

PROBLEMS WITH BROWN'S *GRAMMAR OF MODERN CORNISH*

*kepar ha **flowres** in prasow* 'like flowers in the field' TH 7
*an **flowre** a ra clamdera ha cotha the ves* 'the flowere wilts and withers' TH 7
*kepar dell ra an gwels seha, an **flowre** a glomder* 'just as the grass shrivels, so the flower wilts' TH 7
*eff a deffe in ban kepar ha **flowren*** 'he shoots up like a flower' TH 7
*lower **flowrys** a bub ehan yn place ma yta tevys* 'behold growing in this place an abundance of flowers of every kind' CW 363-34
*me a vyn mos tha wandra omma yn myske an **flowrys*** 'I will go to stroll here among the flowers' CW 538-39.

The word in Middle Cornish for 'flower' was not *blejen* but *flowr*. This is the word which should be used in the revived language.

19.41 *kador* 'chair'

Brown uses the word *kador* [*cador*] for 'chair', but this word is unattested in Middle Cornish, where the word is *chayr*:

cheyrys ha formys plente 'plenty of chairs and forms' PC 2229
*dus oma ese yth **cheer*** 'come here, sit in your chair' BM 3002
*setha in **chare** moyses* 'to sit in the chair of Moses' TH 34
*then stall po **cheare** an scribys han phariseis* 'to the stall or chair of the scribes and pharisees' TH 48a.

19.42 Conclusion

I have drawn attention in this chapter to a number of ways in which Wella Brown's grammar of Kernowek Kemyn gives a false impression of the traditional language. There very many further criticisms I have of this book; but space prevents me from setting them all out in detail. A really thorough critique of GMC2 would take a very long time indeed. It is clear, nonetheless, from the above pages that Brown's grammar of Cornish is unsatisfactory. If revived Cornish is intended to be as like the traditional language, it should imitate the texts as far as is humanly possible. Wella Brown's grammar describes a form of Cornish remarkably different from the language of the Middle and Late Cornish texts. Quite apart from the unhistorical and mistaken orthography in which it is written, GMC2 gives such a misleading picture of traditional Cornish that learners would be wise to avoid it.

CHAPTER 20
Final observations

20.00 Kernowek Kemyn
Dunbar and George call their book *Kernewek Kemmyn: Cornish for the Twenty-First Century*. It must be apparent to anybody, however, who has followed the language debate in the last few years that Kernowek Kemyn is open to very serious question. I would go so far as to say that Kernowek Kemyn is not Cornish at all. Because of the vigour of my criticism of Kernowek Kemyn I have been accused of being abrasive and undiplomatic. I would point out here it was only the publication of Kernowek Kemyn which brought me back to the Cornish revival, so disturbed was I by this spurious form of the language. I am by profession a student of the Celtic languages and even now find it difficult to believe that such an unwarranted variety of Cornish could ever have been adopted by Cornish speakers. I am sure that they had the best of motives when they welcomed Kernowek Kemyn. They were, however, unduly precipitate.

Since the adoption of Kernowek Kemyn by the Cornish Language Board in 1987 the language movement has been divided as never before. The fault rests with those who accepted without question an orthography that bore little resemblance to the traditional spelling and which was based on one man's untested understanding of the phonology of Middle Cornish. George himself appears to have no misgivings at all. He believes that we know so much more about the Celtic languages and of linguistics than the medieval scribes, that it should be easy to improve on their orthography (KKC21: 142).

I cannot understand how anyone could believe such a thing. George is not a professional Celticist, nor even a professional linguist. His experience of historical linguistics when he devised Kernowek Kemyn was perforce limited, yet he seems to think that he knows better than the medieval scribes how to write their own language. They spoke and heard it every day; they knew it thoroughly. They did not need to resort to guesswork and comparison with Breton to see how to pronounce their own mother tongue. Their spelling system is what we should imitate for the revival. If we create a new spelling-system based on our own ideas, we are bound to be mistaken. After all George's "increased knowledge of the Celtic languages" did not stop him from suggesting *tj and *dj, nor does it prevent his writing wholly unattested and erroneous forms like *<bywnans> and *<klywes>.

George himself agreed with me that his putative *tj and *dj were mistaken, and the offending items were removed from Kernowek Kemyn. George's orthography remains defective, however, because his underlying assumptions about Cornish phonology are mistaken. George believes that the Prosodic Shift did not operate until the seventeenth century. Moreover, he believes that the

FINAL OBSERVATIONS

shift lengthened vowels as well as shortening them. Neither suggestion can be sustained. My view, which I have attempted to corroborate with relevant quotations from the texts, is that A) the Prosodic Shift occurred before the period of our earliest Middle Cornish texts; B) that it shortened duration and intensified articulation of stressed vowels; C) that it did not lengthen any vowel.

The evidence for the date of the Prosodic Shift seems conclusive to me. At every turn we see good reason for supposing that half-length had been lost in Middle Cornish. All the indications in the texts point in the same direction. This evidence is, in my view, far stronger than the case against *tj and *dj. The only reason that George has for rejecting such conclusive proof, is his desire to defend Kernowek Kemyn. As we have seen, George himself tells us how ashamed he was to acknowledge that *tj and *dj were fictions:

> I'm sometimes embarrassed and covered in shame
> To admit imperfection, and thereby lose face (KKC21: 71).

To admit now that Kernowek Kemyn is based on a wholly erroneous phonology would be for George an even greater loss of face. Ultimately, however, he will be compelled to acknowledge that Kernowek Kemyn is mistaken.

20.01 The future

If the Cornish Revival is to flourish and indeed receive government funding, it requires a *single written form*. That form cannot be Kernowek Kemyn. The Cornish Language Board have for nearly twenty years attempted to make Kernowek Kemyn the single written form for Cornish and have failed. Indeed, since the publication of my own revision of Unified Cornish, Kernowek Kemyn appears, mercifully, to have lost some ground. Of the three forms of Cornish currently in use, only Kernowek Kemyn has been under continuous and sustained attack. This is because observers are sceptical of Kernowek Kemyn's claims to be academically sound. They may object to various aspects of the other two orthographies, but Kernowek Kemyn alone of the orthographies has been described as inauthentic, spurious, and indeed fictional. These criticisms will not diminish. Until Kernowek Kemyn is replaced, it will continue to be the object of intense criticism.

If Cornish is to have a single written form, that form cannot arise from within the movement. It will need to be imposed from outside. I would suggest moreover that single written form when it is imposed, will be one of three things:

1) A completely traditional orthography (CTO). This is an orthography based entirely upon the Middle Cornish texts. Such an orthography does not use any symbol or group of symbols that is unattested in

traditional Cornish. I have given an example of such an orthography in Appendix E of Williams 1997 (pp. 179-81).
2) Unified Cornish (UC). This, Nance's system, is the spelling still used in Gorsedd ceremonies and is familiar to everybody.
3) Unified Cornish Revised (UCR). This, my own revision of Unified Cornish, makes distinctions ignored by Nance and simplifies various aspects of the orthography. UCR also attempts by concentrating on Tregear (and BM and CW) to make Cornish a more easily spoken language.

Which orthographic system is chosen is, however, a matter for others. Two things are abundantly clear nonetheless. First, a single written form of Cornish is essential if the language is to flourish. Second, the single written form cannot be Kernowek Kemyn. I am confident that Kernowek Kemyn will not be the system of choice, and will one day disappear completely.

I pray fervently for the dawn of that day.

INDEX

References are to paragraphs

a 'concerning, about' 19.19
Abram 18.01
'abroad' (*dres mor* in Cornish) 19.27
adro the 'concerning; about' 19.17, 19.18
Afryca 'Africa' 18.02
alenna 'thence' 5.02; *alenha, alena* 14.03
Almayn 'Germany' 18.25
alternation of *g* ~ *k*; George cannot explain 17.02
alternation of *y* ~ e 10.00
ambos 'contract' 18.61
ambosa 'contract, agree' 18.62
a'm govys 'for my sake' 19.16
Anglo-Saxon 5.02
anothe, anydha 'of it' 12.12
ap Thomas, Robat 7.23
Archæologia Britannica 2.04
argument / **argyans* 18.03
arluth 'lord'; **arloedh* in Kernowek Kemyn 0.03
Arthor Gornow 'Arthur the Cornishman' 18.76
*arvor 'coast' in Kernowek Kemyn 18.45
arvorek 'coastal' 18.04
assibilation of Old Cornish -d- 15.00-08; George's four different "explanations" 15.01-06
'at the one time' 19.13
*<au> in place-names 7.27
Austol 'St Austell' 18.77
avorow 'tomorrow' 19.27

banneth, benneth 'blessing' 14.00, 14.08
'because' 19.22
bedneth, bedna 'blessing' 7.19, 14.08
ber 'short' 19.39
bes 'world' 11.02
beth 'be!' 11.02
bethens 'let him be' 10.08-10
Beunans Meriasek "Life of St Meriasek" 2.06, 3.05, 6.04, 7.20-21, 14.08, 14.10-11, 17.01, 18.64; **Bywnans Meryadjek* in Kernowek Kemyn 2.04
bew / byw 'alive' 12.01-02, 12.06, 19.19; *bêu* 13.03
bewa 'to live' 12.01, 12.03, 12.06
bewnans 'life' (**bywnans* in Kernowek Kemmyn) 0.03, 12.01, 12.04, 12.06, 12.13
Bewnans Ke "Life of St Kea"; Late Cornish features in 14.12; absence of pre-occlusion 14.12; source for revived language 2.06

beys 'world' 11.01
beyth 'be!' 11.01
*blejen 'flower' 19.40
Blessed Virgin Mary 14.12
blethen 'year' 10.03; [pl] *blethynnyow, blethydnyow, blethanniau* 4.01, 14.04, 14.05, 14.06; *blydhen* in Kernowek Kemyn 1.00, 4.01, 10.00
blêu 'hair' 13.03
bloth 'years of age' 7.08, 7.10
bohosek 'poor' 3.03; George's "explanation" of *bohogek*, etc. 15.07
Borde, Andrew 7.07, 7.24, 9.00, 9.05, 14.10, 18.54
bos, boys 'to be' 7.12, 7.32; means 'have' 19.31; with present participle for simple present 19.33
bos 'dwelling' 7.25
Boson, John 9.04, 14.04
Boson, Nicholas 3.08, 5.02, 6.06, 7.08, 7.31, 11.04, 14.04, 14.12, 17.00, 18.12
Boson, Thomas 14.12
Bosons 19.00
boys, bos 'food' 7.12, 7.32; *buz* 17.17; *bous* 7.19
Britheinig 0.04
broder 'brother' 6.06
Brown, Wella; author of GMC2 19.00; firm supporter of Kernowek Kemyn 19.00
*brueslys 'court' 18.44
budhek 'victorious' 18.06
bys 'world' 11.03
byth 'be!' 6.06, 11.03
bythqueth 'never' (in the past) 18.07, 18.51; **bythkweyth* in Kernowek Kemyn 0.03

*cador 'chair' 19.41
cafus, cafos 'get' 7.18; **kavoes* in Kernowek Kemyn 0.03
Camborne 7.24
*can 'white' (**kann* in Kernowek Kemyn) 14.00, 18.36
can, canow 'song(s)' 14.02
*cannaf 'I bleach' (**kannav* in Kernowek Kemyn) 14.00
captyvyta 'captivity' 18.37
Caradar (A. S. D. Smith) 0.01, 2.06, 5.00, 7.01, 8.00, 12.00, 15.00, 18.21, 19.00
caradow 'beloved' 6.06; *karadow* in Kernowek Kemyn 0.03
carharow 'shackle'; **kargharow* in Kernowek Kemyn 0.03
carnacyon 'incarnation' 18.37
carrek 'rock' 17.02
casadow 'hateful' 6.06
certan 'certan' 16.01
chayr 'chair' 19.41

chy 'house' 3.07, 9.00, 9.04-05, 9.08; **tji* in Kernowek Kemyn 12.11
claf 'sick, leprous'; **klav* in Kernowek Kemyn 0.03
Clappya Kernowek 2.06, 20.01
clevegow 'diseases' 15.07
clew / clow 'hear!', *clewes, clowes* 'hear' 12.08-11; **klyw, *klywes* 'to hear' in Kernowek Kemyn 0.03, 1.00, without basis in traditional Cornish 12.09, 12.10; George admits it is wrong 12.11; reason for George's mistake 12.12; **klywewgh* 18.55
colon 'heart' 16.01
color 'colour' 13.04
coltrebyn 'candlestick' 18.39
compas 'straight'; *kympez, cumpaz* 12.12
Completely Traditional Orthography (CTO) 20.01
con 'dinner'; **koen* in Kernowek Kemyn 0.03
concludya 'silence in argument' 18.42
conditional sentences 19.34; periphrastic conditional tense 19.25
conquerrour 'conqueror' 18.40
conquerrya 'conquer' 18.41
constryna 'force, constrain' 18.43
'contrasting rhymes' 16.07, 16.09
Cornish Language Board (Kesva an Tavas Kernewek) 0.00, 0.04; "has cast aside the aims of its founders" 19.00; follows "the theories of a false prophet" 19.00
Cornish Today (CT) passim; George's "humorous" eulogy 0.01
cort 'court' 18.44
cos, coys 'wood' 7.06, 7.12-13, 7.25, 7.28, 11.00; *cous, kuz* 7.17, 7.31; **koes* in Kernowek Kemyn 0.03
cost 'coast, region' 18.45
cosyn 'cousin' 18.46
cot 'short' 19.39
coth, coyth 'old' 7.12; *couth* 17.19
coth 'falls' 7.12; *kothaz, kydas* 'fell' 12.12
coys / cos 'wood' in place-names 7.28-29
creacyon, creacion 'creation'; **kreashyon* in Kernowek Kemyn 0.03
Creation of the World (CW) 2.06, 14.12
crehylly 'shake'; **kryghylli* in Kernowek Kemyn 0.03
cres, crees 'peace' 11.04
cresy 'to believe' 5.08
cry 'cry' 9.00
Cryst 'Christ'; **Krist* in Kernowek Kemyn 0.03
Crystyon 'Christian'; [pl.] *Cristonnyan*, etc. 6.03, 6.05; **Kristyon* in Kernowek Kemyn 0.03
cur 'court' 18.44
Cusgarne (Gwennap) 7.29

Cusvey (Gwennap) 7.29
Cusveorth (Kea) 7.29
Cuskayne Farm (near Probus) 7.29
cyta 'city'; **sita* in Kernowek Kemyn 0.03

dader, dadder 'goodness' 6.06
dampnacyon 'damnation' 18.08
deglena 'tremble' 18.09
del 'as, that' 19.37
delatya 'delay'; George's mistaken etymology 18.10
Densher 'Devonshire' 18.11
departya 'depart' 18.12
desyrya 'desire' 19.27
deth 'day' 11.02
dethyow 'days' 10.05
Dew, Du 'God' 3.04, 13.00, 13.05, 13.06; *Dêu* 13.03
dew, dyw 'two' 19.19; *deaw* 14.12
dewla 'hands' 17.18, 19.19; **diwleuv* in Kernowek Kemyn 0.03
dewlagas 'eyes' 19.19
Dewnans 'Devonshire' 18.13
dewolow 'devils' 6.05
deyth 'day' 11.01
dialect; in BM 7.21; in Cornish 7.24; George expounds it in Cornish 7.23 George denies it exists in Cornish 7.23; George admits it exists 15.06
diglon 'faintheartedness; fainthearted' 18.14
diphthong in *ow* 17.01
disobediens 'disobedience' 18.53
Donald 14.01
Donal 14.01
dos 'come'; between *mar* + verbal noun in protasis 19.34; *mar teffa* in unreal conditions 19.35; *dof, duef* 'I come' 19.29
dowr 'river, lake' 18.15
dre reson 'because' 19.22
drehevel 'to raise, to build' 3.03
du, diu 'black' 13.00, 13.05, 13.06
duk 'duke' 18.16
Dunbar, Paul 0.00; accuses Williams of propagating errors 0.01; calls UCR orthography "lamentable"
dyber 'saddle' 5.03-04
dyhow 'right, south' 18.33; **deghow* in Kernowek Kemyn 2.05
dynnyta 'dignity' 14.11
dysquethes 'appear' (in Late Cornish) 19.32
dyth 'day' 11.03
*dyvroa 'exile' 18.19

<ea> 3.01
Early New English 3.00-01

INDEX

edyak 'idiot' 18.92
<ee> 3.01, 5.09; for [e:] 11.04
eglos, egglos 'church' 17.18
eles 'angels' 17.17
ending of second person singular 19.26
Engothall 18.29
enys 'island' 10.04; **ynys* in Kernowek Kemyn 0.03
Everson, Michael 0.01
Evrok 'York' 18.21
ew, yw in UCR; George's misrepresentation of 13.03; rhyming with *-u* 13.07; George's "explanation" 13.09
ew > ow; took place in 16th century acc. George 17.01; in PA (15th century) 17.01
expedyent 'expedient' 18.20
"experimental error" alleged by George 2.07
exylya 'exile' 18.18

falladow 'fail' 6.06
fannya 'fan' 18.22
fatel 'how, that' 19.08, 19.37
fenten 'spring' 18.23
feth 'faith' 11.02
fevyr 'fever' 18.24, 18.86
feyth 'faith' 11.01
final unstressed *a, e* and *o* confused in PA 16.05
final *g*/*k* 17.02
final long *i* 9.00-08
flehes 'children' 16.01
flowr 'flower' 19.40
fos 'wall' 7.26
Francis II (†1544), king of France 13.08
future of the Revival 20.01
fyth 'faith' 11.03

gallogek 'mighty' 15.07
ganso 'with him' 15.02, 16.02; **gantjo* in Kernowek Kemyn 12.11
gansans 'with them' 16.02
geminate consonants 6.01; single consonants written as 6.02
gemination of consonants 6.00-05
Gendall, Richard 2.06, 3.08
George, Ken J.; lecturer in ocean science 0.00; accuses Williams of poor scholarship 0.01; acknowledges his debt to Williams' scholarship 0.01; says Williams writes "nonsense" 15.00; says Williams' article is "brilliantly argued" 15.03; says Williams' "credibility is tending to zero" 0.01,17.02; says Williams is right and he himself wrong 15.00; George's "orthographic profiles" 0.02; his database inaccurate 0.02, 1.00, 2.04, 5.01, 18.00, 18.18, 18.27, 18.31, 18.50, 18.54, 18.59, 18.70, 18.85, 18.89, 18.95; his attitude to scribal tradition 0.04; his lack of theoretical approach 2.00; dismissive of traditional orthography 0.04, 2.01; his changing attitude to Cornish orthography 2.07; fails to understand problem with **bywnans* 2.04; his inconsistency *vis à vis* Welsh 2.04; his avoidance of discussion 5.01; his special pleading 5.01; inconsistent about scribal tradition 7.18; believes BM differs from all other Middle Cornish texts 7.20; says Williams is "naughty" for using evidence from BM 7.20; George's place-name maps 7.28-29; denies long *a* is raised 8.00; admits long *a* is raised 8.00-01; "explanation" for rhymes with long *i* 9.03-04; uncertain about diphthongization of long *i* 9.05; believes <e> represents *[iˑ] 10.01-02; invokes Welsh and Breton when in difficulty 12.01, 13.00; misrepresents Welsh phonology 13.02; can identify eye-rhymes without knowing the pronunciation 13.09; thinks attested form is "incorrect" 14.04; has silently changed his chronology 14.10; invents chronology 14.10; his *<tj> and *<dj> 15.00; his four different "explanations" of *s*/*j* 15.01-06; can describe precisely the phonetic nature of **tj* and **dj* 15.02; compares Cornish phonology with that of Serbo-Croat 15.02; criticizes Nance for not having noticed **tj* and **dj* 15.02; admits **tj* and **dj* never existed 15.00; embarrassed to admit the truth 15.00, 20.00; ignorant of the nature of *-s-* < *-d-* 15.04; knows exactly the nature of *-s-* < *-d-* 15.05; not a professional linguist 15.08, 20.00; asserts final <e> is schwa 16.04; denies final <e> is schwa 16.04; invents his own "rules" for Cornish rhyme 16.07; invents his own terms for Cornish rhyme 16.07; his metrical "theories" easily dismissed 16.08-09; asserts *ew > ow* took place in 16th century 17.01; says we know much about Cornish phonology 17.02; says we cannot know about Cornish phonology 17.02; Mills says very little right with George's analyses 17.03; Wella Brown extols George's analysis 19.00
ger, geer 'word' 11.04
Gerlyver Kernowek Kemyn (GKK) inconsistent 1.02-03; full of errors 18.00; errors in 18.01-94
Germany 'Germany' 18.25
gew, gu 'spear' 13.06
gew, gu 'woe' 13.06
Glasney 3.01, 3.05, 3.08, 7.18
glew, glu 'sharp' 13.06
Godhal 'Irishman' 18.29
Godhalek 'Irish' 18.29

287

godreva 'three days hence' (Lhuyd's *gudreva*); **godrevedh* in Kernowek Kemyn 0.03
gof 'smith' 7.26
gorra 'put'; *uyraz, woraz* 12.12
gortos 'wait' 16.01
gos, goys 'blood' (Old Cornish *guit*) 7.06, 7.17, 7.20; *gudzh* 7.17; **goes* in Kernowek Kemyn 0.03
*gos 'it is known' (verbal form invented by George) 18.26
goslowes 'listen'; *gyzyuaz, gazowas* 12.12
gothfos 'to know' 3.03
govenek 'hope' 6.02
Grammar of Modern Cornish (GMC1, GMC2) 19.00; language described in it not Middle Cornish 19.00; errors in 2nd edition (GMC2) 19.01-41
graph 1.01
gull 3.02
gull 'to do' 3.02
guris 'done'; "contrasting" with -*ys* 16.09; rhyming with -*ys* 16.09
gwel 'field' 18.30
gwely 'bed' 18.28
gwer 'husbands' 18.27
gwerhes 'virgin'; **gwyrghes* in Kernowek Kemyn 12.13; *an worthyas ker marya* 'BVM' 14.12
gweth, gwyth 'trees' 11.00, 11.02; <gweth> & <gweeth> 11.04
gwetha 'to keep' 2.00, 5.07
gwethen 'tree' 10.07
gweyth 'trees' 11.01
gwreg, gwreeg 'wife' 11.04
Gwydhelek 'Irish' 18.29
gwyf / gweff 'worthy' 12.13
*gwynsella 'fan' 18.22; recommended by George in GKK 18.22; omitted from GKK 18.22
gwyr, gwyer 'true' 14.12
gwyth 'trees' 11.03
gwyw 'worthy' 12.14, 19.19

Halabezack 15.07
half-long /iˑ/; shortened by Middle Cornish period 10.02
hedre, hadre (**hedra*) 'while' 18.31
henna, hana 'that one' 14.09
Henry VI (1422-61)
herwyth 'according to' 18.32
Hiberno-English 7.27
honen 'self' 16.01, 19.32
'how' 19.08
'how long' 19.11
'how many' 19.06
'how often' 19.09
howlsedhas 'sunset' 18.33

huny 'one' 19.01
hypothesis of the two long *o*'s (HTLO) 7.01 *sqq.*
hythev 'today' 13.07

Ihesu, Ihesus 'Jesus' 13.07
Illogan 7.24
indirect statement; Brown's discussion very defective 19.37
intrethans 'between them' 16.02

Jackson, Kenneth H. 7.01, 7.11
Jenner, Henry 0.01, 2.06, 5.00, 5.10, 7.01, 7.12, 8.00, 11.00, 12.00, 15.00, 19.00
jentyl 'gentle, gentile' 4.02
Jordan, William 3.05, 3.07-08, 6.07, 14.08
jorna 'day' 11.04, 18.35
kellyn 'we lose' 6.01
kelyn 'holly' 6.01
Kennedy, Neil 0.01
kenyver 'as many, all' 19.02
kerensa 'love' 3.03; **kerentja* in Kernowek Kemyn 12.11
Kerew, Wella 3.08, 4.02, 5.09, 11.04, 17.00, 19.00
Kernewek Kemmyn: Cornish for the Twenty-First Century; childish insults in 0.01; arguments easily refuted 17.03
Kernowek (*Kernewek*) 12.13; **Kernywek* 12.13
Kernowek Kemmyn; its orthography inauthentic 0.03; inconsistencies in 1.03; theoretical arguments against 2.02; is not Cornish 0.01, 2.07, 20.00; criticisms in CT 1.00-1.02; not phonemic 4.01-02; a mistake 17.03, 20.00; will disappear 20.01
keskerth 'walking together, procession' 18.64
kist, kyst (Kernowek Kemyn)1.03
klyuaz (for *klouaz*) 12.12
korrdonner (Kernowek Kemmyn) 'microwave oven' 18.93
ky 'dog' 3.07, 9.00, 16.07
kyng 'king' 18.47

lader 'robber', [pl.] *laddron* 6.06
lagajak 15.07
lagasow 'eyes' 19.19
lengthening; alleged lengthening of half-long in Late Cornish 5.04; alleged lengthening in LC verbs 5.09
leverel 'say' 3.03
*lew 'lion' 13.01, 18.49
lewd 'wicked' 18.48
lewdnes 'wickedness' 18.48
Lewis, Henry 7.01
Lhuyd, Edward 0.01, 2.04, 5.04, 5.09-10, 7.17, 7.31, 8.00, 9.01, 9.03, 9.07, 10.00, 12.12, 13.01, 13.03-05, 13.09, 14.00, 14.04, 14.09, 17.00,

INDEX

18.04-06, 18.10, 18.12, 18.14, 18.27-29, 18.33, 18.49, 18.69, 18.71, 18.75-76, 18.82, 19.27, 19.39
'lives, is living' 19.38
lo 'spoon' 7.09
long *a* in Cornish 8.00;
long consonants 6.01
long *o*; alleged two kinds 7.00-30
long *u* in Late Cornish 7.17
longya 'belong' 18.50
lowen 'joyful' 3.03
loys 'grey' 17.20; *luz* 'grey' 17.17
lu 'host' 13.07
lyes termyn 'often' 19.14
lyon 'lion' 13.01, 18.49
lyw, lew 'colour' 13.04, 13.05, 13.07; *liu* 13.04

malaria 18.86
Manx 2.03, 2.07, 4.00, 14.01
marthojak 15.07
Mary Queen of Scots 13.08
may hallo 'in order that' 19.23
me, my 'I, me' 9.06-07
mennas 'will'; for future 19.27; *mynnaf, mennaf, mannaf* 'I will' 14.08, 19.30
meras 'to look' 2.00, 5.07
*Meryadjek 'Meriasek' in Kernowek Kemyn 2.04, 12.07, 12.11
mes 'but' 19.21
Mills, John; dismissive of George's work 0.01, 0.02, 0.04, 2.00; 17.03
moghhe 'to increase' 7.16
mois 'table' 7.12
mos, mois 'go' 7.12; *mos dhe ves* 'go away'; recommended by George but barely attested in Cornish 18.12; *mos yn kerth* 'go away' 18.12
mosquito (*Anopheles*) 18.86
moy 'more' 7.16
mur 'great'; *mear, meer* 14.12
mytern 'king' 6.06, 18.47

Nance, Robert Morton 0.01, 2.06, 5.00, 7.01, 7.12, 7.20, 8.00, 10.08, 12.00, 14.02, 15.00, 15.02, 18.04, 18.26, 18.31, 18.38, 18.51, 18.57, 18.59, 18.69, 18.71, 18.78, 18.82, 18.89, 18.91-92, 18.94, 19.00, 19.19-20, 20.01
nef, neeve 'heaven' 11.04
nefra 'never' (in the future) 18.51; wrongly used by George 18.51
neppyth, nappyth 'something' 19.04
Norman French 5.02, 7.18
nessa 'next, nearest' 19.20
nos, nois 'night' 7.12
noth, yn hoth 'naked' 7.20, 17.00
ny 'we' 9.00-02

o 'he was' 7.09
<oa> 3.01
obedyens 'obedience', **obayans* 18.52
obedyent 'obedient' 18.54
occasyon 'occasion'; **okkashyon* in Kernowek Kemyn 0.03
odl wyddeleg 16.08
<oe> 7.02-04
of 'I am' 7.10; *of/yw* 7.16
'often' 19.14
os, oys 'thou art' 7.12
oys, ois 'age' 7.12
oma 'I am' 6.04
omamendya 'improve' 19.32
omassaya 'attempt' 19.32
ombrena 'redeem oneself' 19.32
ombrevy 'prove oneself' 19.32
omdenna 'withdraw' 19.32
omgemeres 'undertake' 19.32
omglowes 'feel' 19.32
omma, oma 'here' 6.04; *ybma, obba* 12.12
omsensy 'consider oneself' 19.32
omthysquethes 'appear' 19.32
omthyvlamya 'apologize' 19.32
omwetha 'protect oneself' 19.32
omwul 'pretend to be' 19.32
onen 'one' 6.04, 16.01
onnen 'ash' 6.04
<oo> 3.01
"orthographic profiles" 0.02
Ó Searcóid, Mícheál 0.01, 7.22
ow tuchya 'concerning' 19.18
oy 'egg' 7.09; [pl.] *oyow* 18.54
oy, <oy> 7.06; confusion of *oy* and *o* 7.11-12; *oy* in place-names 7.13; *oy* < *ui* in absolute final 7.14; *oy* in loanwords 7.15; <oy> and scribal tradition 7.18; *oy* in rhymes in PA and *Ordinalia* 7.19; *oy* in rhymes in BM 7.20
oyeth 'attention!' 18.55

pan vaner 'what kind' 19.07
parde 'by God' 18.56
parkya 'enclose' 18.57
*parti 'party', [pl.] *partys* in Kernowek Kemyn 4.02
Peder 'Peter' 6.06
Pedersen, Holgar 7.01
peswar 'four' 15.00; **pedjwar* in Kernowek Kemyn 15.00, 15.02
Penglase, Charles 0.04
*Penntorr 'Torpoint' 18.58
pesy 'to pray' 3.03, 5.08
phonemic orthography 4.00-02
place-names; evidence for *oy/o* in 7.23
playnya 'plane' 18.59

289

TOWARDS AUTHENTIC CORNISH

plew, plu 'parish' 13.03, 13.06
pluperfect 19.25
pobel 'people' 16.01
poken 'or else' 19.10
polat, pollat in Kernowek Kemyn 1.03
polta gwel, pylta guel 'much better' 12.12
Pool, Peter A. S. 0.02; calls K. J. George "a false prophet" 19.00
preder 'thought' 6.06
prenna, etc. 'buy' 14.11
pre-occlusion 3.05. 14.00-13; parallels in Gaelic 14.01; inconsistency in Kernowek Kemyn about 14.05-14.06; in Scilly 14.07; George invents a chronology for 14.10; arguments against George's invented chronology 14.11-12
preeve 'reptile' 11.04
pref 'insect, reptile' 11.02
pres 'time, meal' 11.02
present participle 19.30
preves 'insects' 10.06
prevyon 'reptiles' 10.06
preyf 'insect, reptile' 11.01
preys 'time, meal' 11.01
procedya 'proceed' 18.63
processyon 'procession' 18.64
procurya 'procure' 18.60
proest 16.08
promys 'promise' 18.61
promysya 'promise' 18.62
Prosodic Shift; 5.00-11; date of 5.02
Pryce, William 5.10, 14.04, 18.33, 18.54, 18.82
prydyth 'poet' (**prysydh* in Kernowek Kemyn) 18.65
pryf 'insect, reptile' 11.03; *pryf* > *pref* 11.00
prys 'time, meal' 11.03
pub termyn 'always' 19.12
py ehen 'what kind' 19.07
pybel 'pipe' 5.03-04
pynag oll 'whoever, whatever' 19.05
pyw, pew 'who' (**piw* in Kernowek Kemyn) 13.04, 13.06, 19.19

Quenya 0.04
quyt 'quite'; **kwit* in Kernowek Kemyn 0.03

rag 17.02
rag kerensa 'for the sake of' 19.16
ragthans 'for them' 16.02
raunsona 'ransom' 18.70
re Varya, arya 'O heavens' 18.05
recompens 'recompense' 18.66
reflexives 19.32
reportya 'report' 18.67
"rhyming ensemble" 16.07-09

robbys 'robbed' 6.05
ros 'promontory' 7.25
res 'ford' > *rose* 7.25
Resohen 'Oxford' 18.71
restya (read *wrestya*) 'twist' 18.68
rhyme in Cornish 16.06; in Welsh and Breton 16.08
*rimyow perfydh, *rimyow isperfydh (terms devised by George for his invented prosody) 16.07
rond 'round' 18.69
roys, ros 'net' 7.12
ry 'to give' 9.00-02; *ros* 'gave' 7.12

Sacrament an Alter (SA) 14.12
Saint Erth 7.23
salvacyon 'salvation' 18.72
Saunders, Tim 7.01
savyour 'saviour' 18.73
saw 'but' 19.21
Scilly 7.23, 14.07
Scot 'Scot' 18.75
scoth, scouth 'shoulder' 7.19
Scotland 'Scotland' 18.75
screfa 'to write' 5.07; **skrifa* in Kernowek Kemyn 0.03, 5.08, 7.04, 10.01
scribal tradition in Cornish 3.00-06, 7.18
secund 'second' 19.20
secunda manus in BM 3.05, 7.19-21, 14.08
seera, syra 'father' 2.00, 5.03, 5.06
selwador 'saviour' 18.74
selwyans 'salvations' 18.72
shortening of /i·/ 5.03
Single Written Form (SWF) 20.01
skyber 'barn' 5.03-04
sompna 'summon' 18.78
spelling reform 2.03
spryngya 'spring' 18.79
squyer 'squire'; **skwier* in Kernowek Kemyn 0.03
ster, steere 'star' 11.04
sterradnou 'stars' 14.04
Stert, An 'Torpoint' 18.58
Stewart / Stuart 13.08
*strothhe 'force' 18.43; both recommended and omitted by George 18.43
subjunctive; confusion of past with present 16.03, 16.05, 19.28
supposya 'assume' 18.80
syra wyn 'grandfather' 18.76

tabel 'table' 18.81
taran 'thunder' 14.04
tarednow 'thunder' (called "incorrect" by George) 14.04

INDEX

tarenner 'thunderer' (wrongly **taraner* in Kernowek Kemyn) 18.82
tavas 'tongue, language' 18.83
te/ty 'thou, thee' 9.06-07
teg, teege 'fair' 14.04
temptacyon 'temptation' 18.84
termys 'terms' 18.85
ternoth 'on the next day' 19.27
terthen 'tertian fever, malaria' 18.86
tevy 'grow' 18.87
têu 'fat' 13.03
the'n dor 'down' 19.15
thethans 'to them' 16.02
thewortans 'from them' 16.02
thys/thes 'to thee' 5.10; *thyso/theso* 'to thee' 5.10
tomder 'heat'; **toemmder* in Kernowek Kemyn 0.04
Ton, Radulphus (or Richardus), scribe of BM 3.00, 6.04, 7.20-21, 17.01; George surmises about his age 14.10
tramor 'abroad' (adjective) 19.27
trega 'to dwell' 5.07, 6.06, 10.01; **triga* in Kernowek Kemyn 5.08; *yma tregys* 'he lives' 18.38
Tregear, John 4.01-02, 6.07, 9.00, 11.02, 14.10, 16.02, 18.26, 18.38-39, 18.48, 18.52, 18.60, 18.63, 18.67-68, 18.73, 18.92, 19.27, 20.01
Trelagossik 15.07
trewa (vb) 'spit' 13.06; *tru* 'spits' 13.06
tru, trew 'sorrow; alas!' 13.06-08
Truro 7.24, 14.07
tros 'noise' 7.32
tros 'foot' 7.32; *truz* 17.17; **troes* in Kernowek Kemyn 7.18
try 'three' 9.00-02
*trygh 'victory' 18.90
*tryhy 'triumph, be victorious' 18.89
tu, tew 'side' 13.06-08
tubm, tybm 'hot' 12.12
tuchya 'touch' 18.88
tuchyng 'concerning' 19.18
turning point in the Revival 0.05
tyra (vb) 'land'; *tyreth* 'country' 5.09

un 'one' (<unn> in Kernowek Kemyn) 14.06
Unified Cornish 2.02, 2.06, 15.03; 20.01
Unified Cornish Revised (UCR) 17.01, 18.65, 20.01; its approach to spelling 0.03, 2.02, 2.06, 18.80; "inferior" to Kernowek Kemyn 0.05; and vocalic alternation 10.00, 11.00
unreal conditions 19.35; negative ~ with *na ve* 'had it not been' 19.36
unstressed syllables 16.00-05
usy/ugy 'is' 3.03
Vannetais 16.08

variant spellings; in BM 6.04; in TH, BK, CW 6.05
verbal paradigms 19.24
Virgil 18.65
virtu, vertu 'virtue' 13.07
voiceless sonants (*lh* and *nh*) 17.00
Volksetymologie 7.25
vu 'sight, view'; *fvu* 13.07
vyctory 'victory' 18.90

warleny 'last year' 18.91
warlergh 'according to' 18.32
Welsh phonology; George's misrepresentation of 13.02
whath 'still' 8.00-01
whelas 'to seek' 5.07, 5.09-10, 10.02; **hwilas* in Kernowek Kemyn 0.03, 10.01
Whevrel 'February' 18.34
why 'you' 9.00-02
whythra 'examine'; **hwithra* in Kernowek Kemyn 0.03
Williams, Nicholas; vilified by George and Dunbar 0.01; "is scraping the barrel" 0.01; "has made a hash" of Cornish phonology 0.01, 17.02; "propagates errors" 0.01; "his credibility is tending to zero" 0.01, 17.02; George's opportunity to show Williams is wrong 2.07; Williams right "in the narrow sense" about **klywes* 12.00; right about *-d-* 15.00; wrong about everything else 0.01, 12.11
wosa 'after' 15.00, 15.03; **wodja* in Kernowek Kemyn 12.11,

y > e (in *byth/beth*, etc.) 11.05
y 'his'; *e* 14.12
y'm bues 'I have'; three developments 19.31
ydyot 'idiot' 18.92
yeynell 'refrigerator' 18.93
yma 'is'; *ema* 14.12
ymach 'image'; **imaj* in Kernowek Kemyn 0.03
yn kerhyn 'about' 19.17
yn kever 'with respect to, regarding' 18.95, 19.18
yn neb maner 'somehow' 19.03
ynjyn 'ingenious; engine' 18.94; [pl.] *ingynnys* 14.11
ynnans 'in them' 16.02
yth yw 'is'; *eth ew* 14.12
yw/ew 'is' 3.04, 13.05

"zone of uncertainty" 2.07

RESOURCES IN UCR

Ashworth, Heather. 2006. *Whedhel Gyttern*. Ewny Redreth: Spyrys a Gernow. ISBN: 978-0-9548451-5-5

Litchfield, Jo. 2004. *Everyday Words in Cornish*. Cornish language consultants Ray & Denise Chubb. Portreath: Agan Tavas. ISBN 1-901409-08-2

Palmer, Myghal. 2001. *Rebellyans*. Ewny Redreth: Spyrys a Gernow. ISBN 0-9535975-3-9

Phillips, Andy & Nicholas Williams. 2004. *Lyver Pejadow rag Kenyver Jorna: Cornish Daily Prayer*. Redruth: Spyrys a Gernow. ISBN 0-9535975-8-X

Prohaska, Daniel. 2006. *Kornisch: Wort für Wort*. Bielefeld: Reise Know-how Verlag, Peter Rump GmbH.

Williams, Nicholas. 1997. *Clappya Kernowek: an introduction to Unified Cornish Revised*. Portreath: Agan Tavas. ISBN 1-901409-01-5

Williams, Nicholas, translator. 2002. *Testament Noweth agan Arluth ha Savyour Jesu Cryst*. Ewny Redrteth: Spyrys a Gernow. ISBN 0-9535975-4-7

Williams, Nicholas. 2005. *English-Cornish Dictionary: Gerlyver Sawsnek Kernowek*. Second edition. Redruth: Agan Tavas. ISBN 978-1-901409-09-3. Westport: Evertype. ISBN 978-1-904808-06-0

Williams, Nicholas. 2006. *Cornish Today: An examination of the revived language*. Third edition. Westport: Evertype. ISBN 978-1-904808-07-7

Williams, Nicholas. 2006. *Writings on Revived Cornish*. Westport: Evertype. ISBN 978-1-904808-08-4

Williams, Nicholas. 2006. *Towards Authentic Cornish*. Westport: Evertype. ISBN 978-1-904808-09-1

www.ingramcontent.com/pod-product-compliance
Ingram Content Group UK Ltd.
Pitfield, Milton Keynes, MK11 3LW, UK
UKHW041415180426
11947UKWH00007B/140